The Education of Ministers for the Coming Age

Disciples Higher Education Series

General Editor

D. Duane Cummins

Manuscript Editor

John M. Imbler

The Education of Ministers for the Coming Age

by

Ronald E. Osborn

CBP Press
St. Louis, Missouri

© Copyright 1987 CBP Press
All rights reserved. No part of this book may be reproduced without the publisher's written permission. Address:

       CBP Press
       Box 179
       St. Louis, MO 63166

Library of Congress Cataloging-in-Publication Data

Osborn, Ronald E.
 The education of ministers for the coming age.

 Bibliography: p. 246.
 Includes index.
 1. Christian Church (Disciples of Christ)—Clergy—Training of—United States.
2. Theology—Study and teaching—United States. I. Title.
BX7326.052 1987   207'.11663   87-13246
ISBN 0-8272-0806-5

Printed in the United States of America

Dedication

in memory of

NAOMI JACKSON OSBORN
(1916-1986)

*who taught me more about ministry,
about the church we have loved,
and about the faith which sustains
than I can ever acknowledge,
and who for nearly half a century
shared the labor and the joy.*

*grateful and abiding appreciation
is expressed
to the following contributors
whose generous gifts
made possible the publication
of this volume*

**JOE AND NANCY STALCUP
LILLY ENDOWMENT, INC.**

Table of Contents

FOREWORD xi

ACKNOWLEDGMENTS xiii

Chapter **1**   THE WORLD RUSHING TOWARD US 1
    Peering into the Future, 1
    A World of High Technology, 2
        An Explosion of Information, 2
        The Dominance of the Mass Media, 4
        The Threat of Nuclear Doom, 7
    Magnitudes that Oppress, 8
        Overwhelming Population, 8
        Global Interdependence, 11
        Economic Dominance, 13
        Omnipresent Bureaucracy, 15
        The Demolition of Community, 17
    The Temper of Mind and Spirit, 18
        Secularity as Working Assumption, 19
        Utilitarianism in Education, 21
        Subjectivizing of Questions of Meaning and Value, 24
    Agenda for Mission, 24

Chapter **2**   THE CHURCH IN THE WORLD THAT WAS 27
    Religion in Society, 27
        Primeval Functions of Religion, 27
        Religious Institutions in the Agrarian Epoch, 28
        Religion in the Urban and Industrial Age, 30
    The Great Church: An Overview, 31
        Israel, the Covenant People, 31
        Jesus: Looking Forward to God's Coming Age, 32
        The Church as Outlaw, 33
        The Church as Monitor and Teacher, 34
        The Church as Source of Inner Security and
          Personal Inspiration, 36
    The Churches in the U.S.A., 39
        A New Form of Church, 39
        A Common Religion Outside the Churches, 40
        Impulse-Buying in Religion, 41
        Impact of the Churches on the American Scene, 42
        A Changing Picture, 43

Contents vii

    The Christian Church (Disciples of Christ), 45
        Their Appeal in Their First Century, 45
        Adaptations to a Changing World, 47
        Agenda for the Near Future, 49
    The Congregation Today, 52
        Forerunners, 52
        Contrasting Perceptions, 53
        Temptations, 54
        Mission, 55
        Concern for the Church at the Grassroots, 56

Chapter 3   MINISTRY IN THE CHURCH THAT WAS 57
    Ministry Out of the Past, 57
        Origins of Ministry, 57
        Ministry in the Great Church, 59
        Ministry in America, 61
        Ministry among Disciples of Christ, 65
        The Shrinking of a Public Figure, 67
    The Work of the Minister, 69
        A Question of Office, 69
        Classical Formularies, 69
        Twentieth-Century Expectations, 73
        Ecumenical Consensus, 75
        Ministry on Two Fronts, 76

Chapter 4   EDUCATION FOR MINISTRY THAT WAS 78
    Ministerial Education in Historical Overview, 78
        Archaic and Biblical Times, 78
        The Ancient Church, 79
        Medieval and Modern Europe, 80
        The Churches in America, 82
    Education for Ministry among Disciples of Christ, 84
        The Education of the Founders, 84
        The Colleges, 85
        A Distinctive Program of Ministerial Education, 86
        The Independent Bible Colleges, 88
        The Arrival of the Seminaries, 89
    Appraising the Work of the Disciples Seminaries, 91
        What Do the Graduates Think?, 92
        The Mentality of an Established Church, 93
        A Fallacy of Misplaced Emphasis, 94

viii   Contents

          Education for the Coming Age: A New Agenda,   96
            A Warning Unheeded: The Storm that Passed,   97
            A New Mandate: Readaptation,   98
          Mission to the Coming Age,   100

Chapter **5**   TOWARD A THEOLOGY OF MINISTRY 103
          The Urgency of a Deeper Theological Understanding,   103
          The Divine Activity as Paradigm for Ministry,   104
            Creativity,   106
            The Pathos of the Living God,   108
            Forgiveness,   110
            Self-Giving,   115
            Intention,   117
            Transformation,   119
          Servants of God in Ministry,   121
            The Great Church as Servant Church,   122
            The Denomination as a Servant-People,   123
            The Congregation as Serving Community,   124
            The Ordained Minister and the Servant Ideal,   126
          Models of Ministry Theologically Appraised,   126
            The Managerial Model,   127
            The Therapeutic Model,   127
            The Rabbinic Model,   127
            The Ambassadorial Model,   129
          Covenanting to Address the Central Task,   129

Chapter **6**   ADDRESSING THE NEED FOR MINISTERS 131
          Calculating the Numbers,   131
            Varied Ministries with Standing,   131
            Supply and Demand,   132
            A Ministry for Small Churches,   134
          Sizing up Persons,   138
            Christian Discipleship,   139
            Understanding of the World,   139
            Appropriation of Christian Tradition,   140
            Concern for Persons,   141
            Capacity for Interpretation,   142
            Commitment to the Church,   143
            Christian Creativity in New Situations,   143
          Vocation, Commission, and Appointment,   145
            The Meaning of Vocation,   145
            The Biblical Concept of "Call",   147

Sending and Appointment
              (Commission and Ordination),   149
            The Church Enlists Its Ministers,   150
          Measures to Meet the Need,   152
            Ministerial Enlistment among Disciples of Christ,   153
            Factors in Enlistment,   154
            Attention to Special Groups,   156
            Responsibility for Enlistment,   158
            Screening the Aspirants,   160

Chapter 7 EDUCATION FOR TOMORROW'S MINISTERS 162
          Three Strands in a Ministerial Curriculum,   162
            The Scientific Strand,   163
            The Professional Strand,   165
            The Fiduciary Strand,   168
          Designing a Curriculum,   171
            A Continuing Problem,   171
            The Integration of Learning,   172
            A Radical New Approach,   173
          Some Particular Needs,   176
            Cultivating the Imagination,   176
            Imparting Knowledge of Society,   176
            Preparing Ministers to Teach,   177
            Teaching the Use of Scripture,   178
          Spiritual Discipline and Christian Maturity,   179
            The Evident Need,   179
            The Problem of Responsibility,   180
            Introduction to the Spiritual Heritage,   181
            A Full-orbed Spirituality,   182
            The Seminary as Educating Community,   183

Chapter 8 SEMINARY, CHURCH, AND MINISTERS
          IN PARTNERSHIP 185
          Concerns of the Partnership,   185
            Faculty and Administration,   185
            Seminarians,   188
            Links with Ministerial Practice,   190
            Facilities, Budgets, and Financial Resources,   192
            Ordination and Licensing,   193
            Sustaining a Vital Ministry,   195
            Continuing Education,   197

Covenant and Conference, 199
  The Mission of the Division of Higher Education, 199
  Conducting Theological Dialog, 200
  Church Funding for Theological Education, 201
  A Channel for the Church's Concern, 203
  The Mission of DHE to the Coming Age, 204
At the Center of a Church for the Coming Age, 206
  The Theological Center, 206
  The Missional Center, 207
  The Spiritual Center, 209

NOTES 212

APPENDIX I (A Guide for Curriculum Review, Readaptation) 240

APPENDIX II (Perceived Strengths and Weaknesses of
  Recent Theological Education) 245

BIBLIOGRAPHY 246

INDEX 257

Foreword

The assignment was plain enough: to visualize the ministry needed by churches in their mission to the twenty-first century and to offer recommendations for the education of such a ministry. The study has sobered, even shaken me. It involves an analysis of contemporary society, the situation of the church, and the state of the ministry, with attention to trends likely to intensify. It is forced to conclude that our religious institutions, shaped by the past, are still largely oriented toward a world that was and that the theological seminaries, which like to think of themselves as the *avant garde*, operate more by axioms derived from academic tradition than from serious concern for ministry to the emerging future.

So to my consternation the opening chapters of the book read like an indictment of the seminaries. That situation can only make me cringe, for I have spent my life in theological education after the prevailing pattern. Moreover, I know that to every alleged charge of failure, shining exceptions must be entered. But I have tried to depict the general scene as it really is. That is why I recently observed to a friend, "This book will cause me to lose whatever ill deserved reputation I may ever have had as a nice guy."

The intent of the study is not prosecution but diagnosis and prescription. It is conducted with no assumption of superior personal wisdom or virtue: the indictment, if such it is, grows out of the assignment. If the proper task of the seminaries were to do what they have traditionally tried to do, they would deserve commendation, but if it is to prepare ministers for the future, serious deficiencies must be acknowledged. I trust that my younger colleagues, still in a position to determine the direction of the schools, will recognize that I am questioning institutional patterns, not attacking old and valued friends.

The proposals set forth in the concluding chapters are in no sense iconoclastic and may seem to some readers less radical than the situation demands. But I believe that the seminaries are doing a great many things which they must continue to do. Moreover, no one person can chart the thoroughgoing reform which will be required if the schools are to serve the coming age with maximum usefulness; rather will that process demand the serious engagement of faculties and governing boards in dialogue with the churches.

Commissioned for the Christian Church (Disciples of Christ) in the United States and Canada and attentive to the specific needs of that body, the study nevertheless aspires to a wider usefulness. Called to minister in a strange, new world, all the churches face similar problems, even as we all share the common faith in which we engage them and the common tradition from which we draw our resources for going forward together.

The phrase "The Coming Age" in the title obviously carries a dual meaning. It points us to the impending technological future: as the church is called to serve the new era faithfully under God, so the mission of theological education now is to prepare ministers capable of leading in that responsibility. But the title also carries a hopeful reference to the future as God's new day. It suggests eagerness for that tomorrow which the Gospels present as the central theme of Jesus' ministry. The prayer, "Thy kingdom come!" expresses the church's commitment to that future.[1]

Yet even in a church whose most influential leader named his journal *The Millennial Harbinger*, few contemporary congregations seem to center their primary efforts on the larger aspects of the divine purpose for this earth. It might be supposed that the situation is different in the seminaries, where the term *eschatology* recurs so commonly in the insiders' vocabulary; but that recurrence too often appears to signify erudition possessed by the learned rather than hopeful expectation or eager motivation to serve. This study focuses on ministry to the coming age, both human and divine, and looks forward to that mission.

The coming age will stand in need of the gospel as much as any previous generation has done. Christian faith includes a forthright commitment to the church matched by concern for the future of the world—its preservation from nuclear destruction, and abundance of life for those who come after us. While the new technologies will profoundly affect physical and societal conditions, Christians are supremely concerned with the life of the spirit. So this book cherishes for coming generations the opportunity to see themselves as children of God and to live together in the light of that vision.

Acknowledgments

This study owes much to colleagues in the ministry and theological education, especially the generations of students who have explored with me so many aspects of the church's mission. With these, with my erstwhile associates at the Christian Board of Publication, Northwest Christian College, Christian Theological Seminary, and the School of Theology at Claremont, with companions from many confessions in the Consultation on Church Union, the Commission on Faith and Order, and the Graduate School of Ecumenical Studies, and with comrades in the Commisssion on Theology and Unity, the Association of Disciples for Theological Discussion, and the Western Association for Theological Discussion, I have been talking about Christian ministry for nearly half a century. I mention also the Task Force on Ministry appointed by the Commission on Restructure and the regional commissions on the ministry, from whom I have learned so much, especially those in Ohio, Indiana, and the Pacific Southwest. To them all I am grateful.

Others have contributed more specifically to the development of the study. These include Rodney L. Parrott, assistant dean of the Disciples Seminary Foundation and facilitator of its Oikodome Research Teams, as well as the members of the Theological and Sociological Concerns Team which in 1984 discussed with me a number of the issues taken up here; those members were F. Wayne Bryant, Dwaine E. Cerbin, Earl C. Gibbs, Laurence C. Keene, and Art Morgan. The heads of Disciples seminaries used some hours of their 1984 consultation to explore the venture with me. Participants in the 1984 Disciples Seminarians' Conference, the presidents of Disciples colleges at their meeting just prior to the 1985 General Assembly, and persons who attended a special interest group on the theme of this study at that assembly joined in discussion of various issues and offered suggestions in writing. More than a few ministers contributed through correspondence, and numbers of them, along with most regional ministers, responded helpfully to a series of questions.

Dean Joseph C. Hough, Jr. and Professor John B. Cobb, Jr., my colleagues in the School of Theology at Claremont, generously sent me in advance of publication their manuscript on *Christian Identity and Theological Education* and included me in a consultation of seminary leaders discussing issues raised in their book. Josh Wilson shared an impressive sheaf of his papers dealing with the nature of the coming world and the kind of ministry necessary to serve it. A few particular friends and intimates have talked through more than one knotty problem; these include particularly President T. J. Liggett of Christian Theological Seminary, Dean Donald D. Reisinger of the Disciples Seminary Foundation, the late William Martin Smith of the Pension Fund, Professor Joseph R. Jeter, Jr. and Professor David Polk of Brite Divinity School, minister Jay R. Calhoun of First Christian Church, Vancouver, Wash., and Naomi Jackson Osborn, my wife of forty-five years.

Craig Calhoun, Jay R. Calhoun, Davis Dyer, Prudence Dyer, and David Polk gave parts or all of the manuscript a critical reading. Prudence Dyer also prepared "A Guide for Curriculum Review, Readapation (Appendix I)." My colleagues in the study, D. Duane Cummins and Thomas R. McCormick, have stimulated new ideas in every conversation, and the staff of the Division of Higher Education, especially Lawrence S. Steinmetz and John M. Imbler, who served as manuscript editor, have proved unfailingly helpful. I offer to all of these, and all others who have had a part in this venture, particularly the readers and critics of the manuscript, my heartfelt gratitude.

Chapter **1**

THE WORLD RUSHING TOWARD US

It will be radically different from the world we have known, that strange, new society rushing upon us. The future, of course, has always been uncertain, and people have always concerned themselves about what it might bring. Our ancestors consulted oracles, augurs, necromancers, and fortune-tellers; we look to futurologists.

Peering into the Future

Using sophisticated theoretical models and complex mathematical projections, futurology has gained considerable attention since the advent of the digital computer. It has had a profound effect on corporate and governmental planning and has spawned a new industry of social forecasting or trend-watching.[1] Meanwhile, journalists, filmmakers, and writers of science fiction have given fancy free rein to depict an imagined world of wonder or horror.

The problem even with well-informed efforts to gaze over the horizon is the radical effect of unforseen emergents. U.S. automakers, growing fat on the profits of ever larger and more powerful automobiles, failed to anticipate the oil crisis induced by the OPEC nations in 1970; they responded slowly and reluctantly to the demand of consumers for smaller, fuel-efficient cars. Half a century ago who could have foreseen the devastating effect which popular programs on the radio networks would have on Sunday evening church services? Or forty years ago who could have predicted the impact of television in diminishing family activities and community life? Who foresaw Vatican II?[2] Who expected the rise of the counterculture? Who in the 1960s perceived how quickly a movement as powerful as the counterculture then seemed to be would run out of steam? Who projected the resurgence of fundamentalism half a century after the Scopes trial? Futurology has limitations.

Our purpose in trying to describe the world rushing upon us is concern that the church identify and fulfill its mission to that strange, new age. In studying contemporary society, we can identify trends which seem likely to shape the world to come.[3] We may, of course, overreact to a phenomenon of the moment or project as major a trend which has already begun to falter.[4] Consider the spotty record of economic forecasters and investment counselors.[5]

2   THE EDUCATION OF MINISTERS FOR THE COMING AGE

In any case, there is no need to rehash, ignore, or try to supplant those recent books on the theme already known to the informed reader.[6] As the lurid titles of two early books of this genre had it, tomorrow is already here, and we are stunned by future shock.

The attempt to outline the emerging world scene sets the stage for an extended inquiry throughout the book: What effect are the new developments likely to have on the life of the spirit? How may the church respond effectively to the new situation? How can authentic Christian ministry best serve the new age? What are the implications for theological education in fulfilling its mission to such a future?

A World of High Technology

Technology shapes the new world, offering humanity a dazzling array of unprecedented possibilities.[7] Here we suggest its impact on society and on the human spirit.

An Explosion of Information

More than any previous age our society relies on increasing quantities of data. The computer revolution has radically transformed communications and publishing and is now making over manufacturing, banking, merchandising, inventory-control, education, and medicine. The slide-rule has already become an antique, and for the parades it gives to heroes, New York City must now import ticker-tape by the truckload since Wall Street no longer uses it.[8] Before the eyes of mystified parents a younger generation is growing up computer-literate, and a new knowledge class has begun to rival the old business class.[9] The new technology generates graphics, composes music, deciphers codes, controls robots, substitutes microchips and floppy discs for film in cameras, even accomodates the complex ideograms of Chinese writing. Continuing research-and-development gives promise of ever greater versatility, with capacity for responding to vocal commands, performing some functions of human intelligence, and storing increasing quantities of data.[10]

A mountain of facts now towers over us. Using a modem, even a home computer can communicate by telephone with other computers, gaining access to data of all kinds. Seminary and university libraries cooperate by computer hook-up to locate and display information stored anywhere in the system. Well-equipped church offices use computers for word-processing worship bulletins, newsletters, mailing lists, and membership rolls, for keeping financial records and preparing reports, and for other relatively common tasks. Special computer programs are available for churches; books and articles on the subject are common in the religious press.[11] Computers have been used to prepare a denominational profile of every county in the United States and to produce a concordance to the Revised Standard Version of the Bible.[12] Granted the familiarity of the oncoming generation with the new technology, instruction in its use is hardly needed in the seminaries (the modern equivalent of fabled Mimeographing 101), but professors ought to have some facility with it, to analyze its impact on society, and to utilize the detailed information it makes readily available.

Of far larger concern to the church will be the social changes brought on by the new technology. The ease of transmitting data may enable many office workers, executives, and other professionals occupied with words or figures to do their work at home. Obvious gains will be savings on high-cost office space and on time spent every day in commuting. Offsetting these will be loss of direct contact with fellow workers, a consequent decline in *esprit de corps*, and a less personal quality of supervision. Yet numbers of self-employed persons and workers in service industries have already shifted their work to their own "electronic cottages."[13] Should the trend spread beyond the ranks of a few favored professionals to include large numbers of laborers, it would alter once again the structure of our metropolitan communities, caught for the past two centuries in constant change. As with each previous development—the factory system, mass transit, the rise of the suburbs, the personal automobile, crosstown freeways, the gasoline shortage, the gentrification of old urban neighborhoods—the church will be forced to adapt to an altered dispersal of the population.

Of greatest concern to the churches will be the effect on persons. Already the new technology has confronted society with a new batch of ethical problems. These include rights of privacy, ranging from protection against the nuisance of automatic dialing with recorded telephone messages to the serious invasion of civil liberties by the compilation of files from various data banks.[14] Less ominous for the sophisticated is the "personalized" mass mailing which repeatedly inserts the name of the recipient into a letter promoting a sale or appealing for funds. Yet some television evangelists prey on the simple faith of persons unfamiliar with the new technology who believe the letters they receive asking for their prayers and gifts are written personally to them. The ability of juvenile hackers to gain access to computers in banks, schools, hospitals, and even the Pentagon alerts us to problems of security with respect to confidential information and to the possibility of serious computer crime.

Like every other instrument for human use, the computer multiplies opportunities for good or evil. Christians will celebrate the possible easing or enrichment of human life without undue astonishment that some persons will use the new technology for nefarious purposes. But the church will be particularly concerned with questions regarding the quality of life in an economy running on computers. What will be their larger effect on the human spirit?[15] The story of Eden indicates that knowledge does not make people good. Will working all week at a keyboard and video-display terminal demonstrate that human beings can live by data alone? Or will it intensify the hunger for more than knowledge? In closed societies will the easy availability of information crack the monolithic power of the state? Will coming generations search beyond the wilderness of facts for a promised land of beauty, truth, justice, and love? Will the church prove sensitive to the spiritual longing of persons caught in a world of high technology? And will the oncoming company of ministers be prepared to engage them with a gospel that addresses depths beyond the facts?

The Dominance of the Mass Media

If so, Christians will have to come to terms with the mass media. As a result of new technology, the business of entertaining and informing has gained unprecedented power over the popular mind. Until Gutenberg, teachers, preachers, and advocates were limited to the range of the human voice or to the effect of a treatise laboriously copied by hand. The printing press dramatically increased the reach of personal influence, and much later the phonograph enlarged the potential audience for musicians and actors. But when the invention of the motion picture brought forth a new industry, the "Dream Machine" became a major factor in forming the popular imagination. Radio reached out to listeners everywhere, greatly enhancing the influence of Franklin D. Roosevelt, Winston Churchill, and Adolf Hitler. Now television has become a constant presence; its impact is magnified by the popularity of video cassettes.[16]

The impact of the mass media, especially the electronic devices, has drastically altered the traditional dynamics for inculcating values in the young. For centuries home, church, and school served to instill in the rising generation an understanding of the cultural heritage and a commitment to principles held to be of supreme importance. In Christian Europe and then in America, mother and father, minister and teacher, policeman and mayor imbued the rising generation with a sense of morality, regard for custom, and love of native land. Mentors and role models were respected members of the local community, personally known to the young, yet linked in varying degrees to more remote centers of public life—county seat, college town, state capital, the great market cities, the capital of the nation.[17] If the crisis of adolescence put temporary distance between parent and child, an understanding teacher, neighbor, or minister commonly provided the friendly guidance which enabled the young person to attain an adult autonomy integrated with a commitment to the commonly accepted values.

The media have radically altered this former dynamic of socialization, in which the church played such a significant part and on which it depended for the transmission of faith and loyalty. Whereas children in "favored" homes were formerly sheltered from the seamy and shocking aspects of the real world, every kind of cruel and vulgar situation is now thrust upon them from infancy.[18] They absorb impressions directly from the screen, not through the interpretation of parent or other adult reading to them or telling a story, and they experience as real what they see and hear. The impact of television is intensified by the common resort to it for babysitting.

Strangely enough, the images projected by the media seem more authentic than direct experience itself. It is not unusual for students on a seminary campus or residents of a retirement community to gather in the common room to watch their peers in a program over closed-circuit television, coming from a studio just down the hall. Even though such persons may verbalize the importance of interpersonal relations and lament the loss of community in today's world, they turn to a medium in which interaction between speaker and audience is lost. It seems more impressive, more "with it," to see flickering images of their friends on a nineteen-inch screen than to listen to them in person in the same room.

In an era of media hype we have fallen victim to the tyranny of the celebrity. (A celebrity has been defined as someone "famous for being well known.") The heroes of the young are persons seen on television, video cassette recorders, or film—athletes, rock stars, actors, news commentators, and the rare political leader who did not first attain fame in one of these categories.[19] Mass-circulation newspapers, magazines, and "books" reinforce the impression by giving frenzied attention to the celebrities. The few figures in the religious world who have made it into the inner circle of fame are those who generate their own hype as television evangelists. Besides these, only rare exceptions—Martin Luther King, Jr., Bishop Desmond Tutu, Mother Teresa—have gained attention in the media, along with the pope, of course, attended by medieval pageantry made to order for the cameras. Ministers most likely to make the news are those who stir up controversy, who challenge custom or policy. But few ministers relish swimming in hot water, and the church has difficulty with those who do.

A few church leaders are known to informed journalists and are interviewed on occasion, but not often enough to be recognized by the general public. Presiding bishops, along with national presidents and moderators of churches, are nonentities to the media and so to the people at large. The same is true of national leaders in education, scholarship, humanitarianism, and the arts, while on the local scene useful and creative women and men—teachers, artists, musicians, social workers, business people, ministers, municipal administrators, volunteers in good causes—are ignored. The persons who make a community function and who before the age of television served as heroes and role models for the young now appear to be of little consequence—"just people we know." No one counts but the celebrity.

The value-system absorbed both from programs and commercials is one of conspicuous consumption and all-out hedonism. Far more influential than either home or church, this sybaritic vision of "the good life"—an expression which once belonged to philosophy and religion—creates constant and extravagant desire. If church people had not fallen unconscious victim to acculturation by a pagan society, they would not limit their protests against immorality in the media to profanity, sex, and violence, but would cry against the blatant selfishness at the heart of the fantasy. Apparently, however, the scriptwriters know only three ways to resolve a problem: shoot the villain dead, hustle the couple off to bed, or end your troubles by buying the product. The promise of happiness through self-indulgence, depicted daily in hundreds of thirty-second dramas, provides the substance for peer-pressure on persons of all ages to abandon common sense and climb aboard the bandwagon of mindless consumerism. Yet, ironically, "The most affluent society the world has ever seen is no happier than any other."[20] The media have produced a generation of young adults without idealism and with a moral outlook radically different from that historically espoused in Christian thought.[21]

Regarding the values professed in biblical religion, the masters of media are ignorant or hostile—or both. Increasingly the industries of broadcasting, film, and publishing have fallen under the control of "big money"—either multimillionaire investors or faceless conglomerates concerned with "the bottom line."[22] Lured by the prestige of owning a major network, studio, or publishing house and by the promise of profits, the new moguls demonstrate little concern for artistic vision, cultural integrity, or moral purpose.[23]

The producers and writers are secular celebrities proceeding on non-religious assumptions and evidently ignorant both of our spiritual heritage and of church life. The nation's premier journalists, for example, demonstrated incredible inability to comprehend President Carter's religious motivation for certain policies or the biblical allusions in his speech. The news media give undue attention to fundamentalism, cults, ecclesiastical conservatism, and weird religion generally, while failing to discern the continuing influence of the mainline churches on millions of lives and countless communities, the relevance of their work and witness to major current issues, or the intellectual and moral calibre of their leadership. Even amidst an explosion of information, all that reaches the viewer "immediately" (as the cliché has it) first passes through the "Information Filter."

A high proportion of big-name journalists claims no present tie with any church, operating with notions of religion compounded of childish memories, sophomoric disdain, and an occasional dash of sentiment; a similar situation prevails among influential television writers and Hollywood executives.[24] Religion as a positive force in the common life is virtually absent from the world they present to the public, having last been seen in the days of the civil rights movement, and Christian ministry does not exist except at an occasional funeral or wedding.

The current trend in the treatment of religion by the media shows no sign of changing direction, though journalists frequently reflect on their social responsibility, as the notes for this discussion attest. A society increasingly impersonal, where the images and magnitudes projected on the screen overshadow more and more the realities of the local community and the commitments of home and church and school, confronts us with crucial questions. Can the church discover how to counter the pressure of the mass media by setting forth firmly, clearly, and attractively an alternate lifestyle appropriate for Christians? Can it find effective ways of making itself and its work visible to the general public without compromising its integrity? Can the theological schools contribute to these ends? Can the ministers coming from the seminaries exercise a quality of constructive leadership which will restore vitality to community life and bring the new generation into meaningful contact with "neighbors" whose lives are genuinely significant from a Christian standpoint so that these may serve as honored mentors and realistic role models? Can these ministers themselves qualify as persons of genuineness, depth, and commitment, who provide essential information and offer a meaningful interpretation of human experience?

The Threat of Nuclear Doom

From the implications of high technology for the quality of life we turn to its threat to life itself—not just personal existence or that of a community or nation, but the future of all humanity and perhaps of every living creature. The nuclear arms race has locked the superpowers into a mindless rivalry to multiply weapons far beyond any strategic calculation, contributing to governmental deficits and diverting resources from pressing social needs. The irresponsible construction of nuclear installations for both military and peaceful uses has continued for a generation with no realistic plans for disposal of the lethal wastes.[25] Yet the mad race continues to produce "newer and better" models while our children live in fear. Asked by Studs Terkel what she wants to do when she grows up, a girl scarcely eight years old replied, "I wanna see if I'm gonna grow up first. . . . I could die overnight from the bomb."[26]

The churches have not been silent about the nuclear threat. The World Council of Churches, the World Conference of Religious Workers for Saving the Sacred Gift of Life from Nuclear Catastrophe, the National Conference of Catholic Bishops, the Iowa Inter-Church Forum, and many other representative bodies of Christians have spoken firmly and clearly on this issue. Kenneth L. Teegarden, then General Minister and President of the Christian Church (Disciples of Christ), convened an advisory panel which over a two-year period produced a call to the church entitled *Seeking God's Peace in a Nuclear Age*.[27] Thus representative Christians have joined their voices with those of physicians, nuclear scientists, humanitarians, and advocates of international law to demand a halt in the rush toward nuclear disaster.

8   THE EDUCATION OF MINISTERS FOR THE COMING AGE

As we look forward to ministry in the coming age, we cannot shake off the questions. Can Christians detach themselves from the assumptions of the nuclear arms race and the policy of nuclear deterrence? Will the general membership of the churches offer a witness on this issue which will effect the development of new, pacific policies by national governments? Can ministers assume again a moral and intellectual leadership in community and national life which will make a difference in saving the world from nuclear destruction? Can the theological schools truly serve as intellectual centers of the church's life by helping find an open way to a meaningful human future?

Magnitudes That Oppress

The shaping of the future occurs not only in the processes performed by the new machines but in the concentrations of power required, evoked, or enhanced by the technology. That fact has made for radical changes among leading corporations, bringing new giants to the top. Sovereign nations lavish money and brains on the race to develop ever more sophisticated military technology and to guard their secrets from rivals, while denying funds for acute social needs, for research in the peaceful application of science, and for the humanities.[28] Overwhelmed by new magnitudes of power and unprecedented perils a generation still congratulating itself on its emancipation from an earlier moralism finds its spirit oppressed far more heavily and human liberty threatened even more profoundly. Some of these forces will strikingly alter familiar patterns and confront the church with major challenges.

Overwhelming Population

On a planet of limited resources, human population continues to increase. Despite war and famine, the total number of people has gone from 2 billion to 5 billion in half a century, on an earth with optimum capacity for supporting about half that number.[29] While the rate of growth has slowed in the most highly developed nations, the U.S. Census Bureau projects a continued increase here until the year 2030, with much slower growth, perhaps even a decrease, after that. But in sub-Saharan Africa, Southeast Asia, and Latin America people continue to multiply far faster than resources, bringing on poverty and famine. On our crowded earth plant and animal species disappear at a rate approaching 10,000 a year, more than one species every hour. Demand for crude oil, expected to continue its rise until the end of this century, steadily diminishes America's domestic reserves, and the eroding topsoil of our fertile heartland washes out to sea.[30]

These trends make the limitation of population growth and the care of the earth matters of extreme urgency. While the General Assembly of the Christian Church (Disciples of Christ) has joined various religious and humanitarian bodies in calling for family planning and a wiser stewardship of resources,[31] the Roman Catholic Church and others continue an unbending opposition to artificial methods of contraception. Yet advocates of limited growth need to reflect on some important questions. What effect will a widespread increase in the number of adults without children or with only one child have on patterns of family life, education, congregational activity, the economy? Is the function of sex to be valued only as a source of pleasure or a bond of mutuality between a human pair, but its function in the propagation of the species to be viewed mainly in negative terms? What may happen to values of character and relationship nurtured for countless generations by the responsibilities of parenthood? Is a great increase of loneliness, alienation, and selfishness to be expected? How can the church respond with pastoral sensitivity and social responsibility to the new situation? Can it cultivate a new sense of obligation for the stewardship of the earth and its resources?

Advances in medicine, by prolonging life, have increased the population and radically altered its makeup. The proportion of older persons has dramatically increased and will continue to do so, from about one in eight over sixty years of age in 1960 to about one in six in the year 2000 and almost one in four in 2020; it is expected that by the turn of the century more than 100,000 Americans will be at least 100 years of age.[32] Already, for the first time in history, the number of persons over sixty-five exceeds the number of teenagers. The maturing of society has made for the rise of "Gray Power," for larger attention to the concerns of the aging in medicine, social work, and politics, for heavy strains on the Social Security System, for the rapid expansion of retirement communities and nursing homes, and for a dramatic shift of population from the Northeast and Midwest to the Sunbelt. It has also made for the aging of the church. A generation ago most of the volunteer work in congregations was done by women; today they have joined the labor force, and the work is done by retirees, numbers of them functioning virtually as unpaid staff.

Congregations do reasonably well in ministering to the needs of older people and in providing them an arena of continuing usefulness and satisfaction. Yet we may ask: Does the preponderance of aged leaders place the church in danger of approaching today's problems with yesterday's mindset? Do ministries to the elderly settle for providing worthwhile activities in a congenial world apart? Do they establish opportunities for intergenerational encounter, enabling older persons to continue a vital involvement with the young and with the new world and making it possible for children and youth and young adults to find pleasure and wisdom in the company of the old? Is a congregation likely to fulfill its responsibilities for the evangelism and education of youth through a program designed, consciously or unconsciously, with the needs and interests of their grandparents primarily in mind?

An even more dramatic shift in the character of the growing population results from immigration. A new ethnic, cultural, and religious pluralism is changing the face and perhaps the mentality of America. Hispanics are expected to outnumber blacks as the nation's largest minority by 1990. Asian-Americans, numbering beyond 3.5 million, more than doubled between 1970 and 1980, making up 3.6 percent of U.S. population; yet they constitute 18.7 percent of the freshman class at Cal Tech, 18.6 percent at Berkeley, and 10.9 percent at Harvard.[33] In California whites are about to become an ethnic minority. Newcomers from Latin America, Southeast Asia, the Middle East, and Black Africa, have brought to this country a fresh infusion of hope, confidence, reliance on the work ethic, and determination to make a better world for their children. These young people will take their place as intellectuals, technologists, and mentors of the nation in the twenty-first century.

The influx of immigrants from peoples not largely represented in earlier decades raises a new awareness of ethnic differences. In the United States, Great Britain, and various nations of Europe, racism continues to erupt into violence between whites and blacks or between Anglo-Saxons and Asians. Racism remains the heaviest magnitude of oppressive power in today's world and shows no signs of going away.

For black families in America real income declined during the decade of the 1970s and the percentage with incomes under $10,000 a year actually increased.[34] If the economy offers opportunity to some bright young people of minority stock, their less talented sisters and brothers start batting with two strikes against them. Unemployment in 1980 ran considerably higher for blacks (18.5 percent) and Hispanics (13.9 percent) than for the population as a whole (9.8 percent); every other black teenager (49.7 percent) was out of a job.[35]

Despite the social liberalism of the seminaries, the clear moral position of the churches set forth in resolutions passed by General Assembly or General Conference, and constructive programs like those supported by Disciples through Reconciliation, racism remains endemic in American society. Blacks continue to bear the brunt of its oppression, but it presses heavily also on Hispanics and Asians. Racism remains on the church's agenda for the twenty-first century, as it does for the theological seminaries, which have not yet succeeded in preparing a ministry equipped and ready to effect genuine change in popular attitudes and social structures which continue its injustices.

The new pattern of ethnic diversity is rapidly changing the American religious scene. Since the civil rights movement of the 1960s members of the long dominant white majority have increasingly recognized the distinctiveness of the black church, important not only to its constituency but to the total Christian witness in this country. Now Hispanics are also winning a place. With the continuing immigration of Caribbeans and Latin Americans, it appears that 60 percent of the Roman Catholics in the United States will be Hispanic by the year 2000,[36] and in the Christian Church (Disciples of Christ), Spanish-speaking congregations have become a significant factor.

The most rapidly growing Protestant churches are those in Asian-American communities, particularly among Korean-Americans; although Disciples have not reaped large gains, they are developing some Korean congregations.

A pressing need for the churches now is to demonstrate both inclusiveness and diversity in the body of Christ, to avert the rise of a new sectarianism along ethnic lines. Equally crucial is the response to a religious pluralism of a range heretofore unknown in this country. Hindu shrines, Muslim mosques, Buddhist temples now stand in cities across the land, and the old assumption that Americans are a Christian people, if it ever was true, no longer holds. A century ago Lord Bryce attributed the religious vigor in the United States to the separation of church and state; he saw religion "standing alone . . . by her own strength" as possessing a vitality which the old established churches in Europe lacked.[37] The question now is this: Can Christianity continue to flourish without the traditional support it once received from the culture? Can it effectively witness the gospel to the new immigrants whose heritage does not include biblical religion? How can the churches relate constructively to the presence of other major religions in such a way that understanding and mutual respect may be increased and the life of society as a whole enriched? Can the church discern and respond to the divine purpose in bringing together in this land such a diverse multitude of peoples longing for freedom and a better life?

Global Interdependence

The flocking of immigrants, legal and illegal, to the United States dramatizes the inescapable reality of human interdependence on a global scale. No longer can a great nation conduct its affairs as though the rest of the world did not exist. Our need for oil from the Arab states, our vulnerability to acts of terrorism thousands of miles from our shores, our susceptibility in a time of air travel to epidemics breaking out in any part of the globe, the high level of foreign investment in the United States, our difficulties in maintaining a balance between imports and exports, our inability to impose our will on the world economic order, our weakness before foreign competition—these and many other factors demonstrate that isolation is no longer possible. Some of America's most powerful corporations have found it necessary for their survival to enter into partnership with firms from abroad, and large numbers of American businesses have transferred their manufacturing operations outside the country. While long established habits and human self-centeredness still prompt many Americans to try to deal with our problems in isolation from the rest of the world, it is impossible to fly in the face of reality. The interdependence of all nations and peoples is an inescapable fact.[38]

It is time for Americans to acknowledge the irresistible power of the freedom movements among oppressed peoples everywhere. Few of us have understood the extent to which our high standard of living—e.g., cheap coffee, tea, bananas—has rested on the exploitation of peasants by giant corporations abetted by the diplomatic and military power of the United States. Now from among the peoples of the Third World is emerging a new leadership to whose rise we have contributed through the preaching of the gospel and the establishment of churches, through programs which bring thousands of foreign students to American campuses every year, through depiction by mass media everywhere in the world of a way of life in radical contrast with conditions which millions of the oppressed cannot take for granted, through the continuing appeal of the ideals of freedom and representative government enshrined in the Declaration of Independence and the Constitution of the United States.

While many immigrants who have fled here from political oppression still look on this country with a touch of romanticism, leaders who have stayed among their own people to lead the freedom movements tend to see it with a jaundiced eye. This is hardly surprising, given the aim of our foreign policy to maintain "stability" for the sake of our investments; our tendency to see freedom movements as communist-inspired, almost forces their leaders into the arms of the Soviets as we back oppressive governments in power. Despite television, radio, newspapers, and magazines, Americans are ill informed about world affairs, lacking motivation to concern themselves about the causes of other people's problems. Can the church counter the mindless preoccupation with entertainment and self-indulgence and replace it with a sense of global responsibility? Can it give effective support to movements for freedom and dignity?

Among the most oppressive magnitudes of power which weigh down on us and all peoples of the world, none imposes a greater burden of anxiety than the long stand-off between the United States and the Soviet Union. For more than two generations, except for a brief intermission during World War II, our governments have been at loggerheads, politicians have used the Red scare for their own purposes, every other conflict, international or internecine (except the war against the Axis powers), has been coopted or distorted because of this struggle. The moral leadership of the United States on many other issues has been compromised by preoccupation with anti-communism, the nuclear arms race as well as the rivalry in conventional arms and arsenals for chemical warfare has kept humanity in a state of quiet desperation if not terror—and the churches have accepted the enmity as a fact of life. Their mild gestures toward international friendship and their protest against nuclear arms seem scarcely to have affected the national mood. Is it not possible for a community of faith which hails its head as Prince of Peace to launch a movement for the de-escalation of the contest? Surely an essential element in education for ministry to the coming age is effective preparation of our students to serve the gospel of peace.

Economic Dominance

Massive economic forces which even the experts do not understand, and massive magnitudes of economic power over which the average person, perhaps even the most highly placed authority, has no control increasingly determine the shape of our lives and the direction of the future. The demands of multinational corporations and the momentum of the military-technological complex (if the two can be distinguished) dictate foreign and domestic policy alike.

Major shifts in the American economy, precipitated by the transfer of manufacturing to the cheap-labor markets of Asia and Latin America and by the move from heavy industry to high technology have quieted the smokestacks of the Northeast and Midwest, leaving thousands of skilled wage-earners without work, sounding the death-knell for small businesses which served the employees of the mills, and contributing to heavy migration from the "Rust Belt" to the Sun Belt. Local enterprises which for generations provided the financial lifeblood of a city have been bought out by conglomerates, then closed down by a board of directors a thousand miles away whose only concern is "the bottom line" on a financial statement. With a mixed record of success, employees have occasionally succeeded in establishing a stock ownership plan in an effort to keep a plant open; here and there ministers and their churches have provided leadership to rally the community to develop new ventures. Workers accustomed to high wages for skilled labor have found it necessary to take low-paying jobs in service industries. One pessimist observes that the trend threatens to turn the United States into "a nation of short-order cooks and saleswomen, Xerox operators and messenger boys,"[39] but others note that some service jobs pay well.[40]

The departure of women from home to workplace, while frequently described in the rhetoric of liberation, has come largely from financial necessity. Two-thirds of American women between twenty-four and forty-four now hold jobs, up from one-third in 1950. Yet their wages run only about 62 percent of those paid to men, and most Americans living in poverty are women; two out of five families living below the poverty line are headed by women.[41]

The absence of parents from the home has brought about a massive demand for nursery schools and day-care centers for children. Just as the church has pioneered so often in the past in efforts to respond to a new social need, congregations have done the best they could to deal with this one in many communities.[42] Will such a service continue to be a significant ministry by the churches? Or will it be taken over by government and private enterprise, as has been largely the case with the schools and colleges?

Poverty in the United States remains an unsolved problem. In 1980, 2 percent of American families, with an annual income exceeding $100,000 each, held 30 percent of all financial assets in the country and 33 percent of the businesses. By contrast, 33 percent of the families had incomes no higher than $15,000.[43]

Wealth confers power, and power in turn seeks greater wealth. Increasingly management bases decisions on the appearance of immediate profit: a good annual report brings bonuses for executives. But the approach is too often counterproductive, resulting in obsolescence for major industries. Having scanted investment in research-and-development and modernization, they cannot compete with state-of-the-art equipment overseas. It has led to continued exploitation of the Third World. It has occupied some of the brightest and most energetic minds in American business, not in devising new and better products at a cheaper price, but in plotting corporate take-overs; once the raider has milked a company of its liquid assets, plants are closed, thousands of laborers lose a lifetime job, and a syndicate from abroad takes over the market. It has led to the degradation of the environment, as industrial giants protest the expense of pollution controls while maintaining highly-paid lobbyists in Washington and the state capitals to ward off legislation mandating a cleanup of air or water or landfill. It has made for the entrenchment of the military-technological complex as powerful corporations grow fat on cost-plus contracts, and great cities stake their economic future on military production. How can the churches persuade public opinion to oppose the arms race in communities where thousands of workers earn their living in the manufacture of weapons? How can they pray with effectiveness for the peace of the world when the largest corporations team up with the framers of foreign policy to sell advanced weapons systems all over the world for the sake of American "prosperity?"

The pursuit of wealth obsesses the mind of the people: a person's income has become society's measure of one's worth. We give our highest rewards to athletes and other entertainers, to the point of corrupting higher education through bigtime athletics. We give significant rewards to technocrats, engineers, and top-level managers. We provide generally adequate compensation for organized labor. We offer minimal compensation to persons in the traditional service professions (teaching, nursing, the ministry)—medicine being the exception, partly because of its command of high technology.

Preoccupation with an upscale lifestyle has become a major phenomenon of the 1980s, with its widely recognized symbols of achievement (degrees from exclusive colleges, particular automobiles, designer labels on clothing, luxurious housing, expensive recreation), its ethos of conspicuous consumption, its assurance that "you can have it all." In 1984 Americans had run up debts, public and private of $6 trillion. The old ethic of hard work, frugality, and delayed satisfaction, once called Protestant, no longer bore the name; it was to be found more readily among Korean and Vietnamese immigrants than among white Anglo-Saxon Protestants (WASPs). Americans generally were looking at the bottom line, even artists and entrepreneurs in religion.[44]

How does the church engage these massive magnitudes of economic dominance, these "principalities and powers," these world-rulers of the darkness in our present and our impending future? If it does nothing else, it needs to recognize their pervasive power. Great concentrations of wealth control the mass media to make profits, whereas the mainline churches have never raised the funds to secure a continuing presence on television. While the press is free under the First Amendment to the Constitution, the continually rising cost of publishing has forced major denominations to close down their national magazines, sell their presses, and curtail the issuing of books. The trend may be offset, however, by the rise of desktop publishing, making use of computers.[45] But until the church recognizes that it no longer has a significant presence in the marketplace of ideas, it will not understand the size of the task before it.

The church also needs to face frankly the uphill struggle necessarily involved in trying to enlist bright and creative young people for ministry in a society which accords ministers little visibility and penurious financial consideration. This is not to suggest that to compete with secular enterprises the church must pay princely salaries; it is simply to observe that the church will not be able to challenge its youth until it begins to challenge the culture. The same point may be made regarding all the service professions as well as the volunteerism required to sustain church and community projects of social service and social action. The self-giving required must be nurtured in a biblical tradition that knows itself to be at odds with the reigning hedonism.

Can the church find the integrity to recruit, educate, and sustain a ministry capable of leading it in such a task? Does theological education bring seminarians to a realization that authentic ministry in our time necessarily involves a struggle against the current "principalities and powers?" Does it—or does any other element in the experience of our ministers-to-be—prepare them with the motivation and insight required for such a conflict? Does it instill in them a respect and love for the lay persons who, without benefit of theological education, make up the membership of the church and are essential in the waging of this spiritual warfare? Does it equip young ministers with the ability to work practically and effectively in building up the church as a vital and authentic Christian counterculture capable of standing up to and making an impact on society at large?

Omnipresent Bureaucracy

One other magnitude of power looms in our future—massive and imperturbable bureaucracy wherever one turns. Despite pent-up popular frustration which frequently erupts in minor and ineffective explosions, bureaucracy has established itself in modern times as the dominant order in government, business, education, voluntary organizations, and the church. No sooner is a responsibility assigned to a group of persons, along with a budget, than they open an office, appoint a staff, begin to draw charts depicting hierarchies of authority and the "flow" of decision-making, secure mailing lists, establish files, initiate mass mailings, and launch a campaign for more funds, either through tax levies or contributions—so that staff may be increased to make it possible to carry through the project. As staff is enlarged a high proportion of working time and nervous energy goes into clarification of prerogatives and battles over turf.

In government, bureaucracy proves most maddening. To the people the bureaucrat has seemed, since the time of Andrew Jackson, an individual privileged to grow fat at the public trough, rejoicing in every opportunity to assert authority, intent on enforcing complex and irrational rules, full of evident contempt for the mere citizen unfortunate enough to have to deal with anyone so obviously important, and strangely unable to remember that the citizen pays the taxes which keep the whole top-heavy bureaucracy afloat. Now and again, voters rise up to "throw the rascals out," but even the most determined and high-minded of newly elected governments soon encounters inexpressible frustration as it discovers its impotence to influence decisions or impose new policies on the creaking bureaucratic structure.[46] Despite the seeming inevitability of bureaucracy in government and business and the evident service of the system in many areas of need, it continues to oppress ordinary folk by its faceless imperturbability, its obsession with rules and technicalities.

By some perverse principle bureaucracies in denominational and other voluntary organizations seem to attract persons unfailing in goodwill, indefatigable in attending meetings and devising new rules of procedure, ready to fly to any part of the country on expense account to explain their organization charts, sympathetic with the constituency in the desire to see something happen in their area of responsibility, and remarkably inept at bringing off any noticeable achievement. In business bureaucracy is notorious for its incompetence and lack of accomplishment, although the more effective companies have begun to abandon it for simpler, less cumbersome procedures designed to get the job done rather than establish another permanent structure.[47]

In a future that, despite some taxpayers' indignation and periodic revolts, gives little promise of curing the addiction to bureaucracy, can Christians find some way of redeeming such a time? Can denominations and ecumenical bodies in their own organizational life free themselves of bureaucratic assumptions and habits, curtail expansion, limit the pretensions of structure, keep uppermost a commitment to the task to be done, learn concern for the people supporting the enterprise, and practice dedication to those it is supposed to serve? In trying to exert an impact on corporations and governments is it possible for a Christian, a congregation, a denomination, a council of churches, a seminary, to discover methods to affect the decisions of the bureaucracies? It will not be easy in a world where "Power confuses itself with virtue."[48] But when the church has been truest to its calling it has found ways to challenge the principalities of this world.

The Demolition of Community

At no point has the present age more powerfully impacted the human spirit than in the elimination of community. The intense sense of belonging to tribe or locale and of having one's recognized place within it which characterized the hunting and agricultural eras (i.e., the greater part of human history) has vanished with the onrush of urbanism accompanying the Industrial Revolution. An individual today is subject to anonymity and a sense of powerlessness, even in smaller towns, which the mass media have blanketed along with the rest of the country. We have already seen one result: everyone but the celebrity has been reduced to nonentity. While urban anonymity provides relief from the oppressive nosiness of the small town, for many it also lowers self-esteem and gives rise to anti-social attitudes. "Nobody" tries to announce that one is "Somebody" by flaunting symbols of significance (e.g., designer jeans), engaging in shocking behavior, even committing suicide, while nearly 20 percent of American adults suffer from psychiatric disorders.[49]

At the same time the forces of urbanism have weakened "community institutions"—not only churches, but neighborhood schools, civic organizations, service clubs, cultural groups, fraternal organizations. While these still provide personal satisfaction to the participants, before the new magnitudes of metropolis they have lost the power they once had to impact the local scene. Thus social change has destroyed or rendered inconsequential the "infrastructure" on which church and ministry long depended for influence within the community and which gave the minister visibility and honor. Perhaps not since the Reformation have so few ministers had local recognition as persons of public significance.

The loss of sense of secular community contributes to the much lamented introversion of congregations and other local societies; it is not uncommon for local chapters of secular organizations, or for congregations, to sever their ties with the national institution. The need to belong to something that is "ours," where we are known and our ideas make a difference, has been intensified by the depersonalization of the world outside, so that members feel undue possessiveness over the life of a congregation, a church school class, or a church fellowship group: "At least this is ours." The resurgence of denominational sensibiity at the expense of ecumenical commitment may also be part of this same phenomenon.

A critical question continues to haunt us: how can a congregation today relate significantly to the people of its particular place and to their needs after the old structures and patterns of community have been replaced by impersonal bureaucracies and the mass media? How does a church or its minister gain attention for its witness and service and action? While it must be granted that few churches take advantage of the avenues open to them (particularly press and radio in smaller communities), urban congregations, churches in their regional manifestation, the mainline denominations, and their ministers are all virtually invisible on the local scene. The issue is not how to turn ministers into tinhorn celebrities; rather it is how to win attention for the gospel in its contemporary relevance.

Here is a problem to be taken up by the seminaries if they are truly concerned to serve the congregations and to address the culture. The Study Department of the World Council of Churches sponsored extensive studies on locality and the missionary structure of the congregation, from the late 1950s through the early 1970s.[50] Except for influencing the definition of the goal of Christian unity ("All in Each Place One"), this impressive and significant work seems to have had little permanent influence on theological education or on congregational life and structure. Perhaps the eagerness to find a "new form of church" better adapted to serving the contemporary world induced a certain blindness to the remarkable persistence of the congregation; the fact that the studies offered congregations little practical help doubtless explains their lack of influence. The issues remain. In addressing them the seminaries must engage one of the crucial questions of our times: can the technology which has fragmented human relations be used to cement them?[51]

To some readers this discussion of magnitudes that oppress may seem an unwelcome digression from the proper task of this study. For American Christians, as we shall soon see, have come increasingly to think of personal and familial concerns as the proper realm of the church's concern. The point of this section is to show that in the world rushing at us the principalities, the powers, the world rulers of this present darkness (Eph. 3:12) impinge constantly on the realm of the spirit, that resistance to these forces calls for vigor and conviction on the part of the chruch. As Christians looking forward we will realize that "technological advance does not eliminate moral struggle."[52] If Christianity is to bear an authentic witness in the twenty-first century, the church must acknowledge that it has a battle on its hands. It will do so only if ministers clearly perceive the nature and intensity of the struggle, and that will happen only as the seminaries come to terms with the necessity of such a spiritual warfare. More on this issue will follow throughout the book.

The Temper of Mind and Spirit

We turn now to the realm conventionally considered religious to inquire into the effects of the emerging world on the human spirit. The trends to be discussed show every sign of gathering momentum in the coming decades, and some will surely be accentuated by high technology and the magnitudes of power just considered. Because the church has not learned to cope with these trends, much less master them, theological education must address them head on if it hopes to prepare ministers for the twenty-first century. Not only do the issues require analysis, in which religious scholarship has brought worldly wisdom and theological insight to bear; they also demand prescription.

Secularity as Working Assumption

Though the theme of secularity may be overworked, it cannot be ignored. As used here, it denotes the fundamental axiom of modern science: all investigation proceeds on the assumption of a natural cause of every phenomenon. Any appeal to the supernatural, i.e., to the idea of God, is by definition to be excluded from scientific discourse. This does not mean that science necessarily intends to be anti-religious or irreligious. A scientist as a person outside the laboratory may be a believer, even the devout and practicing sort; in the universities the believers are more likely to be found among the scientists than among the professors of humanities.[53] But as a discipline science deliberately limits its field to that which can be accounted for by natural law or by causes subject to rational explanation. Scientific method thus made possible a new understanding of the physical world, the abolition of a great deal of superstition, impressive advances in technology, and improvement in the material conditions of life. Because of the prestige accruing to it scientific method has become the "methodology" of virtually every discipline in the university—and in the theological seminary. The naturalistic assumption functions as the axiom of modern life.

As a result theological presuppositions and the religious practice derived from them have been increasingly relegated to the domain of "the soul," i.e., the private sphere. The realm of the "sacred"—traditionally an area of mystery and foreboding, beyond the bounds of rational explanation—has shrunk decade by decade since the Enlightenment, and has receded from public view.[54] In downplaying or disregarding attention to religion, the mass media are not perverse nor even uniquely blind; they merely give expression to the prevailing worldview and by so doing reinforce it. The persistence of faith, especially Christian faith, in so large a part of the population amazes many,[55] and the growth of fundamentalism has dumbfounded most observers. Yet even if secularism is less triumphant than secularists and religious liberals imagine, it has taken over the common life. The fact that the sacred remains personally significant to so many makes for the fragmentation of the contemporary mind.[56] It breaks first into "secular" (or "scientific" or "natural") and "sacred" (or "religious" or "supernatural"). Then the sacred fragment shatters into innumerable pieces corresponding to the various religious interpretations which command acceptance.

Today's secular mind gives minimal attention to ethical considerations, which in Judaism and Christianity and some other major religions have been closely united with faith. The scientific or technological mentality is not accustomed to the type of reflection, akin to philosophical or theological reasoning, involved in ethical thought. Technology asks what is possible, not what ought to be done. If something is technologically feasible and presumed to be advantageous for those in power, it probably will be done. The modern world has moved from religious pluralism to moral pluralism,[57] both of which readily lead to agnosticism. Yet the fundamental socio-political-economic problems of our time come down to an ethical question: "who gets what?"[58]

In a time of increasing secularism in the common life, a question already asked under the theme of the new religious pluralism must be asked again: Can the church in America continue to "stand in its own strength" without the traditional support once provided by a society with inherited Christian mores (sabbath-observance, church attendance) and by a culture saturated with biblical images and ideas, especially in literature, the arts, history, and philosophy? After the adoption of the First Amendment, American churches proved they could stand on their own financially. But can they do so without the buttressing mores of a "Christian nation" and a "Christian people?" The uncertainty evoked by the question is surely a factor in the widespread demand for prayer in the public schools.

As Christians disturbed over the godlessness of the present, we tend to remember our recent past rather than our earliest years. In the first three centuries of the church, Christians could not teach in the public schools because they refused to take part in the prayers demanded by the government. The establishment did not regard these as sectarian, but Christians would not join in them because they invoked pagan gods. A Christianity which risked standing against the culture not only survived but brought down the old paganism as well. Is the American church capable of that kind of independence of the culture? No more burning question confronts the ministry today.

To preserve its integrity in this struggle the church will have to come to terms theologically with secularity. That task devolves on every Christian, especially every minister, but preeminently on the theological seminary. Theological liberalism and modernism embraced the scientific method and even secularity itself, as did Dietrich Bonhoeffer, Harvey Cox, Paul Van Buren, and the death-of-God theologians with various degrees of critical reservation.[59] Bonhoeffer saw the modern age as a time when we must learn to live before God without God. In that spirit Christians who cherish the gains of the past three centuries in the expansion of knowledge and of human freedom will gladly give secularity its due. At the same time they will endeavor to keep their intellectual balance as they contemplate the unfulfilled promise of the modern age, the ominous threats to life itself now posed by technology, and the devastation of the human spirit that attends so many features of contemporaneity.[60]

To posit a closed natural universe free of supernatural intervention for the sake of arriving at scientific explanation of particular phenomena in physics, chemistry, biology, even history is one thing. To attempt to live without God (and in no sense "before God") is quite a different matter: it is the essence of pride, discerned by classical theology as the fundamental sin. Yet it is precisely that brand of secularity which has dismissed ethical considerations from decisions of public policy and advanced a cynical hedonism as the contemporary lifestyle. In such a time authentic Christian ministry will declare the claims of God intelligibly and forthrightly. If the church is to have such a ministry, a heavy responsibility lies upon theological education.

Utilitarianism in Education

A major problem of the churches, largely unrecognized, is posed by the dominance of utilitarian presuppostions regarding education—a far greater danger than the much abused "secular humanism." A generation which has dismissed ethics and religion as issues of common concern has come to conceive of education accordingly as an enterprise to be valued for the vocational utility it offers in the society already described. Emphasis falls heavily on technology, engineering, and finance, with a consequent downplaying of the liberal arts, especially history, literature, philosophy, and, of course, religion. To a great extent the fine arts are dismissed also, except as art may be valued as a financial investment or a social interest of the upscale lifestyle. The value attributed is extrinsic, for the artist is perceived as a decorator, whose work may provide pleasant diversion, but not as a revealer or interpreter of truth about the human condition.[61]

The prevailing utilitariansim has resulted in a devastating loss of humane considerations from the life of the mind. Education so conceived fails to stimulate the imagination, gives minimal attention to symbol and myth, and ignores questions of value and meaning. It has cut the roots of our intellectual and spiritual tradition. Few of our contemporaries, most especially those who attack the bugaboo of "secular humanism," seem to know that the title of Christian humanist was long one of the noblest appellations in Western culture, claimed by Petrarch, Pico della Mirandola, Erasmus, Sir Thomas More, John Colet, Ulrich Zwingli, John Calvin, Philip Melanchthon, and many other leaders of the Reformation, or that it involved an appropriation of the classical tradition of the liberal arts into an integrated worldview controlled by the fundamental principles of Christian theology. This type of Christian humanism prevailed in the universities from the Renaissance on and in the American liberal arts college typically founded as an institution of the church.[62]

With the passing of esteem for the "more humane letters" society has experienced the loss of a common universe of discourse among the educated. Not only are people ignorant of literature and history as content; the technological mind has lost through disuse the capacity to think symbolically and parabolically. When the late Glenn Rose joined the faculty of the Graduate Seminary at Phillips University, he soon realized that he could not teach Old Testament to persons unable to deal with a story as a carrier of meaning; so he began his introductory course by requiring them to read and discuss three contemporary novels in order to experience an approach to truth through story, before they turned to a reading of the scriptures.[63]

The disappearance of the humanities from the world of common discourse has coincided with a massive shift of student population to tax-supported schools: community colleges and municipal and state colleges and universities. The overwhelming increase in the number of degrees granted (4.6 percent of the American population held a college degree in 1940, 16.3 percent in 1980)[64] has taken place in a dominantly secular academy largely lacking the concern for value and meaning which characterized the church-related and private liberal arts schools that for so long set the tone for higher education. The emphasis on utilitarianism minimizes commitment to the ideal of service which formerly marked the community of the educated. Hedonism, careerism, and the upscale lifestyle have entrenched themselves not only in the television commercial but in the great universities.

A generation's changes in higher education might be schematized, not unjustly as follows: from small college to mega-university, from educated elite to college-processed mass, from liberal (humane) studies to vocational specialization, from self-contained community to fractured world, from teaching to research, from idealistic service to careerism, from supervision of youth (in loco parentis) to abdication of oversight, from dominance by the church-related college to dominance by the technological sausage-mill, from the teaching of religion to the study of religion, from the study of the Bible to the study of world religions, from dominance by the church to dominance by business.

The result is an "educated" population without an education in the historical understanding of that term.[65] By the teachers of wisdom in the ancient East, the philosophers in classical Greece, the scholars in the medieval universities, and the professors in the liberal arts college in America, education was seen as a road to insight and understanding, qualities believed as essential as knowledge and "know-how" (*technē*) in persons who would come to positions of leadership. Such education ennobled the human spirit in the process of mastering the skills to make a living.

The overwhelming utilitarian preoccupation on the modern scene has even vitiated the teaching of the liberal arts, which are studied not for the exploration of fundamental questions about life and the universe but for meeting professional qualifications to teach, say, English or history. That being the understanding of the purpose of a college education, there is no good rebuttal to the advice not to study philosophy or French "because it won't lead to a job." While such considerations cannot be dismissed as totally without weight, we note the widespread sense of emptiness in higher education, best seen in the attitude of bored resignation with which students, even in seminary, go about fulfilling requirements for a degree, rather than an attitude of eagerness to explore the meaning of their humanity or to seek for truth about life and the universe.[66]

This emptiness in the university, as in the culture, has expanded into a great void only dimly understood by secular society or even by the church. To try to fill it, people turn as if by reflex action to the entertainment industry, which the university itself has joined. Its heavily subsidized and increasingly scandalous athletic programs have been professionalized beyond any justification in the name of education or even of public relations. The sometimes ugly and irresponsible protest of the counter-culture and the black power movement in the 1960s and early 1970s against the irrelevance of the academic establishment to overwhelming social problems and fundamental human concerns led to brief experimentation with "free universities" and "schools without walls."[67] Most of these efforts have collapsed, and the protest has largely subsided, at least for the time being, but the emptiness remains. It can hardly be papered over even by the most glittering success in the attainment of the widely publicized "yuppie" goals.

The utilitarianism of contemporary higher education and the obsession with vocational success which fuels it have gone largely unnoticed and unprotested by the churches. The question now presses on us: can the community of Christian faith resist this trend, at least to the point of making clear its serious limitations and offering an alternative? Can congregations inspire in their members, especially in their youth and in those who are teachers, a greater depth of humane concern? Can they more clearly motivate vocational commitments to human service and the public good?

It is time for the Christian ministry in America to launch a searching self-examination: how much of its work, including the preaching, involves serious reflection on questions of meaning and value, as over against the pop psychology and institutional promotion which it so constantly purveys? Is it possible to awaken in the church an insight into the emptiness of contemporary education, as well as an awareness of the many potential allies in academia, both professors and students, eager for larger emphasis on the liberal arts? Is it possible to raise that insight to such a level of understanding as may begin to gain visibility for an alternative, Christian style of life and intellectual inquiry? Can commitment to such an ideal reach sufficient strength to revive support for the church college, with its emphasis on the humanities, on service, and on intellectually responsible religion? If any such change it to take place in American higher education, the seminaries have a responsibility for getting it on the agenda of the coming generation of ministers.

Subjectivizing of Questions of Meaning and Value

With the dissolution of the broad moral and theological consensus which once obtained in Christendom by the increasingly powerful forces which shape our age of pluralism, people are more reduced to making private, uninformed, even quixotic decisions on issues of ultimate importance. Today religion integrates from within, not without[68]; it has been reduced to an experience, one among many experiences of diverse sorts, on the basis of which a person makes up one's mind.[69] Rather than finding guidance in a book or a body of teaching generally regarded as authoritative or in the counsel of a figure who is supposed to know, a person responds to the most profound issue with the comment, "It seems to me. . . ."[70]

Even religion has fallen into the general pattern of taking a psychological approach to every issue, often to the neglect of biblical and theological perspectives, and usually without attention to its social or sociological dimensions. Preaching in such a vein is acceptable, even popular, because it accords with the current way of "thinking" about one's problems and of evaluating religious options. Furthermore, it is noncontroversial, seldom bringing the minister under criticism or causing members to cancel their pledge. Usually it is nondemanding; it involves no sense of guilt and calls for no commitment. It makes people "feel good"—a development which would surely have raised suspicions in the mind of the apostle Paul or any of the classical Christian theologians.

Nevertheless preachers, religious publishers, and the seminaries have gone along with the psychologizing of religion—courses in counseling are demanded above all others by pastors in continuing education—without inquiring deeply into the reasons for the phenomenon or its possible limitations, if not dangers. Theological scholarship has given some consideration to the critical correlation of psychological and biblical insights[71] but relatively little attention to the effect of therapeutic assumptions on the common life.[72] A pressing issue at the approach of the twenty-first century is the question: can an authentic Christian theology be articulated capable of delivering the church in our generation from the trap of subjectivism? And, can the seminaries prepare ministers to help congregations deal with this issue?

Agenda for Mission

The twentieth century came in with a great surge of optimism springing from an unshaken confidence in progress; the century is on its way out amid widespread confusion and a general feeling of helplessness. Given the temper of mind and spirit in our time, the public mood is subject to sudden and erratic swings, e.g., the conflicting and shifting attitudes toward the war in

Vietnam or energy conservation or the trustworthiness of our public leaders. Yet amidst the confusion one discerns a longing for a public faith that will not be betrayed and for a pride that is justified by the tone of the common life. The crowds who celebrated Liberty Weekend in 1986, the popularity of a president who personifies the theme of "standing tall" after a season of disillusionment and shame, the elation of hundreds of thousands in response to the journeys of Pope John Paul II, all these catching up to some extent even persons who disagree, indicate a deep longing for common symbols of hope and commitment. While people prize their freedom, they feel an increasing discontent with a pluralism that seems to leave no common bond. While they have clearly rejected the moralism of an earlier generation and regard the churches as, for the most part, not very exciting, they are uneasy over the lack of meaning in a wholly secular and utilitarian culture.[73]

Such stirrings of wistfulness for a hope they cannot justify combine with a general feeling of helplessness before overpowering events and issues. The threat of nuclear war, violent swings in the economy, the disillusioning memory of Watergate, unpredicatable acts of terrorism, bureaucratic decisions made far away that close out the future of an entire community, irrational and anonymous crime, the brutalities of modern history[74]—these are only a few of the elements that combine to produce irritation, bitterness, and fear. Add frustration at the ambiguities of contemporary life: the unfulfilled promise of happiness through prosperity as "more" never seems to satisfy;[75] the hidden trap in women's "liberation" as the rhetoric of fulfillment through a career fades before the actuality of "wage slavery" in an economy where it takes two salaries to meet monthly payments and as the demands of two careers put new and intolerable strains on a marriage; a dull sense of the emptiness of monetary measures of value accompanied by low self-esteem in a society that gives little recognition of one's worth or the worth of others. Small wonder that informed students of our society speak of the "crisis of secularity," affirming that the "modern paradigm is in crisis."[76]

"The future is not the answer," our common American faith that time and progress will solve every problem notwithstanding.[77] Despite our addition to "neolartry," the worship of the new,[78] neither technological innovation nor religious novelty holds the solution to our problems. For at least forty years American seminaries have reverberated to the excitement of one fad after another, some of them central to the Christian witness, some eccentric and, happily, ephemeral; but even those which are valid and important—racial equality, spirituality, evangelism—proved limited in power, valued for vogue rather than for verity.

This book proposes no narrow of faddish answer to the spiritual crisis of our time, no simple formula for the renovation of theological education. It looks forward in Christian hope. It sees the task of the church as a response in faithfulness to the holy nature of God revealed in Jesus Christ. It sees the work of ministry as loyal service to the gospel in all its range and fullness. It sees the task of the seminaries as maintaining the wholeness and balance of the Christian witness in honest engagement with the deepest needs of the emerging world.

The failed slogan of the 1960s, "Let the world write the agenda," had it wrong in seeming to imply that the church should take its bearings from the world, for the church's mission is to serve God's Coming Age, undazzled and undismayed by the purported widsom of "the dethroned Powers who rule this world."[79] But the slogan had it right in recognizing that the church must shape its mission to meet the world's needs, to heal the world's ills, to turn the world from its course heading for disaster. It was a measure of the greatness of Pope John XXIII that he was able to discern the "signs of the times"[80] and inspire the church to authentic Christian response. *Aggiornamento* is not a matter of adapting Christianity to the present age or the emerging future; rather it is freeing the faith from its adaptation to an earlier and outmoded order that no longer exists. In that sense we are to understand our call to serve the coming age. It is the call which Isaiah heard in the Exile and which enabled him to proclaim the new thing God was about to do.

> Whose work is this, I ask, who has brought it to pass?
> Who has summoned the generations from the beginning?
> It is I, the Lord, I am the first,
> and shall be with the last.[81]

Chapter **2**

THE CHURCH IN THE WORLD THAT WAS

To clarify our thoughts regarding mission to the future, we reflect in this chapter on the church's past, noting assumptions derived from historical situations far different from our own, but still persisting to confuse its people and compromise its witness. We note also traits essential to the fullness of its character which were better realized in other eras and which we too easily forget. The church is the arena within which the graduates of the seminaries will work. Yet too often they leave our schools with an unrealistic understanding of it. They will find true freedom only as they free themselves both from traditionalism and from faddishness.

It is a long and ambiguous past out of which the church enters the future. In some respects it confines us; yet though we decry its dead hand, our history transmits a precious heritage, in interaction with which we define our identity and find our faith.[1] In looking to our past, we remember our far parents in the faith, Abram and Sarai, whom God called to set out in freedom on mission to a new day.[2] In the same way God calls us to turn our backs on the past and, looking to the grace that has brought us safe thus far, go out to serve the coming age. For us, both past and future find their meaning in the eternal Giver of them both.

Religion in Society

We begin with an overview of religion's place in society across the major epochs of history.

Primeval Functions of Religion

Before the writing of history, when our ancestors lived by hunting and gathering, they looked to religion to help secure their elemental needs. To ward off evil, to find aid in getting food or bringing a child to birth, they sought contact with the unseen powers. Though they practiced a shrewd worldly wisdom, the notion of separating sacred from secular would have been inconceivable. Interwoven inseparably with the customs and claims of the tribe, religion was the conserver of social values; celebrated in song and enacted in sacred dance, its rituals played out "the disciplined rehearsal of right attitudes."[3] But religion was also the source of ethical and cultural innovation, as the shamans perceived in dreams and visions new and nobler possibilities for humankind.[4]

From those far ancestors we have inherited not only the basis of our material civilization[5] but the majestic archetypes of our literature and our religion, the springs of our spiritual heritage.[6] To drink from these waters is to find refreshment in the joy of human imagination, the wonder of creativity, the unchanging poignance of love and birth and death, the sensitivity of the human spirit, and the primordial longing for God. Some of the Bible's oldest stories call up memories of that far time when hunting had begun to give way to herding and the patriarchs had set out for a new land.

In those far-off times religion had already assumed its crucial and characteristic functions in society, and anyone who hopes to use the church primarily as an instrument for radical social change will do well to ponder those aboriginal functions, which still persist, deep and virtually ineradicable: the human community looks to a sacred tradition to maintain social solidarity, to conserve the values it has honored in the past.[7] Equally persistent is the pattern of celebrating the divine approval assumed for a particular way of life (its own!). Anyone who undertakes work in the church not reckoning with this dynamic is in for deep trouble. Unrealistic hopes shatter in disillusionment, while God's bewildered people suffer hurt and even a sense of betrayal.

Yet to perceive religion as merely sanctioning things-as-they-have-always-been is to misunderstand its essential character. Just as culture is a "process [of] unremitting interaction between the past and the present,"[8] so a living religion involves that same dynamic. Sacred tradition simultaneously affirms the common life and stands in judgment over it. In dream and vision the sacred archetypes disclose new possibilities and even hint at a divine universalism transcending the limits of the tribal heritage. This dynamic operated in primitive religion, and the biblical prophets understood it: they saw and proclaimed their radical new demands for justice and peace as implicit in the covenant by which God had brought Israel into being. They looked forward to the future as God's coming age because they saw their people's identity defined by divine action in their past. In the Christian faith, the Holy Spirit presides over and guides this process as the church of the present interacts with its history, seeking to understand its mission to the future.

Religious Institutions in the Agrarian Epoch

Before the dawn of history, a major technological advance came with the discovery of agriculture. It launched a new era, which prevailed almost to our own time. The "biblical world" consisted of dominantly agrarian societies. Classical orators, philosophers, and poets cherished the rustic ideal in contrast with urban depravity. Farming provided the basis for the feudal economy and employed most of the population well into the modern period; at the dawn of the twentieth century less than 40 percent of the American people lived in towns of 2500 or more inhabitants. In 1980 the number fell just short of 75 percent.[19]

The new technology of seeding and harvesting enhanced the power of religion and the growth of the religious institution. The farmer's dependence on the cycle of the seasons led to the development of calendars, stimulating the study of astronomy and mathematics, while the increase of trade called forth the invention of writing. The new knowledge produced the first learned class in history, the priesthood, who led in the building of temples, the elaboration of liturgy, and the codification of law, both religious and secular. The prescribed ritual intended to insure fertility.

Like the hunters and gatherers before them, the tillers of the soil lived in harmony with the processes of nature; their direct dependence on the power which brought new life from seeds scattered in the ground or from the mating of their flocks evoked in them a sense of mystery, induced gratitude for such beneficence, and inclined them toward religion. Rooted in the immemorial routine of planting, cultivating, and harvesting, and relying on hand implements or simple machines operated by muscle power, the agrarian way of life made for attachment to a particular plot of ground, a sense of stability, and a feeling of kinship with the generations gone before.

Long after the rise of civilization agrarian patterns persisted with only slight and gradual changes. Through its first nineteen hundred years the church learned to adapt to the lives of rural people and to minister to their needs. Despite printed books in their hands and steamboats on the inland waterways, the students of Alexander Campbell followed a way of life closer to that of Jesus' hearers than to the life my students knew only a century afterwards. To these Southern Californians whose feet rarely touch the earth, what are seedtime and harvest? What is rain but an affront? What even are summer and winter?

In ancient times famous cities arose and thrived on trade, government, and manufacturing—in the original and literal sense of producing goods by hand. Yet they were always suspect in the agricultural era. To the prophets Babylon and Nineveh were by-words. Jerusalem crucified Jesus. Rome persecuted the Christians. Even though the apostle Paul directed his missionary strategy to the great centers of population, suspicion of the cities prevailed in the classical world and continues even yet. Both Thomas Jefferson and Alexander Campbell looked on urban life as leading to corruption. Our nineteenth-century religious forebearers founded their colleges in rural areas far from the noisome atmosphere of the cities. At the end of the century when Americans were moving to town in great numbers, they still associated their faith with the quiet and innocence of the countryside: "There's a church in the valley by the wildwood. . . ."

Religion in the Urban and Industrial Age

In the eighteenth century the Industrial Revolution shattered the serenity of agrarian society, drew thousands of people from the land to smoking factory towns, and initiated the age of urban dominance. The new system brough wrenching change, and the church did not succeed in shifting as rapidly as the world.[10] Members of long established parishes resented the influx of rude country folk, who came to work in the factories, and few ministers attempted to reach the new urban poor. Yet out of that need arose the Evangelical Revival, the involvement of the new Methodist movement with the working class, and the Sunday school as a dramatically successful instrument for the ministry of the laity. Although the church never fully identified with labor, it managed the transition from rural to urban life reasonably well in the time of small cities. It flourished notably among white collar workers and the expanding middle class.

Gathering momentum in America in the decades after the Civil War, the shift to the cities produced anxiety in the minds of those who left home and those who stayed behind. Leaders from the churches responded by organizing the YMCA and YWCA, the Young People's Society of Christian Endeavor, several comparable bodies tied to particular denominations, and on the campuses the Student Volunteer Movement. The rise of these movements coincided with the heyday of the church college, which took seriously its responsibility *in loco parentis*, the president in nearly every instance being a well known Christian minister, like a majority of the faculty. Probably at no other time in history has the church proved more effective in responding to the needs of older youth and young adults, instilling Christian altrusim along with an understanding of the emerging world, and enlisting large numbers of the most idealistic for lifelong service. In looking after its own, the church responded with discernment to the need needs occasioned by rapid social change. Advocates of the social gospel and leaders in the missionary movement rallied support for significant reforms, though the churches for the most part still accepted the assumptions of white racism.

As city gave way to metropolis after World War I, the church lost its grip on the levers of social influence. In 1980 the United States had 284 standard metropolitan areas, each consisting of one or more central cities of at least 50,000 inhabitants and the surrounding counties. Between 1950 and 1980 the percentage of the population living in such areas increased from 56.1 to 74.8—a total of 169,405,018 persons.[11] But the new magnitudes and impersonal character of the great concentrations of population have made things increasingly difficult for the churches and have overwhelmed the ministry as a public force, so that the minister functions chiefly as the official of a comparatively small, virtually invisible, voluntary organization. Congregations may flourish in the suburbs, but as institutions they exert little perceptible influence on megalopolis.

And now massive changes confront religion, both those which evoked high technology and those induced by it. Perhaps the power of tradition, perhaps readiness to use the mass media has enabled fundamentalist and evangelical denominations to flourish, while ironically, the mainline churches, which have made a serious effort to come to terms with the "modern mind," have slowly lost ground.[12] Dealing with metropolitan society seems to have stumped their leadership. How does the church engage a massive heterogeneous population caught up in the anonymity and diversity of a secularized culture which has destroyed community? If theological education is to serve the coming age, it must find a way to prepare a ministry qualified in mind, spirit, and professional skill to lead the church—its congregations, regions, and general structures—in a more effective mission to a different kind of world than it has ever known.

The Great Church: An Overview

Now to take a closer look at the calling fo the church against the large backdrop just sketched, we double back to trace its story as a distinctive people with a mission for the benefit of all humankind. Reflecting on the people Israel, the ministry of Jesus, and the major epochs in the life of the great church,[13] we note the historical conditioning of much that people assume as permanent, remind ourselves of lessons too readily forgotten, and point to the responsibilities of the seminaries in addressing an ambiguous religious scene.

Israel, the Covenant People

In answer to God's call Abram and Sarai moved from Ur of the Chaldeans to a new land which became the home of Israel their grandson. Back to that land, centuries later, Moses led the Israelites after a long period of enslavement in Egypt. There Deborah and Gideon and other heroes looked to Yahweh for victory over their foes, as did King David, who, triumphant at last, set up his royal capital in Jerusalem and prepared to build a temple. With Abraham, with Moses, with David, God made covenant. In each case Yahweh and the people pledged their loyalty by a sacred oath. Their destiny would be determined, in the mind of the prophets, by Israel's faithfulness or unfaithfulness or disobedience to the covenant.

As the Bible tells the story, God kept shaking the chosen people out of their familiar routine. When they prospered in Egypt, God allowed them to be enslaved. When Moses led them into the wilderness and they had grown accustomed to life there, God sent Joshua to bring them into Canaan. When King Rehoboam's wealth caused him to despise the common people and break the commandments, a prophet from God directed Jeroboam to rebel and so divide the kingdom. When the two nations forgot their calling as God's people and their covenant-pledge of justice, they were carried into captivity. Then just as the Jewish people had grown used to life in Babylon, God laid on them the task of returning to their homeland and rebuilding the temple. Through all their history, God repeatedly overruled their efforts to keep things as they had once been, denied their religion that kind of preservative function, had some new things in store, which are rarely easy to deal with. Still the prophets called on the people to recover their past, when God had dealt directly with their ancestors, and to renew the sacred covenant. That meant faithfulness to God alone in the practice of justice and mercy.

From the beginning the church has claimed Israel's sacred story as part of its scripture, turning to it for instruction as to its mission. But in eagerness to triumph over Judaism, the church has repeatedly misread the narrative, as though God had repudiated the Jews in favor of the Christians. That interpretation misses the point: God is never pleased with people who for their own advantage try to keep things as they are, who while making much of ritual do not practice justice, who understand faith as anchoring them to the securities of the past rather than impelling them into the uncertainty of God's future. The burden of scripture is a call to serve the coming age, to look forward with God.

For all who lay claim to the heritage of Israel a crucial need is a long overdue rapprochement among all the "children of Abraham"—Jews, Christians, and Muslims.[14] Especially pressing in this country is a new relationship between Christians and Jews. While outright anti-Semitism expresses itself less blatantly than in the past, few church people realize that rivalry between the two faiths colored the language of Christian scripture, which in turn prompted hatred and cruelty through the centuries. It is still common to hear in sermons and Bible classes descriptions of the Pharisees or of the Law which are wholly inaccurate and uninformed, even if not malicious in intent. Christian seminaries have begun to correct such errors in the minds of students and have employed an occasional rabbi as an adjunct professor but have done little toward changing attitudes in the churches and among the general populace. But genuine dialog between Jews and Christians is all too rare, even in the theological schools, and even more so in communities where church and synagogue are neighbors.[15] Together we might well explore what it means to be children of the covenant in our kind of world.

Jesus: Looking Forward To God's Coming Age

The human being in whose life, Christians believe, God chose to be most fully revealed lived and taught in eager expectation of God's coming age. In the earliest Gospel, Jesus of Nazareth began his public ministry with an announcement: God's new day is breaking, God's reign is at the door (Mark

1:15). Constantly he spoke of the new world God is ready to give if only human hearts will receive it. Then the first will be last, the meek will inherit the earth, the poor will receive the Kingdom, and the last will be first. The acts of healing which Jesus performed were signs of that new day. He called disciples to follow him, then sent them out to preach the approaching Kingdom (Matt. 10:7); like his own ministry, that of the incipient church was to look forward, to serve the coming age.

The first Christians linked the fulfillment of that hope to the speedy return of the risen Lord. So the emphasis shifted from the coming of the Kingdom to the advent of Christ. But gradually that perspective also changed: Paul's gospel of salvation in the risen Christ increasingly emphasized the grace of his presence, Luke wrote the Acts of the Apostles as a manual for the church's mission in a world with an ongoing history, and John thought of Christ as indwelling the church through the Holy Spirit. The church continued to proclaim the Lord's return, but increasingly thought of the future as an indefinite extension of the present era until the final consummation. Even so, Christians could not escape the claims of God's coming age nor the vision of the divine reign of justice, mercy, and peace.[16] (In the nineteenth century Alexander Campbell founded his journal *The Millennial Harbinger* to herald the plea for the oneness of the church; that would make possible the conversion of the world, the prerequisite for the reign of Christ on earth which Vachel Lindsay hailed as a "secular millennium.")[17]

Despite Jesus' eager expectation of God's imminent new day, his keen analysis of conditions in his time and of their probable outcome establishes a kinship with the futurologist or analyst of contemporary social trends. The Gospels depict him as an observer astute in assessing the mind of ordinary folk,[18] of the religious authorities,[19] and of the rulers who lorded it over his people.[20] With piercing insight he foretold the certain outcome of the smoldering revolution against Rome, just ready to burst into flames: the temple would be destroyed and Jerusalem left desolate.[21] Though he viewed the prospect through tears, he rejoiced in the possibility of a truer spirituality which need not be bound to a particular sacred site.[22]

Like the Christ portrayed in the Gospels, the church in mission is called to discern the signs of the times in a dual sense: to descry as best it can the current trends on the secular scene and to look beyond them to the eternal purpose of God, seeking to discover how best to serve that purpose in the particular historical moment. Such discernment is central to the task of theological education.

The Church as Outlaw

Because it understood loyalty to Christ to demand obedience to God rather than to human authorities (Acts 5:29), the earliest church consistently found itself in trouble with the government. Even though Paul regarded civil authority as divinely instituted for the well-being of society, neither he nor his successors for the next two hundred and fifty years entertained any illusions about the state. They did not confuse their religion with patriotism, but insisted on the supreme lordship of Jesus Christ over every earthly power. Because they refused to participate in the ceremonies of civic allegiance they were imprisoned and executed by the hundreds. Yet for three centuries the church survived as an illicit organization, the power of the Caesars insufficient to stamp it out—"in spite of dungeon, fire, and sword."

A church obsessed by the compulsion to avoid controversy too easily forgets the heritage of the martyrs. Yet that heritage still gives courage to stand against evil. A vocal minority of Christians protests the arms race, repudiates nuclear weapons, denounces racism, offers sanctuary. A smaller minority totally renounces war and the claims of the sovereign nation, even to the point of civil disobedience, ready to bear the penalties that may be assessed. Few Christians, however, have effectively challenged the hedonism and materialism of our age.

The church's heritage as outlaw raises the issue of Christ and culture.[23] Animating the mission to serve God's coming age, the vision of Christ transforming culture requires a certain acceptance of the world and its institutions matched by an undeviating loyalty to Christ above all earthly powers. American Christians can readily conclude that the church in Nazi Germany, except for the bold minority which rallied behind the Barmen Declaration, too easily submitted to the blasphemous claims of a totalitarian state. Only with difficulty can they discern how casually they themselves subordinate their allegiance to Christ under the claims of patriotism.

The memory of the martyrs reminds the church just how demanding its loyalty to Christ must sometimes be. A truly forward-looking church will cherish that heritage, ministers will motivate Christians to such faithfulness, and theological education will help a new generation to trace for our time the lines which Christians will refuse to cross.

The Church as Monitor and Teacher

In time Rome tired of executing Christians. Despite fierce and determined opposition their numbers grew, and in A.D. 311 Constantine and Licinius offered religious toleration. A radically new era began half a century later when the Emperor Theodosius threw the power of the state behind the church. Established as the official religion, Chrisitianity enjoyed that status by law until the Enlightenment brought religious freedom, and until our own century the cultural tradition continued to support the faith. The pattern was exported to European settlements in the New World. Religious establishment prevailed in Virginia and other southern colonies, and notably in New England with a lingering effect on American culture long after Independence.

During the so-called Christian centuries the church was seen as the Ark of Salvation. Even after the schism between Rome and Constantinople and the further shattering of unity by the Protestant revolt, only one church was recognized in each country. To be right with God, one must maintain good standing in that church. Hence it was able to exercise powers of discipline incredible to our free-and easy age. In the Christendom that was, the true church monitored the morals of the entire population, with the support of the state.

The church also held a unique position as guardian of truth. Since salvation depended not only on right living but also on confessing the true faith, orthodoxy or right teaching was a dominant concern. It was promulgated with authority by the teaching office of the church—the bishops and above all the pope; then Protestantism declared the Bible the supreme authority for determining truth.

In addition to morals and dogma the authority of the church prevailed in education, for until the High Middle Ages the church exercised a virtual monopoly of schooling at all levels; even after the rise of the universities, the majority of professors were clerics until the nineteenth century. As mother of learning the church spoke with the authority of secular knowledge as well as of revelation, and few had sufficient education to challenge it.[24] In medieval and renaissance Europe, a vigorous intellectual life flourished, with suprising freedom and diversity, but within a limited circle. Scholars rarely went public with their controversies, for few outside the universities would know what they were talking about. The Reformation began when a printer recognized the dynamite in the Ninety-Five Theses which Martin Luther had proposed for a disputation among scholars and ran off great quantities of them. Refusing to back down, Luther carried the issues to the people; theological debate became a matter of public consequence, and the education of laity took on new importance.

Through the long era of Christendom the church functioned as center of community. In an episcopal town the cathedral dominated the highest eminence and rose above surrounding buildings; in its open plaza or inside its walls all kinds of public meetings took place. The less pretentious parish churches in the villages, or even the monastic chapels in the countryside, towered similarily over the landscape. Their bells rang out the hours of prayer and took note of important events. In the supreme moments of life—birth, marriage, death—people repaired to the church for fitting ceremony. Before the Industrial Revolution a people's life was tied closely to a particular place; those who lived there formed a true community, and the church was at its center.[25]

So from Theodosius to Jonathan Edwards the church was the primary molder of culture. As guardian of the faith, as keeper of the most profound symbols by which human existence was interpreted, as sponsor of education, as center of community, as patron of the arts, the church provided matrix, inspiration, and support for drama, poetry, painting, sculpture, architecture, music, history, philosophy—the priceless treasure of our European cultural heritage. The greatest artists (Dante, Giotto, Leonardo, Michelangelo, Bach, Handel, to mention only a few) dealt with Christian themes, for these were inseperable elements in the fabric of culture.

From the era of Christendom two aspects of the church's heritage raise issues of major importance for its mission to the coming age and consequently for theological education. These are the informing of the culture by Christian symbols and themes and the church's exercise of authority. But before reflecting on them it is necessary to consider the changes wrought by the Enlightenment.

The Church as Source of Inner Security and Personal Inspiration

With the Age of Reason the era of secularization began, as modern intellectuals rebelled against revelation and ecclesiastical authority. First toleration, then full freedom of religion became the order of the day, the latter inaugurated by the First Amendment to the Constitution of the United States and by the French Revolution. "Enlightened" minds put their trust in science and rational reflection, assuming that the world could be more clearly understood as a machine operating in accord with natural law than as a theater for divine intervention. Most intellectuals of the eighteenth century believed in the creation of the universe by a supreme architect and in an afterlife of reward for virtue and punishment for vice; such a view was held to be self-evident to human reason and in no way dependent on revelation.

Religion therefore had a certain social utility because, whatever the differences among the sects on inconsequential points of doctrine, all were presumed to teach morality, so necessary to the making of good citizens.[26] But the sages of the Enlightenment ruled out the kind of involvement with public issues which the church had practiced under the old order in Europe through the intervention of ecclesiastical authorities in the processes of government. Aside from the common ethical responsibility attributed to religion, the Enlightenment looked upon the church as an institution serving private concerns, associated with subjective values rather than objective reality. People turned to faith out of a peculiar personal bent or a longing for security not to be found within themselves.[27]

So the church in Europe began a long decline.[28] Deprived of its power in government and education, ousted from its position as molder of culture, it retained its vigor longest in the area of moral regeneration and social reform; the Evangelical Revival occurred concurrently with the Enlightenment. But only rarely did Christian thinkers succeed in engaging the larger intellectual community, though some undertook to respond to the crisis precipitated by

Darwinism by integrating the new scientific worldview with a responsible theological understanding.

No longer did the church function as molder of culture, nor does it give signs of doing so in the world rushing toward us. For the most part high culture ignores or derides Christian symbols and themes—which was precisely Gabriel Vahanian's point in reviving Nietzsche's phrase, "The Death of God,"[29] though one may list such notable and varied exceptions from the latter half of the twentieth century as T. S. Eliot, C. S. Lewis, Dorothy Sayers, Graham Greene, W. H. Auden, Alexander Solzhenitsyn, Flannery O'Connor, Annie Dillard, and perhaps Leonard Bernstein, John Updike, and Peter DeVries.

Popular culture exhibits faint traces of Christian motifs—in disguise (the Superman story), in recognized ritual (the minister in mandatory clerical dress at a stylish wedding or funeral), in the occult (witchcraft, exorcism), in subservient distortion ("Onward Christian Soldiers" as a nationalistic battle-hymn), in sentiment (the plaster saint), or in caricature (the cornball evangelist, the fanatic). But seldom on film or television do normal, attractive, altruistic people say grace at family table, read the Bible, or attend church, much less articulate a basic Christian idea; rarely do we encounter a robust Christian.

As for the life of the mind, no theologian since Paul Tillich and Reinhold Niebuhr has been considered mandatory reading among secular intellectuals, though Thomas Merton, Hans Kung, Martin E. Marty, Harvey Cox, and John B. Cobb, Jr. have earned fairly wide name recognition. Leadership in the learned societies dealing with religion has passed from the scholars in the seminaries to those in religious studies at the universities, and among the church-founded or still church-related institutions of higher education it is rare to find a vigorous center of Christian thought in active dialogue with secular scholarship at the cutting edge. (Perhaps Notre Dame University is the most gratifying exception.) A surprising number of congregations and a few seminaries have commissioned artists to do sculpture, stained glass, paintings, and sacred music, some of which is unexpectedly good, but virtually unknown beyond their particular constituencies.

The disappearance of Christianity from the culture is an unforeseen price of religious freedom. The efforts of conservative Christians to determine the content of textbooks, control selection for public libraries, and push through a constitutional amendment mandating prayer in the pubilc schools, understandable as they are, are misguided. Conservative Christians of all people should know that if a Christian understanding is to flourish, it cannot and should not be imposed by government; it must spring from a vital faith joyously inculcated by the churches. But the churches are not doing very well at this task, nor have the seminaries given impressive leadership. How can the seminal minds and spirits of the coming age be brought into lifegiving contact with the Christian tradition so that its insights and power may truly inform their work? This question should be high on the agenda of theological education.[30]

The issue of authority is another crucial matter raised for the church in passing from the era when it was monitor and teacher of Christian Europe to the age of secularism and individualism. The world has already denied any public authority to the church in a democratic society: it has only the opportunity to persuade, and efforts to harness the power of the state to achieve what the church cannot do by persuasion should rightly be declared out of order.

But what about the internal life of the church? Here it has had considerable difficulty in freeing itself from the habits and mindset of a former time, despite the insistence of modern-minded persons on making decisions for themselves. Even the Roman Catholic Church, which has a clear doctrine of magisterial authority, has felt increasingly the power of the modern mood; on certain issues the faithful simply disregard the almost frantic insistence of pope and bishops.[31] In Protestantism the connectional churches also experience increasing difficulty in making their constitutional authority stick. In the matter of church discipline churches of virtually every stripe have abandoned the effort to regulate the behavior of their members. It should be noted, however, that the precise appeal of the new religious cults and some conservative Christian groups lies in their authoritarianism over the true believers, persons evidently in psychic need of a closed system.

Among Disciples of Christ, the crucial issue in their restructure during the 1960s was how to conceptualize a form of church which made possible true organic relationships, the power to formulate general policy, and a clearly delineated flow of responsibility without giving one manifestation or person authority over another. They believe they achieved this goal in the Design for the Christian Church (Disciples of Christ). The key is the principle of "mutual consent." Persuasion is of the essence. Those parts of the church that are ready for an action are free to move on the basis of majority vote, but they cannot require others to take the same step.[32]

The authority of the minister is a continuing problem for all churches today because of old assumptions. Most young pastors coming out of seminary evidently presume that they will be accorded some measure of authority, in recognition of their office and their degrees, but they soon discover, often with great pain, that the presumption is false. Even though they articulate their concept of ministry in clichés of enabling, they are frustrated at the minimal deference they receive, and only with considerable psychic suffering, while masochistically verbalizing the sentiment that the minister is not a leader, do they learn how to lead. It is urgent that the seminaries help their students work out a realistic understanding of authority in a Christian community,[33] the demands of leadership, the power of persuasion, and ways in which a Christian leader may exercise with integrity the authority of one who knows.

It would be wrong to end these reflections on the great church on a note of despair. Within congregations, church colleges, seminaries and other Christian communities in every part of the world, along with a discouraging amount of perfunctory piety, one finds authentic faith, amazing intellectual and cultural vitality, and genuine commitment to Christ and the Christian cause. The ecumenical movement, though it has lost the appeal of pioneering which marked its earlier days, continues an impressive work of service and intellectual inquiry. But all this dynamism, from Cross Corners to Geneva, is largely hidden from public view, not being judged newsworthy by the media. Perhaps the church should ask "So what?" The leaven in Jesus' parable was also invisible, but it leavened the whole lump. Here is the real issue for the church and the seminaries: how is the leaven to be placed in the great lump of secularism so that by the power of God it releases its dynamic throughout the whole of modern life?

The Churches in the USA

Turning to the particular religious situation in the United States, we see the historical context producing conditions in the churches which theological education must take into account.

A New Form of Church

The decision to treat religion as entirely voluntary had profound institutional implications. In Europe, where ecclesiastical establishment gave way only gradually to toleration and then to religious liberty, elements of the older pattern lingered long, especially in education and custom; the United States, by contrast, began its national life under a new order of freedom.

Scarcely 5 percent of the population belonged to a church, and any increase depended on the efforts of those few and the free decision of those they tried to convert; it was no business of the government. Even that handfull of members was scattered among several religious bodies roughly equal in size, so that no one church was in a position to dominate. Out of this freedom and multiplicity emerged a new form of church which Americans quickly came to regard as normal. It is the denomination.

Unlike the state church, the denomination had to make its own way without governmental aid. Yet unlike the sects of the radical reformation, it did not cut itself off from society; rather it tried to win a larger place within it. With unbounded hope and competitive zeal, each denomination dreamed of becoming *the* church of the American people. By winning souls as an instrument of mission, it advanced the true faith and built up its own life.[34]

Divisiveness and pluralism were built into the situation from the beginning, but a pragmatic people could not forever maintain the fiction that only one denomination, their own, had a monopoly of gospel truth. Little wonder that cooperation in mission arose early, providing strong impetus for the ecumenical movement. Religious liberty produced both the denomination and the opportunity for joining forces to overcome denominationalism.

American life continues to shape the form of the church. Assumptions as to the need for bureaucratic patterns and elaborate structures have seeped into the ecclesiastical mentality as unexamined axioms. In denomination and congregation alike preoccupation with institution tends to overpower sense of community, and concern for survival to supplement commitment to mission. The denomination has changed from carrier of a particular religious vision to a sociological entity, from an instrument of mission to an engine of financial production. The management model controls the thinking of large numbers of ministers—pastors, bishops, and bureaucrats.

It may be noted that some cults flourish with little structure apart from a network of devotees[35] and that many congregations thrive under the label "nondenominational." May not their appeal indicate a widespread antipathy to the denominations and to traditional religious institutions as popularly perceived? Except for a minority of members deeply involved in denominational affairs, little love appears in the congregations for Indianapolis or Philadelphia or 475 Riverside Drive, New York. Antipathy toward ecclesiastical power was a major factor in the early growth of Disciples of Christ.

A Common Religion Outside the Churches

An unexpected ambiguity resulting from the new freedom and diversity was the emergence of American civil religion as a common spiritual force in the life of the people.[36] Two aspects of the phenomenon require attention here.

One is the pretension of the sovereign nation to ultimacy, which can only be called idolatry. The churches had best keep their guard up, for the public mood is subject to unpredictable outbreaks of nationalistic frenzy, and American Christians may be called on at any time to declare God's sole and supreme sovereignty.

Another aspect of civil religion points directly to a failure of the churches and ought to concern the seminaries. As noted in our analysis of religion's social functions, it is no merely private affair; it performs a crucial task in giving expression to the common values and commitments of a people. It readily did so in primitive society, which did not separate sacred from secular, and in medieval Christendom, where church and state operated in close harmony. But in a pluralistic society with a bewildering diversity of churches, sectarian religion divides the people instead of binding them together. In a land of many denominations the flag rather than the altar symbolizes unity, and national holidays like Thanksgiving and Memorial Day give common religious expression to that oneness in moving public ceremonies which no single church can offer. It is hardly surprising that 87 percent of the respondents to a recent poll favored a quasi-religious moment of silence in the public schools.[37]

To counteract their guilt in allowing their divisions to stultify and negate an elemental function of religion the churches must either sustain the vision of one united people providentially fashioned from "the multitudes brought hither out of many kindreds and tongues"[38] and give ethical content to the phrase "one nation, under God"—or settle for sectarian status in society. The task calls for a new urgency in the ecumenical venture. The oneness of the church is promised as gift of God, not for its own sake, but as sign and promise to the world of God's intention for humanity. Hence the churches are called to overcome the divisiveness which has fractured sacred community and to relate the oneness of this people to that larger oneness of all humanity given by God in creation and promised in the coming Kingdom.

Impulse-Buying in Religion

The constitutional guarantee of religious liberty arose from a widespread conviction, after centuries of persecution, that a person's religion is not a public concern, but a private affair.[39] Determined to get government off their backs, evangelical Christians teamed up with political liberals and deists to win toleration in Virginia and then to pass the First Amendment to the Constitution.[40] Yet an unexpected ambiguity emerged, which should greatly concern theological education: the wholesale subjectivizing of religion.[41] Americans buy what appeals to them at the moment.

This condition resulted from the freedom of speech, press, and religion guaranteed in the First Amendment. In arguing that no one is in so good a position to make up one's mind about one's religion as is the person involved, the seers of the Enlightenment took for granted both human dignity and the rational character of such a decision. Throughout the nineteenth century, the denominations conducted a vigorous polemic, intent on convincing their hearers by scripture and right reason. Disciples of Christ thrived on debate, glorying in their triumphs of biblical knowledge and applied logic.

But many people did not make their decisions on rational grounds. The Great Awakening swept in thousands of converts on waves of emotion, and nineteenth-century revivalism refined the process of manipulating the feelings so as to stampede the hearers to the mourner's bench. The popular hallmark of conversion was established as "experience." In earlier Puritanism an "experimental knowledge" of one's election had rated as an essential of salvation and church membership, but that experience had ensued after long reflection on magisterial preaching of Christian theology and a long regimen of "preparation" including fervent prayer. As the intensity of revivalism waned, Americans nevertheless continued to rely on their feelings as the primary factor in choosing a church.

Subjectivism afflicts liberal and conservative Christians alike, betrayed, for example, in the American penchant for almost always speaking of "a worship experience" rather than just "worship" as though the act had less significance than the effect on the participants. While Disciples long resisted subjectivity in religion and still resist its more blatant forms, it must be admitted that many people in the congregations have chosen to be there primarily because they "liked" a minister or a class or the music or some other attractive feature.[42] Theological education has a mission to impart depth to American religion by a convincing presentation of the biblical witness concerning sin and salvation, by a relevant theology accessible to ordinary people but addressed to the whole person, so that religious decision becomes a total and integrating action of the entire human being rather than a matter of impulse-buying.

Impact of the Churches on the American Scene

Despite unforeseen problems, the remarkable vitality of American religion has resulted in impressive achievement. Under conditions of free choice, the churches have brought into their membership a majority of the nation's population; in a century and half the proportion rose from less than 10 percent to more than 60 percent.[43] While the cultural heritage carried a regard for the Bible and the Christian faith, their decision was seen by all concerned as an act of conversion involving a new loyalty, reformation of life, and commitment to new ideals for personal character, family relationships, neighborliness, and community service. As settlers filled up the continent, Christians established congregations, colleges, and other institutions. In each new place their ministry provided a nucleus for community life. Yet paradoxically, denominational separation simultaneously fractured community.

Drawing on the scriptures and America's brief history, the churches offered an interpretation of human experience and national destiny. Abraham Lincoln's Second Inaugural Address was made possible by the large place of the Bible in popular culture and by a Calvinist interpretation of history. Though it presumed an inferior status for American Indians, blacks, and Hispanics, preaching celebrated an ideal of freedom inevitably erosive of attitudes and institutions which denied it to all. Despite the current secularism and declining church membership, an overwhelming proportion of Americans interviewed in a 1984 Gallup Poll described themselves as Christians and professed adherence to the basic religious beliefs taught by the churches.[44]

The activity of the churches in leading popular movements for social reform is clearly a by-product of modern democracy. In ancient Israel the prophets called the people back to covenant-obedience and rebuked kings. But the historical circumstances of Jesus' ministry closed out the option of social reform except by preaching the vision of God's coming Kingdom and the change of mind (repentance) which it demanded. The outlaw status of the ancient church limited it to efforts to change human hearts and personal behavior. After Constantine the church lived under authoritarian governments for fourteen centuries; spiritual advisers might counsel emperor or duke or king, but popular agitation to achieve social reform was at best a limited option. In Christian thought as in late classical philosophy virtue remained privatized.

Once the people had won the right to vote, the whole situation changed. Bearing a responsibility for governmental decisions, Christians now undertook by preaching and overt political action to change offensive conditions and achieve a larger measure of justice. So the churches in the United States have opposed duelling, the war with Mexico, slavery, child labor, the liquor traffic, the war in Vietnam, and policies that point toward nuclear war. They have carried on special ministries to immigrants, refugees, illegal aliens, and migrant agricultural workers. Despite the much-publicized obscurantists, churches have worked to establish free public schools, secure women's rights, provide education for the emancipated black people, help new immigrants achieve "Americanization," and win civil rights for ethnic minorities.

A Changing Picture

Negotiating the passage between a familiar past and an unknown future, the churches confront a scene of rapid and drastic change.

Since the heyday of the 1950s the mainline Protestant denominations have suffered a slow but steady decline in membership and influence. In a sense, this is nothing novel in America, where older, well entrenched denominations have commonly lost their dominance (though not absolute numbers) to the raw vitality of new movements. After 1800 Episcopalians, Congregationalists, and Presbyterians gave place to Methodists, Baptists, "Christians," and Disciples.[45] In time these upstarts joined the "mainline," but now—except for Southern Baptists and other equally conservative Baptist bodies—they are falling behind fundamentalists, Pentecostals, and evangelicals. Their losses may be explained in part by the collapse of the cultural allies on which liberal religion had relied—a philosophy concerned with metaphysics, a science rich with promise, a biblical scholarship in touch with the churches, a kind of history written for the general public rather than just for academic specialists.[46] Their forthright stand for civil rights in the 1960s and their continuing commitment to a liberal social agenda, reflected in resolutions passed at denominational assemblies and by the National Council of Churches of Christ, have caused disenchantment among conservative constituents. While these churches possess the vitality to sustain a high level of giving, they have not mustered the imagination or the resources for a major new assault on the national consciousness and have gradually ebbed toward invisibility in the age of mass media.

By contrast, some conservative churches enjoy spectacular growth. Their best known ministers have mastered the use of media and computer technology and in the spirit of free enterprise have built huge personal ventures in broadcasting and publishing. Fundamentalism has joined with political conservativism and the patriotic front in the political arena to promote a vision of Christian social responsibility strangely different from that of the mainline churches.[47] Among evangelicals (one can only lament the loss by default of this magnificent word) are scholars of impressive learning and readiness for dialogue with more liberal Christians. But the great mass of conservative Protestants write off the mainline churches as hotbeds of secular humanism and avoid them almost entirely. By choice, the Christians of this vast bloc are almost without representation in the ecumenical movement.

Another drastic change in the religious landscape is the mushrooming of cults, both religious and psychological.[48] The American environment has produced "far-out" groups in abundance since the early nineteenth century, but the counterculture of the 1960s gave new impetus to the tendency, which flourished unabated through the narcissism of the 1970s. It is sobering that the cults and psychological "isms" have had their greatest appeal among educated youth from relatively well-to-do homes.[49] One wonders if the seminaries cannot come to a deeper insight into the spiritual void which prompts a new generation to go prospecting in religion and if they cannot work with the churches to develop a fresh and vibrant style of congregational life which will not strike the young as so predictable, so boring, so passé.[50]

The emergence of the Roman Catholic Church as a vigorous presence in the public eye has brought yet another change on the religious scene. No longer identified mainly with recent immigrants, it has clear public visibility, enhanced in recent years by the "Bishops Letters" on nuclear war and the economy. Although its positions on birth control, abortion, and the ordination of women resemble those of the fundamentalists, the ecumenical involvements of Roman Catholicism have made it increasingly more congenial to mainline Protestants. Bilateral dialogues with other churches, including Disciples, have led to warm friendships among the participants and considerable theological consensus, though to little formal change.[51] Representatives of the Catholic Church appear frequently in the media. Yet despite new visibility and sense of belonging in American life, attendance at mass has declined, as have religious vocations,[52] while recent efforts to silence dissent have introduced new strains with American Catholicism, as between it and liberal opinion in the churches and outside.

The current scene in religion is enough to baffle the churches and their ministers to the point of discouragement. After a century of effort to come to terms with the "modern mind," to work out an understanding of the Christian faith in which the worldview of science and a biblically informed spirituality can live together in honest harmony, to demonstrate the relevance of the gospel to the major issues of the times, the very churches which have pursued these goals most consistently now find themselves in decline. "It is not fanciful to say that American churches flourish today in negative correlation to their degree of *aggiornamento*."[53] The oft-remarked aging of the membership among mainline Protestants appears to be explained not so much by the presumed otherworldliness of the churches or the fear of death by the aging but rather by the remarkable persistence of those members who flocked into the churches after World War II. Nevertheless the cool and careful mood of classical theological liberalism does not seem to address the spiritual yearnings of today's young,[54] who veer to the right to enter the tight box of fundamentalism or to the left to seek fulfillment in the cults. "Where have all the flowers gone?"

On this somber note let us turn to the specific situation of the Disciples.

The Christian Church (Disciples of Christ)

The particular church which commissioned this study is part and parcel of the American experience. All four of its most prominent early leaders, in their effort to bring a faithful Christian ministry to their time and place, broke away from the churches that had been. The history of the movement initiated by Barton W. Stone, Thomas Campbell, his son Alexander, and Walter Scott does not need recounting here, except for the observation that two movements originating among a few congregations in the Ohio Valley converged and grew into "a great people," numbering about 2 million at the end of their first century. Here is offered, almost in outline form, a brief analysis of that history as it pertains to our understanding of the church, called from the world that was to serve the coming age.

Their Appeal in Their First Century

In an age of denominational rivalry, sectarian shattering of the frail community slowly building among a lonely people, and partisan bitterness, here was a plea for the unity of all Christians, who were urged to "consider each other as the precious saints of God."[55]

In a time when the "mainline" churches insisted on subscription to confessions of faith elaborating abstruse formulations of complex theological issues, here was a proclamation of the "simple gospel" centered on Jesus Christ as Son of God—"No creed but Christ."

Among a people elated at having taken political government into their own hands and impatient with ecclesiastical restraints, which they dismissed as human "traditions and inventions," outmoded accretions from the age of superstition and repression, here was an appeal to the clear teaching and demonstrable practice of the early church: "Where the scriptures speak, we speak; where the scriptures are silent, we are silent."[56]

To a generation in terror of a literal hell and agonizing after assurance of divine election, here was the gracious offer of a sane, scriptural, objective pattern of conversion, with commands to be obeyed, gospel facts to be believed, and promises to be enjoyed, all neatly summarized in a five-finger exercise: faith, repentance, baptism, remission of sins, and gift of Holy Spirit and of eternal life.

In a context where denominational titles advertised a peculiarity of polity, doctrine, or ordinance, here was a name for all. Rather here were names—Christian, Disciple, Church of Christ. And here was an insistence on "the whole gospel" which, though it too often boiled down to the plan of salvation or the necessity of immersion, envisioned nothing less than "the restoration of primitive Christianity: its doctrine, its ordinances, and its fruits."[57]

To a people zealous for their newly won liberties in civil society and equally devoted to freedom in religion, here was a stirring commitment to that ideal, which repudiated the authority of ecclesiastical courts and dogmatic systems while holding fast to the heart of the faith: "In essentials, unity; in non-essentials liberty; in all things, charity."[58]

In a setting where settlers going West kept outrunning the advance of institutions, both governmental and ecclesiastical, here was a pattern for church and ministry well adapted to frontier conditions yet vowing to conform wholly to "the original faith and order," to "take up things exactly where the Apostles left them"[59]

Among a scattered people living a hard and perilous life without the ministrations of a professional clergy except for brief visits at spasmodic intervals here was provided, under authority of scripture, an authentic sacramental life through the "standing and immutable ministry of the Christian community," i.e. elders and deacons chosen from and ordained by the congregation of believers.[60]

To a popular mind that honored John Locke as "the Christian philosopher," readily acknowledged the authority of scripture when read with "common sense," and was as yet unshaken by the skepticism of Hume or the critiques of Kant and Feuerbach, here was offered a formulation of the gospel that fit their (Lockean) worldview.[61] The position could be stated clearly enough for ready apprehension by the majority who were largely deprived of "book learning," but it accorded responsibly with scripture and so convincingly with prevailing intellectual patterns that impressive numbers of thoughtful people, well read in the classics, political theory, and current literature, found joyful haven among the Disciples.

For a generation which heaped adulation on its heroes, thinking of them as larger than life, here was a leadership readily idealized for devotion to "the good cause," intellectual powers, quick wit, and ability to discuss profound issues with ordinary folk. Not only the four founders, but "Raccoon" John Smith, Caroline Pearre, James A. Garfield, Isaac Errett, David Lipscomb,

Z. T. Sweeney, Alexander Proctor, Helen E. Moses, J. W. McGarvey, to name only a few, were idolized by hosts of followers, if not by all Disciples.

To a people scattered across a still empty land, hungry for news from home or even the sound of a familiar voice, here was (as in a number of the denominations) a sense of belonging to a larger "family." As yet unsensitized to inclusive language, Disciples spoke fondly of the "brotherhood." They addressed one another as Brother and Sister. They travelled long distances to attend cooperation meetings or general convention. Because their "evangelists" (itinerant preachers) did not hold membership in conferences or presbyteries organized geographically, they travelled widely, and when they began to "locate" in settled ministries, they still moved readily from one part of the country to another. Scores of leaders were known throughout the brotherhood by name and even by face, and to those who were genuinely involved, it meant something to be a Disciple.

Work was hard, resources limited, tensions within the movement troublesome, and opposition sometimes fierce. But the plea was sublime, the victories heartening; to some it seemed that Disciples were about to take the country.

Adaptations to a Changing World

Then the world changed. The founders had not intentionally cut their cloth to the patterns and presuppositions of their time and place, for they were convinced that they were reading their program straight from the New Testament. But in evident sensitivity to the needs of their situation, they had found the scriptures addressing them with exciting relevance. From the early successes of the plea Disciples had deduced a highly romanticized and triumphalist vision of their destiny. Only as drastic changes overtook society after the Civil War, did it begin to dawn on them that their inherited formulations had been designed for a world that no longer was.

The process of adaptation to new conditions and new ways of thinking, always painful, became traumatic after the death of Alexander Campbell: at odds over emphases in the plea which now seemed contradictory, though few had perceived the problem before, Disciples could turn to no interpreter who commanded general assent. Parties coalesced around particular positions, and what seemed right and necessary to some proved offensive and ultimately intolerable to others. Among those who emerged as the Christian Church (Disciples of Christ) significant adaptations occurred.

Scarcely had the pioneers dissolved their ecclesiastical associations before they realized a need for structures of relationship and mission. They instituted cooperation meetings, state societies, a general convention, missionary and benevolent organizations, and colleges, which together evolved into "the great cooperative work of the brotherhood" and profoundly affected its ethos. Generations of the faithful denied that all this had an ecclesiastical character (despite Campbell's losing battle for "church organization"), but that denial, along with the insistence that Disciples were not a denomination, was an article of faith, not a sociological description.[62]

So also their rhetoric of anticlericalism gave way before the evident need of a settled ministry in the new urban context.[63] Subsequent demand for specialized education called forth ministerial programs in the colleges and the emergence of theological seminaries, though none dared use that name until mid-twentieth century.[64]

Critical study of the Bible and other academic disciplines in religion evoked restlessness with the legalism which had hardened in the middle period. Genteel sophistication and the prestige of science encouraged a liberal reformulation of the plea emphasizing Chrisitan liberty, opposition to creeds and ecclesiastical authority, loyalty to the person of Jesus above particular dogmas, progressive revelation, rationality, teaching as precursor to conversion, and the social implications of the gospel. All this echoed the evangelical liberalism then bringing release to many Christians trapped in the tight theological systems of the past, and it had genuine roots in the Disciples tradition. From the 1890s on increasing numbers of teachers and leading preachers espoused the reformulation; by mid-twentieth century it had taken over the colleges and seminaries.[65]

The ecumenical movement attracted Disciples of liberal temper, who saw it confirming their witness to Christian unity. Despite restiveness about "recognizing the denominations," accepting denominational status, and seeming to minimize believer's baptism, zeal for cooperation increased. Disciples led in the ecumenical movement and were profoundly influenced by it; from it came the rationale if not the reasons for the practice of inclusive membership.

Meanwhile changes occurring in society, the unwieldiness of the many cooperative agencies and institutions, and a realization of their implicit churchly character, so long denied, led to the process of "restructure" and the adoption in 1968 of what is now The Design for the Christian Church (Disciples of Christ).

Two schisms arose from the efforts to adapt to a changing world, as sectional bitterness after the Civil War and diverse rates of response to new developments in society and culture bred misunderstanding, suspicion and estrangement. The Churches of Christ separated about 1906 in protest against "digression" (missionary societies, musical instruments in worship, and early manifestations of liberalism); and the "independent" Christian Churches and Churches of Christ claimed separate identity about 1968 in opposition to liberalism, ecumenical relationships, open membership, and restructure. The desire of all three groups to distinguish themselves by names which stem from the common tradition makes for awkwardness and confusion.

The two schisms have had a shattering effect on a people who once thought of themselves as a major religious body in America; whereas the three groups claim some 5 million members, the U.S. membership of 1,116,326 in the Christian Church (Disciples of Christ) in 1985 falls short of one-half of 1 percent of the population. Morale has been damaged by the loss of perceived significance and the insufficiency of the "plea" to hold its adherents together—or to reunite them, despite signs of a more charitable spirit and occasional dialogue. It has suffered even more from decline in actual numbers, waning of ecumenical zeal, symptoms of "tired blood" in liberal theology, and difficulties that confront all mainline churches.

The world has changed once again, and promises to change even more. The original slogans and the liberal maxims alike assume a worldview which no longer holds. Significant reformulation will require a dialogue with tradition—the biblical witness, the heritage of the larger church, and Disciples' own history—as well as with the emerging future and its needs. In their responsibility for the health of the church, this situation calls for serious attention from the theological schools of the Disciples.

Agenda for the Near Future

Here are some of the issues confronting this church:

1. *A theologically responsible formulation of their "noncreedal" or "nontheological" stance.* At the outset Disciples could be both noncreedal and authentically Christian because of their emphatic adherence to the New Testament witness to Jesus Christ. "No creed but Christ" was not empty and shapeless; "Where the scriptures speak, we speak" gave it substance. The liberal reformulation, espousing noncreedalism but abandoning biblicism, turned out to have no "rule of faith," and many Disciples have reduced the original slogan to the two words: "No creed." While remaining free from the specious finality of historical creeds, Disciples need to reappropriate the dynamic of the gospel concerning Jesus Christ by coming with a new seriousness to the biblical witness—as we now understand the Bible. Otherwise the names "Christian" and "Disciples" are but empty shells.

2. *Working out a forthright theology of the sacraments.* Disciples put the two dominical sacraments, which for a century they insisted on calling "ordinances," at the center of their preaching and church life; rarely did a sermon end during their first century without a thorough discussion of baptism, never did a congregation assemble on the first day of the week without the ministry of loaf and cup. Their significance transcended the limitations of the biblicist rationale and liturgical sterility which too often attended them, and they functioned truly as means of grace. Embarrassed at the legalism and exclusivism into which the preaching on baptism had fallen, the liberal reformula-

tion fell silent on the subject. Whereas earlier generations had heard little but baptism, a new one heard it hardly at all. Evangelism ground to a halt, the Easter season brought the annual immersion of a few children, and theologizing showed more concern to avoid old pitfalls than to enunciate a doctrine of grace.[66] The typical ritual for the breaking of bread was brief and spare, overloaded with explicit Zwinglianesque vocabulary ("memorial," "emblems," "only symbols") and other rationalist weights gratuitously imposed on the wings of biblical imagery. Yet communion meditations and hymns sung about the table tend to emphasize presence, grace, solidarity with the suffering and oppressed, and the oneness of the church rather than the nineteenth-century themes of "the first day of the week," "every Lord's Day," atonement, and memorial. Evidently the operational theology of the eucharist is richer and more catholic than traditional popular doctrine, and Disciples scholars have provided substantial fare.[67] Unexpected readiness to discuss the document on *Baptism, Eucharist and Ministry* indicates a genuine popular interest. It is time to give responsible theological affirmation to these holy mysteries, so long central in practice, that they may justifiably have an equal place in Disciples thought.

3. *Thinking through a consistent doctrine of ministry.* Since this issue will be discussed at greater length in the next chapter, it is enough to note here that the realism of experience led Disciples to alter in practice the "standing and immutable ministry" which Campbell had perceived. Today the church recognizes an order of the ministry made up of ordained and licensed ministers with standing who exercise within congregations the offices once reserved to elders. Disciples know how to describe this ministry functionally, but are far less clear theologically. They do not know whether elders, who perform sacred eucharistic functions reserved by all other churches to the ordained, are ministers or laypersons. Not a few voices among them assert the notion that any Christian may properly preside at the Lord's Table. In restructure, Disciples gladly abandoned the title "state secretary" for that of "regional minister," but again there is little clarity concerning the specific ministerial character of this officer. Largely administrative in its functioning, the office as now exercised better fits the historic Christian understanding of deacon than it does that of bishop, to which Disciples tend to liken it. A clearer doctrine of ministry would have important effects on the kind of education offered persons preparing for ordination and those preparing for eldership.

4. *Faithfulness to the vision of oneness and wholeness for the church.* Excitement over the ecumenical movement as "the great new fact of our time" has subsided; perceived by a new generation as part of the status quo, it has dropped in the lists of priorities kept by denominations, congregations, pastors, and seminaries; ecumenical meetings are forums for discussion, not cells for reformation. Where Christians know themselves to be in the minority, they band together for the sake of the common mission or even for very

life, but in the United States the illusion persists that we can manage without each other. The ecumenical movement urgently needs a revival of impetus and vision if its promise is to be realized and if the church is to engage the emerging future. The call for the oneness of Christians is still a matter of urgency for Disciples.

5. *A new confidence and effectiveness in evangelism.* For more than a century Disciples grew, relying on a simple pattern of evangelism that spoke to earlier generations and offered a reasonable biblical alternative to the frenzy of the camp meetings. But for too long now they have neglected the task because of its association with religious show business, organizational gimmickry, shallow concepts of church growth, and minimal regard for Christian social witness. The times call for a new surge of evangelism, growing out of profound reflection on the meaning of Jesus Christ for our world, motivated by genuine concern for persons outside the Christian community, and committed to serve the coming age. For Disciples such evangelism demands a new openness to ethnic diversity; our fastest growing segment is Hispanic. It will require a new way of thinking about what we do; 98 percent of our church programs, denominational and congregational, proceed on the assumption that they are designed for the people who already belong. Theological education has given insufficient attention to the essence of Christian witness to a world like ours or to the process of conversion in our increasingly pagan society.

6. *Growing into the vision of the church articulated in the Design for the Christian Church (Disciples of Christ).* Restructure occurred during a rare florescence of theological interest among Disciples;[68] its architects drew on the doctrine of the church enunciated by the founders, the "biblical theology" current in the 1950s, and fruitful studies in Faith and Order and the Consultation on Church Union, to conceptualize a form of church truly organic and genuinely free, centering in the ideas of covenant and mutual consent. Written as a constitution, not an ecclesiastical "confession" after the Reformation model, the Design only suggests these notions. Widely discussed before its adoption, the ecclesiology implicit in them has not yet been fully realized. That animating vision and distinctive spirit require continued nurture.[69]

7. *Discerning God's particular intention for this age as clearly as Stone, the Campbells, and the other founders did for theirs.* The need to find the basis for Disciples identity is a theme much bruited about at the moment. Such talk too readily overlooks the genius of denomination as form of church: it is an instrument of mission. Unless Disciples discern together an essential mission to God's coming age, they will wither and die. Or they should.

With the lamentable observation that the seminaries do not seem to have shown much interest in the issues raised in this section on Disciples, we move to a closing word on the congregation.

The Congregation Today

All the issues taken up in these first two chapters involve the congregation, the company of people gathered for worship and mutual ministry in a particular place. Here the generalities we toss about so easily concerning religion, the church, the denomination come to concrete expression or exception. Here ministry engages the lives of real persons and theological education is put to its ultimate test.

Forerunners

While the congregation may seem part of the unchanging order of things in religion, it has not always been so. In the archaic world of the hunters and gatherers, the entire village turned out for worship, to sing and dance in all-inclusive communal rites; but this "congregation" was a people on the move, a tribe without a fixed place. With the coming of agriculture and the sacred city, the temple established religious observance at a holy place, though it ordinarily involved a transaction between an individual and the priest rather than a corporate service. But when a multitude gathered, bringing their offerings, liturgies were sung; in Israel, the throng which assembled for the annual feasts was called the great congregation.

The emergence of the synagogue as a local gathering of the faithful, presumably during the Babylonian Exile, introduced a new epoch in spiritual history. Organized wherever ten men bound themselves together to study the Torah and to worship God, the synagogue was literally a "bringing together," a local "congregation." The same word designated the meeting, the building in which it was held, and the community of members.

The apostolic church took over the pattern of the synagogue as a local company rather than of the temple. Perhaps to distinguish itself from the Jewish community, the new Christian body adopted a political term, *assembly* (*ekklesia*), instead of the religious word *synagogue*. This word *church* also applied both to meeting and to membership, but evidently not to a building until much later. The early literatue uses *ekklesia* in at least three ways: a) inclusively, for the entire company of Christian everywhere, or throughout an extensive region, b) for all Christians in a city, c) for a group living or meeting in a particular house.

Soon the church in a town or city became known as a *parish*—a secular term meaning *district*[70] having its chief pastor or bishop and a staff of presbyters and deacons. As numbers swelled after toleration, Christians held meetings at numerous locations, but still spoke of only one church with one bishop for each city. By the sixth century the term parish had devolved to a section of town whereas the term diocese now applied to the total area served by a bishop. In medieval Christendom both diocese and parish shared two primary meanings: a) the people of the church as a worshiping community and

b) the entire population of the place. Thus a parish was both a church and a "field" of mission; the church and its ministers owned their responsibility for everybody in the place and their concern about every force affecting life there.

Contrasting Perceptions

In common usage "parish church" and "congregation" have become virtually synonymous, but only after a crucial shift in meaning made evident in three radically different perceptions of the congregation.

1. *The congregation as an instrument of reform.* On the Continent Protestantism advanced by winning the support of local political powers, e.g., the German princes or the councils of the Swiss cantons. In England, by contrast, reform was first prevented, then minimized by a combination of royal and episcopal power. There preachers who refused to abandon their demands for purity of the church, appealed to the initiative of congregations.[71] So a gathered community of Christians, acting under the authority of Christ as head and taking the scripture as rule, began the work of reformation. In response to the divine initiative, the people bound themselves to God and to one another in sure confidence that by this sacred covenant Christ constituted them a true church. When charged with breaking the laws of religious uniformity, they countered that the congregation as the body of Christ is the rightful interpreter of scripture, better qualified than parliament or bishop to declare its meaning.

Here is no notion of the will of the majority as governing principle. On the contrary, the common mind of the faithful, by searching the scriptures, is to determine and obey the will of Christ. This is classical congregationalism.

2. *The congregation as local outpost of a denomination.* With the coming of religious liberty, and especially the end of ecclesiastical establishment, the gathered community inevitably became the standard ecclesial pattern, even in traditions that used the language of parish. A congregation was the local branch of its denomination. It was common to find the buildings of two churches, sometimes even of four, located at the same corner. One could tell from the brand name on the oustide what one would find within.

Yet sometimes in thinly settled areas, a congregation which stood alone in village or countryside still functioned like a parish, serving the community for miles around. Among the Disciples the church at Bethany or Hiram, and many an open-country church ministered as a parish except for the conditions attendant on religious liberty and American voluntarism, as a genuine local church, fully identified with its place and people, its ministry undivided.

3. *An artifical community in a broken community.* In America the congregation became as a self-selecting community, reaching outside its locale to draw in persons of the type who already belonged and tending to neglect the people near at hand if they did not "fit in." This practice diluted its character as a community gathered by the gospel, and denominational rivalry accentu-

ated the drift toward social stratifcation as congregations vied for supremacy, then struggled for survival.[72] Such "community" as each group now enjoyed was artifical, deriving from homegeneity of class or culture and only vaguely related to its "place," where divisions in the church had made for brokenness of the secular community.

In such a context, a congregation is not a "local" church. Nor is the suburban "parish," even if it has carefully selected a site a decent distance removed from other congregations, for the principle of single-class homogeneity still applies. Denominational loyalty or personal preference still draws members from far away while near neighbors commute elsewhere to find their kind of congregation. The socio-economic forces which created suburbs have separated the place where people live from the places of power and decision.

The local significance of the congregation is not what it once was. The links between religion and power having been cut, the areas subject to religious influence continue to shrink.[73] A generation ago critics decrying the "suburban captivity of the church" lamented that religion had been reduced to personal and familial concerns; today, given the power of the mass media, the weight of peer pressure, and the force of the drug traffic, it seems that family, church, and school have lost even the capacity to influence the young.

Temptations

In such a situation of powerlessness the congregation is subject to grave temptations.

In its frustration with forces it does not understand, it may cast itself as a serene retreat from the ugly realities of the world; adopt an attitude of possessiveness toward "our" church where "we decide what we want"; focus its interest and attention on internal satisfactions and concerns; tremble at the very suggestion of controversy and so resist taking a stand on any real issue; cultivate homogeneity by looking for "our kind of people" who will fit comfortably into "the way we do things"; translate resentment against an impersonal society and its bureaucracies into estrangement from the denomination; insist on "doing things our way."

No temptation is more subtle or more devastating then the delusion that "congregational autonomy" is an item of Christian faith. The word *autonomy* should give the deception away, for any true church confesses Christ as its head. But for almost a century, since they picked it up from secular law, Christians in the congregationalist tradition have fallen victim to it, though it derives neither from scripture nor theology, and asserts an unbiblical doctrine of the church. English Reformers maintained the independence of the congregation as a means of asserting "the crown rights of the Redeemer" against a corrupt hierarchy, and American Christians on the frontier insisted on the competence of a covenanted body of believers, acting under the authority of

Christ as head, to constitute themselves as a true church with the power to appoint a ministry and to provide valid sacraments. But neither of these movements understood popular sovereignty as a valid principle for the church.

Assumptions about political democracy and congregational freedom, however, have coalesced in the popular mind to form a notion of local autonomy in the church which has no basis in scripture and totally overlooks the lordship of Christ. The Design for the Christian Church (Disciples of Christ) clearly affirms the rights and responsibilities of congregations, as of other manifestations of the church, under that lordship, without once using the term "autonomy." Unfortunately the word lingers in the common speech, with its connotations of suspicion, going it alone, and running our own show—all sustained by the mistaken belief that it is a biblical principle.[74]

Because few church people and not many ministers seem to comprehend the shift of forces in our society which makes it so much more difficult for a congregation to "succeed," unrealistic hopes and expectations turn to frustration, feelings of guilt, and nominations for scapegoat. If a minister's program draws a large following, few stop to ask if it presents the authentic gospel. It is disillusioning to analyze the motives appealed to by most of the celebrities on religious television or in the advertising by churches in the public press. But for many, if "folks like it," that is enough.

Mission

Yet despite all temptations and limitations, the congregation performs the basic ministries essential to the life of the church. It functions as the continuing community where Christians meet for the ministry of the word and sacrament, where they know and support one another, and through which they render much of their service to the church and to the world, reaching out in evangelism, response to every kind of human need, and social action. Though a particular congregation often seems so much less than the great church, here is its cutting edge, and for the denomination also, whether in encountering the onslaughts of an unfriendly culture or engaging specific persons with the grace and demands of the gospel.

The congregation has filled a vital place in the life of the American people. The steeples of white frame churches towered over the greens of the New England towns and the rolling prairies of the heartland. Imposing "cathedrals" of every major denomination rose on the main thoroughfares of the nation's growing cities. After World War II the new churches of suburbia spread out over sizeable properties, as though to make up in added parking space and activity rooms for the diminished reach of arch and spire, and, sometimes, the sense of transcendance. In all the settings mentioned, and many more, hundreds of thousands of local companies of believers have gathered in the name of Christ. Disciples of Christ worship in 4214 congregations across the United States.

Concern for the Church at the Grassroots

Strangely enough, the congregation has not claimed much attention from Christian intellectuals. Though none of the trends described in these first two chapters is unknown, little work has been done by theological faculties to think through a strategy of Christian mission for such a time. Some ministers turn to the slogan, "The church is not called to be successful, but to be faithful." True enough. But is the church faithful when it struggles on in the survival game, mounting an occasional campaign to lift the level of giving or turning hopefully to a program for church growth, but failing to address the trends which have so powerfully impacted its life? Is theological education helping church and ministry to understand these forces and to deal with them? Or will it be content with its familiar academic routine until the ship goes down? If the new interest in the congregation expressed by some leading theological educators proves to be more than a passing fad, it could bring reformation to the enterprise and send the church into the twenty-first century with renewed strength and insight.[75]

Questions which have arise explicitly or implicitly throughout our discussion really come to focus in the congregations.

Can congregations cultivate effective discipleship in the oncoming generation of youth and young adults? A heavy load of their volunteer work is now carried by retirees. That is not inappropriate, assuming they have more discretionary time than younger adults. More disturbing is the fact that the percentage of income contributed by those under forty is much smaller than that given by those who are older.[76] Will the new generation increase its stewardship as it is relieved of some present responsibilities? Or will the mission of the church decline for lack of support?

Can congregations find ways to look beyond their present hardcore church constituency and again to reach people from outside with the gospel of God's coming age?

Can they rally people of goodwill and organizations from their communities to participate in the struggle for peace with justice? Can Christians who were effective in the struggle for civil rights and the effort to stop the war in Vietnam, work again through their churches to mobilize widespread moral consent for a new social contract among a people who have lost their sense of obligation in a narcissistic world of hedonism and subjectivity?[77]

In short, can American congregations in the power of the Spirit find grace to hear and believe and witness to the gospel of Jesus Christ, to look forward in the certainty of Christian hope to the fulfilment of God's purposes? In large measure the answer to that question depends on the vision, wisdom, skill, and commitment of the ministers who will be available to serve the coming age.

Chapter **3**

MINISTRY IN
THE CHURCH THAT WAS

Ministry as we know it took shape in the church that was. Doctrines and rules of order, ethos and expectations, role models and programs of theological education all come to us out of a past that was radically different from our world and that could scarcely imagine the world rushing toward us. Yet reflection on ministry in that past can serve a threefold purpose: 1) it enhances our understanding of the present situation; 2) it deepens our awareness of our Christian identity; 3) it helps disentangle from our assumptions about ministry notions that belong to another age, not to our present or our future. The backward look is for the sake of looking forward.

Ministry Out of the Past

Origins of Ministry

The sign of holiness first marked out select women and men for ministry. In the archaic age of the hunters and gatherers these were the shamans, certified by ecstatic seizure; a vision revealing the spirit-world constituted their call. Their primary work was to heal the sick and accompany the spirit of the dying across the rainbow bridge to the unseen realm of the ancestors. As already noted, the great archetypes of religion and literature derive from the songs in which the shamans recounted their visions.

With the age of agriculture worship moved to the temple. Holiness now inhered in the religious institution and was imparted by it to those admitted to the priesthood. Marks of holiness now were distinctive dress, style of speaking, and education in the sacred lore; with notable exceptions, priesthood was routinized and rational rather than ecstatic. Among the archaic peoples, both women and men were shamans and priests, though particular societies might limit either office to one of the sexes.

In Israel the priest combined the ideal of holiness and ritual duty with the obligation to righteousness or justice. Early prophecy there showed affinities with shamanism, coming also out of ecstatic experience, but the canonical prophets emphasized ethics as the test of genuine piety. A third form of minister, the sage or teacher of wisdom, combined pragmatic rationality with epigrammatic wit in commending uprightness to the young and offering counsel to kings. The spirit of the wise reappeared in the rabbis of early Judaism, but rather than condense their own insights into gnomic sayings, these teachers devoted full energy to the understanding of scripture, summing up their interpretations in pungent aphorisms. While priesthood was restricted to males, women as well as men were inspired to prophesy and by their sagacity won a place among "the wise"; rarely, however, did a woman gain recognition as a rabbi.

Jesus of Nazareth evidently taught in the style of the sages, and the content of his teaching also recalled the wisdom tradition. But his words carried an urgency characteristic of the prophets, arising from his expectation of the imminent advent of the Reign of God. His acts of power, moreover, signified the arrival of that new age. From such demonstrable contact with the holy, people took him for a prophet; they also regarded him as a teacher of wisdom, though not of course as a priest.

At the heart of Jesus' ministry was the controlling ideal of the Servant, embodied in life, work, teaching, and death. Isaiah of the Exile had expressed the vision in moving poetry, but no other so consistently gave it flesh and blood as did Jesus. The early Christians proclaimed their risen Lord as the Holy One, the Sufferer of whom the prophet had sung, and their Christology depicted God's glorified Servant still engaged in a ministry of intercession.[1]

Consistent with their gospel was their concept of their calling as "slaves of Jesus Christ" and of leadership in the church as service: the highest office was that of minister. Virtually all their titles for representative position in the Christian community express that ideal: apostle, deacon, servant, worker, officer, waiter, steward, pastor, overseer, ambassador, herald, evangelist, preacher, helper, healer, administrator, leader (i.e., trailblazer).[2] The word that summed them all up has become so shopworn that we forget its revolutionary implications. But a true minister follows in the holy way of, does the holy work of, exemplifies the holy spirit of, the Servant Christ.

Across the decades made known in the various books of the New Testament we see the church evolving from a Spirit-filled fellowship poised for the imminent return of the Lord to a community with incipient institutions and an understanding of the Spirit as indwelling the processes of its ordered life. Ministry moves from primary emphasis on particular function to the more general notion of office, with accountability to the church. Consistent with prevailing social patterns of male dominance, most ministers were men; but the example of Jesus and the gifts of the Spirit combined to open various ministries to women as well.[3] So long as the emphasis fell on function, it appears, zealous Christians simply worked into or were co-opted for particular tasks; but by the laying on of hands the church signified its appointment (ordination) of chosen persons to particular ministries. All Christians had a part in the corporate ministry of the church, but *minister* was not a term applied indiscriminately to all; it was a title of office.[4]

Ministry in the Great Church

The long history of ordained ministry and of theologizing about it, which ought to receive careful attention in the seminaries, can only be touched upon here.[5] Urban T. Holmes III periodized it neatly: the sacramental person, the sacramental rite, the sacramental word.[6] In each age ministry provided a channel for contact with the holy, and epochal changes of channel radically altered the shape of ministry itself. Its modern diminution suggests a more profound cause than social change: when secularity seeped into the mind of the church in the wake of the Enlightenment, the sense of the holy diminished, and, with it, the sacramental understanding of the minister's work. Every step in our analysis raises the question: can the seminaries put their students in touch with a theological understanding of ministry capable of sustaining solid conviction as to its necessity in a secular world?

The Sacramental Person. In the generations after the apostles the bishop emerged preeminent among the varied ministries evolving in the church. As pastor of the entire Christian community in a place, he was a servant with authority. That authority derived from faithfulness to the message of the apostles, leadership among a sizeable corps of ministers, responsibility for discipline in a church surrounded by paganism and bloodied by persecution, administration of the care for widows and orphans and others in need, eminence as chief preacher and teacher and interpreter of scripture, and exemplar embodying the moral and theological virtues. The church was blessed in the calibre of its bishops, especially in the fourth and fifth centuries: in mental power and skill in oratory, the chief means of communication, they were unsurpassed by their secular contemporaries; in spiritual stature they tower even yet as giants unequalled. Despite an intensity of conviction that offends the modern mind as intolerant and an austerity almost incomprehensible to our laid-back generation, their winsomeness charms even yet. Most of all, they conveyed to those who knew them, and even to those who read them today, a sense of the immediacy of God, of divine judgment and grace. They fulfilled the apostolic ideal, for "The preeminent ministry is that of those who, not only in word but in their very person, embody the Christ."[7]

Accepting the current social pattern of male dominance, an exclusively male clergy prevailed by Constantine's time, and suppressed the memory of anything different. Now scholars are rediscovering important ministries held by women in the age of persecution, when the church was a private association living by the standards of God's coming age rather than a public organization trapped in secular mores. Even after secular patterns took over in the church, certain Christian women carried the aura of the sacramental person, though ordination was limited to men.[8]

Minister of the Sacraments. In the social disorder of the early Middle Ages, with a clergy far more numerous than before, but generally undistinguished and frequently uneducated, the church began to locate its encounter with the holy less in the person of the bishop or priest than in the rite which he celebrated. Clearly a sacerdotal officer, on whom the church bestowed holiness by ordination, the medieval priest alone possessed the power to effect the miracle of transsubstantiation by which the faithful received the real presence of Christ in the eucharist; while the definitive doctrine took centuries to mature, its roots reach back to some of the earliest Christian writings.

Discussions of the sacraments necessarily entailed concepts of priesthood; throughout the Middle Ages these excluded women from sacramental ministry, as they still do in Roman Catholicism and Orthodoxy, but other issues captured attention. From the earliest controversies (Cyprian against the Novatianists, Augustine against the Donatists) theologizing about ministry has concentrated on arguments about "orders." Currently this debate seems sterile and unreal, despite the convergence in *Baptism, Eucharist and Ministry*; for, though concerned in a roundabout way with the issue of holiness, it misses the essential point: ministry in its true character, that is, after the pattern of Jesus Christ, embodies holiness through servanthood, and servanthood is the crucial issue.[9]

Minister of the Word. The Protestant Reformation found the power of the holy in encounter with the Bible: the faithful proclamation and hearing of the Word confronts the people directly with divine judgment and grace. While every Christian is a priest, the minister is an interpreter of scripture, educated and ordained to be a preacher of divine truth. The Holy One touches the lives of the hearers through rational and ethical discourse, and preaching itself becomes sacramental.[10] In self-understanding and fervor, however, the Reformers identified with the prophets more than with "the wise."

The Reformers flatly repudiated the medieval division of one church into separate and unequal parts: clergy and laity. Luther firmly insisted that all seven of the functions or offices which tradition assigned to the priesthood devolved in equal measure on all Christians.[11] "The universal priesthood of believers" became the watchword of the Reformation. Yet the Christian community would not leave the performance of these sacred tasks to haphazard, but would choose and ordain ministers to serve as its public leaders.

Despite insisting on the universal priesthood, the Reformers did not open the ministry to women. Conditioned by the continuing male dominance in society, they held to the "Pauline" injunctions that women should not instruct men; even so, a glimmering here and there suggests that the gospel had overturned the old order.[12]

Until the Enlightenment, and even later in some circles, it was common to think of the natural and the supernatural and to regard religion as having to do chiefly with the latter. Not only did the miraculous fail to embarrass the Christian mind; it validated faith. Theologians saw the essence of the medieval eucharist as a miracle, and the Reformers attributed comparable power to the preaching of the Word.

Now that the seminaries have taught ministers to understand God as working within natural processes and to discard the notion of the supernatural, how are people to think of encounter with God? A bishop is, let us hope, an attractive and forceful personality; the eucharist is a powerful symbol; a sermon is, at least now and then, a great speech. But does the minister have any direct and acknowledged way of bringing people into encounter with the Holy One and imparting divine grace to forgive, redirect, and empower? If so, can the seminaries teach prospective ministers what this way is and how to follow it? And do the seminaries see this method as a professional skill, a technē which can be learned from a manual? Or if, in essence, it is a matter of the gospel entrusted to the church, can the schools help their students understand it honestly and appropriate it inwardly as faithful servants of the Word and of the people who faint and die for want of it?

Ministry in America

Among the diversity of ministerial styles produced in pluralistic America[13] it will be useful to mention five distinctive types within the Protestant tradition.

The Magisterial Puritan. The contemporary minister may well feel twinges of nostalgia for the days when the parson held sway in New England. Ministry was an office esteemed by both church and society, attracting the ablest youths and exerting large influence.[14] Normally the best educated person in the town, the preacher labored to produce massive sermons, each an intellectual *tour de force*, delivered them to large and discriminating audiences, pursued a major theme for some months, then commonly gathered the "chapters" into a book of considerable weight. Preaching gave direction to religious, moral, and political life.

The learned Puritan preachers have an undeniable appeal to theological faculties. What professor would not wish for students of such competence, discipline, and influence? Yet the power of these magisterial divines derived from a synthesis of disciplined intellectuality with the zealous spirituality of the convert.[15] The churches required an "experimental knowledge" of salvation for admission to membership; theology was no cold abstraction in a book; it was an existential grappling with the grandest themes of earth and heaven, meditating on the divine grace which had entered one's life in an experience never to be forgotten or denied.

The Voice of Revivalism. The primacy of experienced grace found a powerful voice, after some decades of spiritual cooling off, in a sermon by revivalist Gilbert Tennent on "The Danger of an Unconverted Ministry."[16] It installed subjectivism at the heart of American religion half a century before the First Amendment. The preacher bade the truly converted to examine their ministers and forsake those who lacked "experimental knowledge" of their own salvation. Despite the prominence of Jonathan Edwards and other undisputed intellectuals in the Great Awakening, revivalism carried Tennent's theme afar, sowing seeds of prejudice against theological education for allegedly replacing the power of the gospel with the pretensions of unconverted reason.

Driven by an intense sense of mission, the revivalists won thousands of converts as religious excitement spread through the colonies in the 1730s. At the beginning of the nineteenth century the Second Great Awakening stirred the frontier, brought multitudes into the churches, and established the camp meeting as a primary mode of evangelism for decades to come; subsequent revivals flourished in the major cities as well as in the back country. Despite the intense individualism of the appeal for conversion, the concentration on personal holiness, the oversimplification of theology, and the frenzied emotionalism, the movement aroused popular zeal for abolition, temperance, foreign missions, and other Christian causes.[17] For the first time in mainline Protestantism women preachers came to prominence, as the converting and empowering Spirit of God evidently showed less regard for masculine monopoly of ministry than did the long-established rules of the churches; this phenomenon characterized the Evangelical Revival both in Britain and America. For more than a century the Holiness tradition has ordained women much more freely than have the older denominations.[18]

Revivalism poses two major questions for theological education. The first has to do with prospective ministers. Do the seminaries—do the churches—consider religious "experience," whether crisis-type conversion or a gradual unfolding under Christian nurture, an essential qualification for ministry? If so, and if the students have found such experience, how do the schools deal with it and help them integrate it, in the manner of the magisterial Puritans, with the intellectual disciplines and with professional expertise? If not, how do they understand the relationship between the ministry and holiness? What is sacred about the minister's work, and how, if at all, is that element of holiness related to the intellectual disciplines and professional skills taught in the seminaries? Do the schools consider such questions inconsequential, properly to be ignored in the classroom and left up to the graduate to work out in one's first parish after the rude discovery that its members had no intention of calling an academic instructor or social reformer?

The second question is more general. Do the seminaries understand the gospel as confronting persons today with a staggering challenge to their autonomous course, calling for redirection of life, offering God's forgiveness, and imparting grace and power? Can they help ministerial students appropriate such a perception of the gospel, integrate it into their theology, and give it effective expression in every aspect of their ministry? If not, evangelism is a dead issue and what masquerades under that name is no more than a periodic drive to recruit members with the hope of underwriting the budgets of the churches.

Servant among the People. Conditions on the frontier and in rural America called for a servant-ministry. Even though preaching offered an escape from the drudgery of the farm, few ministers got rich, and many lived sacrifical, often lonely lives. Celebrated in the sentiment of a later time, the Methodist circuit-riders typified the "home missionaries" who criss-crossed the back country to convert sinners, organize congregations, conduct funerals and weddings, and provide Sunday services in cabins, barns, courthouses, and, at last, white frame churches.

As the towns grew, the itinerants settled down as pastors, and frequently as proprietors of academies or rude colleges. Many women's names appear among these pioneers, not only as teachers, but as evangelists, organizers, and pastors, traveling under the hardest conditions and holding discouraged little bands of believers together.[19] Few of these gallant women received honorary degrees, promotions to "better" churches, or even anonymous mention in the denominational histories.

Throughout the nineteenth century, lay leaders, both women and men, took a prominent part. Zealous church members organized Sunday schools which became nuclei for new congregations. They conducted midweek prayer meetings, met with the young people in Christian Endeavor, kept congregations afloat through money-raising projects by the Ladies Aid, organized missionary and temperance societies and local branches of YWCA and YMCA, and gave leadership to state and national organizations associated with these enterprises.[20] Christians who prospered in business frequently became major benefactors. Some of the religious activists naturally eased into fulltime ministry without formal ordination, but most continued to earn their living by secular work. Many of these lay leaders were young, especially in the raw settlements of the West, where single men and newlyweds made up most of the adult population; in the churches, as in politics, they assumed high offices long before their hair had turned gray, and religion flourished.

Among such "do-it-yourselfers" the minister did not try to "call the tune." People who broke the sod of their homesteads, built their own houses and barns, doctored their own ailments, organized their own schools, incorporated their towns, and even started their own railroads, did not expect to be told how to run their church. The minister's distinctive task was to conduct services, which centered in the preaching—esteemed for knowledge of the Bible, intensity of conviction, plainspokenness, and off-the-cuff eloquence—and to preside at rites of passage: baptisms, weddings, funerals. Outside the pulpit people wanted a minister who was a "good mixer" and a friend to all.[21] One led by establishing trust, identifying with the people, relying on the power of suggestion, and offering counsel when it was asked. If ever an "enabling" ministry flourished it was in nineteenth century America where lay persons took on great tasks and then welcomed a boost from the minister.

The Pastoral Director. With larger congregations and the demand for urban niceties, church buildings became more pretentious, thus more expensive to erect and maintain; institutions grew more complex with the many activities of a flourishing congregation, its array of subsidary organizations, and its involvements in the community. To conduct a major evangelistic meeting, running nightly for six weeks, even to set one up for a guest preacher, required careful planning, strong leadership, the motivation of many workers, attention to detail, and energetic follow-through. The denomination, with all its agencies and institutions, state and national, discovered that the local minister was the key to every emphasis, promotional campaign, or special day; and the minister soon learned that "playing ball" with the larger church won recognition—and recommendations for a "call to a larger field of service." The successful pastor was not only a good preacher but a skillful organizer, a promoter, a go-getter. Through the twentieth century, the ministry was shaped more and more after the ideal of management.[22] The role model for other ministers, the bishop, came to resemble a corporate executive in mode of work, public image, and style of life.

The new preoccupation with "church management," along with an emphasis on professional skills throughout American society, and the rapid growth of theological education resulted in the virtual elimination of the type of vigorous lay leadership which had flourished in the nineteenth century.[23] The shift began with the advent of the religious education movement; soon after World War I every up-and-coming congregation of any size was expected to have a paid staff member in this department, and control of the Sunday school passed from the lay superintendent and corps of volunteers to the professional director of religious education. Ministers who were held responsible for a successful program on the part of a congregation or general organization assumed the role of experts and wrested control from the amateurs. For a while things went reasonably well, but it has become harder to enlist inexperienced lay workers in projects which they do not really run; the concept of the minister as "enabler," romanticized by seminarians in the 1960s and '70s, foundered on this rock.

Nevertheless the major study of theological education conducted at midcentury led H. Richard Niebuhr and his colleagues to acknowledge that the minister's base of operations had shifted from study to office; the administrative model of ministry had come to prevail, and consequently the seminaries should prepare their students as "pastoral directors."[24]

The supplanting of holiness by efficiency has prompted the plaintive question: is the minister today, as in former times, the energizer of a sacramental community, or is the minister now the manager of a small firm? To put the question more bluntly: is it not time for the seminaries to undertake with the churches a critical assessment of the managerial model for ministry, which has been building in America for a century and has had free rein among Disciples for fifty years? Granted that a degree of administration is valid and essential. Should this phase of the work be allowed to stand as the measure of a minister's success and so to preempt time, energy, and priority? Would it not be useful for the schools to project various models appropriate to our time, to help churches and ministers move toward a rough consensus as to the primacy of contact with the holy over the secular details of organizational life and of teaching over busyness? The seminaries could offer a biblical and theological critique of the current pattern, as well as historical and pragmatic analysis. They could press the question: is there a causal connection between the decline of the mainline churches and a reigning model of ministry which subordinates sacramental service to professional expertise and managerial mode?

The Black Preacher. Nowhere on the American scene has the minister cut a larger figure than the preacher in the black community, a towering example of human dignity and inner power. Combining the experience of a divine call to preach with knowledge of the Bible "cover to cover" and the melodious eloquence derived from an oral culture, the minister exercised the influence of the sacramental person and simultaneously channeled the power of the sacramental word. The Holy One was made present through this ministry. Holding virtually the only post of leadership permitted to blacks through a long and tragic history in America and being among the few with opportunity for education, the black preacher attained an eminence and authority much like that of the bishop in the ancient church. With a double portion of charisma, augmented by innate intelligence, courage, and eloquence, the outstanding black ministers of the twentieth century have exercised an influence far beyond the black community to alter the larger patterns of American life.[25] Even so, the seminaries have done little to appropriate this tradition for the reshaping of ministry in all the churches.

Ministry among Disciples of Christ

The founding patriarchs of Disciples of Christ were ministers of the Word, Barton W. Stone and Thomas Campbell having been ordained by presbyteries before breaking their denominational ties, Alexander Campbell and Walter Scott afterwards by congregations. But their efforts to unite Christians on the Bible alone led them to oppose the "kingdom of the clergy" by contending for the "original faith and order." As enunciated by Alexander Campbell: "The standing and immutable ministry of the Christian community is composed of Bishops, Deacons, and Evangelists."[26] Evangelists were the fulltime educated "professionals" who made their living, such as it was, by the preaching of the gospel. Deacons never really achieved recognition as ministers. But the bishops, better known by the alternative title of elders, "ruled" the affairs of the congregations which elected them.

The elders were the designated teachers of the congregations, presenting a lesson or sermon when no evangelist was present, or inviting a guest to fill the pulpit. They presided over worship and conducted the ministry of the Lord's Table. They had charge of the "spiritual affairs" of the congregation, theoretically deferring to the deacons in matters temporal. They exercised discipline in cases of serious moral offense. They visited the sick and explained the plan of salvation to sinners. They were ordained to their office and held it so long as they remained with the authorizing congregation. By any measure customarily used to denote ministerial status, other than a diploma from a theological seminary or financial compensation for their services, these nineteenth-century elders were ministers in the fullest sense. They earned their living at secular occupations and gave their service in devotion to the church. So long as the system functioned in its purity Disciples had a bivocational ministry.

The emergence of a settled pastorate wherever a congregation could afford it manifested practical wisdom, despite the failure to come up with any generally accepted biblical or theological rationale. For a long time Disciples nurtured the fiction that the pastor was one of the elders, but the role of the latter suffered diminution as pastorates became longer, much as the presbyterate in the ancient church had been subordinated by the rise of the monarchical bishop. Disciples now seldom referred to the ministry of elders or to their ordination; they were "installed" in office along with deacons, chairpersons of committees, and other congregational leaders. Their power was broken in the 1930s and '40s by shifting responsibility for "program" to functional committees and especially by introducing rotation in office, usually after a term of three years, for everyone but the pastor. In time Disciples began to infer that the elders' offering of the prayers at the Lord's Table signified the propriety of any lay person's taking a turn, without ordination, at performing this most sacred act—the very antithesis of the original doctrine of the eldership. Thus did the professionalization of ministry smuggle into a church no longer tutored in biblical doctrine the alien, and once unacceptable, notions of clergy and laity.

Not until Restructure did Disciples begin to hammer out a theology of ministry in keeping with current practice. The Design for the Christian Church (Disciples of Christ) affirms the foundational ministry of Jesus Christ, the corporate ministry of the believing community, and the need for appointed ministers "to equip the whole people to fulfill their corporate ministry." Accordingly it provides for an "order of the ministry," consisting of ordained ministers and licensed ministers related to regional commissions operating under policies and procedures enacted by the General Assembly. The eldership and the diaconate are referred to as "offices ordered by the congregations." In most particulars Disciples thinking about ministry has drawn closer to that of other mainline churches, being markedly influenced by the ecumenical dialog, and theological education has become a requirement for ordination.

We have noted the inextricable association of holiness with ministry, from archaic and biblical times on through the history of the church: in varying ways ministry has signified the reality of the transcendent God and put people in touch with divine grace. Disciples have not commonly used such language, yet examination of their traditional practice will discover the reality and disclose its power.

The encounter with the divine occurs for Disciples, as for other Christians, in sacrament, Word, and service to human need. While the Lockean epistemology of the founders left no place for mysticism and denied subjective experience as a trustworthy ground of religious certainty, they believed that the "positive" (i.e., objective) ordinances are divinely appointed means of grace. Baptism brings assurance of salvation based on God's unshakable word. To each disciple receiving the broken bread and the cup, Campbell wrote, the Lord says, "For you my body was wounded; for you my life was taken." And on passing the symbols, one in effect greets the neighbor "now brought home to the family of God" and affirms, "Under Jesus the Messiah we are one."[27] Similarly the preaching of the whole gospel brings the hearers in touch with divine grace. Hearing the word, their minds convinced by the facts set forth in the biblical testimony, the hearers believe and obey, claiming the promises of God. In the same way the preaching of Christian unity and of the coming millennium of justice and peace likewise opens responsive minds to the realization of God's holy purpose. The faithful service of deacons in ministry to human needs likewise demonstrates God's concern for "the least of these" and expresses the holiness of servanthood. Thus despite their rather crabbed formulations and their distrust of runaway emotionalism, Disciples encountered divine grace through the ministry of elders, evangelists, and deacons, even as the contemporary ministry of sacrament, word, and care still holds the possibility of relating them to the transcendence of the Holy One. It must be confessed, however, that the emphasis of this paragraph is seldom heard in congregation, regional assembly, or seminary chapel.

The Shrinking of a Public Figure

To return to the larger religious scene, the forces of secularity and pluralism discussed throughout these chapters have made for the decline of ministry as a social force. With the increased emphasis on professional education early in the century, the influence of the generalist abated; lawyers, executives, city planners, newscasters, and other specialists displaced the urban pulpiteer in giving direction to public policy.[28] Yet the seminaries, while paying extensive attention to the termination of religious establishment, the end of the theological *Weltanschauung*, and the loss of the sense of transcendence, take little systematic notice of the waning of intellectual leadership by the ministry. Students now in seminary, as children of secularity and, for the most part, innocents in historical knowledge, scarcely imagine the wide influence of the ministry in the Christian past. While some hold to romantic notions of the minister as "change agent," most of them will go to the churches with sadly attenuated concepts of what ministry may be, unless the issue is addressed directly against the kind of historical background suggested here.

By a bitter irony, church and seminary have added to the problem. Fifty years ago conventions and other general meetings of the churches were primarily occasions for preaching, with at least half a dozen sermons, addresses, and lectures every day by as many ministers; scores of them were public personages throughout their denomination, and they heard each other speaking of their deepest convictions. The current ecclesiastical style has put business to the fore, with formal liturgies and perhaps an evening address by a dignitary from another denomination. The result is that, after leaving seminary, ministers have few opportunities to hear other ministers preach or bear witness to their faith; they meet casually in sessions of boards and committees, which seldom sound the spiritual depths and offer less inspiration than a company sales meeting. As for the seminaries, even the dullest student quickly perceives that the persons esteemed there are scholars from Tuebingen or Oxford, the first female bishop in the denomination, celebrated social activists, and the faculty member who has published half a dozen technical works. But condescension hangs like tattered banners from the ceiling when a nearby pastor is invited to preach in chapel.

The problems of morale, too much discussed when ministers get together, is clearly related to the decline of influence in society and of esteem in the church. Ministers who have served for two or three decades have themselves experienced it. One can observe it in the culture shock of a successful pastor called in the prime of life from a county seat to metropolis, from the South or the Midwest to the Northeast or the Pacific Coast. In contrast with a cultural era extending from the rise of the universities through the nineteenth century, ministry rarely occurs to a promising young person today as a serious option and is rarely presented by vocational counselors or even by ministers. The Catholic Church has suffered a damaging decline in vocations; in Protestantism the problem seems not so much a matter of numbers as of persons with the potential for genuine leadership.[29]

The frequent issue of ministerial "burn-out" may be more closely related to this phenomenon than to overwork, underpayment, crisis of faith, or other commonly mentioned considerations. The same must also be true of the "new quest" for status so evident among ministers in recent years. Symptoms are the upgrading of nomenclature for theological degrees,[30] efforts to establish standing as a "profession" which may expect appropriate recognition in society, and the increasing tendency of ministers to refer to themselves as "clergy"—a term as culturally archaic as the title "Reverend" which it has displaced in ministerial usage. "The clergy" is an outmoded sociological term belonging to the era of religious establishment when ministers had a recognized and honored place in British society; they have no comparable position in American democracy. Furthermore the concept has no authentic standing in the theology of the Reformation or in the tradition of Disciples of Christ. It becomes ludicrous when a young minister, meticulously avoiding sexist language, ostentatiously refers to oneself as a clergyperson.

A solid foundation for ministerial self-esteem requires a clear understanding by church and seminary of what a minister is expected to do and of the importance of that work.

The Work of the Minister

A Question of Office

Suspending for the moment any sweeping suggestions on reshaping the structures of church and ministry for the sake of more effective service to the coming age, we turn to a simple question: *What is the minister supposed to do?* To use the language of an earlier time, that is a question of "office" or function, and the answers of the past are enshrined in tradition. Christian ministry was practiced longest in the era of agriculture, then in the industrial age. Having now entered an epoch of high technology, increasingly service-oriented, we are driven to inquire: how does ministry fit this new situation?

The clue lies in separating the essential from the ephemeral, in asking why the church in every generation has found it important, even necessary, to ordain persons as ministers. This requires theological reflection about ministry, a process not practiced overmuch by American Christians, including Disciples,[31] nor pursued yet in this study, despite its expressions of uneasiness over the emptiness of secular models and categories (celebrity, manager, profession, career). Now we ask about the essence of ministry.

After the example of Jesus Christ, servanthood is the heart of the matter. But the nature of that serving calls for definition. What is the difference, if any, between the "ministry of Christ" and humanitarian services?[32] To specify the nature of the minister's offering to church and world, we reflect on certain classical formulations from the Christian tradition.

Classical Formularies

The New Testament itself has fundamental importance for any consideration of Christian ministry, an importance which can only be suggested here.[33] The Letters of Paul (notably the Corinthian correspondence and Philippians), Luke-Acts, the Epistle to the Ephesians, and the Pastoral Epistles all give major attention to this theme. They all emphasize the ministry of the Word, a self-denying concern for persons, the upbuilding of the church, the witness of the minister's life and character, a boldness of missionary strategy in a daring effort to capture attention for the gospel, a clear-eyed understanding of the inevitable conflict between commitment to God's coming age and the purposes of the world, an exuberance of joy in the power of the Holy Spirit. Strangely enough, no passage in the New Testament clearly designates a minister (or any one besides Jesus) as presiding over the eucharist, although several narratives recount baptisms by an apostle or evangelist. The Pastorals list qualifications for bishops, deacons, and widows (a ministry?), but do not spell out their duties.

The literature of the second and third centuries contains fleeting references to various forms of ministry, disclosing problems precipitated by wandering charismatics and the increasing importance and nobility of the bishops.[34] We note their crucial role in maintaining discipline and admire the balance between firmness and grace in their imposition of penance on Christians who under persecution had concealed their faith.[35] From the fourth century we have several sets of catechetical lectures delivered by well known bishops as they prepared coverts for baptism.[36] These brief glimpses reveal three classical functions: the ministry of the Word, the ministry of the sacraments, and the ministry of pastoral care or discipline.[37] The same century also produced several small treatises dealing directly with the work of the minister.

A charming piece in this vein is a sermon by the young Gregory Nazienzen to the church he has been appointed to serve as priest, apologizing for having run away to a monastery instead.[38] He specifies the demands on a priest for holiness of life, the grave burden of setting an example to the flock, the fearful responsibility of ministering at the holy table, the ineffable glory of Christ that overwhelms the powers of the preacher, the diverse spiritual states among the people. He confesses his longing for the solitude of the desert and his decision to return in deference to duty. Evidently his oration overcame the outrage at his truancy, for the people received him back, and he became a distinguished bishop and theologian.

A generation later John Chrysostom of Antioch produced a dialogue, "On the Priesthood," enlarging on Gregory's arguments as justification for his own reluctance to accept ordination.[39] Both works indicate that ministry was not a career eagerly sought by spiritually minded youths, no matter how great their promise or the insistence of older Christians. The serenity of the monastery held more attraction than the clamor of the city and the demands of the parish, but the determination of the church to appoint its ablest young members to this office prevailed over personal desire. Both Gregory and John became celebrated preachers, sensitive spiritual counselors, and courageous bishops who resisted political pressure as they contended for authentic Christianity.

In the same century Ambrose of Milan composed a work *On the Duties of Ministers*, borrowing his title (*De officiis*) and much of his material from

Cicero's handbook for public officals. Ambrose develops a profound ethic of leadership, but despite his title gives little theological attention to the "offices" of ministry.[40] His most brilliant convert, Augustine of Hippo, wrote *On Christian Teaching* to set forth principles of biblical interpretation and the Christian use of rhetoric; it remains significant for attention to the ministry of the Word and of care. Treatment of the sacraments occurs in works on baptism administered by schismatics; Augustine insists that divine grace does not depend on perfection in the minister, else no recipient of a sacrament could ever feel secure.[41]

At the end of the sixth century Pope Gregory the Great composed his *Book of Pastoral Rule* to describe the kind of person required for ministry and to offer guidance in dealing with various spiritual states. Drawing on Gregory Nazienzen and informed by classical literature, he brings psychological subtlety, biblical perspective, and theological insight to the work of counseling and disciplining persons caught up in pride, anger, fear, greed, and other conditions inimical to their psychic health as Christians.[42]

By the early medieval period ministerial offices or duties had become clearly established. As the complete or normative Christian priest, the bishop was charged with all these functions, assisted by presbyters or parish priests who had pastoral responsibility for particular churches and by deacons who carried the administrative tasks, especially care for the poor. The bishop's oversight (*episkopē*) over the entire diocese included liturgical and doctrinal supervision as well as discipline of both clergy and laity, and the bishops of a province or larger region frequently conferred collegially to determine issues of general importance. Because the church was the strongest and most stable institution in society and because the entire population, Jews excepted, belonged to it, medieval bishops exercised considerable political power; as princes of the church they consulted with dukes and kings, and some devoted more attention to secular interests than to ecclesiastical matters.

Encountering bishops most commonly as opponents, the Protestant Reformers could not regard them or their office as essential. Within the priesthood of believers Lutherans made the local pastor (*Pfarrer*) the crucial figure in ministry, responsible for Word, sacrament, and care; for the work of oversight the Christian prince served in place of bishops, and in some regions ecclesiastical superintendents were appointed.[43] The Reformed churches, by contrast, developed a system of collegial oversight through presbytery, a body composed of pastors and ruling elders.

John Calvin produced the clearest and most definitive formulation of Reformed theology in his *Institutes of the Christian Religion*, taking up in Book IV the church and the doctrine of ministry. Its functions imitate and serve the three offices of Jesus Christ as Prophet, Priest, and King; to these correspond the Ministry of Word, sacraments, and discipline[44]—duties which Alexander Campbell would later assign to bishops/elders in each congregation. The prophetic office of preaching, that is, leading the congregation in systematic study of the scriptures, held highest importance. Throwing out the lectionary with its selection of brief passages suited to the liturgical calendar, the great Reformers read and preached their way through an Epistle, Gospel, or Prophet, then moved to another book of the Bible. The Geneva gown, i.e., the academic robe, displaced priestly vestments as standard dress for the minister conducting services; it designated the preacher's educational attainments at a time when few members of the congregation held university degrees, and it emphasized ministry as primarily a teaching office. Church discipline received large attention, for it involved regulating the morals of the entire population in a Reformed canton. The minister also administered baptism and celebrated the eucharist, but both the theology and the ethos of the churches gave this sacramental function less emphasis than preaching and discipline.

In the English-speaking world the great Protestant classic on the work of the minister is Richard Baxter's *The Reformed Pastor*.[45] Composed as a series of lectures to meetings of Puritan ministers, it breathes the spirit of biblical piety and experiential faith which motivated the more zealous advocates of Reformation in England. Urgently the book inculcates responsibility to know and call regularly on every member of the parish, the whole town or district, not just persons active in church, not as a matter of social visiting but to inquire after the state of their souls and to impart guidance and motivation. More than any other book, *The Reformed Pastor* shaped the ideals and practice of ministry in English and American Protestantism; though few now read it, its influence lingers.

The most significant book on ministry produced by nineteenth-century Disciples was *The Care of All the Churches* by Thomas Munnell, state evangelist for Kentucky.[46] At once doctrinal, practical, and spiritual, it deals with the duties of evangelists, elders, and deacons, and provides a rite for their ordination. Written at a time when churches were beginning to call fulltime pastors, the book sees them as preachers and leaders, sharing with and guiding the elders in their common responsibility. Munnell emphasizes discipline, offers counsel on preaching, and gives suggestions for the orderly conduct of the sacraments, which he calls ordinances. The common-sense reading of the New Testament and pragmatic piety characteristic of Disciples at their best run through the volume.

Except for Calvin's *Institutes*, these classic works have been generally ignored through most of the twentieth century during a student's progress through seminary. Theologians and church historians have chased after other game, and professors in the "practical field" rarely mentioned them, perhaps thinking them archaic or irrelevant. Any theology of ministry which filtered through to the student was likely to be traditional, unsystematic, and thin, based largely on documents pertaining to denominational polity and tending to ignore the larger history. Hampered by superficial notions of ministry unrelated to the grand scheme of theology and unrooted in history, the graduates went out to serve the church confused as to what is essential in the work and operating from an idiosyncratic doctrine of the office.

But this bleak situation may have begun to change. Two impressive studies on the history and theology of ministry, Bernard Cooke's *Ministry to Word and Sacraments* and Thomas C. Oden's *Pastoral Theology* now offer resources hitherto not readily available, and vigorous new discussion is going on in practical theology, with a serious effort to integrate the two terms in the title of the field.[47] It is high time. Otherwise pastor and people alike pick up secular ideas of "success" and feel frustrated over ministerial performance, for no one clearly understands what ought to be done.

Twentieth-Century Expectations

A striking anomaly of ministry in the twentieth century is the vast divergence between the traditional understanding of its offices or functions and the actual expectations of both minister and church (congregation and denomination). The traditional doctrinal summaries, the ordination ritual and sermon, and the routine job description for a pastor, all focus on the ministry of Word, sacrament, and care: the preacher is expected to come up with a sermon every Sunday, preside over the eucharist and administer baptism, visit the sick and bereaved. But all that falls in the area of minimal expectations, analogous to a schoolteacher's showing up for class; a minister may discharge all these duties faithfully and well, but after a time will begin to feel, along with the congregation and the denominational staff, that little is happening. The three traditional functions, spiritual in essence, do not readily lend themselves to that quantitative measurement so esteemed by the ethos of our competitive society. Let a minister spend a lifetime preaching, baptizing, conducting worship, marrying, burying, visiting the sick and afflicted, then retire old and full of years and loved by all, with the congregation at peace and in good health, but not substantially larger; most Americans would have difficulty finding great significance in such a ministry. "Success" demands impressive numbers: growth in membership, increase in giving, a major building program, a notable gain in attendance at services, new programs that attract wide attention and many people.

The result is not surprising, especially where seminary courses in church administration propound an operational doctrine of ministry modeled on business school theory. (Happily the practice is not universal.) Reinforced by the system of rewards in congregation and denomination, such teaching supplants traditional formulations regarding the essential offices of Word, sacrament, and care. What is really essential is raising the budget and enlisting new members. H. Richard Niebuhr's use of the concept of "pastoral director" has given impetus to this managerial notion of ministry, even though he took care to relate the concept to the traditional "offices" and subordinated it to "the purpose of the church and the ministry," namely, "the increase of the love of God and neighbor."[48] Sociologist Samuel W. Blizzard's listing of their six "practicioner roles" sounds more realistic to today's ministers and more natural to seminarians than the three traditional "offices." These roles are administrator, organizer, pastor, preacher, priest, teacher.[49]

A more recent survey of expectations was a project designed to determine readiness for ministry, conducted by the Association of Theological Schools in the United States and Canada in the 1970s. Responses from approximately 5000 church members and ministers gave highest important to the following "themes" in a person's ministry: open, affirming style; caring for persons under stress; congregational leadership; theological competence; ministry from a personal commitment of faith; development of fellowship and worship; and denominational awareness and collegiality. Two other themes were regarded as "somewhat important": ministry to community and world and priestly-sacramental ministry. Two themes were regarded as "undesirable" or "detrimental": a privatistic, legalistic style and disqualifying personal and behavioral characteristics.[50]

Responses from Disciples, ministers for the most part, indicated the following concerns as of highest importance: personal honesty, paraprofessional counseling, empathetic ministry, personal faith, skill in group leadership, responsibility as spouse and parent, recognition of one's own needs, self-understanding, concern for responsible church membership, and theological clarity.[51]

A rough indication of congregational expectations among Disciples may be derived from a survey of regional ministers conducted as part of the present study. Asked for the most common complaints about ministers heard from congregations, 23 regional ministers responded. More than half of these (12 of 23) reported a strong desire for more pastoral calling, an indication of the high value which congregations place on the traditional ministry of care in its traditional form. (Paging Richard Baxter!) Closely related is disappointment over clumsy, inept personal relations (8 of 23)—inability to relate to the people, who get the feeling that the minister does not understand them, their needs, and the daily pressures on them. Regional ministers report complaints about bad preaching (7 of 23)—wordiness, inadequate preparation, sermons that are not biblical. A fourth area of complaint is incompetence in leadership (6 of 23)—apparent incapacity to provide direction and motivation within a pattern of democratic decision-making, reluctance to take risks, inability to deal with conflict, fear of breaking the pastoral relationship if one stays with a policy to which some object, lack of good judgment and common sense, a tendency to be too radical and impatient, failure to keep the congregation informed about activities of the larger church and about current resources. Related to this theme is a frequent complaint about poor administration (4 of

23)—unwilling to work hard and hampered by poor work habits; similarly it is felt that the minister is insufficiently concerned about evangelism or church growth (4 of 23). Dissatisfaction arises from the impression that the minister is not spiritual enough (5 of 23)—coming across as too political, spending too much time on issues and interests not helpful to the church, giving the impression of "professionalism" rather than of "vocation."

While the tendency is strong to read such complaints (along with the themes and concerns of the ATS study) as evidence of need for the seminaries to require more courses in church administration, pastoral counseling, preaching, and other arts of the ministry, the integral relationship of the reported deficiencies to the classic "offices" should not be overlooked. Calling, relating to the people, administrative style, and work habits all have to do with the ministry of care; preaching and evangelism with the ministry of the Word. "Spirituality" and evangelistic concern may have a closer relationship than is evident at first glance with the ministry of the sacraments. The real problem may be not so much a matter of professional skills as of ministerial self-understanding and its correlation with the day-to-day life of the congregation.

Ecumenical Consensus

The most searching, widely representative, and theologically responsible discussion of ministry during our lifetime has gone on under ecumenical auspices. Since the churches have allowed the question of ministerial orders to preempt the place of priority wherever broadscale union is being discussed, that vexed issue has come in for far more attention than it merits here, except to observe that denominations historically seem to end up with three kinds of ministers, whatever they are called, and that if calling them "bishops, presbyters, and deacons" will hasten the coming of union, there should be no serious objection to so naming them.[52]

Far more important than the preoccupation with orders has been the insistence on thinking holistically of ministry, moving from that of Jesus Christ to that of the entire Christian community and then to that of the ordained.[53] The reflections of particular churches about their particular ministries have been profoundly influenced by this pattern of ecumenical thought, from the Constitution on the Church issued by the Second Vatican Council to The Design for the Christian Church (Disciples of Christ).[54] A crucial aspect of this way of thinking is the principle that ordained ministry must be at once personal, collegial, and communal.[55]

Within this holistic context the emerging ecumenical consensus gives careful attention to the "offices" or responsibilities of ministers, addressing simultaneously the nature of their work and its theological significance. The Consultation on Church Union, for example, lists the functions of presbyters ("the biblical name for persons today designated pastors, elders, ministers, or priests") as follows: preachers of the Word, celebrants of the sacraments, teachers of the gospel, pastoral overseers, pastoral administrators, leaders in mission, servants of unity, and participants in governance.[56] These functions simply spell out or elaborate the ministry of Word, sacrament, and care.

Ministry on Two Fronts

Reflection of this kind can seem irrelevant and even boring for one primary reason—the introversion of so much of our thinking about the church and especially about ministry. For too long "pastor" or "priest"—and now "administrator" have been the terms that come to mind as synonyms of "minister." These terms focus inward on the life of the congregation or denomination (as does the current substitution of "church growth" for "evangelism"), and ignore mission. Equally essential to any biblical doctrine of ministry are the terms "prophet" and "apostle" and "evangelist." These portray a minister facing the world, engaging the world, serving the world—with the support and at the calling of the church. Any discussion of the minister's work is defective if it emphasizes only one of these fronts. Ministry properly understood necessarily involves pastoral-priestly-administrative responsibility directed toward the church and prophetic-apostolic-evangelistic responsibility directed toward the world.

Viewed with such twenty-twenty vision, the traditional offices of Word, sacrament, and care take on vital contemporary significance. These services are needed fully as much in our technological age as in the agricultural and industrial age.

The ministry of the Word includes the pastoral-priestly function of teaching the gospel to members of the congregation, especially as it relates to their own interests and problems, but also the prophetic-apostolic-evangelistic function of preaching the Word to outsiders, bringing the Christian message of repentance and hope to persons who are confused, discouraged, or uncaring, and ringing out its challenge to unjust and oppressive practices everywhere. As Alexander Campbell pointed out, preaching in the New Testament sense is proclamation to those outside the church—a task which the mainline churches have all but forfeited in the age of mass media.

The ministry of the sacraments is of course a ministry provided within the church, but the Christian perception of its significance is too often radically internalized. The covenantal character of the sacraments has inevitable implications for the identification of the church with the suffering and helpless in the world and for a new vision of the ordering of its life.[57] Since the promises to which they bear witness are offered to all people, every sacramental act should be understood as an invitation to those who have not yet received the blessings it proclaims and conveys.

The ministry of care in its pastoral-priestly-administrative dimension is directed toward persons within the Christian community, to the institutional health of the congregation, to the effective functioning of the denomination, and to the work of the ecumenical movement. But this ministry also has its prophetic-apostolic-evangelistic side in meeting the needs of confused, friendless, hungry, and homeless in the community, efforts to change conditions which degrade, and service to institutions and causes committed to the ennobling and enrichment of life.

Thus each office of ministry is directed inwardly to the church and outwardly to the world. Such a vision has obvious elements of glory. It also poses a problem, for in an age of specialized professions, the minister necessarily remains a generalist,[58] and it is not easy to maintain the competence, outlook, and public confidence required for such a role. Yet the wisdom of sensitive and informed generalists is precisely what contemporary society needs—the guidance of persons who see the whole picture, who are concerned for the welfare of all, who are attuned to the purposes of God for the coming age.

But consider now how theological education has prepared students for a ministry that was . . . in a church that was . . . in a world that was.

Chapter **4**

EDUCATION FOR MINISTRY THAT WAS

Traditional assumptions and inherited practices to a large degree shape education for ministry. Diverse forces interact with them, such as opportunities, resources, and limitations associated with culture; calculated responses to specific conditions; attempts to give expression to particular visions, hopes, and convictions; notions regarded as axiomatic; and the understanding of mission to the emerging future. This chapter will sketch the history of education for ministry, with particular attention to Disciples of Christ. It will assess the effectiveness of the enterprise among Disciples, reflect on the mission of the seminary to the coming age, and propose a new agenda.

Ministerial Education in Historical Overview

Archaic and Biblical Times

In the archaic world a young person marked by the gift of religious ecstasy was taken by a mature shaman for a long period of tutelage in the mythology of the tribe, the sacred dance, and the ethos of one chosen to serve the holy. Instruction was oral and kinetic, as the neophyte chosen by the spirits lived out the apprenticeship.[1] Education for priesthood involved new elements: location at a sacred site, a temple; a company of students; memorization of sacred texts; the use of written materials; instruction in studies regarded today as general or secular (mathematics, astronomy, history) but then known chiefly to priests; rehearsal of the music and choreography of the liturgy; extensive work in the law.[2]

In Israel, where priesthood was hereditary, ethos and lore would be absorbed from the family and the hieratic community. A similar process must have gone on in the "schools of prophets"—companies of ecstatics living together in countercultural communes where religious zeal was sustained at a high level and frequently broke into ecstatic utterance.[3] The "wisdom schools" flourished under the monarchy as centers for the training of courtiers. While some of the work was not unlike that of a business college, the curriculum included elements that came to dominate classical education, instruction intended to cultivate skill in speaking and reasoning. Koheleth, the eloquent "Preacher" of Ecclesiastes, represents the teachers in the wisdom schools. The ethos was akin to that of a church-related college in the nineteenth century, charged with religious and ethical concern, even though the students were not preparing for "ordination."[4] The spirit of the sages continued in large measure in the rabbis, as noted in Chapter 3. Wherever there was a synagogue, small companies of those who loved the Law gathered daily to discuss it, and one perceived to have trustworthy knowledge of the Torah, with insight and a gift for pungent commentary, was accorded the title "Rabbi."

In the Gospels various persons so honor Jesus. He frequents the synagogues and teaches there, presumably following the customary format of rabbinic discussion. But he also carries on a popular teaching ministry outside the synagogue, using the rhetoric of the sages and the rabbinic storytellers rather than of the formal exegetes of the Torah. Jesus devotes much effort to "the Training of the Twelve,"[5] leading them away from crowds to quiet places for instruction and in Mark explaining the secret meaning of his parables. Students of the Bible have conventionally held that his ministry covered a period of three years; is this the reason for the tradition of a three-year course of study leading to the degree in divinity?[6]

The apostolic church regarded teachers as public ministers, gifted by the Holy Spirit with the charisma for that function, and the qualifications for the office of bishop included the ability to teach.[7] The gift had academic as well as spiritual dimensions: the Book of Acts presents the apostle Paul as a man of impressive education, including advanced studies under the most eminent of the rabbis, a familiarity with Greek literature, and a mastery of those skills in oratory which were the focus of the classical schools; in the epistles he reasons like a rabbi, makes use of classical rhetoric (despite his oft-quoted disavowal), and occasionally echoes a pagan poet or philosopher.[8] Stephen's speech in Acts idealizes Moses as educated in all the wisdom of the Egyptians (7:22).

The Ancient Church

That kind of openess to secular learning marked the first great Christian schools. In the second century Justin Martyr taught at Ephesus and Rome, and at Alexandria Pantaenus founded a catechetical school for converts from paganism; his student and successor, Clement attracted women and men from cultivated families by his brilliant correlation of Hellenistic and Christian thought. Where the insights of the Greek philosophers could be harmonized with the gospel, Clement regarded them as "Christians before Christ." An attractive and seminal mind engaged with the key issues of his time, he presided over the preeminent center of Christian intellectual life, and some future ministers studied there. The greatest of them, Origen, went to Palestine, where he became a noted exegete, preacher, theologian, and commentator; he built a great library for the school at Caesarea and by his teaching and writing profoundly influenced the Christian intellectual leadership of the next generation.

The Christian preachers and interpreters who came on the scene in the new age of religious toleration include the greatest minds of the fourth century. Eusebius of Caesarea, Basil the Great, Gregory of Nyssa, Gregory of Nazianzus, and John Chrysostom in the east, Ambrose, Augustine, and Jerome in the west, all had superb classical educations in philosophy, literature, and rhetoric. Their particular preparation for ministry, by contrast, was not highly institutionalized, but involved intensive study in the scriptures and reflection on issues of theology, combined with a monastic or quasi-monastic rigor of spiritual discipline; they studied on their own initiative, for the most part, with counsel from older presbyters, bishops, or lay teachers, including some notable Christian women.[9] The preaching which they heard and practiced involved profound theological work. In a famous series of orations on the Trinity, Gregory of Nazianzus admonished all who undertook to consider the sublime mysteries:

> Not to everyone . . . does it belong to philosophize about God; . . . it is permitted only to those who have been examined and are past masters in meditation, and who have been previously purified in soul and body.[10]

Medieval and Modern Europe

The monastic ideal of spiritual discipline held sway for more than a thousand years, the most important centers of learning in the early Middle Ages being the monastic schools.[11] Bishops also established cathedral schools for their secular priests, required to live under rule as canons regular. Hrabanus Maurus, Archbishop of Mainz during the ninth century, composed a manual *On the Education of the Clergy*, dealing with baptism, the mass, unction, the tonsure, vestments, fasting, penance, the confessional, and reading and singing in worship. He continued to claim classical learning for the ministry in arguments and phraseology taken from Augustine's *Christian Instruction* and Pope Gregory's *Pastoral Rule*.[12]

In the twelfth and thirteenth centuries cathedral schools flowered into universities—chartered corporations devoted entirely to learning, with faculties of philosophy, theology, law, and medicine. Among the most brilliant doctors of philosophy and theology were members of the new preaching orders devoted to mission in the world, which furnished some of the ablest interpreters of Christianity in the High Middle Ages. Nevertheless the social disorder so common in the feudal era, the ignorance of the population, and the secular preoccupations of many of the bishops wore down the efforts of noted reformers, so that the general educational level of the parish clergy remained in a sorry state until the Reformation; some priests did not even understand the words of the Latin liturgy which they recited by rote.

The Christian humanists of the Renaissance brough new excitement to learning and to preaching, giving impetus to the ideal of a learned ministry. Their enthusiasm for classical rhetoric, for the recovery of ancient manuscripts and the publication of texts, for the production of grammars and lexicons, for a synthesis of faith with liberal learning, profoundly affected the Protestant Reformers, producing both the tools and the cast of mind for an appeal to scripture in protest against popular ignorance and corruption. Both the magisterial Reformers and those northern humanists who retained allegiance to Rome embodied a cultural ideal which later flowered anew in the Christian liberal arts college; though intended for a learned elite, it provided a singularly effective preparation for ministers, supplemented, of course, by reading in theology.

A key emphasis of the Reformed tradition, was a learned ministry, and Protestant candidates enrolled in the universities as a matter of course. Then the Council of Trent mandated every Catholic bishop to provide solid educational preparation for prospective priests through the establishment of theological seminaries;[13] Rome would no longer countenance an ignorant ministry.

A radical change in the wake of the Enlightenment established the modern pattern of study for the ministry by the introduction of the theological encyclopedia. In the beginning theology had been a profoundly religious exercise of the intellect reflecting on the mysteries of salvation made known in scripture. The medieval scholastics had distinguished between theology as wisdom given by revelation and as "science" or knowledge demonstrable by reason, and the "scientific" or academic approach inevitably triumphed in the universities. Even at the cost of abandoning the intellectual leadership of the clergy, Pietism advocated greater emphasis on the spiritual and the practical.[14] But after the eighteenth century the "Theological Encyclopedia" became the prescribed course of study for ministry, involving four branches of scholarship: biblical studies, dogmatics, church history, and practical theology.[15]

A strange paradox marked this development. On the one hand these four branches were deemed to be related in their intention of preparing students for ministry; on the other hand, secularization and specialization made for the continuing refinement of each discipline, with its own scientific methodology, and a constant narrowing of the range for each professor. The trend has accelerated—in European theological faculties, American seminaries, and departments of religion in American universities.

A noteworthy exception to the pattern of narrow specialization is furnished by the English theological college, where the principal carries responsibility for a relatively small group of students from a particular denomination studying for degrees in the university. The post requires competence in the various disciplines, leadership in liturgical life, pastoral ministry to students, and obligations to the church—a heavy burden but one that makes for a holistic approach to the education of ministers. That ideal is an impressive aspect of British theological scholarship, in which each separate discipline of the "encyclopedia" is enriched and made relevant by considerations from the others.[16]

The Churches in America

In British North America the founding of the colonial colleges sprang in large measure from a concern for the education of ministers. The Puritans of Massachusetts Bay made explicit their motivation in establishing Harvard, the first such school, in 1636 as they confessed "dreading to leave an illiterate Ministry to the Churches, when our present Ministers shall lie in the Dust."[17] In 1701, to meet the need for ministers in Connecticut, church leaders there secured a charter for the college that became Yale University. Anglicans meanwhile had established the College of William and Mary in Virginia in 1693, and Presbyterians followed with Princeton in 1747. William Tennent, Sr. had already set up his Log College in Pennsylvania in 1736 to train revivalist ministers, and it contributed important leaders to the Great Awakening. But all the eighteenth-century colleges gave major attention to the education of the clergy;[18] one-third of the graduates of Harvard became ministers.[19]

The nineteenth century was the great era of the denominational college, as each of the major religious bodies moving westward with the frontier planted new schools in state after state. These institutions offered the traditional classical curriculum, to women as well as men, in preparation for various walks of life, but providing a supply of ministers was a dominant concern, and justified the colleges' existence.[20] After graduation a prospective minister spent some months "reading divinity" under the direction of an established minister, frequently under the president of the college. As early as 1784 the Dutch Reformed Church appointed a professor of divinity at New Brunswick, New Jersey to direct the studies of its college graduates.[21]

The founding of Andover Theological Seminary introduced a new pattern in American higher education, a graduate *school* after college; in the preparation of ministers the approach soon became standard.[22] Congregationalists opened Andover in 1808, Presbyterians followed with Princeton Theological Seminary four years later, other denominations started similar schools, and a few nondenominational ventures were launched.[23] Although revivalists and popular preachers on the frontier scoffed at the seminaries, some faculties strongly supported the revivals. As the number of institutions grew, several schools arose within a denomination—to serve regional needs or to promote particular emphases. In 1889 Hartford began to admit women on the same basis as men.[24] By the end of the century the ideal of the fully educated minister, with four years of college and three years of seminary, had taken hold in American Protestantism, even though only a minority realized the ideal and Methodists and Disciples, in their dislike for academic pretension, avoided the term theological seminary, preferring to call their own ventures biblical institutes or colleges of the Bible.[25]

The first American seminaries advertised a three-part curriculum, consisting of biblical studies (with emphasis on exegesis in the original languages), divinity or theology, and church history-and-polity, but it soon became common to think of sacred rhetoric and other elements of practical theology as constituting a fourth area of primary concern.[26] By the second half of the nineteenth century American seminaries generally were offering the chief elements of the "theological encyclopedia."

Increasing emphasis on academic rigor within each discipline and the association of professors from the various schools in common intellectual enterprises made for convergence in Protestant religious scholarship. Students showed decreasing interest in the peculiar emphases of their own denominations, focusing rather on the problems raised by the recognized authorities whose books all of them studied. A sense of common interest among the seminaries led to increasing consultation, cooperation, widely publicized studies, and the formation in 1936 of the American Association of Theological Schools, which emphasized the academic strengthening of all the member institutions.[29] The triumph of "modern scholarship" in the seminaries, as in the denominational colleges and publishing houses, in the first quarter of this century, resulted in the virtual exclusion of fundamentalist professors from the established intellectual institutions of the churches.[30]

The growing academic commitment of the seminaries and the considerable prestige enjoyed by higher education during the two decades after World War II began to shape the seminaries more and more after the model of the secular university. The Ph.D. degree became mandatory for theological professors, with an occasional exception in the practical field, and students intending to teach religion increasingly bypassed the professional divinity degree to go straight for the academic doctorate; within a brief time the ideals and sensitivities of seminary faculties resembled those of the graduate school rather than those of the church.

The overshadowing of the old denominational college by tax-supported institutions meant that a growing proportion of students entered the seminaries with a totally secular undergraduate education, their spiritual sensitivity stunted by the decline in humane studies noted in Chapter 2. Moreover the rapid growth of university departments and graduate programs in religion meant that secular intellectuals, frequently detached from the church, from experience in the practice of ministry, and even from Christianity itself, increasingly set the agenda and tone for scholarship. Recognition by the guild required adherence to its methods and spirit, often a great distance removed from the needs of the parish minister or the problems of the average church member. In the 1960s and '70s, leaders in theological education insistently called on the seminaries to develop their programs in a university setting, even at the price of relocation.[31]

The postwar decades brought an increase in seminary enrollments as every major denomination except the Southern Baptist Convention and some of the black churches established the basic divinity degree as its minimal educational requirement for ordination. This fact alone gave the seminaries greater control over ordination than any other institution.[32] From 1969 to 1978 the number of students enrolled in the program for the M.Div. degree in schools belonging to the Association of Theological Schools increased from 20,620 to 26,618, and the number working toward the D.Min. degree from 201 to 4,833.[33]

Yet signs of dissatisfaction were increasingly evident. Regarding traditional theological education as irrelevant to the present social situation and virtually bankrupt, a number of radical reformers lauched various experiments in "action training" in the late 1960s; most of these did not survive into the '80s.[34] A more sobering development has been a shift of students in mainline denominations from the seminaries of their own churches to the newer nondenominational, evangelical schools, e.g. Fuller, Asbury, Gordon-Conwell.[35] Thus from the left and from the right have been coming indications of deep dissatisfaction with the dominant pattern of theological education in the mainline denominations.

While all these developments were taking place, Disciples of Christ increasingly patterned their programs of education for ministry after the seminaries of the mainline denominations in America. We now turn our attention to that story.

Education for Ministry among the Disciples of Christ

The Education of the Founders

Given the prevailing level of formal education on the nineteenth-century frontier, the founders of the Christian Church (Disciples of Christ) were learned men. Barton W. Stone met the academic qualifications for the Presbyterian ministry by studying at David Caldwell's Academy in North Carolina, an institution not unlike the Tennents' Log College. Thomas Campbell graduated from Glasgow University and then attended the seminary of the Old Light Anti-Burgher Seceder Presbyterians at Whitburn. Delayed by shipwreck when the family set out from Northern Ireland for America, Alexander Campbell put the winter in Glasgow to good use, taking courses at the university and at the Haldanean Seminary. Though he did not attend college in this country, he continued a demanding course of study with his father as tutor, built an impressive personal library, sustained a regimen of intensive reading throughout life, and was reputed to be one of the erudite intellectuals of the American West. Walter Scott took a degree from the

University of Edinburgh before coming to the United States; in Pittsburgh he studied the Bible and the history of the early church under the tutelage of David Forrester, pastor of the congregation of "Kissing Baptists."

All four of the founders were frontier intellectuals: they preached and lectured and edited journals, and three of them taught school; Alexander Campbell attained fame as a debater. All these activities required continuing study, and the four may be fairly described as well read in the recognized British and American works. The younger Campbell was also acquainted with books of substance intended for the general reader in that day before academic specialization. The four gave little attention to the work of contemporary German philosophers and biblical scholars, or even of Immanual Kant, who died just before the Campbells came to America. In the best sense of the term, all four were folk-theologians:[36] their doctrine was in intention derived from the New Testament and argued on scriptural and logical grounds; their intellectual universe was that charted by John Locke and the Scottish Common Sense School; the issues they addressed were those which most concerned the lay mind and the welfare of the congregations. They had little interest in the technical work of contemporary theologians, which they regarded as unprofitable speculation in relatively inconsequential matters of opinion. On everything that truly mattered, God had uttered saving truth in the revealed Word. They intended to speak where the scriptures speak.

The Colleges

Like the Western pioneers of the various denominations, the founders saw the need for institutions to educate a new generation of leaders in church and state; they could not long be satisfied with informal efforts like the "School of Preachers" that brought neophytes together for just a few days.[37] In 1836 Bacon College, named for the famed seventeenth-century intellectual, opened its doors at Georgetown, Kentucky, with Walter Scott as president; soon it merged with Transylvania University in Lexington. Campbell launched a new "Seminary of Learning," Bethany College in western Viriginia in 1840.[38] Just after mid-century, Western Reserve Eclectic Institute (now Hiram College) in Ohio, Northwestern Christian University (now Butler) in Indiana, Walnut Grove Academy (Eureka College) in Illinois, and Christian University (Culver-Stockton College) in Missouri began operations. As president of Bethany, Campbell placed his mark on the entire enterprise, for the other schools acquired luster by calling Bethany graduates to their faculties.

Concerned with the education of leaders for the churches, the colleges served the ideal of the responsible Christian well versed in the Bible and the liberal arts; education for future preachers was the same as for members of the congregations. Determined that Bethany College should not be confused with or develop into a theological seminary, Alexander Campbell wrote into its charter a proviso prohibiting the establishment of a theological professorship there. From the campuses a stream of young leaders grounded in the faith returned to the churches to strengthen their life, and for generations Bethany and Hiram were "household words" among Disciples.[39] In their eagerness they founded many schools which could not scrape up the resources to survive, but a few in the South and West managed to endure; the youngest of the liberal arts institutions, California School of Christianity (Chapman College) was established in 1920.

A Distinctive Program of Ministerial Education

With the passing of the founders, a new generation of leaders worked out a program of ministerial education peculiarly suited to the genius of the Disciples and the situation of the churches: an intensive course of specialized study concentrated on the scripture.[40] The College of the Bible pioneered the new approach in 1865 as part of Kentucky University, with which Transylvania had been consolidated. Like the theological seminaries of the denominations, it offered a three-year program, but rather than theology it emphasized the content of the Bible, with some work in preaching. Designed for college graduates, it was open to others as well.[41] Until the end of the nineteenth century, most students pursued the program leading to the diploma while also working toward a baccalaureate degree in liberal arts; but relatively few completed both courses of study. That was no great matter, for the churches welcomed the young preachers so well versed in biblical knowledge.

The pattern of intensive Bible courses, designed for ministers with an education in the liberal arts, spread to other Disciples colleges: Hiram, Butler, Eureka, Drake, Add-Ran (Texas Christian), and Oklahoma Christian (Phillips) ran flourishing Bible departments or Bible colleges in the period between the Civil War and World War I (and even later), open to undergraduates, but in most cases leading to a diploma or M.A. degree.[42] The concept reached its most grandiose expression in 1908 when Eugene Divinity School in Oregon changed its name to Eugene Bible University.[43]

Designed for students who intended to be—and in most cases had already begun to be—preachers, these programs were "professional" in intent. Large ministerial associations on the campuses cultivated zeal, fellowship, and high morale. Although the curriculum had a particular focus, the location alongside or within small liberal arts colleges exposed ministerial students to professors and fellow students from other departments and to the intellectual atmosphere and broad culture of the general community, while the curriculum itself called for some work in the humanities. Yet despite the obvious service of the Bible programs to the churches and the sizeable number of students they attracted, some faculty members in arts and sciences, along with some trustees, resisted their rapid growth, believing that they compromised the character of the colleges.[44]

In a time when congregations exercised all too readily and sentimentally their power to ordain, the academicians struggled to build a consensus establishing the B.A. degree as a minimal requirement for ordination. In 1915 the Disciples Board of Education, comparing the ideal "preacher's preparation" to that of "the best qualified lawyer, physician, teacher, or scientist," urged that those entering the ministry should have a "recognized academic degree" and be "especially trained in biblical subjects and pastoral ministrations." But not until 1939 did the International Convention of Disciples of Christ adopt educational guidelines for ordination: "A full college course and, if possible, graduate training in religion."[45] Even then, a three-year reading course, with approved experience as a licensed minister, was suggested as an alternative for the person not in a position to earn a degree.

At midpoint in the twentieth century, terminology shifted from the Bible department or college to department of religion. The stronger programs raised requirements for entrance, added professional degrees, and gradually evolved into theological seminaries. We shall come to that story shortly.

One variation on the program of the Bible departments was the Bible chair, an original contribution in higher education, established by the Christian Woman's Board of Missions at the University of Michigan in 1893, then at the University of Virginia, and other state schools; it seemed evident to Disciples at that time that an introductory course in religion should be a course in Bible content. While the Bible chairs were intended as a service to students generally, they succeeded in recruiting a number of ministers.[46] Another variant was The College of Missions set up by CWBM in Indianapolis, adjacent to the campus of Butler University. Under the dynamic leadership of Charles T. Paul, it offered work in what would now be called missiology, history of religions, cultural anthropology, and apologetics as preparation for the large number of young persons preparing to go into service overseas.[47] Similar to the training schools then flourishing in several of the denominations, the institution attained a strong reputation.

While historians customarily note the influence of editors during the Disciples' first century, they have accorded insufficient recognition to the professors of Bible and the ministerial presidents of the colleges. In an age before the Ph.D. degree was expected, the "gentleman scholar" dominated American higher education. He possessed keenness of mind, love of learning, wide erudition, strong convictions, and the ability to inspire—or at least discipline— youth. In a church that had no "teaching office" other than the local eldership, and at a time when its intellectual life was largely self-contained, the influence of such stalwarts as W. K. Pendleton, C. L. Loos, J. W. McGarvey, Robert Milligan, H. W. Everest, Jabez Hall, D. R. Dungan, E. V. Zollars, Clinton Lockhart, Frank H. Marshall (the last two of these men earned the Ph.D. degree), and others of their type, can hardly be overstated. Not only did they instruct hundreds of preachers-to-be, imparting "sound doctrine" and zeal for the plea; they wrote the textbooks and the Bible lessons in the popular journals, spoke as headliners at state and general conventions, conducted evangelistic meetings, served as arbiters of doctrinal disputes, and provided role models for generations of ministers. Most of them doubled as editors of or contributors to "brotherhood" journals and played a leading part in the organized life of the movement. When the stirring of new ideas in the world at large began to agitate the serenity of Zion, Disciples concerned with the intellectual issues organized annual Congresses to hear divergent viewpoints on such topics as evolution, biblical criticism, and federation (the emerging ecumenical movement), and these professors from the colleges had star billing.

The Independent Bible Colleges

The new intellectual movements in the world at large and the readiness of some preachers and professors to discuss them, or even modify their thinking in the light of them, led to two diverse movements: the evolution of theological seminaries and the emergence of a new type of Bible college. One of the first of these latter was the Nashville Bible School (1891), where the emphasis fell on memorizing the sacred text.[48] Another early starter was Johnson Bible College, begun as the School of the Evangelists in 1893 in the mountains of Tennessee. The Nashville school provided leadership for the Churches of Christ, but Johnson furnished hundreds of preachers for the Disciples.

As secularism and liberalism gained a footing in the liberal arts colleges and the seminaries, and as conservatives stepped up their attacks on the United Christian Missionary Society and other cooperative institutions, scores of new independent Bible colleges sprang up to offer an alternative program for the education of preachers. While at first glance it seemed to resemble that of the early College of the Bible at Lexington and the other colleges already discussed, there was a crucial difference—inspired by a fear of modern learning, intense opposition to religious liberalism, and suspicion of urban culture, all exacerbated by rivalry between publishing houses and emerging schism between cooperatives and independents. Isolated for the most part from the larger world of higher education, the new schools conceived of their task as one of indoctrination.

For many years the Bible Colleges promoted their program as offering sufficient preparation for ministry, but after World War II the pattern of going on to seminary took hold, with Butler School of Religion (now Christian Theological Seminary) and Phillips serving as the most common destinations. As dissatisfaction with all the Disciples schools increased and as some of the independent Bible colleges raised the academic standing of their faculties, a few institutions evolved seminaries of their own. At the time of Restructure, all of the "Bible colleges" left the Disciples. Only one liberal arts institution, Milligan College, identified primarily with the "independent" churches, as did its affiliated seminary, Emmanuel School of Religion. Northwest Christian College, continuing a program like that of the Bible colleges, but holding regional accreditation, persisted in its efforts to relate to both Disciples and "Independents."

Compared with the number of pre-ministerial students now enrolled in the liberal arts colleges of the Disciples, the independent Bible colleges have clear numerical predominance. They have largely achieved their purposes of indoctrination, for the uniformity of viewpoint among "independent" ministers is striking.[49] Measured however against the trends described thus far in this study, one can only consider their program a cultural anachronism in need of radical revision. Few of their recent graduates have entered the ministry of the Disciples.

The Arrival of the Seminaries

By 1890 Yale Divinity School had begun to attract young Disciples who went beyond college to pursue their education for the ministry, and several young scholars entered the Ph.D. programs in religious studies at Yale University and the University of Chicago. By 1894 the Disciples Divinity House had been established in affiliation with the new Divinity School at the latter institution. Exposure to the ferment of scholarship in the larger religious world caused excitement and consternation among Disciples. Ministers who were open to discussion of the new ideas organized the Campbell Institute in 1896, a somewhat elite intellectual fellowship since it required the B.A. degree for membership. For two generations it was an important forum—until the daring notions which had once seemed so startling became commonplace to a seminary-educated ministry.[50]

The involvement of Disciples at the cutting edge of theological scholarship had a profound effect on the College of the Bible at Lexington and on the departments of religion in the liberal arts colleges, which began to move toward the new standards and methodologies. In 1914 the school at Lexington replaced its diploma with the then standard postcollegiate degree for ministers, Bachelor of Divinity. The old Bible department at Butler University became the College of Religion in 1924, with emphasis on postgraduate work, after an earlier brief attempt at the end of the nineteenth century. At Drake, Phillips, and Texas Christian universities, the Bible colleges placed increasing emphasis on the M.A. and B.D. degrees; as early as 1928 the Conference of Bible Teachers from schools affiliated with the Disciples Board of Education formally recommended "two to five years of graduate training for our ministers."[51] Nevertheless ordination with the B.A. alone remained common until World War II, and the schools offered various options for conflating the three-year B.D. program with studies taken for the B.A., so that most students managed to complete the two degrees in five or six years. (The pattern was common among American seminaries at the time.)

The formation of the American Association of Theological Schools in 1938 put considerable pressure on institutions to conform to the standards of the strongest seminaries, though among Disciples at the outset only College of the Bible at Lexington could qualify for accreditation. (The Disciples Divinity House at Chicago was of course affiliated with an accredited school). The other Disciples "seminaries" were ineligible because of their practice of using the same faculty for college and seminary work and of mingling undergraduate and graduate students in the same classes. By the formation of the Graduate Seminary in 1944, Phillips became the first school to adopt the nomenclature; Drake and Brite opted for the name Divinity School, following usage which prevailed at Yale, Chicago, Vanderbilt, and other universities. When the School of Religion separated from Butler University in 1958 it took the name Christian Theological Seminary, the first institution among Disciples to avow a title which would have been anathema two or three decades earlier, and College of the Bible became Lexington Theological Seminary in 1965. The new nomenclature did not introduce a new ideal of education; rather it acknowledged a change that had already occurred in the character of the schools.

Meanwhile Disciples Divinity House at Vanderbilt had begun operation in 1942 and the Disciples Seminary Foundation launched its association with the School of Theology at Claremont in 1960; for a time also a Disciples House operated in connection with Yale Divinity School. Disciples institutions now affiliated with the Christian Church (Disciples of Christ) are Brite Divinity School, Christian Theological Seminary, Disciples Divinity House at the University of Chicago, Disciples Divinity House at Vanderbilt University, Disciples Seminary Foundation, Phillips Graduate Seminary, and Lexington Theological Seminary.

Seminary education became normative for ministers of the Disciples, as for the other "people's churches" which had flourished on the frontier, only after World War II. During the postwar prosperity and religious boom of the 1950s the seminaries enjoyed a period of rapid expansion, being flooded with the normal contingent of recent college graduates, large numbers of veterans studying on the G.I. Bill, and a considerable number of ministers in mid-career who now saw the necessity of a professional degree. Not until 1957 did Disciples of Christ in International Convention vote to establish the B.D. degree as the minimal educational standard recommended for ordination. The current "Policies and Procedures for the Order of Ministry," adopted by the General Assembly in 1973 list the A.B. degree and the first professional degree from an accredited seminary as basic standards.

During the postwar decades of rapid growth, an impressive expansion of faculties took place; the total number of fulltime professors in the four Disciples seminaries increased from 26 in 1945 to 58 in 1986. (At the time of its closing Drake Divinity School had seven professors, not included in these totals.) Virtually all the new teachers had the Ph.D. or Th.D. degree, which, if not exactly a rarity in these schools before World War II, had been regarded as a mark of unusual distinction. Today the entire teaching force, with hardly an exception, and that usually in the practical field, holds earned academic doctorates. Disciples predominate in the faculties, but scholars belonging to other denominations are numerous, called both for mastery in their disciplines and with the purpose of enhancing the ecumenical character of theological education. In the faculties at Chicago, Claremont, and Vanderbilt, Disciples are, of course, a small minority.

Professors in the seven institutions enjoy intellectual collegiality in scholarly organizations representing the various disciplines, in such organizations as the Association of Disciples for Theological Discussion[52] and the Commission on Theology of the Council on Christian Unity, and in occasional guest lectureships. While each school has a distinctive ethos and particular strengths, the mutual suspicion regarding theological stance which lingered only a few decades ago has dissipated. A professor in any of the schools could now be intellectually at home with the faculty of any of the others, though one might feel less comfortable with unfamiliar regional mores or colleagues whose research interests do not fit with one's own. Since all hold common assumptions, one faculty can hardly fault another on academic commitment, curricular requirements, or library resources; though the schools offering Ph.D. programs may acknowledge a stronger institutional obligation to advanced research than do others. A study of the catalogs, however, suggests that all seven schools are trying to do pretty much the same thing in the education of ministers and offer remarkably similar programs.

Appraising the Work of the Disciples Seminaries

How well are the seminaries of the Disciples fulfilling their mission? We may begin our search for an answer to that question with an analysis of requirements for the Master of Divinity, the degree requisite for ordination.

Table I

Requirements for M.Div. Degree in 7 Institutions
Affiliated with the Christian Church (Disciples of Christ)
(figures represent semester hours)[53]

	Brite	CTS	DDH,UC	GS,PU	LTS	STC	DDH,VU
Bible	12	12	12	12	18	18	12
History	12	12	12		6	16	6
Theology & Ethics	9	18	4	12	6	16	6
Society, Culture & Personality	9	6	-	6	18	4	-
Work of Ministry	28	20	8-16	18	18	26	15
Orientation to Theol. Study	-	-	4	3	3	-	-
Project Thesis	-	-	8	-	3	-	3
Electives	18-26	19	40	27	9	16	19

Course requirements in the seven Disciples institutions show a high degree of similarity and have remained relatively constant across the decades, even though elective offerings have changed with the times.

What Do the Graduates Think?

Ministers generally hold their work in seminary in considerable esteem for what it contributed to them in their profession. As part of this study a set of questions was distributed to ministers in various meetings and mailed to at least twenty representative graduates of each of the seven schools related to the Christian Church (Disciples of Christ), as well as to some alumni of other institutions. Responses numbered 140. Designed to elicit comments and individual concerns rather than answers subject to quantification,[54] the questions evoked medium to strong approval, with forthright expressions of gratitude, for the general quality of instruction, for processes of critical thinking, for particular areas of study (commonly biblical studies or theology), for lessons learned serving as a minister while going to school, for the inspiration of particular professors, and for fellow students who continue as colleagues and friends in common vocation.

Asked about elements of their education which they perceive as having had least significance for their ministry, some respondents designated a certain course (Hebrew, Greek, world religions, church history, theology, field education), but frequently specified that the problem was in the way the subject was taught; others mentioned these same courses as being particularly useful. A number specified particular pedagogical procedures (field exams, the requirement to learn quantities of data rather than techniques of research, failure to address newer concerns like racism and sexism, busy-work), but one lone soul spoke up for the value of field exams, and twenty of the respondents ignored the question, while 36 (more than 25 percent) countered with an assertion that every course has value. With almost no partisan declaration of loyalty to *alma mater* (except for older graduates of Chicago and Vanderbilt), the replies to these two questions convey a strong positive feeling about the work of the seminaries.

On another question, however, respondents showed overwhelming agreement in naming elements of decisive importance to ministry which they found lacking or altogether insufficient in their seminary education. Of 140 respondents, 108 confessed inadequate preparation for practical aspects of ministry (baptisms, weddings, funerals, budgets, campaigns, stewardship, evangelism, Christian education); for working with people, resolving conflicts, motivating, enlisting, and organizing volunteers; and for spirituality or growth in personal Christian faith and discipline. Their declaration of their own unreadiness for the practice of ministry agrees to a remarkable degree with the assessment by congregations as reported by regional ministers, which we have already noted, as well as with other studies.[55]

Complaints of inadequate preparation or useless classes in practical ministry and supervised field education indicated that the required courses in these areas did not give the insights and resources they needed. Repeatedly the alumni mentioned professors who, despite evident competence in their scholarly discipline, had little experience in or comprehension of the work of a minister in the parish and whose teaching, while impressive and intriguing in the seminary setting, seemed to have no potentiality for carry-over to the life of the congregation. Many of the respondents called for increased emphasis on the arts of ministry, with a realistic introduction to life and procedures in the churches, but a voluble minority insisted that the business of the seminary is to teach the classical disciplines, to help students learn how to think, to engage them in the struggle with great issues, and argued that they can quickly learn the skills once they get on the job.

So the answer to our question, "How well are the Disciples seminaries fulfilling their mission?" depends on the way in which the mission is perceived. The degree requirements listed above indicate some formal concern for the traditional tasks of the minister, even if most of the faculty has little interest in them. But respondents corroborate the impression registered throughout this study that seminary professors generally inhabit, and project for their students, a world far removed from the parish and the work of the women and men who serve as ministers there. As a guild, professors seem not much interested in what goes on in congregations, where ordinary people, few of them academics, meet to give common expression to their faith and to seek help in living out their vocation as Christians.

The Mentality of an Established Church

The irony of this situation can hardly be overlooked, for the triumph of the new ideal among Disciples—a ministry with a professional education obtained at a theological seminary—was accompanied by the decline of this once evangelistic people. Along with the other mainline churches with whom they so eagerly sought to identify, Disciples have suffered a slow but uninterrupted loss in membership across a period of two decades. Perhaps unwittingly, they accepted the model and assumptions of an established church, assuming faith to be inherited from generation to generation and looking to society to exert the pressures of tradition to sustain religion; they lost the missionary and evangelistic outlook which characterized their first century.[56]

The anchor of that establishment presupposition is the theological seminary, which justifies its existence on the grounds of providing leadership to perpetuate an institution and which has encouraged the faculty to fashion itself after the ultimate role model of the theological professor in the German university, with one's research as one's primary commitment. By its very nature research tends to be recondite and theoretical. Though government offers grants to faculty members in the sciences, especially for projects that may lead to new weapons systems, any special consideration to induce professors in the seminaries to devote their most intense intellectual efforts to the problems of life or death in the church is rare.

In an earlier day, when the schools of Disciples centered their education for ministry on the study of the Bible, they consequently dealt with the basic realities of saving faith and churchly life, even if they gave little formal attention to the problems of the modern world. When, in rightly turning from a biblicism which critical study had rendered obsolete, they embraced the presuppositions of modern scholarship in religion, they exposed students to a bewildering assortment of notions, principles, hopes and prejudices with no central organizing principle. Presumably most theological professors had found for themselves a solid basis for belief and action, and their example enabled some students to do so. But there was no corporately professed common understanding, such as the Christocentric "biblical doctrine" had provided in the Disciples' first century, or as the early liberal commitment to working out an honest Christian faith for free minds had done for those who entered that quest.

Whereas young ministers in some denominations can look to a confessional or liturgical tradition to provide a structure of faith, Disciples have only a brief tradition, derived from a view of the Bible which no one in the seminaries any longer holds. Little wonder, when all comes down at last to subjective judgments, that the seminary campuses have been swept by gales of imitation and faddishness, that gimmickry appeals to those intent on careerism, that social action offers the most readily available sense of common endeavor for idealists, that the vision of evangelism as good news of God in Christ to challenge and change both persons and social structures seems almost incomprehensible, that so many ministers feel and even manifest a sense of spiritual emptiness. Still, Alexander Campbell scored an indisputable point when he allowed, "I have a little more faith in an educated than an uneducated ministry."[57]

A Fallacy of Misplaced Emphasis

Our argument to this point calls for a response from the seminaries which takes seriously the life of the church, but in more than traditional fashion. They all require courses in the work of the minister, however adequate or inadequate these offerings may be. But if we shift our attention to the challenge of the world rushing upon us, the eyes of the curriculum-builders seem blind. Here we have sketched the shape of a society and culture strikingly different from the world that was; in this situation the church that was finds increasing difficulty in functioning effectively and the ministry that was expends its energies just in trying to cope with new and unfamiliar conditions. Yet the courses the seminaries require suggest little effort to help students understand that world. (It might be argued that courses in church history, theology, arts of ministry, and even in Bible, should be taught in such a way as to provide such understanding, but evidently that is not always the case.) Required courses in the area of society, culture, and personality hold a minimal place among the requirements and are slanted largely toward religious education and pastoral care. Some of the schools require one or two courses giving special attention to global issues, and many seminarians emerge as doctrinaire liberals on such matters. But do they really understand the dynamics of contemporary society? Do they know how to lead traditional church members to a larger vision of justice, peace, and care for the victims of life? Have they an idea how to confront pagans on the outside with the challenge of a persuasive Christian witness?

The signs are not encouraging. The theological seminaries have long indicated by their very name, which Disciples adopted a generation ago, an implicit commitment to theology as queen of the sciences, at least in the curriculum for ministers; and the proposal for the reintegration of theological education which has stirred the greatest excitement in recent months undertakes to unify the curriculum by an explicit theological approach to every area of study.[58]

Yet theology at the present moment seems a weak reed, hardly capable of supporting the burden of educating ministers for a new day. Whereas a generation ago the names of Barth, Brunner, Tillich, Niebuhr, Bonhoeffer, Dawson, Murray, and Rahner (along with preachers like Fosdick, Buttrick, Sheen and Marney) commanded wide respect among secular intellectuals and even some attention from the media, Christianity has few such recognized spokespersons today, except for fundamentalist celebrities. Theology has "lost its voice" in the conversation with high culture.[59]

Moreover, as a rising chorus of observers has noted, theology is out of contact with the church, its native community, and with the Christian tradition.[60] Having fallen victim to a disease of intellectuals, scholars in the seminaries commonly seem to disregard, if not actually disdain, the laity and their concerns.[61]

The irony that such a great gulf separates seminary faculty members from the concerns of the ministry and of people working in the congregations is a major cause of the irrelevance so often charged against theological education. In contrast with schools of education, accused of all method and no substance, seminaries have little esteem for or interest in methods, even in courses on the "Arts of Ministry."[62]

Committed to scholarly concerns within their particular disciplines—concerns which are honorable in themselves, and demanding of time and energy—professors in any field manifest the behavior typical of human beings with vested interests to protect; for all their sophisticated discussion of original sin or Niebuhrian insights or even liberation theology, they behave like oppressors everywhere. The privileges they cherish are not crassly financial, but academic: required courses, additional faculty appointments in their field, specialized degree programs, foundation grants.[63] They may hear but can scarcely comprehend, much less empathize with, the cries for change in the system, particularly those which arise outside academia. Moreover the highly competitive ethos of the graduate school in the secular university increasingly manifests itself in seminaries, as the self-aggrandizement of the free-enterprise system shows up in theological teachers and ministers alike.[64] The dynamics of the seminary as a branch of the academy assigns primacy to performance as a scholar, whether in the appointment of a new professor or in recommendations for promotion; usefulness to the church in some indirect fashion may be more or less assumed, but rarely does it function as a criterion in selection or advancement.

How shall ministers be prepared for the coming age? When we repeat the question now, having considered the present state of the seminaries, our consciences reel under the word of the prophet Isaiah concerning those who are asked to read for a troubled people.[65]

> A scholar . . . answers,
> "I cannot; the scroll is sealed."
> An illiterate person . . . answers,
> "But I cannot read."

Those of us who dare to teach in the seminary find ourselves in the situation of the distraught householder, beating on the neighbor's door at midnight:[66]

> A friend of mine has arrived on a journey,
> and I have nothing to set before him.

Education for the Coming Age: A New Agenda

Only the most hard-hearted would give a stone to a child begging bread or a snake to one asking a fish. Nevertheless good intentions could deceive, and in more than one way. An overriding preoccupation with pastoral methods and administration could mislead the unwary into offering a stone of "how-to" training while forgetting the bread of life, to serve up a serpent of techniques for sure-fire success without asking what it means for a minister or congregation to do God's work with faithfulness. But such a prospect is no more likely than it is desirable in our seminaries. We must also turn the figure in another direction. Does it not appear that we have set before our students the stone of abstract theory, too often secular and irrelevant, in place of the bread of insight into the nature of authentic Christian ministry, its spirit, intention, and mode of operation. Instead of the food that alone nourishes, the reality of the living God ever confronting a people called by grace, we have been beguiled into offering the serpent of a smug intellectualism far removed from the pressing concerns of plain people and their pastors, the perplexities of congregations and regional commissions, the problems of denominations and ecumenical bodies, an intellectualism which blithely ignores the troubling realities which confront our graduates as soon as they leave our classes.

The burden of this section is a call for all concerned to develop a new agenda: to design our education for ministry so as to address with full Christian responsibility the central problems of the church's life in its mission to the coming age. Such a redesigned program may well include much of the substance of traditional theological education, but we cannot take such inclusion for granted nor dare we even permit it without searching reflection. The program may call for radical shifts in some of our academic presuppositions. Before proposing agenda for such a reconsideration, let me recall a fairly recent crisis of ministry, which has now abated, but perhaps only for the time being.

A Warning Unheeded: The Storm that Passed

A floodtide of radical criticism regarding traditional ministry lashed at the churches in the 1960s, whipped by high winds of disenchantment with the congregation and driven by the tempest of anti-institutionalism then raging in American society. Although secular magazines were full of articles on "Why I Left the Ministry," a host of bright, idealistic young people continued to enter seminary—chanting the refrain, "I don't want to serve in a parish." They were bound for "experimental ministries," sustained by brave talk, some high-level studies on "new forms of ministry," and some genuine experimentation. For the support of all such ventures, however, the new pioneers soon discovered, they had no place to look except the much-maligned institution. Shortly after graduation most of them settled for work in a congregatoin or on a denominational staff.[68] Before long the storm subsided; most of today's seminarians know nothing about it.

The theological schools rode out the gale, the old hands on the faculties trying vainly to persuade their students of creative possibilities in parish ministry, the *avant-garde* joining in the critique with concerns not unlike those set forth in Chapters 2 and 3. In any case very few changes took place in congregations or seminaries, aside from adding student representatives to faculty committees. Most of the experiments ended inconclusively for want of funds. Who knows how much of today's ministerial "burn-out" traces back to those wild years in seminary when students ignored or inwardly rejected everything designed to help them develop into the conventional parish ministers they have outwardly become?

As for theological faculties, we responded only partially to the charge of irrelevance then so freely hurled at church and ministry: we pressed the liberal-to-radical social agenda with new vigor. Resistance to the Vietnam War and the nuclear arms race, along with advocacy of liberation theology, inclusive language, and gay rights, achieved the status of a new orthodoxy on the campuses and in the national assemblies of the mainline churches.

The deeper issue of "relevance," however, has received little attention. Aside from "taking a stand" through resolutions in ecclesiastical conventions, how do the churches significantly engage the principalities and powers of our society? How do they get a hearing for the gospel? How does a congregation, or any other body of believers in whatever new shape, become an authentic force for justice and goodness and truth in the life of its community? How does it bring a redemptive and transforming ministry to bear on continuing white racism,[69] the plague of drug-addiction, urban crime, the aimlessness of youth, the hedonism of young adults, the materialism of the elderly? How does a minister go about changing this kind of world while genuinely caring for the people of a congregation, building up its strength for mission, and maintaining its integrity?

The seminaries show few signs that their faculties have collectively addressed such issues even in a general way, much less with the intention of radically reconsidering their curricular requirements, course offerings, degree programs, and unexamined presuppositions about theological education. Most faculty members, moreover, would insist, for reasons already noted, that their competence and interest lie elsewhere, pleading that they are not really qualified to address the crucial issues of congregational witness in today's kind of world. Is that state of affairs perhaps the real problem with theological education? If ministry is to serve the coming age, must its reshaping take place outside the seminaries?

A New Mandate: Readaptation

To fulfill their mission of educating a Christian leadership for the future, the seminaries will have to address head-on the crises in culture, church, and ministry, then take a radical new look at their programs and presuppositions.[70] Observations in a recent study of industry equally apply to theological education: "Although organizations can get by for a time being only efficient or only innovative, over the long term there must be simultaneous achievement of both efficiency and innovation." Citing the American automobile industry as an example of organization characterized by efficiency without innovation and hospitals as an example of institutional innovation without comparable efficiency,[71] the authors call for "readapation"—the repeated discovery of ways to introduce innovations, while maintaining or enhancing efficiencies and member involvement.[72]

Such a dual process of readapation is now incumbent on the church, the ministry, and the seminaries—unless the children of this world are still wiser than the children of light (Luke 16:8). If the seminaries, as intellectual centers for the church, are to take the lead, they must find the secret of readapation first of all.

As for the two components of readaptation, the seminaries seem to have been the more concerned with efficiency, seeking to upgrade their own institutional life through academic excellence: they have given great care to faculty appointments, standards for accreditation, regular research leaves, lectureships, and improved physical facilities. One would like to add expansion of libraries to this list, but on the grim day of budget-cutting year after year, the item for new books always seems to suffer. One would also like to include greater selectivity in admissions, but the need for increasing income from tuition tends to override the best of intentions toward raising requirements for entrance. With respect to concern for church and ministry, the seminaries' implicit goal for courses in the practical field is evidently efficiency—to help ministers carry through with professional skill the various tasks which the church lays on them. Responses to our questionnaire suggest that this teaching tends to be uneven and insufficient, some of it ranking among the most useful courses, some as a waste of time.

With regard to innovation, the seminaries do not have a notable record. They changed the nomenclature of their basic degree from Bachelor of Divinity to Master of the same, without notable upgrading. In the 1960s two schools to which Disciples are related, Chicago and Claremont, instituted a four-year doctorate as the basic professional degree, with heightened academic demands, and in 1970 a commission of the American Association of Theological Schools recommended the general adoption of such a program with an exacting set of standards; but the schools unable to meet them, a majority of the association, voted down the recommendation. The Doctor of Ministry degree is now generally awarded for advanced study undertaken by ministers some years out of seminary; as such it seems to have proved its worth. In the 1960s and 1970s some of the leading schools instituted new programs of supervised internship designed to apply to the general work of ministers methods and precision comparable to those used in clinical pastoral education, but such efforts have proved more frustrating than successful.

The large-scale entry of women into ministry, perhaps the most far-reaching innovation of recent years, occurred in their own response to the gospel, with the seminaries playing the role of bystanders, first astonished and then grateful, persuaded more by the positive impact on enrollments than by early conviction of rightness for the churches. A degree of excitement has attended ecumenical ventures in academic cooperation, which have brought Protestant and Catholic students together in some courses and enabled Disciples to study with Orthodox Christian, Roman Catholic, Jewish, and Buddhist professors; increasing exchanges are also occurring between seminarians and professors of the Third World and their American counterparts. But now that these things are happening, the wonder is that it took so long to bring them about.

Theological education, in short, like higher education generally, has not shown itself to be remarkably innovative within its own house. Our argument contends however that faithfulness to mission requires readaptation by the seminaries, with a commitment to innovation in church, ministry, and study of divinity. What if the faculties were to set aside the term "theological education" and speak instead of "education for ministry"? If they were to take the change in terminology seriously, it might bring on true innovation and sweeping readaptation. Not that theology should be minimized or its place in the program reduced, but that the focus is changed. Students will still be educated *in* theology, but not as an end in itself nor just as a subject to be explored, for they are to be educated *for* ministry. The point here is not novelty for its own sake or for scoring points in public relations. The kind of innovation urged here is for the purpose of helping the Christian movement to break out of its introversion and irrelevance to the issues within contemporary culture, to bear authentic witness to the gospel, and to fulfill the calling of its Servant-Lord.

Mission to the Coming Age

Approaching the twenty-first century, Christians are called in mission to a culture in which secular hope has collapsed; as has been wryly noted, "The only convinced Marxists are the dissidents in the west, and the only convinced liberals are the dissidents in the east."[73] Any popular consensus regarding a common obligation to the public good has likewise vanished; the hedonistic appeal of advertising and a mindset that reasons primarily in psychological assumptions have combined to produce an individualism no longer capable of articulating or affirming the covenantal faith on which our commonwealth rests.[74] If the medieval worldview, at least in a state of ideal purity, saw "no dichotomy between the private and the public, between the believer and the citizen,"[75] such is no longer the case. The contemporary mind has effected an apotheosis of the capitalist faith in self-interest, before which even the iron knee of Marxism has begun to bend.

In a world where the primacy of personal preference has become almost axiomatic, liberal churches have all but rolled over and played dead. Nowhere has this been more obvious than in their response to the sexual revolution; while fundamentalists and Roman Catholics march in often vulgar demonstrations against abortion, prostitution, and homosexuality, liberal Christians have limited themselves to feeble outcries about the overemphasis on sex and violence in the media, but have virtually ceased to use the word chastity, much less commend it as an "alternative life-style" in a culture where "anything goes." Fifteen years ago a keenly perceptive mainline minister who had always maintained good rapport with his young people told me that he had stopped trying to give them guidance about sex, lest they conclude he was so far "out of it" that they would discount his views on everything else. Failing to understand our society and how to make it work, ministers have become increasingly frustrated at their irrelevance to the common life and their lack of power, not only in the community at large, but even in the church.[76]

Yet the church hardly lacks opportunity to engage this generation. In increasing numbers sophisticated adults are turning to the arts, not so much for investment as for a means of announcing their status: "a large and sophisticated white-collar public . . . are searching for artistic flair and the personal touch."[77] Here is a potential opening for dialog which too many stodgy congregations and unimaginative ministers will miss out on altogether, unless the seminaries begin to broaden churchly interest and sensitivity. A similar opportunity presents itself in the area of music, as a few alert congregations discovered during the Bach Tercentennial. The Cathedral of the Resurrection in Coventry and of St. John the Divine in New York maintain an active dialog with artists and musicians and give notable support to their work.

It requires no very bright observer to see that our contemporary hedonism has failed to produce happiness. Even the relatively well-to-do are restless in their search for something "more," not only quantitatively but qualitatively. When that hunger turned briefly in the 1970s to the realm of spirituality, mainline religion cannot be said to have struck out; it did not even come up to bat. At best, ministers went along with the development by diminishing an already too feeble social witness in favor of even greater privatism, but there was no great outburst of spiritual renewal in congregations, much less any imaginative approach to outsiders. Even the seminaries which offered faddish courses on the cults and psychological exercises for expanding the inner consciousness failed to engage their students in any robust way with the great tradition of biblical and Christian spirituality.

Our mission to a pagan culture lies before us, largely unattempted as yet because of the long-held illusion in Europe and America that ours is a Christian society. That illusion is no longer credible. When the weight of contemporary secularism and paganism begins to press upon the churches as the burden of the millions in Asia and Africa who had never heard the name of Christ weighed upon the noblest Christian spirits of the nineteenth century, we may expect a new thrust in Christian mission. That new sense of calling ought to arise in the seminaries with the sobering acknowledgement that in our world the Christian enterprise is a minority movement. Liberal Christianity, moreover, is a minority within that enterprise, and Disciples of Christ are a minority within liberal Christianity. This reminder is not a cry of pessimism; on the contrary it affirms that realism which is a necessary condition for Christian hope.[78]

Time and again the world has seen the power of a minority that knows its distinctiveness and is committed to maintaining its integrity. From a human standpoint, a good part of the power of the early church, living for nearly three centuries under the prospect or the actuality of persecution, was its clear understanding that to a dark world it offered the alternative of light. The free churches in early nineteenth-century America, smaller in absolute numbers and in proportion to the population than they have ever been since, had not the slightest doubt of their minority status—and they exerted an influence on the culture and on the national policy greater than they could manage after their members fell under the illusion that this is a Christian nation.[79] By contrast,

> contemporary British (and most of western) Christianity is an advanced case of syncretism. The Church has lived so long as a permitted and even privileged minority, accepting relegation to the private sphere in a culture whose public life is controlled by a totally different vision of reality, that it has almost lost the power to address a radical challenge to that vision and therefore to "modern western civilization" as a whole.[80]

The nineteenth-century minister, especially among Disciples, enjoyed no automatic status as a public figure; rather in most places the servant of God had to earn recognition and influence in a stubborn fight against a hostile or indifferent majority. A few twentieth-century Christians have managed the same feat by beginning with the knowledge that they were a minority; the later M. R. Zigler of the Church of the Brethren, one of the smallest Christian communions, made a massive impact for good in times of hostility and want by organizing the National Service Board for Religious Objectors, helping to establish Church World Service, the Christian Rural Overseas Program (CROP), and the Cooperative for American Remittances to Europe (CARE), and by developing the Heifer Project, which enabled ordinary church people in rural America to participate creatively in the ministry of reconciliation.[81] Once Christians in a congregation or denomination or seminary manage to see themselves as a principled minority, they may begin to discover some creative options.

Much of the substance of these first four chapters is familiar to those who have given attention to the current crisis in church and society. Ironically, a great deal of material, especially that in the first three chapters, has been overused by presidents, deans, and development officers of theological seminaries as rhetoric to rally support for the institutions and programs now in operation. In this book it is not intended as propaganda to provide sanctions for what is now being done, but rather as an agenda for readaptation on the part of the church, ministry, and theological school. And our contention is that readaptation must begin with the seminary.

Chapter **5**

TOWARD A THEOLOGY OF MINISTRY

Like the students whom they undertake to educate, the seminaries themselves are called to a servant ministry. Yet this central element in their vocation has suffered displacement to the margins of the enterprise by the compelling clamor of other concerns, generally legitimate in themselves, but not rightly the determining core of the schools' business. What is wanting from the common mind of theological faculties and their graduates is a vital theology of ministry. Prevailing notions, a mishmash of popular expectations, traditional doctrine, and intellectual faddism, have allowed school and church alike to fall into the irrelevance which recurs as such a painful theme throughout the first half of this book and have left seminary-educated ministers insufficiently prepared for their task.

No theology is worth a dime to a Christian minister if it does not illuminate, fortify, and commend the gospel. Theology and evangelism are not contradictories. Rather evangelism announces the good news of God, while theology reflects on that gospel, seeks to comprehend it intellectually, and undertakes to correlate that understanding with the questions and concerns of our particular time. Properly understood, theology is a distinctive mode, an abstract and intellectualized mode, of talking about the gospel. Too often in the seminary we seem to give students the notion that theology is something to talk about instead of the gospel. Theology's task is to clarify our thinking regarding our affirmation of faith.

To sketch the outline of a theology of ministry capable of redirecting the schools, the churches, and the graduates in the strange new world opening before us is our undertaking in this chapter.

The Urgency of a Deeper Theological Understanding

It might appear that the emerging ecumenical agreement widely publicized in *Baptism, Eucharist and Ministry* and reflected in "The COCU Consensus" would provide a strong theological base for the work of the seminaries.[1] These documents employ the idiom of most theologizing about ministry, tending to treat it as part of ecclesiology, too often as the largest part. Concerned with vexed questions of episcopacy, priesthood, and primacy, the relation of Word and sacrament, and other historically divisive issues, the texts of the emerging consensus neatly sidestep the old arguments about the essence of ministry, to describe it operationally, replacing normative nature with normative function. Except for brief suggestions that the character of authentic ministry in the church derives from the ministry of Jesus Christ (a theme more fully developed in the earlier literature of Faith and Order), the chapters on ministry, though written in theological idiom, seldom relate it to the central themes of theology. The overwhelming quantity of doctrinal and often polemical literature on the work of ministry produced in the various confessional traditions tends to be apologetic and admonitory.[2] This vast ecumenical and confessional literature on the doctrine of ministry rarely excites interest in the seminaries.

Despite the "emerging ecumenical consensus" concerning some issues long disputed, there is little theological agreement within congregations as to the nature or primary work of ministry, little consensus in the seminaries as to the essence of the task for which they presume to educate their students, little general interest in working together as a faculty to come to a common mind. Such theological reflection about ministry as goes on takes place in introductory surveys, denominationally required courses in polity, and seminars for seniors; otherwise it is left to professors in the practical field, many of whom tend to skip lightly over archaic arguments about ecclesiology. To the seminary at large, theology of ministry is pretty dull stuff.

In this chapter I hope to approach the topic more profoundly by focusing on the central concern of theology, to inquire how our understanding of God and the way God works affects our understanding of ministry and what a minister does. While the chapter draws on insights from process thought, the intention is not so much to promote a particular brand of theology as to invite reflection on the activity of God as a paradigm for ministry. Whatever we may say regarding the essence of the being of God is philosophical speculation, whereas our confession regarding the work of God is biblical faith expressed in biblical lanugage, having to do with particular events in history experienced as revelation. In the Fourth Gospel, Jesus reflects on his ministry in the manner suggested here: "My Father is working still, and I am working" (John 5:17), then follows with a promise, "Greater works than these will [you] do" (John 14:12).

The Divine Activity as Paradigm for Ministry

My thesis proposes that we look for the essence of ministry, so far as its *modus operandi* is concerned, in the divine way of working, and that we seek to cultivate a ministry which replicates the divine mode of action insofar as this is possible for human beings. I am advocating no spiritual athleticism nor prideful presumption; rather I propose a humble and obedient effort to show forth and to rely on God's own way of dealing with humanity, and to echo it in the world.

It could be argued with just a dash of cynicism that this proposal is not so new as might first appear. The model of God as autocrat was long affected by the church, the right of ministers to rule was claimed in God's name, and controversies over prerogative and primacy raged in society as well as in the church. Perhaps such thinking about ministry becomes understandable when we see in it an imitation of the prevailing secular pattern. The emperor served almost axiomatically as the model for God in Augustine's *City of God* and Dante's *On Monarchy*, though these great Christian minds understood themselves as thinking from God to emperor, rather than vice versa. Such imperial notions of God led ecclesiastics in the feudal era to see themselves as "princes of the church," much as our own generation of ministers senses a certain fitness in seeing ourselves as professionals or executives.[3] Despite the explicit warning of Jesus, our humanity as ministers loves such titles as Master, Father, Doctor. The course advocated in this chapter is not to assume the divine prerogatives, but to exhibit, insofar as humanly possible, the character of God.[4]

A theology of ministry ought to be a *real* theology; that is, whatever theology one espouses in the intellectual articulation of one's faith ought to underlie and determine one's doctrine of ministry. Our central affirmations about God should shape our thinking about this particular work. To speak thus is not to imagine that we as creatures possess the ultimate power of creation or redemption (for such power is God's alone) any more than Athanasius's aphorism, "God had to become man so that man might become God," should suggest that we should worship ourselves as divine. But Athanasius and the Cappadocians did hold that in Christ the deity of the Only-Begotten was inseparably and eternally united with the whole of our humanity; that in and through Christ the lost image of God, effaced by the sin of the first human pair, was restored to humankind; that in the ascension of Christ our humanity was carried up to the heavenly places, irrevocably taken into the Godhead; that in our baptism we are incorporated into that redeemed humanity of Christ and called to manifest the image of God in holiness of life. The end and result of the whole scheme of salvation, they maintained, is to catch us up into the likeness of God. We are made divine; this is *theosis*. Pretentious? Yes. But orthodox!

For our theology of ministry I propose a similar orthodoxy: there is a legitimate parallel between a mundane model and our image of God, and so between our understanding of God and our theology of ministry. In *The Atonement and Psychotherapy*, Don Browning rehearses the familiar secular models of atonement in the soteriologies of the past (ransom, moral influence, etc.), then proposes the therapist as a contemporary model. He argues that the effectiveness of the therapist rests on the client's perception that this person represents the structure of reality. Affirming the parallel, I suggest that the good therapist therefore effects healing by acting in the way in which God acts.

To think theologically about ministry, we must necessarily ask: How does the corporate ministry of the whole people of God manifest the nature of God and the activity of God? How does my own work as a minister manifest God's nature and replicate or duplicate God's way of working? How does the institutional life of the seminary reflect the way in which the faculty teaches that God works? Whatever in our theology we consider central to the nature of God, we must study to make central also in the way we work in our ministry, in the way we conceptualize our task, in our determination of what we will do and how we will do it, in the kinds of relationships and structures we develop to express the common life of a Christian community and to enable it to do its work, in the declared purpose and institutional conduct of the seminary. The activity of God and the nature of God provide the fundamental paradigm for our theology of ministry.[5]

Creativity

When we say "God," we speak of the ultimate power which brings into being the worlds and everything in them, a power constantly at work in wisdom and in grace, unfailingly offering and offered to make all things new. One of our hymns addresses God as "Eternal Spirit, evermore creating." Here we begin to work out our theology of ministry.[6]

All the major theological systems related to the biblical tradition deal with God as Creator, a crucial theme for our venture. At this point process thought conceptualizes God in a way that can accommodate the biblical witness to *The Living God* without destroying the essence of that concept as classical philosophies do in defining ultimate perfection as divine apathy. It conceives God rather as ultimate vitality, as the energy of that creative process which underlies and makes possible all existence. Bergson's *élan vital*, Whitehead's lure, Kazantzaki's cry, Teilhard's Omega Point, Williams' attraction of love, Ogden's reality that underlies our will to live, Cobb's The One Who Calls—all these give systematic conceptuality to Paul's doxology of faith which climaxes Romans 11 (magnificently translated in the NEB): "Source, Guide, and Goal of all that is—to God be glory for ever! Amen" (Rom. 11:36).

Here is the secret of apostolic ministry: "the power of [God] who is mightily at work with me" (Col. 1:29 Wey). The essence of ministry is letting that power work. Yet more and more we leave it to the evangelicals, the cults, and the lunatic fringe, while for a hundred years mainline churches have tried to rely on business methods applied to religion, on the latest secular theory in Christian education, counseling, and exegesis, on managerial gimmicks in administration and church growth. Now all that, except the gimmicks, has a certain legitimacy. Christians should refuse nothing merely on the ground that it is secular, for God the Creator creates the *saeculum*, the world, and properly we thank God for it; thanksgiving for creation marks genuine worship, as in the eucharistic liturgies. But when human beings worship and serve the creature rather than the Creator (Rom. 1:25), that is idolatry. It is not hard to find professors and seminarians and pastors and denominational bureaucrats whose witness suggests greater reliance on secular wisdom than on the creative power of God working through Word, sacrament, and the ministry of the church, through prayer and the gospel and a life of humble discipleship.

For two decades I have puzzled over seminarians turned on to Whitehead and to the whole glossary of technical Whiteheadean argot, but totally bored by worship or preaching or Christian education or the prospect of any other sort of ministerial task except the discussion of process thought, as though all the rest of it were totally beneath them now that the true light had been revealed. Granted, a lot of preaching and worship and church school activities are boring enough. But if so they are boring for one particular reason: they are dead! All the life has gone out of them! Yet for the life of me I cannot understand how anyone can become excited about the process of creative advance and then poormouth the tasks of the minister or blush with embarrassment at the mention of evangelism. Here we are talking about a God who makes all things new! And the immediate corollary of that concept ought to dazzle us with excitement about the work of ministry, a work which replicates the creative work of God—or if that sounds too presumptuous—which offers a human channel for the operation of the divine creativity.

Think of the joy of creation: myriads of stars flung across the darkness of space—and, on one small blue marble of a planet circling one of those stars, zebras and cheetahs and mockingbirds and bluebonnets and the way of a man with a maid. No wonder that Gen. 1 and Ps. 104 and Job 38 hymn the joy of creation. No wonder that the Yahwist celebrates the joy of human creativity—old Tubal-Cain with his forge, and Jubal with his harp, and Lamech with his song, grisly though it be.

Creativity in the ministry of the church mirrors the joy of the creative power of God. At times the church has drawn into the service of the gospel creative talents like Giotto, Michelangelo, and Rembrandt, Dante and Milton and Donne and Browning and Eliot, Bach and Handel and Haydn and Verdi, though only Donne was ordained. But in too few congregations does one see signs of free spirits given range for their creativity. So many ministers and members seem so dull and unimaginative, so mired in the rut of routine, so weary in well doing, so fearful of upsetting the ecclesiastical apple-cart. We forget the voice of the God who says, "Behold, I am doing a new thing," who in the words of Berdyaev, "created the world by imagination."[7]

Some congregations are beehives of joyful creativity. I think of Coventry Cathedral, of the Protestant monastic community at Taize, of the Cathedral of St. John the Divine in New York, and in ordinary places of scores of drama groups and musical combos and people designing banners.[8] I think of

Disciples who have loved the arts—Vachel Lindsay and Edwin Markham and Jessie Brown Pounds, Mother Ross and Cynthia Pearl Maus and Rosa Page Welch, W. E. Garrison and Thomas Curtis Clark and B. Fred Wise, Wilfred Evans Powell and J. Irwin Miller and Xenia Miller. In St. Louis you can see sculpture by Garrison at Union Avenue Christian Church, by Professor Grant F. Kenner of Culver-Stockton in the Beasley Building which houses the Division of Higher Education, by Hillis Arnold at Webster Groves Christian Church. Vachel Lindsay dreamed of a new Athens in Springfield, Ill. and then at Spokane, Wash., and the leaders of both cities stared at him with leaden eyes, unable to see the dream. Their descendants would turn all our young people into engineers, computer programmers, and money managers.

In such an age the divine creativity calls on the church for a ministry which will give full range to the human spirit, which will make known once again the joy of engaging in the creative activity of God—in word and music, in prayer and witness, in handiwork, and in the dance of life.[9] For our God is a living God.

The Pathos of the Living God

An essential element in the divine creativity is the intimate interrelatedness of God with everything God has made. We shall explore various aspects of that relatedness as a basis for our theology of ministry, beginning with the concept of *pathos*.[10]

In classical philosophy and in most subsequent theology, both Jewish and Christian, God is conceived as perfect, as totally fulfilled in the divine Being, hence as untouched by anything that happens in creation. God is the unmoved Mover, characterized by *apatheia*, the total absence of *passion*, which to the ancients always threatened *reason*. Hence God is without emotion and is beyond vulnerability. That is why the apostolic preaching of a crucified god was a laughingstock to the Greeks.

In deference to that philosophical notion of divine perfection thousands of theologians have played all kinds of hermeneutical games with the Bible. For the God of the Bible and especially of the prophets is characterized not by *apatheia* but by *pathos*, by intensity of feeling and, yes, by suffering. "In all their affliction he was afflicted" (Isa. 63:9); so the prophet of the Exile marveled at the Servant of God—the Suffering Servant—and the note of divine *pathos* is struck with equal poignancy in Hosea, Jeremiah, and Ezekiel. At the outset of the Gospel according to Luke it is suggested by Simeon and Anna, and all four Gospels come to a climax in the story of the Passion. To my mind, one of the chief virtues of process thought is its capacity as a philosophy to relate the concepts of divine perfection (the primordial nature of God) and of divine *pathos*, to conceive a living and responding God.[11]

So we speak of the *suffering of God*.[12] Of God's Servant the prophet sang, "Surely he has borne our griefs and carried our sorrows" (Isa. 53:4). Long before liberation theology, the prophets proclaimed God's identification with the poor and the oppressed, and Jesus declared, "As you did it to one of the least of these . . . , you did it to me" (Matt. 25:40). In the Incarnation that identification with the helpless necessitated terrible risk: even God's Christ refused to be a special case by asking for a miraculous intervention (Matt. 26:53-54).

If the activity of God, the suffering of God, is indeed paradigmatic for a theology of ministry, the conclusion is inescapable: where people suffer, the church is called to be. A true minister cannot evade that suffering, no matter how many trappings of professionalism or how many degrees. Witness in our own century Corrie Ten Boom, André Trocmé, Martin Luther King, Jr., Bishop Cesar Romero, Dorothy Day, Mother Teresa, Buena Stober, Minnie Vautrin.

The seminaries manage to repeat the rhetoric of liberation theology and bring some students into the presence of human suffering through clinical pastoral education. But does not the temper of their common life generally reflect the detachment and even irresponsibility of the secular college campus? Yet, theologically speaking, their task is to involve their students with the suffering of the world's forgotten, students who as ministers will bear the responsibility of so involving their people; in both cases the task is to bring to life in them an experience like that in which God addresses sulking Jonah: "You pity the plant, for which you did not labor, nor did you make it grow. . . . And should not I pity Nineveh, that great city, in which there are more than a hundred and twenty thousand persons who do not know their right hand from their left, and also much cattle?" (Jonah 4:10). The divine pathos involves God in the agony of every created being.

The concept of divine *pathos* also requires us to return to the notion of the *wrath of God*. Under the influence of liberalism the mainline churches have sentimentalized this idea right out of their working theology, even though it has meant flying in the face of the witness borne by the prophets and Jesus and the apostles and resisting the full weight of Jewish and Christian tradition. Granted that the notion has often been preached vengefully in contradiction of the revealed love of God. Yet distortion of the notion in much popular theology does not justify rejecting a concept so central to biblical and Christian thought.

This concept is the flip side of the coin called *pathos*. The obverse is a God who suffers with the oppressed, the reverse a God whose wrath blazes simultaneously against the oppressor, even though the latter may be personally decent and sincerely religious. Why did the prophets' eyes flash and their words sear? Because they had seen and felt with God. As Lactantius put it in the fourth century, "God is moved and indignant when injustices are done."[13] The divine pathos is terrible in wrath.

Should not the seminaries help their students to this kind of biblical and theological approach to issues of social justice? Most church members are at least mildly conservative in politics and economics, and we only antagonize when from the pulpit we sound like a left-leaning politician, much less like Castro or Marx. If only we could get people to see with God's eyes! To feel with God's heart! Then the church would be prepared to enter a new era of corporate ministry, afflicted with the world's afflicted, indignant at the world's indifference.

Once we feel its burning heat as a paradigm for ministry, the *pathos* of the long-suffering God expressed as divine wrath, moves us to repentance and prepares us for forgiveness.

Forgiveness

When we come to the heart of the gospel, we find ourselves in the place called The Skull, and from a cross we hear a tortured Victim praying, "Father, forgive them; for they know not what they do" (Luke 23:34). There most poignantly we meet the Everlasting Mercy, there grace speaks in judgment more telling than any we have known, yet there we know ourselves accepted and claimed and loved, no matter what our past has been, and there—unless we harden our hearts like stone—we find ourselves at one with God. So "we preach Christ crucified, . . . to those who are called, . . . Christ the power of God and the wisdom of God" (1 Cor. 1:23-24).

Knowing this gracious power and startling wisdom, we find the divine forgiveness on every page of the Gospels: in parable and admonition, in Jesus' scandalous acceptance of publicans and sinners, in the restoration of Peter and the other failed disciples, in the central petition for ourselves in the prayer Jesus taught: "Forgive us our sins, for we ourselves forgive every one who is indebted to us" (Luke 11:4).

The gospel is the good news of another chance. The debt is paid. The writ is cancelled. The burden is taken away. The prisoner is set free. The slave is liberated. The wounded is made whole. The wanderer is restored. The wretch is accepted. The outcast is loved. Whatever biblical image you use, you are speaking the heart of the Christian experience of God in Christ. You are using familiar, though somewhat shopworn poetry to describe the God who is making all things new.

This description startlingly parallels that given by the process thinkers when they describe God—except that their abstract language with its cosmological and ontological preoccupation sounds bloodless and cold to the simple soul struggling with life's perplexities and perils and accustomed to the warm imagery of evangelical piety. Yet biblical imagery and the conceptuality of the theologians both alike speak of the God who makes all things new—and that word is the heart of the gospel.

To the soul caught in despair over failure, plagued by a sense of worthlessness, burdened by guilt, fearful of a future without deliverance or hope, the characteristic action of God in offering a new occasion, another chance, in opening the door at every moment to the possibility of new life, is the supreme expression of the divine way of working. It is nothing less than grace. Forgiveness wipes the slate clean; if offers us the chance to start over again, sustained by the same parental love and lured by the same beckoning hope that we knew in the time of innocence.

Whether we think of our inmost life of the spirit, our intimate relations with those who are dearest to us, our daily contacts with associates and strangers, or the ambiguities and oppressiveness of social systems, we are lost—except for the possibility of another chance. When the issues are not too overwhelming, a good night's sleep and the freshness of a new day rejuvenate us, and we take a new start. Our quadrennial involvement in the campaign for the presidency, with its flood of rhetoric on perils and promises, provides a telling parable, no matter how flawed, of our need to start over again.

Yet our human predicament is such that a good night's sleep will not solve many of our problems and often after the election the country is no better off than it was before. But still the unwearied patience of divine grace unfailingly offers in every moment the chance to begin anew. I am not writing sentimentality. It is tragically clear the the objective results of prior decisions and actions carry over into the present and future; we cannot undo the past. But by the grace of God we can in this moment make a fresh start. If you will accept my rather homiletical way of putting it, I would say that is the religious essence of process thought; I insist that it is the essence of the gospel. "Behold, I make all things new" (Rev. 21:5).

Without that constantly creating activity of God, the universe itself would perish. Without forgiveness all creative possibility for good vanishes from our failed human relationships, and the burden of guilt banishes hope from the human soul. Creativity, forgiveness, grace—all these words denote the necessary and characteristic activity of God if life is to go on. That very grace of the creative event, that setting forth of a new opportunity by the generosity of forgiveness, provides our fundamental paradigm for ministry.

In a profound sense the church has always known that theologically. The two dominical sacraments image dramatically the promise of new life which is heard in the reading of the scripture and the preaching of the gospel. The Protestant Reformers asserted the authentic presence of the true church wherever the word is rightly preached and the sacraments rightly administered. The great liturgies and the classic pastoral prayers of the free churches regularly include both a confession of sin and the assurance of forgiveness. Formally, all the churches rooted in the historic Christian tradition declare the forgiveness of God and announce the offer of a new birth. Even those pale churches at the shallow end of liberalism which have lost all sense of divine transcendance continue to serve up some offer of hope in their promulgation of pop psychology and their allegedly sure-fire formulas for success. In the vast majority of cases the rites and habits of the church's public ministry repeat some evangelical word about grace or forgiveness or new life. To the extent that people who cling to the churches have heard in that utterance the promise of an answer to some inner need and have responded by reaching toward that promise, we should like to believe that the creative advance is served.

Yet we must examine the situation more deeply, for not all preaching of forgiveness accords with the gospel of Jesus nor with the revelation of God given in his life and ministry. Much so-called evangelical preaching presents a vindictive God who threatens puny mortals with eternal punishment for minor infractions against an archaic code of behavior and who seems totally lacking in concern about the weightier matters of justice and mercy and faith. The long and micawber history of the church's exercise of "the power of the keys" is an ugly tale of authoritarianism, judgmentalism, and self-serving. At the other end of the religious spectrum, the easy tolerance of the liberal churches and their genial permissiveness of both human foibles and diverse opinions have prompted psychiatrist Karl Menninger to the plaintive query, "Whatever became of sin?" The discouraging evidence yields a clear conclusion: Not all religion is good for people. Not all religion confronts persons with the righteous demands and gracious offer of the living God. Not all religion serves the creative advance.

Shifting from the realm of abstract ideas to the operational level of the church's life and the actual functioning of its corporate ministry, let us ask ourselves: If the activity of God provides the paradigm for ministry, how effectively does the corporate ministry of the churches we know, as expressed in their common life, convey or replicate the unfailing creativity of God in making all things new?

To answer first for the affirmative, I must say that in ministering to persons in bereavement, illness, or disaster, the churches I have known have been at their best. Again and again I have seen a company of Christian people surround a wounded, bewildered, and lonely member with concern, prayer, love, and companionship—mailing cards, bringing in food, taking on outings—until that person was brought back from the depths and enabled once again to affirm the joy of living, even in a radically diminished world. Surely this ministry authentically replicates the activity of God in making all things new.

To be quite honest about it, I should quickly admit that this kind of ministry is most effectually offered to, and most readily received by, persons vitally related to a community of Christians. Outsiders who receive some expression of such ministry often seem incapable of engaging sufficiently in that interpersonal interaction which is the essence of its effectiveness; they cannot seem to muster the psychic energy for even a friendly involvement with persons who are more or less strangers, and they may be inhibited by repressed hostility and guilt or by overt suspicion of the motives of these church folk. Nevertheless for those who have been able to receive such a ministry, it is not only an expression but, one must say, the primary instrument of the activity of God in making a horrid interruption in life an occasion for the creative advance. Never underestimate the significance of this pastoral ministry offered by ordinary believers fulfilling the universal priesthood. In such a situation, the paradigm proves out.

But now for a less positive word, as we move to the center of that divine activity which we term grace or forgiveness or inner renewal. If we ask how accurately the churches we know best might be characterized as communities of the forgiving, a different answer must be given. We are compelled to confess that in dealing with sinners (allow me the use of the term despite its antiquated sound) most groups of Christians fail to manifest that marvelous openness of Jesus to all manner of persons, and especially to the morally outcast, which so perfectly revealed the grace of God. Despite our ritual language about sin and grace, and especially our traditional affirmation that the church is a company of forgiven sinners, we don't really think like that or act like that. With no intent to cast aspersions on the best people of Jesus' time, it would be more accurate to say that the church is a company of Pharisees or a company of the conventionally religious.

We acknowledge that we are sinners in constant need of forgiveness. But we have in mind the petty immoralities and natural shortcomings which are permitted to religious folk. Most of us in the seminaries feel no intense need of forgiveness for our complicity in the systemic evil of our society; rather we commonly assume an inflated self-righteousness when the oppressiveness of our institutions is mentioned, for we are social liberals, perhaps even closet radicals, and we have often spoken out—on the safe haven of our campuses—against the evils of the system. Even though we benefit in a small way from its inequities, we really feel clean because of our liberal prejudices, and when we read aloud those eloquent unison prayers of confession which we have written to excoriate social evil, we do so with unction and enthusiasm, for we are really confessing the sins of the fat cats and the members of the ruling establishment. Such confession causes us no searching of heart, no pain. In fact, we rather enjoy it. ("That chapel prayer I'll have to use at church next Sunday.") And we are not forgiven.

But let us move to that area of personal behavior or private morality which most readily comes to mind when the discussion turns to sin and forgiveness. (After all, most folks are not prophets like ourselves!) Almost no church known to me overtly and consistently practices that openness toward sinners which is such a beautiful feature of Jesus' ministry in the Gospels and which brought the derelicts and the outcasts flocking to him. We do not really understand that church is for that kind of people—"extortioners, unjust, adulterers, or even . . . this tax collector" (Luke 18:11).

Of course, if one should cross the line and sin in such a way, and if it became known to some in the church, we should expect that out of Christian charity they would keep the matter quiet and the pastor would assure us of

God's forgiveness. But that expectation arises from our perception of ourself as a good and decent person who properly belongs among the good and decent people of the church and who, being human, in a moment of weakness, made a little slip that is really understandable if the circumstances were known. So we make confession and take communion and continue on our respectable way.

But let a known ex-convict or person under criminal indictment or prostitute or womanizer or victim of drug abuse show up in church, and the customary ease in Zion goes suddenly rigid and self-conscious. After all, these aren't Sunday school types, and we don't know how to respond. We tell ouselves that we ought to be friendly, but these intruders would not be a good influence on our youth. The liturgy may rehearse the familiar words about forgiveness, but these outsiders are not likely to feel the warmth of divine love mediated through the open hospitality of the congregation. For who in the membership of the church dares to say to them. "I was once where you are, and look what God has done for me."

So the poor devils who really need and want help band together as Alcoholics Anonymous or other companies of persons with problems. They often meet in church parlors, and they recite slogans which translate the gospel of grace into nontraditional terms which they find helpful, and they discover the forgiveness of God. Or a searching soul may take advantage of the anonymity of a great evangelistic crusade and, lost in the crowd, heed the preacher's call to come to Christ and pray through with one of the kindly helpers who will never know one's story. But in neither case has the paradigmatic activity of the forgiving God come to expression through the common life of the church, except in the most marginal way.

Sociologically, the situation I have described is thoroughly understandable. H. Richard Niebuhr described it long ago in *The Social Sources of Denominationalism*. If a church begins as an incredulous gathering of forgiven sinners like that nondescript congregation gathered by Paul on the Corinthian waterfront, it soon becomes a company for the cultivation of the Christian life and a school of character for the children of Christian families. Even if the language of revivalistic crisis lingers anachronistically in the routine formulae repeated in the public meetings, and even though surges of emotion attend the singing of the old gospel songs, the dynamic has changed.

That is largely the condition of religion in American today, particularly in the so-called mainline churches, including the Christian Church (Disciples of Christ). Despite the importance which they hold for a diminishing portion of the population, these churches seem to be exerting ever less influence on the people at large, especially on the young and those who set the trend in mores and lifestyles. Yet despite all the rhetoric about freedom and emancipation, one has to characterize the new ways as frantic and even desperate rather than happy and to acknowledge an inestimable toll of misery attendant on the culture of drugs and alcohol and sex and violence. I have no desire to come on like the voice of the oldtime revival hour. So, leaving the problem largely unsolved, I return to theological assertion.

The corporate ministry to which God has called the church is a life-in-community which gives expression to the divine activity of making all things new. By his own openness and freedom Jesus evidently evoked freely and without overt condemnation a dual realization in the lives of those he touched: (1) a longing for the joy and freedom they saw in him, so different from the misery and unworthiness they felt within, and (2) a sense of acceptance without embarrassment, of forgiveness, of grace, with the glorious promise of a new life. We should not understand that the church is called to be Christ or to supplant Christ, but rather to minister Christ, to make Christ known; and a crucial element in that disclosure of Christ is to find ways of expressing through its own common life the grace of God which Jesus so fully revealed. That is an essential element in a theology of ministry.

Self-Giving

Our sense of need to be forgiven makes us know our dependence on the grace of another, and grace is always costly, even when that Other is God. It is to this reality that the old ransom theories of atonement attest. In our sophistication we would laugh them aside—if we could—for some of the doctrines were crude, even downright bizarre, but they speak a truth we cannot evade.

> Alas! no one can ever ransom oneself
> nor pay the price of that release;
> one's ransom would cost too much,
> for ever beyond one's power to pay,
> the ransom that would let one live on always
> and never see the pit of death (Ps. 49:7-9 NEB).

If we cannot pay it because it is too costly for us, even God can pay it only at terrible cost; not because God is stubborn, but because we are. So we sing:

> Just as I am, without one plea
> But that thy blood was shed for me . . . ,
> O Lamb of God, I come.

There is no need to rehearse the old notions of soteriology nor their expression in the vivid language of the revivalists, which, for all the crude archaisms, we moderns cannot fully shake off. The point here is this: God's forgivenss is but one example, though a powerful one, of a constant element in the activity of God, *God's continuous and costly self-giving*, and that is a paradigm for ministry.

Self-giving became the supreme and climactic form of God's self-revelation in Jesus whom we confess as the Christ. "Unique and absolute truth has in

Christianity the form not of a rule, a law, a Dharma, nor of ideas or theologies. Christian revelation has the form of a person."[14] Because of God's supreme self-giving in the event of the Incarnation, our ministry is possible. For the God we serve was supremely revealed in human life, in a particular life of lowliness and self-giving.

The Synoptic Gospels witness to the evident reluctance of Jesus to claim for himself the glory of the Messiah. He spoke so obliquely of the Human One (the Son of Man) that scholars are divided over the question: did he mean himself, or another? "What do you think of the Christ?" he asked (Matt. 22:42). With unaccustomed sharpness he repudiated the notions associated with Messiah as Son of David, as king and conqueror. Rather the Christ is God's Servant, a Deliverer made perfect through suffering (Heb. 2:10, cf. vs. 14). That perfection we see not only in the human Jesus, but even in the Godhead, where perfection also comes through suffering, through self-giving. "Christ gave himself in the Last Supper as mortal; to the disciples at Emmaus as risen; to the whole church as ascended into heaven."[15]

Self-giving, then, is necessarily the pattern for Christian ministry—the corporate ministry of all Christian people, the work of the ordained, and the ethos of the seminary. In arguing that all seven functions which the papal church reserved to priesthood belong to all believers as "the common rights of Christians," Luther comes fifth to "sacrifice":[16]

> ... in the New Testament there is no sacrifice except the one which is common to all, namely the one described in Rom. 12:1, where Paul teaches us to present our bodies as a sacrifice, just as Christ sacrificed his body for us on the cross. In this sacrifice he includes the offering of praise and thanksgiving. Peter likewise commands in 1 Pet. 2 [:5] that we offer sacrifices acceptable to God through Jesus Christ, that is ourselves, not gold or animals. ... The sixth function is to pray for others. ... Christ gave the Lord's Prayer to all his Christians.

Sacrifical service is the authentic mark of ministry. The Gallup Poll keeps telling us that nearly all Americans profess to believe in God, pray frequently, if not regularly, and consider themselves religious. Yet the world is sick from too much religion—from Iran to Lebanon to Northern Ireland, and if our politicos do not tone down the piety act, America will be sick of it. The issue in ministry is not how religious we think we are, but whether our common life replicates and mirrors God's self-giving.

To come more particularly to the ministry of the ordained, the graduates of our seminaries, the self-giving of God manifested in the self-giving of Jesus provides the model for their life and work. At this point our theology of ministry, which finds its paradigm in the activity of God, collides disastrously with the sociology of ministry as actual fact. For reasons already suggested in this volume, our generation of ministers has been inordinately preoccupied with questions of status. The seminaries "upgraded" the Bachelor of Divinity degree to Master of Divinity, then introduced programs leading to the Doctor of Ministry. We talk *ad nauseam* of professional standards. Ministers clutched desperately at any sociological semblance of status and took to referring to themselves as "the clergy." (This even among Disciples!) Jesus, Peter, Paul, Priscilla, knew nothing of such a distinction. Alexander Campbell directed his most sarcastic shafts at the "kingdom of the clergy." And ministers pompously refer to themselves as "clergypersons."

Increasingly we speak of the work of ministry as *management*, usually assuming the model of management in which the boss calls all the shots and the underlings fall to, to produce the results which the boss wants. Yet two shrewd observers of American business have looked at this "numerative, rationalist approach to management" which "dominates our business schools" and have concluded that it is not even good management in business: "It doesn't teach us to love the customers" or the product.[17] Such revisionist studies, with their critique of business management, contain significant implications for a theology of ministry. But the warning should hardly be necessary for ministers of Jesus Christ:

> You know that among the pagans their so-called rulers lord it over them and their great men make their authority felt. This is not to happen among you. No; any one who wants to become great among you must be your servant, and anyone who wants to be first among you must be slave of all (Mark 10:42-43 JB).

The document entitled *Baptism, Eucharist and Ministry* states forthrightly: "The authority of the ordained minister is rooted in Jesus Christ. Because Jesus came as one who serves . . . , to be set apart means to be consecrated to service."[18] Before the self-giving God, what other authority can we ask?

Consider the medieval papacy. Never in history had the world seen such a massive, rational, splendid, and efficient administrative machine as that developed by pope and curia toward the end of the Middle Ages. Yet for all its superb efficiency the finished machine was incapable of fulfilling the spiritual functions for which ostensibly it was devised. By a bitter irony the Servant of the Servants of God had forgotten how to serve.[19] Have we here an admonitory parable for the theological seminary?

Phoebe was content to be a minister of the church at Cenchreae. Epaphras was a faithful minister of Christ. Paul identified himself as a minister of the gospel. The only degree Thomas Campbell appended to his name was D.V.M., *Dei verbi minister*, Minister of the Word of God. All were content to be ministers, servants of the suffering, self-giving God most fully revealed in the One who came as Servant of all.

Intention

The creativity, the pathos, the forgiveness, the self-giving of God all have a majestic intention in view: the realization of the divine purpose of life-in-community for all God's creation. The central petition in the Lord's Prayer is

"Thy will be done," the very petition which formed the core of Jesus' praying in Gethsemane. The purpose of God is a dominant theme of scripture and of Jesus' ministry; consider the various sayings presented in the gospels as summaries of his ministry:

> I seek not my own will, but the will of [the One] who sent me (John 5:30).
> I came that they may have life, and have it abundantly (John 10:10).
> For this I was born, and for this I have come into the world, to bear witness to the truth (John 18:37).
> For the Son of Man came to seek and to save the lost (Luke 19:10).
> Even as the Son of Man came not to be served but to serve, and to give his life as a ransom for many (Matt. 20:28).

These considerations all make clear the supreme importance of the divine purpose in any theology of ministry.

It is at this point that church life in America is most dangerously confused. So many secondary aims, legitimate enough when kept incidental to the primary purpose of realizing the divine intention, obscure that purpose by themselves claiming primary attention: survival goals for the congregation, building up the denomination, achieving a more acceptable public image for an ecumenical venture, advancing one's career in the ministry, winning greater prestige for a seminary.

Even more perilous is the displacement of the divine intention by goals taken over from secular society and a pagan value-system, for these subvert the rightful purpose of ministry: the substitution of numerical aims for concern for persons and society, a preoccupation with particular doctrinal formulations to the downplaying of other Christian concerns, doctrinaire commitment to a single cause which loses sight of personal needs and the value of individuals, an institutionalism which coopts the time and attention of pastors and leading members to the point of eliminating time for their families or for cultural and intellectual pursuits, the subjectivism which measures the worth of a church by the degree to which it satisfies one's inner desires and conforms to one's prejudices, a quest for celebrity and the trappings of "success," a professionalism which emphasizes status and know-how rather than witness and service, the pursuit of kudos for scholarship while neglecting the claims of Christian mission.

Over against all these partial and distorted aims towers in authentic grandeur "the purpose of the church and its ministry" and also of the theological seminary: the increase of love for God and neighbor. Loving life-in-community according to the divine intention expresses the essence of Jesus' proclamation: "The kingdom of heaven is at hand." It is the burden of the petitions,

> Hallowed be your name,
> your kingdom come,
> your will be done,
> on earth as in heaven.

The eschatological vision of the ultimate fulfillment of the divine purpose dominated the worship and shaped the social vision of the church throughout its early centuries.[20] The Christian witness against the pretentions of sovereign nations, the arrogance of political and economic power, the demonic violence of war and oppression, and every other kind of social evil springs from reflection on God's will for the whole creation: the voluntary and joyous harmony of every created entity responding fully to the divine intention.

> . . . already my desire and will were rolled—even as a wheel that moveth equally—by the Love that moves the sun and the other stars.[21]

Ministry which seeks to replicate God's own way of working will ever center its attention on the divine purpose. Ministry itself will be understood not so much juridically nor officially as personally and relationally.[22] For its genius is to fulfill the intention of God.

Transformation

Faithfulness in ministry to the service of the divine intention becomes the primary and ultimate mode of changing persons and society, for it is the way in which God has chosen to work. When I first read *Adventures of Ideas*, I observed whimsically to the metaphysicians I knew that Whitehead's model for God is neither philosopher nor theologian. Rather God is conceived after two other human models: (1) God as historian (every occasion, though it perishes, passes into the memory of God), and (2) God as rhetor, as orator, as persuader (God's instrument of creative advance is not coercion but persuasion, lure, cry). As a historian of preaching, these notions excited me to the core.

Preaching, understood theologically, is not so much talking about God, not projecting theological abstractions, not passing out advice or political opinions or pop psychology cloaked in religious verbiage and crowned with a text, not hurling denunciations at people in an effort to coerce them through fear or authority, not manipulating one's hearers by the dominance of personal charisma or psychological pressure of specious argument. Rather preaching is doing the work of God in the way God works. It is holding forth the Word of Life, the possibility of new being, the vision of the peaceable kingdom in such a way that the divine possibility either attracts a positive response or elicits a decision of rejection. In either case, the response is free, the integrity of the person is wholly honored and kept inviolate, and the person acting in freedom lives with the results of a choice made in integrity, by oneself and for oneself—and yet a choice made possible only as a response to the divine possibility that comes from beyond oneself.

This understanding of God as Supreme Power who does not hurl thunderbolts or otherwise coerce a recalcitrant creation to obey the divine will has radical implications for ministry. Sometimes all that God or the preacher can do is to cry: "Is it nothing to you, all you who pass by?" (Lam. 1:12). Preaching has no ultimate power but the power of the cross. From this core for an authentic theology of preaching I propose the expanding of that notion to an over-all theology of ministry.

Some insights gained from reading about religion in primitive or archaic societies offer matters of great importance for a theology of ministry which takes the mode of divine activity as paradigmatic. From sampling the literature in fields of specialization far from my own, as part of my investigation into the cultural roots of preaching, I have been driven to theological reflection on the divine method for transforming life and culture across countless generations prior to or apart from the divine self-revelation proclaimed in scripture. My conclusion: God's mode of transformatoin is to offer a new vision with the power of expanding the mind and spirit of a people.

The mythologies of our distant ancestors from every part of the world, recorded and commented on by anthropologists, enthnologists, specialists in linguistics, folklorists, historians of religion, and other scholars, contain a vast storehouse of sacred story and proverb. Much of it is so alien to our experience and outlook that a casual modern reader can hardly exegete it at all. But again, some of it seems to carry a built-in hermeneutic. These ancient stories about animals and spirits and gods and heroes come through to us as allegories of human existence and human possibility, carrying an explicit moral.

What was the source of these stories? They came from the visions and inspired songs of shamans, the holy men and women whose lives had been manifestly touched by the spirits. Tutored by older shamans in the sacred lore and from time to time granted a vision as one or another crossed the rainbow bridge into the other world, they provided their people with an imagery and vocabulary for poetry, religion, and ethics. One may take as representative the account by John Neihart of a holy man among the Lakota, *Black Elk Speaks*. Margaret Mead has proposed that such visionaries were the mentors of our race in ethical advance, and other anthropologists and theorists of literature support the thesis. The notion is given implicit theological substance in Whitehead's *Adventures of Ideas*, with an ontological interpretation of the history of human freedom: a vision released into the common imagination by the teachings of Plato and Jesus at last produced a moral consensus for the abolition of slavery.[23] (When all this began to come together, I was off the the races on a theology of preaching!)

God's mode of transformation, for persons and cultures, is to set loose in the world a new vision of the divine intent and to let the quiet leaven of its persuasion do its work—until at last the created order is drawn up to a new level of possibility. The process thinkers have a technical vocabulary for all this, but it is the native idiom of faith, too often discarded by the seminaries for the abstractions of academic theology. Jesus knew the method well. "How shall we picture the kingdom of God or by what parable shall we describe it?" (Mark 4:30 NEB).

Dante's vision of the other world was at the same time a bitter commentary on and a daring program for the life of the world. Elias Hick, the early American Quaker, painted over and over again his vision of "The Peaceable Kingdom" which united biblical faith with a concern for making peace in his own time. Abbott Book, minister of Christian education at Union Avenue Christian Church in St. Louis half a century ago, inspired a generation of youth by his work of collecting masterpieces of religious art. Martin Luther King, Jr., stirred the conscience of a nation by his eloquent reiteration, "I Have a Dream." And Peters and Waterman in their study of well-run companies, present the effective executive as "the keeper of the myth," the inspirer and motivator of all who work there.[24]

Is not this the ministry of the church—to hold ever before the world, before desperate and perplexed men and women, youth and children, the transforming vision of the Old, Old Story?[25] Consider the transforming power of the liturgy, as evidenced by Geoffrey Wainwright's recurring use of the term "vision" in his *Doxology*.[26] The saint closest to me for forty-five years began her ministry in a consecration service at a young people's conference when she was still in high school; the group was singing "Open My Eyes That I May See."

Our work as ministers is not primarily to scold, to organize, or even to console, but to hold out the vision and to follow through with teaching. Thus we replicate the work of God and serve the Christ in the transforming of persons and of culture. All this is the work of grace, to which God's people are called. It is the mystery of which we as ministers are appointed trustees.

Servants of God in Ministry

Reflection on the way God works has brought up some of the major topics of theology: creation, judgment, redemption, atonement, eschatology, sanctification, though for the most part we have avoided these shopworn terms. None of these topics is trivial, marginal, or faddish.

To base our understanding of ministry on the nature of the divine activity suggests a new approach to Faith and Order issues. It thrusts relatedness and motivation to the place of central importance, pushing questions of form into a secondary position, as the apostle Paul did with the Law; nothing counted but a new creature in Christ. And what counts in ministry is a people and their ordained leadership doing the work of God.

This paradigm unites the varied tasks of ministry in integrity and wholeness, for "God is one"; therefore the minister's diverse work is one, [27] no matter how frustrating the diversity. The mission of the seminary is also one, in recognition that the calling of the church is to do God's work in God's way, that this is the assignment of the ordained, and that the seminary's vocation is to bring all the scholarly discipline and creative intelligence of its faculty to the preparation of graduates able to lead the church in such a ministry. The mission is service, not sentimentally understood, but defined as living out in our calling the very work of God. This is our mission.

The Great Church as Servant Church

The innovation required of the church for readaptation to such a mission[28] calls for closer attention to the gospel and renewed commitment to it. It requires the seminaries to grapple with the question: In this age of self-seeking can they help the church recover its calling as servant-community on behalf of the world, a servant-community called to do the work of God? This would mean a radical overturning of the present state of affairs, with the prevailing notion that religion is a private concern. Under this delusion, "Churches become exactly what the early Church refused to be. They become spiritual societies for the spiritual development of their members."[29]

The innovation-renovation required for a truly God-like ministry will necessarily upset the unheroic prudence of institutional life.

> When the churches might have been putting moral capital into the race issue, they were busy guarding their investment in the standards of WASP culture; when they might have been sinking ethical substance into the protest against warfare they were busy pulling in returns from the national crusade against communism; and when they might have demonsrated the ethics of love by their investment in the cities, they were amassing captial from shrewd ventures in suburbia.[30]

By contrast the outspoken Christian witness for justice and freedom by Archbishop Desmond Tutu of South Africa has caught the world's attention. His protest against apartheid is no mere political activism. As with Martin Luther King, his social message arises inevitably out of the gospel. Ministry involves him in what God is doing.

A South African priest writes:

> The Bishop points toward the Church of the future, a Church freed from its dogmatic trappings and its denominational divisions, that are no less misleading than the ethnic divisions imposed by the apartheid system.[31]

Any proper vision of the church of the future imparts ecumenical urgency. By many seminarians ecumenism is understood as just not making a "big deal" out of denominational differences; it commands acceptance but little excitement. No wonder it seems to have "settled down for a long winter's nap."[32] Seminaries committed to a servant-church will hold forth the vision of engagement in the very work of God, striving to fulfill the divine intention for life-in-community embracing the entire human family in joyful response to God's holy will.

The Denomination as a Servant-People

A perplexing anomaly is the persistence of the denomination as the prevailing form of church in America. Yet contemporary theological scholarship offers almost no recent critique of the denomination as a form of church and pays little attention to the particular traditions except in the courses in denominational history and doctrine required by the churches for ordination. Despite the theological and sociological irrelevance of the denomination, seminary faculties devote little attention to its limitations, seeming inevitability, responsibilities, and prospect. Only a minority of professors participate actively in the institutional life of their denomination or devote much effort to serious engagement with their denominational tradition.

If students take their denomination seriously, it is as prospective employer. While many feel only minimal loyalty to a particular institution or its distinctive tradition, depending on the route of their spiritual pilgrimage, some students acknowledge their denomination as their spiritual "home" or family. But from seminary classes they learn very little as to the way in which it actually operates, and many enter the ministry with virtually no sense of loyalty to it or inclination to participate in its general life. Such aloofness does not arise from a larger and more intense commitment to the church ecumenical, replacing lesser loyalties, but from a failure to grasp the institutional reality of the church. On graduation they soon find their ministry being shaped less by their own intentions or the theology learned in seminary than by the effect of denominational programs and demands, generated by assorted bureaucrats with no intention of reshaping ministry, no realization that they are doing so, and certainly no overarching vision of the ministry required by the times.[33]

With a church too largely determined by a world that was and a ministry designed and educated for that church and that world, but now being shaped by many pressures with no over-all design, it is time for seminaries to examine the effect of an outmoded past and of uncoordinated denominational expectations on the shape of ministry. A good place to begin is the problem of ministerial "invisibility," not just in our impersonal world dominated by the media, but particularly in the church itself. How is it that the denomination today accords little recognition to pastors, unwittingly exacerbating the effect of an already powerful social trend? Few mainline denominations give star billing to pastors. Only rarely do Disciples elect the minister of a congregation as moderator[34], as president of one of the major units of the church, as head of a college or seminary, never yet as general minister and president. No wonder that younger ministers, hungry for recognition and fulfillment, find themselves attracted to even minor positions in the denominational bureaucracy, which seem to offer a "career path," that so many mature ministers of ability with good records and reasons for deep personal satisfaction in their ministry suffer a nagging sense of insignificance, the feeling that their "career path" is not leading anywhere and that neither society nor the church attributes to their vocation the worth it properly deserves.

Is it not incumbent on the seminaries to reexamine theologically, sociologically, and from the standpoint of dynamics for mission, the situation of the denomination today and its impact on ministry? At a time of hesitation and confusion, Disciples seminaries could well give attention to those elements in the Disciples tradition which may be regarded as strengths in the life of today's church and to those elements calling for reinterpretation and reform.[35] It is high time that our contemporary denominations learned how to fulfill their calling as a servant-people.

The Congregation as Serving Community

In working out their agenda for the future, the seminaries owe a large measure of attention to the life and vocation of congregations: to discover ways in which ministers can guide them in realizing their destiny as servant-communities doing the work of God. These basic Christian communities deserve greater understanding and attention from theological scholars than they have received, for here those actions which are absolutely essential to ecclesial existence and mission take place.[36] Without proposing a complete agenda for congregational readaptation, and keeping in mind the needs indicated in previous chapters, we mention some specifics as matters of particular urgency.

People today are hungering for community, for pattern in their chaotic lives, for a sense of meaning amidst the seeming absurdities of their experience. In an age of secularism new cults flourish precisely because they offer community, structure, and meaning; in 1980 an estimated three million Americans belonged to a thousand religious cults.[37]

A fundamental goal of ministry is the realization of Christian community, and the process for achieving it, a major theme in the New Testament, is *oikodomē*, "building up," archaically rendered as "edification."[38] Emphasis falls on growth toward Christian maturity by the whole company of believers as well as individual disciples, looking toward fulness and completion in the quality of churchly life, in faithfulness to the mission of witness and service to humanity, in personal growth toward the likeness of Christ, all resulting in the release of powerful influences in society for the realization of justice, the ennobling of life, and the transformation of a decadent culture.

In this process, realism obviously requires attention to the institutional health of the Christian body, but the concern is legitimate only as the institution serves the goal of building up the Christian community in the fulfillment of its calling. Unfortunately, the seminars to which perplexed pastors flock, like the books and tapes sold to help them with church problems, tend to emphasize gimmicks and programs to further institutional prosperity, on the unexamined premise that such a goal is obviously good. On the contrary, it can be good only as it serves the authentic purpose of the church, replicating the activity of God. The seminaries have the responsibility of providing a biblical and theological understanding of authentic Christian community, along with a sense, both historical and practical, of how to build up such a community in institutional health and effectiveness for mission.

As the basic unit for the education of the laity,[39] the congregation has not in most instances discharged this task with distinction; consider the ignorance of most church members regarding the most elementary assumptions about the study of the Bible. While it is easy for Christian intellectuals to deride such ignorance, church members are not to blame for it, but rather those ministers and professors who have not learned how to communicate with them about such basic matters. After decades of sophisticated critical study of the scriptures, why does this approach, even in it most rudimentary conclusions, remain a secret closely held by religious professionals? Could it be because conventional biblical scholarship leaves the student confused as to the implications to be drawn for faith when the text is approached "scientifically" and seems to attribute more significance to technical trivia than to the central religious witness of a passage? While it may be possible to operate with such aloofness in the groves of Akademe, young ministers in their first congregation quickly discover the vanity of attempting to do so there. Proving unsuitable for transfer to the parish setting, the mode of biblical study conventionally followed in the seminary is quickly abandoned, and with the mode the substance.

Ministers may keep interior faith with the hermeneutical responsibility learned in seminary, refraining from the blatant propagation of traditional views discarded by scholars. But few really open intellectual doors for their people to the modern understanding of the Bible. Faithful members of mainline congregations, after two or three generations of seminary-educated ministers, still lack a systematic understanding of the Bible as conveying the Word of God, except for bits and pieces of the fundamentalist view which they pick up literally out of the air. Confusion is compounded by the all too common resort to proof-texting on the part of religious liberals seeking a divine cachet for their social views. Could the central problem of biblical study in the seminary be the discovery of a mode of approaching the scripture with both intellectual honesty and spiritual openness, an approach which enables modern persons to find illumination, guidance, and power in the living Word?

Moving on to theology, we note the desperate need of congregations for help on problems of faith, particularly those having to do with belief in God, achieving a sense of the reality of God, a helpful interpretation of failure and suffering, a Christian understanding of death and hope beyond death, a realistic and constructive theology of intercessory prayer.[40] All these are profound theological issues, posing pressing existential questions which sensitive pastors confront every week, but for the most part they receive minor emphasis in seminary, where excitement tends to focus on the sweep of magisterial systems, the technicalia of methodology, and theoretical discussions of little relevance to the life of faith.

Careful reflection is also needed on the central elements of ecclesial life: the worship of God, confession of Jesus Christ as Lord; the reality of sin in all its dimensions, personal and corporate; the offer of forgiveness; baptism; eucharist; the universal priesthood of believers; the nature of the church; the oneness of all Christians; the fullness of the church.[41] Young ministers need a theologically responsible and spiritually compelling grasp of topics like these in order to invest their ministry with meaning and power, to deal with their members "where they are," to provide an authentic alternative to the easy "gospel" of cheap grace, guaranteed success, and certain healing so commonly offered in nondenominational tabernacles and on television.

Congregations need help from the seminaries, a kind of help which the schools have not made central to their mission. A radical overhaul is in order.

The Ordained Minister and the Servant Ideal

Finally, ministers need help. Caught between the upper millstone of popular expectation (too often in insubstantial fantasy projected by "successful" pastors and religious celebrities), and the nether millstone of their underlying theological convictions, many endure intolerable pressure. Their duties are only vaguely defined, the expectations of their members for a miracle-worker defy reason, even though not written into the contract, and too often no clear consensus prevails. The seminaries are called to address crucial questions: In the conflict between spiritual goals and secular standards of achievement how is the ideal of servanthood conceived after the activity of God to be rightly articulated?[42] What is a proper model of ordained ministry in keeping with its essential nature and the character of God?

Models of Ministry Theologically Appraised

A discerning inquirer has asked: "Do developments in theological education precede or follow changes in ministry?"[43] Our survey of the world scene in the first four chapters indicates profound and even demoralizing changes in ministry in recent decades, with even more radical developments to be expected, and little systematic attention by the seminaries to their responsibility in coping with the new situation. Before recurrent efforts at curriculum revision can amount to much more than a minor tune-up on an antiquated jalopy, there is need for systematic corporate reflection by seminary faculties on the condition of the ministry and a theology of ministry along the lines suggested in this chapter. Could not the schools project various models of ministry more or less appropriate to our time and submit these to theological assessment with the intention of helping churches and ministers move toward a deeper understanding?[44]

The Managerial Model

We have noted the pressures in church and society toward conceiving the minister as essentially the manager of a voluntary organization. Is such an understanding of the minister's work necessary in our culture? If it involves the danger of assuming mistaken priorities, how can the contemporary church help its "presbyters," and especially its bishops and regional ministers, who serve as role models, recover their primary functions?[45]

The Therapeutic Model

It is not to be wondered at that in a society which has multiplied on every hand its number of professional counselors, the role of the minister should be profoundly affected. We have taken note of the tendency toward pop psychology in preaching and of the large interest among seminarians in courses in pastoral counseling. Theologically we need to ask: Is the counselor an appropriate model for ministry? Is this a sufficient model in our time of grave societal ills? (Carlyle Marney "once observed that dealing with the trivial problems of middle-class people was like 'being stoned to death by popcorn'."[46]) Does it offer too easy a refuge for "avoiding all controversy?"[47] Is there a distinctively Christian perspective for ministry conceived on this model?

The Rabbinic Model[48]

An irony of our day is that the best educated generation of ministers the American church has known has lost the position as public educator or even as Christian teacher enjoyed by its predecessors. The ministry has for the most part surrendered its position of intellectual leadership.[49] Several reasons come quickly to mind. The populace as a whole has spent more time in school than did previous generations, and every community has a number of persons with advanced degrees; the ministry now makes up only a small portion of the "educated class." Moreover, people today look to the media as their authoritative source of information, and ministers have barely begun to make educational use of their parish newsletters and Sunday bulletins, much less of newspapers, magazines, radio, television, and video cassette recorders.[50]

Yet today's seminary graduates have rare if not unique qualifications to meet a pressing social need: among a people fractured by specialization their education has qualified them to take a holistic and coherent view of life. Betrayed by "experts" in government, industry, technology, and finance, who narrowly consider only what is possible or advantageous to their special interest, society stands in desperate need of "generalists" on the issues confronting civilization.[51] Yet even including journalists, educators well grounded in the humanities, an occasional political leader, and a few public-spirited amateurs, generalists are exceedingly rare. Despite the limitations of theological education, the minister with a baccalaureate degree in the liberal arts, a professional degree from a good seminary, a commitment to continuing education, and an ongoing program of personal reading is likely to be one of the best informed persons in the community on many issues with experience in responsible research and the organization of information. The seminaries need to help the current generation of ministers take their place as generalists in the contemporary world.

The fact that many ministers are opting to teach in the public schools, in colleges, universities, and seminaries, and in community organizations underscores a general affinity and basic qualification for such work. This is nothing new. Throughout the centuries, the church has been closely allied with general education, and the move from the pulpit to professor's podium and back again has always been an option within ministerial careers in America.

What is needed now is a new exaltation of the teaching office of the minister within the church. This will involve a greater emphasis by the seminaries and denominations on the educational function of the pastor: an educational vision for the total life and program of the parish, more careful planning of areas to be dealt with in sermons and other public presentations in worship, opportunities presented through the church school and the regular program of various organizations within the congregation, special courses with limited enrollments designed for persons ready to commit time and money (for tuition and solid books) to serious study, developing and promoting the use of the church library, working with the public library and community groups, cooperation with denominational and ecumenical programs. New attention within Protestantism also needs to be given to the issue of magisterium and the problem of authority.[52]

The rabbinical model for the minister is that of sage, the responsible guru, the great teacher, rather than the research scholar or the academician in the ivory tower. We have noted elsewhere the speedy disillusionment of young seminary graduates who imitate in their preaching the didacticism of their professors. But a new concern with effective teaching appears here and there in the schools, where some faculty members exemplify the art of teaching at its best. Fortunate the congregation whose pastor has learned from such teachers.

It will require no small effort to turn the church from its preoccupation with managerial and therapeutic ideals of ministry to the ampler and more basic concept of minister as teacher, within the church and within the larger community. But the seminaries should make the effort.

The Ambassadorial Model

The minister who exercises significant teaching function within the community has moved to an intellectual frontier, working along "that boundary between church and world," which has been referred to as the proper place for Jesuits to be.[53] It is the proper place for anyone professing an apostolic view of ministry, recognizing that one's ordination has appointed one as a representative of the church, indeed of Jesus Christ, in all of one's contacts.[54] Ministers working on the frontiers have an obligation to the church also to report back what they are learning and to try to involve their members in meeting community needs. Many pastors devote hours every week to such ambassadorial responsibilities, although most seminary students know far less about such service than about counseling or administration.

Certain specialized forms of ministry are located "on the boundary": campus ministry, institutional chaplaincy, some forms of street ministry, ecumenical representation of the churches on public issues, offices of information (representing the churches to the media). A few notable figures in theological education have fulfilled with distinction this ambassadorial role on the intellectual boundary between the church and secular culture—Paul Tillich, Reinhold Niebuhr, Henry Pitney Van Dusen, Douglas Horton, and John Courtney Murray. The times call for seminary faculties which will seriously engage the possibilities of the ambassadorial model—for themselves as institutions, for professors fulfilling their ministerial calling, and for the ministry generally.

Covenanting to Address the Central Task

The education of ministers for the coming age is clearly the central responsibility laid upon our theological seminaries. They have done some things remarkably well. But institutional patterns have prevented them, for the most part, from seriously and existentially assessing the present state of the world, the condition of the church, the situation of the ministry, and their own proper response. Despite the warning of our Lord, it still seems to be true that "the children of this world look further ahead . . . than the children of light" (Luke 16:8 Moffatt).

This chapter has undertaken to explore a theology of ministry by asking what God is doing and proposing that as paradigm for our task. We close this consideration with a call to seminary faculties to reflect together on this theme, to ask what such an understanding of God means for the reshaping of the pastoral task today,[60] and to accept the demands on the seminaries for their own reformation. Such a consideration might well have revolutionary effects on both curriculum and faculty, as will be suggested in subsequent chapters.

It may be necessary, however, to offer a preliminary assurance: what is needed is not a "trade school." But a preliminary warning is in order as well:

what is needed is not necessarily "theological education" in the traditional sense. That terms begs the question. What is needed rather is "education for ministry" in a strange, new world. By addressing their task theologically, the seminaries may wind up paying much closer attention to the students preparing to be ordained ministers, to the situation of ministers now in the field, to the condition of churches, and to the state of the world.

Chapter **6**

ADDRESSING THE NEED FOR MINISTERS

Congregations tend to assume an ever ready supply of ministers. Is that assumption sound? Statistics can suggest only a partial answer, for when a congregation searches for a pastor, a unit of the church for a responsible leader, a seminary for a new professor, qualitative considerations far outweigh numbers. This chapter, therefore, after a brief quantitative analysis, will devote major attention to concerns of mind and spirit.[1]

Calculating the Numbers

Varied Ministries with Standing

The Design for the Christian Church (Disciples of Christ) recognizes "an order of the ministry, set apart or ordained, under God, to equip the whole people to fulfill their corporate ministry." The church inducts into this order women and men granted the office of ordained minister and the office of licensed minister,[2] and awards "ministerial standing" to those whose positions require "continuous accountability" to a congregation, related institution, or regional or general unit of the church.[3] On change of employment one's standing is subject to review.

The diversity of services performed by ministers with standing is suggested by Table I. Slightly more than 22.5 percent of those persons are retired, but still render such service to the church as their circumstances permit. Of the remaining 5336, not quite half (49.17 percent) serve as pastors of recognized congregations. If student pastors and non-Disciples ministers serving Disciples congregations are added, the figure reaches 51.705 percent; the inclusion of persons engaged in other employment but still preaching raises it to 64,914 percent, and the number of retirees serving as interim pastors would increase a bit more. Still it must be noted that more than one-third (34,083 percent) of the active ministers with standing serve in a capacity other than that of fulltime senior pastor. The number and diversity of these ministries cannot be overlooked when considering the needs of the church in the coming decades.[5]

Table I
Totals by Classifications

A	Associate minister	374	NE	Non-Disciples minister serving local congregation	42
C	Armed Services chaplain	94	NP	Non-Parish minister	84
CE	Christian education	51	OP	Other employment but preaching	705
CM	Campus minister	36			
D	Disciples minister serving non-Disciples congregation	109	P	Pastor of a recognized congregation	2609
EM	Minister employed by national ecumenical organization	7	R	Retired, Retired missionary or Retired but preaching	1550
ER	Minister employed by regional ecumenical organization	53	SP	Student pastor	108
			SA	Student associate minister	73
G	General ministry in general units	116	SC	Student chaplain	9
GR	General ministry in regions	149	SZ	Ordained pastor returning to school for limited time-not working in the ministry for said period or ordained students not presently employed in the ministry	56
HE	Higher education	199			
IC	Institutional chaplain (Federal institutions)	13			
IR	Institutional chaplain (Non Federal institutions)	112			
M	Missionary	97	Z	Other	139
MC	Minister of counseling	85			
MM	Minister of music	14		Total	6886

Changes of occupation within the order of ministry itself, involving the movement of ordained ministers from one category to another, ordinarily have no effect on standing, but movement from a clearly defined ministry of the church (for congregation, region, general unit, related institution, or ecumenical organization) to clearly secular employment or to a form of idealistic service not explicitly religious raises a question as to continued recognition as a minister. The issue hinges on "accountability"—responsibility *to* the church and approval *by* the church. Statistical information, to be useful, refers to ministers whose standing is current.

Supply and Demand

The diversity and complexity of the general religious scene make it difficult to analyze trends, much less offer valid predictions about the supply of ministers. The decline in vocations in the Roman Catholic Church has caused concern since mid-century.[6] By contrast, an excess of priests confronts the Episcopal Church in the United States; if recent trends should hold until the year 2004, that church would have one priest for every lay member.[7] The number of ordained ministers in mainline American-Canadian Protestant denominations somewhat exceeds the positions offering a living wage.[8] This situation limits mobility when pastors and congregations desire a change. The relatively small number of larger congregations dampens for many the sense of achievement which measures success by the statistical norms of the culture.

How many ministers do Disciples need? Two studies during the past decade conclude that the supply of ministers is adequate for congregations able to support a seminary graduate, that it has remained relatively constant since the shakeout after Restructure, and that the situation is likely to continue.[9] The average number of replacements needed is about 120 per year, the annual number of ordinations in the decade which began in 1966 averaged approximately 119.[10] These figures indicate the relatively static situation of an "established church" noted in Chapter 4, a condition not much changed by the launching of new congregations, an average of about eight a year[11] and the demise of others. These are, moreover, "raw" figures. They do not differentiate, for example, the situation of black or Hispanic congregations and ministers; with both these ethnic groups a critical shortage of qualified younger ministers has already developed.[12]

The most striking trend in this superficially static situation is the dramatic shift from a virtually all-male ministry; in the past eight years more than 28 percent of the ordinands have been women, and in the past three years the figure has risen to nearly 38 percent. Among mainline denominations The United Church of Christ and the Disciples have the greatest number of women in ministry.[13] Even so, congregations and a number of regional ministers have been slow to respond to the new situation. In late 1984, 117 women served as pastors of Disciples congregations, 121 as associate pastors, 53 as members of regional or general staffs, 18 as institutional chaplains (in addition to those in federal institutions); 4.5 percent of Disciples pastors, 31.5 percent of associate pastors, were women.[14]

Thus, while Disciples march near the van of churches ready to ordain women, their reluctance to appoint them as pastors and regional or general ministers causes them to lag behind secular society. Thirty-eight percent of the students in American law schools are women, comparable to the proportion of women graduating from Disciples seminaries, but approximately 15 percent of the nation's judges are women, about the same proportion as among lawyers generally;[15] by contrast, Disciples in late 1986 have named only one woman as regional minister; they have no women serving as head of a major unit in the church.[16] And congregations which have called women as pastors are, with rare exceptions, small, with their salaries at the bottom of the pay scale for seminary graduates.[17] Statistics as to numbers of women leaving the ministry, at least temporarily, because of limited job opportunities and restricted mobility are not available, but the problem is sufficient to dampen morale.[18] Even so, says one commentator on the American churches, "By the year 2000, the majority of the clergy may be women."[19] It is easy to foretell that congregations and other institutions of the Disciples which insist on male ministerial leadership will find their pool of potential candidates drying up. It is virtually impossible to predict the effect on the tone and vitality of church life as the proportion of women in ministry continues to increase.

The seminaries have, as already indicated, welcomed the influx of women students in a decade when total enrollments have remained relatively static.[20] While faculties and administrations twenty years ago tended to take a dubious and patronizing stance toward women students wanting to prepare for the pastorate, they have become their strongest advocates. Is this conversion to be explained by institutional self-serving, radical chic, or a discovery through experience that gender is not a factor in the way in which students manage the seminary curriculum or ministers the work of a parish?

A more crucial issue of supply and demand may lie hidden within the "raw" statistics. While ordinations have for some years approximated with almost uncanny exactness the losses from active ministry by retirement, disability, and death, the changing demographic picture could radically alter that comfortable situation. If Disciples continue to ordain 125-130 new ministers each year, they can replace those coming to retirement in the next two decades. But in 1985 ordinations fell to 105 (from a high of 136 in 1980), and seminary enrollments also declined that fall—generally and among Disciples also.[21]

More critical yet, the sharp drop in the number of young people now of high school age in Disciples congregations, with severe decline predicted through the early 1990s, will mean fewer candidates for college and then a smaller pool of potential seminarians.[22] As the incipient shortage of young adults intensifies competition on the part of secular graduate schools and major corporations, persons who might otherwise be attracted toward ministry will be actively wooed for other careers.

Another factor not to be overlooked is the rise in the average age of seminarians as a result of mid-life decisions for ministry. Terms of active service will be shorter, requiring more replacements than in the past just to maintain a static situation.

So an apparent equilibrium in supply and demand could soon shift to a shortage. Moreover with the population as a whole expected to expand and with persons past sixty-five constituting an ever larger proportion of it, the churches would seem to have new opportunities for growth and a somewhat increased need for ministers. From the standpoint of quantity, the situation among Disciples calls for continued close attention. Any impression of adequacy in numbers, it must be repeated, rests on the mentality of an established church, the assumption of, if not satisfaction with, a static condition. Furthermore, statistics purporting to show adequacy in numbers ignore the issue of quality.

Before addressing that concern, however, we must take note of the situation of the small churches, few of which can support a seminary graduate on a fulltime basis.

A Ministry For Small Churches

Disciples have never solved the problem of providing and adequate ministry for small congregations. Yet they make up a sizeable portion of a church in which the median size of actively affiliated congregations is 136 members.[23] In

1979, 2677 congregations, just a shade less than 60 percent of the total number in the church, had fewer than 151 members; with 22.09 percent of the denomination's participating members, they had the services of only 870 pastors, of whom 255 supported themselves by other employment and 103 were students. Forty-eight were ministers from other denominations. Of the ministers with standing who served these churches, 79.32 percent were ordained, and 20.68 percent were licensed.[24] If congregations of 200 members or less are considered "small," this category includes 3117 congregations, 69.56 percent of the total, with 31.13 percent of the membership. A total of 1474 ordained ministers and 431 licensed ministers serve this group of churches, 49.07 percent of the 3007 active ordained senior pastors and 86.54 percent of active licensed pastors.

The numerical importance of the small congregation is evident; moreover, since virtually half the ordained ministers of the denomination now serve churches of 200 members or less, their needs should be of primary concern to seminary faculties. A strong case can be advanced for the small congregation as preferable on relgous grounds to the larger church, primarily because of the more direct encounter of person with person. Yet ministers and members alike, confused by values of the culture, tend to think of bigness as a mark of importance. In the "new world a-coming," however, the small church may well be in the vanguard for the future. A depersonalized society which privatizes religion produces intense need for interpersonal relationships, quite possibly making for the increase of Christian "cells," house churches, and small urban congregations in coming decades. Obviously, few such groups can support a fulltime minister at a living wage.[25] How then is the need for ministerial leadership to be met?

The classical Disciples solution of earlier times was the eldership composed of two or more men chosen out of the congregation to serve as its ministers of Word, sacrament, and care. It provided a ministry suited to the frontier and to rural situations even in later times, but was found wanting in a more sophisticated setting. Some elders had an education comparable to that of the itinerant evangelists or located preachers; one of Campbell's purposes in establishing Bethany College had been to supply the churches with such leaders well grounded in scripture and the liberal arts. In the British Churches of Christ in the first half of the twentieth century, William Robinson brought the training of their eldership to a high level, especially their prepartion for liturgical responsibility. Yet despite our rightful tribute to this ministry in an earlier time and our tendency to idealize it, we must remember that the churches abandoned it (and the general notion of "mutual ministry," of which it was an essential part) and instituted the "one-man pastorate" instead, and we must take the reasons for the shift into serious account.

Another solution frequently advanced by idealists and those on lower-than-average incomes is salary equalization for ministers, funded through the denominational treasury. As a strongly connectional body, the United Methodist Church operates such a scheme. But it would take a radical conversion of Disciples from the mindset of congregational independence and the ethos of free-enterprise prevalent in the profession to adopt such a scheme.

A more probable procedure to enable seminary graduates to serve smaller churches is "bivocational ministry": One's ministry is one's vocation; one's second vocation, another income-producing job, makes one's first vocation financially possible. The celebrated "worker-priests" in postwar France undertook such a dual vocation more to establish solidarity with the working class, largely estranged from the church, than to supplement income; because it seemed to compromise the sacred character of the priesthood as "set apart" from secular concerns, the experiment was ended by papal order. But current economic reality has brought something similar back in through the back door: 1700 priests in France now serve bivocationally because of the limited means of their people; most of them are ready for this, but not all, and the necessity has tended to discourage new vocations.[26]

For Disciples such a scheme is not so new as it might at first appear. In the nineteenth century, most of their educated "professional" ministers also farmed, taught school, or practiced medicine to supplement the meager support from the churches. In the early twentieth century, pastors frequently took time off from their regular post to conduct evangelistic meetings elsewhere, and even today a few of the more fortunate earn outside honoraria as visiting speakers. In 1979, nearly 18 percent of Disciples ministers with standing who served churches of 150 members or less worked also at another job; in 1985, 705 ministers relied on outside employment for support while carrying on their ministry—that figure represents 13.212 percent of ministers not retired, more than one in eight.

A third possibility for enabling a small congregation to have a minister with a seminary education depends on the earnings of a spouse to augment the ministerial salary. In a time when it is increasingly common for both husband and wife to hold jobs, this arrangement has proved possible in a number of situations. Yet since most young families today require two full incomes, this scheme pinches both minister and spouse financially. The pressure may be somewhat eased if the church can provide an adequate parsonage or allowance, since housing costs constitute such a large part of a family budget. It should be emphasized, however, that this "solution," like bivocational ministry, depends on considerable sacrifice and a high degree of dedication, both by the minister and the family.[27] That has been true of ministry in most small churches through the years.

A fourth arrangement is the "yoking" of two or more small congregations in a single "parish" with sufficient resources to support a minister and staff. The scheme seems to work best in connectional churches, e.g., a two-point or five-point "charge" in Methodism, or the "mission" served by an Episcopal rector as a remote part of his parish. A generation ago the Dale Hollow Larger Parish in rural Tennessee creatively involved congregations and ministers of several denominations, including Disciples, in a voluntary unified program, since suspended. Any such scheme requires give-and-take among the yoked congregations, as well as dedication and stamina on the part of the minister.[28]

A fifth arrangement offers a small church with a fortunate location the ministry of a seminary student who divides time between church and school. Until the early 1960s the Disciples seminaries relied almost entirely on this practice as a means of supporting their students and giving them field experience along with classwork, reducing the school week to four days or less. Pressure from the American Association of Theological Schools led them to lengthen their school week, and the expansion of urban populations into once rural areas enabled a number of the churches to grow to the point of calling a fulltime minister. Yet the practice continues among all the seminaries and divinity houses (and a few of the colleges) of the Disciples, with such students holding the office of licensed minister; in the metropolitan centers, however, most students gain their field experience as pastoral assistants or workers with youth. In regions where Disciples have a seminary or a college with a strong department of religion, small congregations have relied largely on student pastors. In other parts of the country a few may secure students from seminaries of other communions, but most are deprived of this source of supply.

Apart from college and seminary students, the office of licensed minister makes possible a bivocational or paraprofessional ministry by persons without a divinity degree. In this case one's secular job is usually one's primary means of earning a living, with ministry undertaken as a service "on the side." Before educational standards for the various professions, including ministry, had become so clearly established in America, this kind of ministry was common among Disciples, frequently with no other ordination than the call of a congregation to serve. Even the Roman Catholic Church is coming to rely on "lay pastors" for a great deal of its parish leadership and visitation, though of course it reserves sacramental ministries to the priesthood. In 1979, 14.2 percent of Disciples ministers serving congregations were licensed; with congregations of 150 members or less the proportion was 20.68 percent; these 431 persons constituted 86.54 percent of all licensed minister.[29]

A crucial problem for persons seeking this office is the securing of an adequate education for ministry. Among Disciples few licensed ministers have had the opportunity to take courses in seminary. Yet in a society with increasing numbers of college graduates, 71 percent of whom go on to graduate or professional schools,[30] it would be unfortunate to regard ministry as a vocation requiring no special education. While regional ministers, especially those in parts of the country not served by Disciples seminarians, feel intensely the need of an educational program designed to prepare licensed ministers, the theological schools have been uneasy about the matter, keeping it at arm's length; indeed, both the seminaries and the colleges have resisted designing such programs. (Exceptions have been the now defunct Bible College of Missouri, Culver-Stockton College, the Christian College of Georgia, and Northwest Christian College). Reading courses required for license have proved insufficient. Yet after the General Assembly of 1981 called on the Department of Ministry to consider developing a program for the training of licensed ministers, that department found little evident desire for or consensus regarding such a venture and threw the matter back to the regions.[31]

A key concern is the morale of licensed ministers. If the church at large authorizes such ministries, it is obliged, as are its ordained ministers, to provide support for the pastors of its small churches, to honor, not downgrade their ministry. A study of small Disciples congregations in Missouri took note of the disposition of these churches to look after themselves. What they want primarily from their minister is preaching and pastoral concern rather than program. Such congregations value a minister for relational skills more than for professional expertise; that is why a dedicated licensed minister without theological education but with a concern for persons and small groups can often serve such churches effectively and why seminary graduates without such ability often fail there.[33]

The certainty of one who spent her ministry among such churches puts the matter in a proper light: "No matter how few in numbers the congregations I was called to serve, there are no little churches in the Kingdom of God. There is no such thing as a small church when it is a church of Jesus Christ."[33] That observation moves us from the numbers of ministers needed to the qualities required to serve the coming age.

Sizing Up Persons

As we consider the need for a new generation of ministers, licensed and ordained, to serve the coming age, our concern is larger than keeping the wheels turning with the church; we look for women and men of various ethnic and cultural backgrounds whose high calling it will be to forward God's purposes for the transformation of that world. Those who enter on such a ministry will require certain personal qualities as well as qualifications obviously acquired; they are essential spiritual gifts or personal attainments. Another writer drawing up such a list would phrase it differently,[34] but both the seminaries and the churches, if they would fulfill their mission to the future, must give careful thought to the kind of persons needed, then find ways to attract students possessing those qualities or capable of developing them.

What are the essential traits?

Christian Discipleship

A true minister must be a fully committed Christian, mature in the faith and sincere in discipleship.[35] The task requires abundant inner resources of courage, patience, wisdom, and joy, along with faith, hope, and love. While no minister is perfect, nothing undermines one's witness as servant of the holy faster than insincerity, hypocrisy, or lack of commitment. The quality of a person's life cannot be assured by fulfilling a particular course of study or even a siege of indoctrination. Not what one believes (or, we may add, what one knows) but what one loves measures the goodness in a person, St. Augustine wrote long ago.[36] An evident love for God and for persons is central to the life of the disciple and to ministry in the spirit of Jesus Christ.

Authenticity as a Christian is the *sine qua non* of ministry conceived as service offered through a person in distinction from ritual performed by an office-holder. While free from smugness, self-righteousness, clerical mannerisms, and pietistic clichés, it requires an unapolgetic forthrightness about one's convictions and commitments and the ability to speak naturally of one's faith. The ministry of the "sacramental person" continues in the witness of a faithful life. Power in preaching and teaching derives less from knowledge, eloquence, and logic than from the contagion of genuine faith. The conduct of worship, even of sacraments, is enhanced by the evident involvement of the celebrant, despite St. Augustine's assurance that the ministration of God's grace is not contingent on perfection in the priest. Service as a pastor occurs minimally in the discharge of administrative duties necessary to the life of the congregation, but it reaches its highest effectiveness in the concerned involvement of a true Christian with the needs of persons, the agony of the world, the problems of the church. The three great offices—Word, sacrament, and care—all call for faithful discipleship sustained by a life of prayer.

Understanding of the World

As the arena of mission and the object of God's all-inclusive love, the world must be understood by ministers who would be more than caretakers of a flock or operators in an organization. While it may help the minister to be "street-wise," a far greater need is that understanding commended by the biblical tradition of "wisdom" and represented in Israel's sages and in Jesus. Such understanding today, at its fullest, requires a Christian appropriation of the cultural tradition of humankind: acquaintance with the powerful spiritual symbols set forth in mythology, art, and literature; awareness of the actual and symbolic importance of crucial historical events (e.g., the triumph of Greek democracy, the fall of Rome, the rise of the universities, the Declaration of Independence, the United Nations Declaration of Human Rights); and some familiarity with the scriptures of the great world religions.[37] It also requires a somewhat sophisticated comprehension of social structures and dynamics (attainable through more undergraduate work in sociology, economics, history, and biography than most entering seminarians bring to their theological studies, and sustained by lifelong reading in newsmagazines and journals of commentary).[38] Writers known for honest realism, like Machiavelli and Reinhold Niebuhr, can help a minister guard against romantic notions of human goodness or deceptive assumptions about human motivation.

Understanding of the world requires a knowledge of the problems, needs, and resources of one's particular community: investigation into such matters and reflection on them belong high on the agenda at the beginning of any new ministry. Essential also is a global consciousness, ever mindful of the needs of the whole world, informed by the concern of the citizen for responsible governmental policies toward other nations, and inspired by the Christian's sense of solidarity with all who suffer want or endure oppression. Such an outlook once provided powerful motivation for ministers because of the emotions associated with the worldwide missionary enterprise, but with the emergence of mature leadership in the "younger churches" the old romanticism and paternalism have passed. Global concern today is more likely an intellectual awareness of economic problems or a zeal for the liberal social agenda; presented as such by the minister, global concern fails to "turn on" many parishioners. Yet it still have tremendous appeal when shown as Christians caring about human beings like ourselves overwhelmed by great need; witness the outpouring of contributions at the extravaganzas produced by rock musicians on behalf of the victims of famine ("We are the World"). The populace stirred by such events, even the church members among them, remains largely ignorant about the work of Church World Service, the World Council of Churches, and even of Disciples through such programs as Week of Compassion, Reconciliation, and the continuing mission of the Division of Overseas Ministries. Consequently congregational giving to the general work of the church languishes, even though it moves beyond ministry to physical need (hunger, disease) to include evangelistic witness and educational and social programs. Christian global awareness is still minimal throughout much of the church.

Understanding of the world in the fullest sense will include an awareness of the interdependence of all created things. It will issue in a responsiveness to the beauties and wonders of nature, environmental concern, and faithful stewardship of the earth and its resources.

Appropriation of Christian Tradition

Protestant ministers, and particularly Disciples, have gloried in their familiarity with and love for the scriptures—until our own time. While it is easy to fault the seminaries for turning out ministers who do not know the Bible, or do not preach it, the real cause of the current ignorance is the decline of long-established patterns of Bible-reading as central to Christian devotional life. All Christians, and especially those pointing toward ordained ministry, really ought to enjoy familiarity with scripture gained through daily reading. (By doing a Psalm, a couple of chapters from the Old Testament, and a chapter or two from the New Testament each day, one can go through the entire Bible in about a year; following this plan, I had read it through five or six times before seminary.) And one ought not to have to go to a theological school, or enroll in a college course in religion, for responsible study of this literature; classes in biblical studies, drawing on the work of contemporary scholars, should be a part of the general program of religious education in congregation and region. Along with the scripture, one needs to know and appropriate the classics of Christian devotion, especially the hymnal and the *Book of Common Prayer*. By daily use of such spiritual treasuries along with the Bible, one learns the spirit and language of communion with God.

The minister-to-be needs to acquire an intellectual and existential comprehension of Christian doctrine, an understanding of the church's history and the ecumenical scene, and the ability to relate the Christian faith to the contemporary world. (Again, classes should be available in congregation and region.) Essential to mature understanding is a knowledgeable participation in the life of one's denomination and in ecumenical ventures, giving personal knowledge of the life of the great church. Moreover, the minister needs the ability to synthesize and correlate all such knowledge and experience of the Christian tradition and life with the evident need of persons and of society; the study of theology is intended to inform and enhance this capacity. From one's appropriation of the Christian tradition and prayerful reflection on it will come the ability, in dependence on the Holy Spirit, to bear authentic witness to the gospel.

Concern for Persons

Ministry is service to persons. Like all the caring professions, it requires a concern for them, a love for them one by one, not just as a mass abstraction, the ability to relate to them, and the capacity to work with them.

A minister is called upon to work with persons in groups, small and large—persons who may be ill informed or misinformed, who may not share the minister's goals, who have their own agenda, whose view of the particular task assigned them may be distorted. If such a company of persons is to be "equipped" for their corporate ministry, their minister needs no little skill as teacher, leader, motivator, and, above all, pastor—who cares as much for these persons individually as for any program and who lets them know that they are valued in the church and in the sight of God. The minister whose concern for persons is evident, who does not panic and hide when someone disagrees, who states a position and the reasons for holding it while respecting the right of members to make their own decisions, will enjoy great freedom and win a surprising degree of loyalty. But the minister who gives the impression of not caring for people can expect little support.

Much of a minister's most important work is helping and counseling persons one at a time. Some of this is crisis counseling, for which today's seminaries provide impressive programs of preparation. Much of it is less portentous—help in preparing an assignment for church or school, friendly advice about tennis or golf, suggestions about a cultural or educational or recreational opportunity. A few persons have a remarkable gift for relating to everyone they meet, even in casual contacts, a gift highly to be prized in a minister. The ability of others to relate naturally to persons operates within a more limited range (e.g., church people, academic types, those who share the same interests, those who approach one as minister), but even such persons can cultivate the capacity for openness and for interest in others. People long to be valued, to receive personal attention; they wish they had more opportunities for time with the minister, that the minister would visit more often, and come to know them better. Pastors long for the same kind of care from regional ministers,[39] seminary students from their professors, professors from their dean or president, while persons in high administrative positions in school or church long for an occasion to step outside the role of "parent" and pour out to another their own human hopes and fears.

Capacity for Interpretation

In an age when information multiplies, the capacity of the minister for teaching is of crucial importance. She or he is called on for knowledge about many aspects of religion and of secular life as well. Throughout Christian history the office of teaching, the ministry of the Word, has been central to the pastoral task. In carrying out this responsibility the minister has available a number of traditional channels—preaching, teaching, the liturgy, counseling, work with groups—and needs to develop both the sensitivity to opportunities and the determination to make the most of each one. Yet despite the crucial importance of the educational task, seminarians for a generation have typically avoided courses in Christian education and resisted requirements in this area; of 140 ministers responding to an inquiry connected with this study 25 acknowledged that they were not equipped for this responsibility when they began their ministry.

Besides conventional churchly ways of teaching, every minister should acquire the ability to work effectively in some area of public communication, e.g., community structures and organizations, journalism, radio, video, music, drama, poetry, film, one of the plastic arts, sports, activities for youth. Some of a minister's most important teaching, especially in its prophetic-apostolic-evangelistic dimension, may be done by such means.

Commitment to the Church

Ordination is appointment to work in the service of the church and under its auspices. One who accepts the laying on of hands should therefore bring to one's ministry a deep love for the church as community and as institution, a great loyalty to it, and zeal for its mission. One has a right to expect mutuality, responsiveness, support, and love in return, and in most instances, one will receive these in large measure, if one is faithful and uses good judgment. But one must also expect resistance, for many have not yet come to the minister's position, either in Christian insight or in commitment, and some do not want to be there. Moreover, if one feels called to a prophetic ministry crying down judgment and doom, one should recall the price the prophets paid for their trouble and remember that they acted in response to a call from Yahweh, expecting no salary from those they condemned.

Commitment to the church includes a readiness to sacrifice, as generations of ministers have done in the past. While not implying a readiness to be exploited, it does involve willingness to subordinate one's own ambitions to the welfare of the Christian community. Fifty years ago J. Warren Hastings pleaded unforgettably with a company of ministerial students: "Don't hurt the church. Don't hurt the church!"

The commitment reaches beyond the congregation or other employing institution, for a minister also has obligations to the church in the region, to the general work of the Christian Church (Disciples of Christ), and to the "Coming Great Church" envisioned in our ecumenical hopes. The general fracturing of community in our century has deprived many young ministers of significant association beyond the congregation or campus Christian fellowship; they do not know experientially the larger church as it was once known in the Student Christian Movement, the Disciples Student Fellowship, the Christian Youth Fellowship Commission, young people's summer conference, Christian youth meets and rallies, and Sunday school conventions. Many seminary graduates have had little experience with regional assemblies or General Assembly or ecumenical meetings. Their personal knowledge of the church's life is stunted.

Yet a minister is not merely a pastor of a congregation or member of an institutional staff, but a representative of the Christian Church (Disciples of Christ) responsible for the life of the whole body and consequently authorized to vote in the General Assembly. In the free church tradition, the ordained minister represents the "great church" to the congregation one serves.[40] One's commitment to the church therefore involves the obligation and joy of participating in regional, denominational, and ecumenical affairs and sharing the larger vision with those who do not have such opportunities.

Christian Creativity in New Situations

Our times have been marked by extreme changes and radical shifts of the public mood; contrast the 1980s with the 1970s, the 1960s, the 1950s. Churches constantly confront new and unexpected situations, and the minister's task is to help them respond to the new situation with creativity and

Christian faithfulness. In 1969 Robert A. Thomas looked back over eight years of ministry at University Christian Church, Seattle, recalling for his congregation some of the situations they had faced together:

> I brought with me to Seattle a view of the Faith and the Church that seemed very strange to many of the members of the congregation, and dangerous heresy to others. I found some people hungry for serious wrestling with the theological issues and the biblical problems modern science and the twentieth century world view pose for [persons] of faith. I found others anxious to see the church minister to the needs of youth without the hypocrisy of former times and in a way that would present the Faith and the Church as viable choices in a time of radical change. And I found many who wanted the Church to speak out on social issues and be involved in the life of the community as it confronted the fact of change. But, as in every large institution, there were many others who wanted no change, who were threatened by the open entertainment of doubt and question, and who expected the ministers on the staff to comfort and soothe and proclaim judgment on the traditional sins. There were people who had no interest in the university, or who saw it only in negative terms as dangerous, radical and godless. And when we made a positive response to the new attitudes of Roman Catholic leaders there was a good deal of quite bitter criticism.
>
> The counseling ministry, the youth ministry, the educational ministry, the social action ministry—all have been at one time or another under attack, and sometimes all of them at once. But my colleagues on the ministerial staff and I have persevered . . . because we are committed to love above law, inclusiveness before exclusiveness, involvement in this world rather than singing and praying about one another. We have been committed to the necessity of renewal in the life of the Church, a renewal that comes only from confrontation with the world and the God who loves the world. We have believed that a congregation must be led to see itself in its setting, determine its direction and purpose, and exercise the ministry of which it is capable under the guidance of the Holy Spirit. We have been more concerned for the whole Church and the great issues for the institution and the Faith in the whole world than we have been for the particular issues of denominational tradition. And we have long since rejected the pietism and puritanism characteristic of our nineteenth century American Protestant heritage.[41]

Such responsible ministry demands great psychic resilience, constant engagement in study and dialog, courage, and alertness to the movement of the Holy Spirit. No reading course, no class in seminary can anticipate or offer solutions for such unforeseen situations.

The wide prevalence of ministerial burnout, the demand by pastors for seminars in career assessment, and the frequent evidences of low ministerial morale indicate that theological education may have prepared them for the church that was, but has not prepared them to understand the new world or to respond to situations without precedent. Running into a blank wall, pastors frequently react by looking for a seminar in sure-fire methods, signing up for a program of self-evaluation conducted by a counselor, flight to the bureaucracy (or if qualifed by the Ph.D., escape to a faculty), or leaving the ministry. The rash of departures in the 1950s and '60s, followed by a spate of confessional articles should have alerted us to the impossibility of coping with today's problems with yesterday's assumptions.

To a young person with the intelligence, psychic health, and interpersonal skills here described, the prospects for vocational success will open doors to a number of possible careers. Yet it is persons of just such rare gifts, along with authentic Christian faith, spiritual sensitivity, and devotion to persons, that mission to the coming age will require; in fact, it is difficult to foresee significant ministry without these qualities. During college years, some of them may be only incipient, waiting to be evoked and directed. But the present generation of ministers, the leaders in the congregations, the people in the theological seminaries, and denominational officials must launch a new initiative to mark out such young people and confront them with God's call to ministry if the church is to meet the challenge of the coming age.

Vocation, Commission, and Appointment

To serve the coming age, the church will need new ministers. Yet the inclination to think in economic terms of supply and demand, or to call for a realistic program of enlistment, both so characteristic of moderns, runs into resistance from many Christian people. "Does not God call people into the ministry, as Saul of Tarsus was called on the Damascus road?" they ask. "Do we want a generation of ministers who have entered on this work as a career choice without being called of God?" Such questions arise so persistently that they must be dealt with—biblically, theologically, historically.[42]

The Meaning of Vocation

Vocation is simply the English form of the Latin word for *calling* or *call*. Webster's Unabridged Dictionary discriminates three meanings of *vocation*:[43]

1. a call, summons, or impulsion to perform a certain function or enter a certain career, especially a religious one.
2. the function or career toward which one believes oneself to be called.
3. any trade, profession, or occupation.

In general useage Webster's third meaning is tricky; especially when converted to an adjective, as in "vocational guidance," it refers less commonly to professions than to blue-collar jobs.[44] Can this fact underlie the strange downplaying of the language of vocation in ministerial circles in recent years and the eager embrace by the seminaries of the term "profession?" Does preoccupation with the status of minister affect even our speech? Jesus had no status except as a carpenter, an honest vocation, and in the occupational hierarchy of today's world, ministers can hardly claim more.

The second meaning confronts us with a major concept of the Reformation which had a powerful impact on society. In protest against the idea of superior holiness in the "indelible character" of the priestly mediator at the altar (sacerdotalism) or in the monastic quest for perfection through life under the Rule, Protestants proclaimed the sanctity of daily work in the world, pointing to the spiritual significance of the service of every Christian in his or her "calling." (In theologically muddled form this notion enjoyed a recent, and disastrous, vogue in the insistence that every member of the church is a minister—which was not what the Reformers said.)

Now for Webster's first meaning: a call to a particular career, especially a religious one. If any axiom of traditional piety still holds in the popular mind, it is the assumption that ministry is a vocation properly restricted to those who have received a divine call, like Saul of Tarsus on the road to Damascus. One might be excused for asking why else a young American in the late 1980s or 1990s would want to enter the ministry. It would not be for financial reward, nor for status in our secularized society. It would probably not be for upward social mobility, a factor which once brought some of the brightest youth from the farms to the small church colleges; nor the the lure of a life of intellectual leadership and genteel culture which ministry offered a century ago; nor as a likely means of effecting profound social change, since idealistic ministers seem to feel more trapped by the demands of the ecclesiastical system than placed by it in a position to change patterns, Martin Luther King, Jr. being regarded as a rare exception; nor because a devoted mother or aunt prayed for years that this child might become a minister or because one's parents dedicated the child to this service before its birth or because one's minister or professor made stirring appeals that one would give one's life in this way. The social, psychological, cultural, and religious factors which once operated to direct many of the most promising young people into ministry no longer seem to work that powerfully.

Still it is widely believed that God will call gifted persons into this service. Once it was supposed that God's action was limited to young men, except perhaps when choosing someone as a foreign missionary. Now, however, it is argued concerning women seeking ordination: If God has called, who is man to deny?[45] Some day, devout Christians believe, a dazzling light will fall across a young person's path, a voice will sound from heaven, and one will emerge from that experience with the unshakeable knowledge that one is a chosen vessel, called of God as a minister.

Hardly any minister of my acquaintance can honestly report that kind of call to ministry. The mode of experience is more common in the dominantly black churches and perhaps in conservative evangelical groups.[46] But in 32 years as a seminary teacher, eleven years as dean, rarely if ever did I hear students speak of such a call as we discussed their reasons for coming to theological school, and of 55 Disciples responding to questions at the 1984 Seminarians Conference only ten made note of such. Frequently my students (especially Methodists and Baptists) seemed apologetic about not having experienced such a call, but so pervasive is the popular notion of its being the proper mode of coming to ministry that they assumed their cases were exceptional and perhaps deficient. Nevertheless, few biographies or autobiographies of modern ministers recount a sign in the sky or a voice from heaven. Entrance into ministry seemed natural rather than miraculous.

Yet the notion that an experience of a supernatural call is essential to authentic ministry pervades the popular understanding so profoundly that the reader can almost hear the objections: "That's what's wrong with the American churches today!" "That's why conservative churches are growing." "How can the church be empowered if its ministers do not believe they have been called of God?"

It is now time to ask: where did this notion come from, this notion of the necessity of a miraculous call to ministry? In American Protestantism it arose with the Great Awakening. The assumption that a legitimate call to preach must be conveyed through a supernatural experience paralleled and accompanied the understanding of conversion as the work of the Holy Spirit manifested through unmistakable signs or undeniable inward encounter.[47] It fixed itself into the religious mentality of revivalism and the popular theology of Methodists, Baptists, and the evangelical parties in the Reformed churches.

In Catholicism the idea of a vocation to the priesthood arose in imitation of the vocation to life as a monk or nun. (As we shall soon see this notion involved a significant departure from the mode of entering the ministry which prevailed in the first few centuries.) In monasticism the "call" was an authentic feature from its beginnings: St. Antony, St. Francis of Assisi, St. Catherine of Siena, St. Ignatius Loyola all experienced a vivid "conversion" or "calling" by a word from God at a particular moment. (With Antony and Francis, however, it came through the public reading of scripture rather than as a "bolt from the blue.") Yet it must be remembered that a monk was not a priest unless ordained as such, and a nun could not be ordained; the monastic call was a call to life under Rule in quest of Christian perfection through discipline, prayer, and obedience.[48]

Disciples of Christ rejected the notion of a supernatural inward experience of a divine calling to preach and for a long time even lampooned the accounts of such experiences as delusions. Yet widespread theological illiteracy and seepage from evangelical folk piety have produced a generation that does not know this, fixing in the popular mind of Disciples, along with others, the notion that such a call is rightly to be expected. Hence the uneasiness of many seminarians, convinced that they ought to be in the ministry but unable to recount an experience of "calling." This is a good point at which to reexamine the biblical material.

The Biblical Concept of "Call"

As a dramatic instance of a call from heaven, there is of course Saul of Tarsus. But who else in the New Testament? The answer is: No one. No one else is reported to have had this kind of call to ministry.

The term "call" is, however, one of the most prominent words in the early Christian vocabulary, recurring throughout the literature. Jesus of Nazareth called the four fishers from their nets. Later he called Levi from his post as tax collector. He called them to follow him; they were called to discipleship. The call was a confrontation between persons in the real world, not a mystical experience, though in Luke's account it was accompanied by a miraculous haul of fish. Other disciples were drawn into the circle by those who were already disciples or by reports of Jesus' ministry; their calling to discipleship was a natural process. Of these disciples Jesus appointed (ordained) twelve to the apostolate.

Throughout the New Testament, *every* Christian is called to belong to Jesus Christ. The verb *chosen* or *elected* is likewise applied universally to all disciples.[49] As for a call to preach or to serve in the office of a minister, only the apostles receive such a vocation—the Twelve, and, as he never ceased to insist, the apostle Paul. And he alone was the only apostle whose calling is described as a miraculous experience. The "prophets" of the New Testament were believed to speak under direct inspiration of the Holy Spirit, though retaining the ability to control their utterance rationally, but we have there no account of a prophetic call.

The idea of a "call to every Christian" has deep roots in the Hebrew scriptures. They tell of the call of Abram and Sarai, not to "ministry," but to the founding of a people. They recount the call of Moses and other deliverers, such as Gideon and Samson, and the call of the great prophets, Samuel, Amos, Isaiah, Jeremiah, Ezekiel, Hosea. In all of these stories, God "spoke" directly with the person being called, and the accounts in Acts of Saul's conversion and call show clearly the intention of describing a comparable event. It should be noted, however, that other deliverers (Ehud, Deborah, Esther) simply responded to evident needs. The dominant ministry in ancient Judaism was the priesthood, assigned to the tribe of Levi; vocation as a priest was received not by a special call, but by birth. Yet Hebrews says that "every high priest . . . is called by God" (5:4). With the idea of a special or direct call to ministry holding such a prominent place in their religious heritage from Judaism, it is remarkable that the Christians in the primitive church did not take over this pattern. But they did not.

Rather the New Testament gives numerous indications of the concept of a ministering community: the church is a corporate ministry to which all Christians are "called," to which they are commissioned and ordained by baptism, in which all participate. Their "calling" and "election" is to discipleship in the company of servanthood which is the church. Through its common life and work they exercise their various gifts (*charismata*) for the upbuilding of the body of Christ and the good of all. This call to ministry has come to every Christian.

Yet, despite the oft-heard sentiment that every Christian is a minister, the church of the apostolic era had a corps of recognized and authorized workers, whom it appointed or ordained to specific tasks and to general leadership, and for them it used a specific vocabulary of order. The titles are well known, and continue to be used in various ways in the various denominational traditions: ministers or servants (deacons, liturgists, helpers, assistants, officers), stewards, bishops, elders, workers, etc.[50] These titles were applied not to all Christians indiscriminately but to persons holding recognized positions of responsibility, either temporary or lifelong, to which they had been appointed. (The "servant"-title applied to all Christians, whether apostles or the humblest of believers, was "slaves." They acknowledged themselves slaves of God or of Jesus Christ. But outside the gospels the other words are used in the more limited sense.)

How then were people drawn into the ministerial ranks?

Sending and Appointment (Commission and Ordination)

For bringing qualified persons into special or representative ministry the key words in the New Testament were not *call* but *send*, not *vocation* but *appointment*. *Commission* and *ordination* seem to us to have more of an ecclesiastical ring and are legitimate translations of the two respective concepts, but the language of the early church was the simple speech of every day: *send* and *appoint*.[51] Sometimes God or Christ or the Holy Spirit is the subject of one of these verbs, but commonly it is the church or even a single minister who initiates the action, with or without specific mention of divine guidance. Thus the Holy Spirit directs the church at Antioch to separate Barnabas and Saul for missionary work (Acts 13:1-3) or speaks through the prophets to appoint Timothy (1 Tim. 4:14). Sometimes the believers designate persons to perform a task, as the church at Jerusalem, instructed by the apostles, selects the Seven (Acts 6:1-6). Even more commonly, a leader chooses a helper; just as Moses enlisted Joshua; or Deborah, Barak; or Elijah, Elisha, so Jesus appoints and sends out the Twelve, Barnabas goes to Tarsus and brings Saul to lead the new community of Christians at Antioch, Paul and Barnabas choose Mark to assist them on their missionary journey, later Paul chooses Silas and Timothy and a score of other helpers.

The vocabulary for these actions is the normal everyday terminology of persons concerned about a cause who take common-sense action to find leaders and workers. When a need arises, these Christians "do what comes naturally" yet to do it in an orderly fashion, developing the rituals and terminology which have come to mark ordination and even the idea of "standing."[52] While the commission or "sending" always takes place within the community of the "called," the two concepts are fused only in the case of the apostles *called* to be apostles and *sent* as apostles (emissaries, missionaries—literally persons who are sent); all the others are called to be saints (people belonging to God), and some of them, whose gifts fit them for the task, are sent on particular missions or appointed to offices of ministry. The first to be sent by the risen Lord are the women who come to the tomb on the morning of the resurrection.

Sometimes the sending or appointment is to a particular task, presumably for a short term. But both words are also used for appointment to a work with no foreseeable terminus. Such an ordination does not imply a change of "character" as in the later Roman Catholic understanding of ordination, but does seem to presume a lifelong commitment to ministry.

The Church Enlists Its Ministers

Through the early centuries of its life the church continued to follow the normal practice of the apostolic era: a minister would co-opt a talented young person for the work of ministry, a congregation would choose a leader from the community, a relative would encourage a gifted member of the family to take up this service. The first great defender of the apostolic tradition, Irenaeus of Lyons, writing late in the second century, argued that the teaching of those ministers to whom the apostles had entrusted the churches offered proper guidance for Christians, whereas the innovations of unauthorized teachers who claimed to be the only prophets of saving knowledge were not to be trusted. Bishops kept on the lookout for persons qualified to lead the Christian community: during the intense persecutions of the third century, Cyprian of Carthage, soon to be martyred, ordained as lectors two young confessors who had suffered for refusing to deny the faith; thus he started them on the road toward priesthood.[53]

The number of early leaders who came from notable Christian families or were nurtured by at least one devout Christian parent is impressive: John Mark, the daughters of Philip, Timothy, Origen, Basil the Great and his brother Gregory of Nyssa, their noble sister Macrina, Gregory Nazianzen, John Chrysostom of Antioch, Augustine of Hippo. Again and again in Christian history, a tradition of ministry has run in families.

Accustomed to the notion of a miraculous call to ministry or to the idea of choosing it as a profession, the reader may be shocked by stories from the fourth century of young persons conscripted for ministry against their will, even kidnapped and hauled off to the bishop to be ordained. Such was the experience of three of the greatest preachers of all time, Gregory Nazianzen, John Chrysostom, and Augustine of Hippo. Equally striking is the case of Ambrose of Milan, the chief Roman official of the city, who on going into the cathedral to quiet a crowd on the verge of rioting over an election for bishop, suddenly found himself nominated, then chosen by acclamation, even though he had not yet been baptized. Because of such persons the church of the fourth century had in its ministry a high proportion of the most gifted and influential minds of that time.

None of these just named "chose" the ministry. None was "called" secretly by the Holy Spirit. They were "chosen" and "sent" by the church, and for spiritual power their ministry has never been surpassed. The church required the best minds and spirits of the age for its ministry, it went after them, refusing to take "no" for an answer, and their influence still continues. Even in later centuries, bishops continued to "recruit" priests to care for the church.

In the Reformation, John Calvin reaffirmed the church's initiative as essential to the understanding of the call. He evidently regarded it as the duty of the presbytery and session to keep an alert eye on the members of the congregations looking for signs of those spiritual gifts which might indicate divine intention for ministry. On agreeing that someone had the necessary qualifications they were to convey their judgment and ask the person to spend time in prayerful self-examination, seeking the confirmation of their judgment.[54] But no one who had completed theological studies, regardless of the manner of being led to undertake them, was considered to have been "called" as a minister until an invitation came by vote of a congregation to serve as its pastor. Only then would presbytery allow one to be ordained. So Presbyterians speak of God's call "by the voice of the church."[55]

Alexander Campbell regarded the claim to have been called by the Holy Spirit as, at best, a strong inward feeling which could not be outwardly proved. The only legitimate call to minister comes from a congregation whose members discern in one the marks of Christian character, knowledge of the Word of God, and the disposition to teach it faithfully, and who enter into covenant with such a person to serve it as a bishop (Campbell's term for elder). Ordination is proper only after both parties agree to the covenant.[56]

Later generations of Disciples insisted with equal vehemence that one does not need, should not expect, a secret or inner call to preach. My old professor of Christian doctrine, C. C. Taylor, used to glory in his insistence: "No, I was not called to preach. Christ gave his Great Commission to all the disciples, and that is enough for me."

At the peak of its influence, the Student Volunteer Movement for Foreign Missions pushed that logic even farther. Forty years ago I heard J. J. Handsaker, an aged veteran of service in Japan, tell of attending a YMCA Conference in his student days. A representative of the Student Volunteers approached a group of youths with the question: "Can you give one good reason why you should not go as a missionary abroad?" They could think of none more compelling than the Great Commission. So they enlisted.

Alexander Campbell believed that anyone who would serve as minister should have a strong conviction that this work is the proper work of one's life, that providential circumstances point in this direction. And he established Bethany College to provide such circumstances for a new generation. Like the Christians of the apostolic age, he saw it as the duty of the church and its leaders to try to attract the most promising youth of their own time into the service of the gospel. Charles Kemp speaks clearly in this tradition:

> One decides for the ministry essentially the same way [one] decides for any other vocation—by finding out all [one] can . . . so that the decision is based on adequate, realistic information, and by making an honest evaluation of [one]self.

To this basically rational comment he adds words equally crucial to an understanding of this tradition: "It is most important . . . that one seek self-understanding, through knowledge of the vocation, and *the guidance of God.* In 1945 as a young pastor Barton Hunter expressed this concern in a memorable poetic appeal to youth,[58] with the recurring question,

> What are you going to do with your life?

and the thrice repeated query,

> How and for what will you die?

How then are persons drawn into ordained ministry? By the action of the Holy Spirit working through the church. Not only in our time of secularism is it rare for the call to come privately or subjectively; rarely did it come that way in the church of the New Testament. Even in the accounts of Saul's conversion and call in Acts, it is Ananias, the representative of the church at Damascus, who tells the blinded convert that God has chosen him to carry the gospel to the Gentiles (9:15-16, 22:15). So it has been through much of the history of the church and specifically in the history of Disciples of Christ. In no sense does the action of Christians to seek out the best qualified young people for ministry usurp the work of the Holy Spirit. Rather do these Christians become instruments of the Spirit, who normally chooses to work through the church.

Measures to Meet the Need

With the likelihood that changing demographics and cultural values may reduce the current flow of students into the seminaries, the sheer quantitative side of supply and demand could soon become an issue for Disciples. To rise above their recent mentality as an "established church," moreover, and to reverse their current decline by bringing in significant numbers of new members, launching new congregations, and initiating new programs regionally and generally, will require continuing additions to the company of ministers.

Particularly crucial is qualitative concern: the urgency of securing creative, courageous, and faithful ministers with commitment to serve in hard situations, strength to resist overwhelming cultural pressures even within the church, intelligence to chart a course for church and society, ability to work with persons and groups in effective leadership, and vital faith in God to animate the Christian community. Moreover, if an adequate ministry is to be provided for congregations of 150 members or less, i.e., 60 percent of the total, and for the new communities of believers which may well arise in the new society, even more ministers of superior ability and commitment will be called for. One has the impression that not all of today's ministers and seminarians fit that description.[59] Persons of the kind most needed are not likely to push forward on their own, without specific prompting, even urging, by the church.

Without a new and urgent assertiveness on the church's part, too many of the brightest young people will be lured by the aggressive recruiting of business corporations, the armed forces, and university departments offering graduate scholarships, all abetted by the drag of a hedonist, consumerist culture which rates persons and professions by their income. Technology, management, psychotherapy, and the big-money professions now attract many of the bright young people once drawn to ministry. Part of the problem is a church so beguiled by the values of the culture that through inattention it has allowed the morale of its ministers to suffer. Can the seminaries help it to develop a sound theology of the vocation of all Christians and a renewed conviction as to the necessity of choosing and commissioning those best qualified for ministry? If so, the church may once again take prayerful initiative in enlisting the type of persons required to serve the coming age. To do this is to open channels for the work of the Holy Spirit.

Ministerial Enlistment among Disciples of Christ

In the days when America was dominantly rural and Disciples were more concerned over the need for preachers than over ministerial standing, able young people were drawn quite naturally into the ministry. A bright young person with a good presence and a flair for public speaking would be asked to fill the pulpit for a small church which had no minister. If the neophyte did well, encouragement of the people and satisfaction from the experience led to repetition. Some such persons might preach "off and on" for the rest of their lives without ever earning their living at the task. Others felt the need to go away to college. Some graduated and found jobs but continued to preach on the side. James A. Garfield preached, debated on religious topics, and taught school before going into politics; though he was never ordained, Disciples claimed him as one of their ministers. Cynthia Pearl Maus was engaged as the Disciples' first national superintendent of young people's work on the basis of abilities demonstrated in teaching school and in business as well as in church. Before much thought was given to "women in ministry," she served essentially as a minister and for some years must have "preached" as often as any one of her generation.[60]

The format in religous education encouraged development toward ministry. The Sunday school put articulate Christians to work as teachers or superintendents, and Christian Endeavor trained young people to speak. It was but a short step to a pulpit somewhere on a day when there was no regular preacher; and such early unschooled attempts frequently led to a call to serve as pastor.[61] It was not unusual for a minister, a Sunday school teacher, a college president to press the claims of the ministry on a promising youth.[62]

The influence of the Christian family has been a key factor in turning young people toward the ministry in every period of Disciples life. One can see this by consulting the indices of proper names in the histories of the movement. While few families among the Disciples have given six or seven generations of ministers, as is the case in some older denominations, the names Ainslie, Cole, Errett, Harmon, Henry, Humbert, Owen, Snodgrass, Stauffer, West, to list only a few, designate well-known lines.

The campus of the church-related college, as already noted, provided from the outset a concentration of ministers on its faculty, a magnet for idealistic youth, and a context in which decisions for the ministry naturally formed.

In the years between the two World Wars, the young people's summer conferences emphasized consecration to Christian leadership, enlisting many volunteers for service as ministers, missionaries, and workers in Christian education. The emotional appeal at some consecration services was heavy, some young people made commitments they later did not want to keep, and the new generation of Christian educators abandoned the procedure. The Department of Ministry sponsored a number of useful manuals and in the 1960s developed its most thorough approach to this concern in its Disciples Guidance and Recruitment Program,[63] but since then the church has had no sustained approach to ministerial enlistment.

Most of the seminaries and several of the colleges sponsor annual conferences on the ministry to interpret the varieties of career patterns,[64] deal with the notion of the "call," explain the educational programs, and recruit students for their own institutions. From 1954 to 1976 the Disciples seminaries, along with other schools in ATS, participated in the Rockefeller Brothers Scholarship Program, designed to finance outstanding students who had not yet made a career decision through a "trial year" in seminary, with the option of attending any accredited theological school. Similar programs have also been available for particular minorities but have brought few persons into the Disciples ministry.

Factors in Enlistment

Several factors may be suggested as of particular importance in leading young people to decisions for ministry.

The importance of role models. The personal equation should be evident from previous observations on ministerial families, church colleges, and young people's summer conference; it may also be seen in the notable record of certain pastors in attracting young people into ministry. Yet increasing secularization and the loss of community have lessened the opportunity for many young people to know a number of ministers, even their own pastor, as friends. The campus minister or a professor of religion in a secular university now provides virtually the only "ministerial" role model for many; for minority students and women the situation is even more bleak.[65] Seminaries concerned for the future of the ministry need to develop opportunities for getting their faculty members before groups of college students and young adults.

Esteem for Ministry. A technological and materialistic culture with a secular system of education rarely holds ministry before young people as an ideal. Preoccupation with income rather than finding significance or satisfaction in one's work tends to eliminate ministry from most discussions about "vocational" decision.[66] More serious is the church's hesitance to present the ministry to the new generation. Whether the failure is due to an uncritical acceptance of secular values or to a low state of ministerial morale or to some other cause, the situation needs to be redressed. A frank facing by congregations of the minister's finanical dilemma would be a step—to raise salaries where possible, to honor ministers and their families for sacrifice where it is not. Even more crucial is continuous demonstration by the church at large of its esteem for ministry. It is particularly important that the seminaries manifest such esteem.

Prayer. "The harvest is plentiful, but the laborers are few; pray therefore the Lord of the harvest to send out laborers into hs harvest" (Matt. 9:37-38). That dominical word, which held such a large place in the piety of the missionary movement, is largely ignored in congregations and seminaries today. The Episcopal Church still follows the practice of praying for the increase of the ministry on the stated Ember Days four times a year, but it is rare to hear such petitions in any current gathering of Disciples.[67]

When the church is most truly itself, the openness and genuineness of true prayer pervade its life. Of the seminarians at the 1984 conference, 30 reported a particular event in the Christian community as precipitating that reflection which turned them to ministry: one's baptism, a memorable service of worship, being asked to "preach" on a special occasion, an ordination, a Sunday at the old home church, visiting a mission field, working with the Order of Andrew, participating in CYF, taking part in group discussion of a film, defining one's own position while listening to a Moral Majority debate, attending Chi Rho camp or youth conference or retreat, working in the regional program, attending sessions of the Southern Academy or CWF Quadrennial or General Assembly or World Council of Churches; five of these persons mentioned a specific sermon or lecture. In all but two or three cases the speech or the event had to do with the church's witness and mission; it was not set up for enlistment, but the Christian authenticity of the occasion set them to thinking about ministry.

The church's intercessions express its deepest longings. If Christian people let the Spirit of God pervade their common life and if they begin to care enough about the quality of the ministry to pray for its increase, a new generation may catch that concern, and the prayer be answered.

Individual Concerns. Even so, persons continue, one by one, to turn toward ministry for various reasons: encouragement by a pastor, a relative, a teacher; an inner conviction that this is God's purpose for one's life; an open-ended decision to give ministry a trial run; frustration with another career; desire for time of exploration in seminary to think through what one believes or to work through problems; an attempt to find personal fulfillment. Such concerns bring diverse kinds of persons to the ministry. Curtius has categorized a variety of "personal value types" and delineated the particular ideal which each presents in its "models for emulation":[68]

the artist	the pleasant
the director	the useful
the hero	the noble
the genius	the intellectual
the saint	the holy.

Although one's first impulse may be to rush toward arranging these types in a hierarchy of importance with regard to ministry, one soon realizes that, with its distinctive charisma, each makes its necessary contribution to the good of all. While a particular type may seem to have predominated in the ministry of a given time, examination will show that all have been needed and all have been given in every period. So today. Though a culture-bound church may too readily presume that the ideal minister is the director, each of the others brings gifts essential for upbuilding.

Attention to Special Groups

Certain groups of persons are important potential sourεces of new ministers. Chief among these are gifted adolescents. Many students of high school age, and some considerably younger, have inquiring minds and superior intelligence, which the church rarely challenges and too often insults by trying to entertain. The frantic effort to keep the youth "interested" with childish amusements betrays the suspicion that they will not respond to anything of substance. Perhaps some will not. But the kind the church needs for ministers are being lured to the limits of their powers by statewide and national events which require the creative use of abilities in music, art, science, politics, and, of course, athletics.[69]

Against the excitement of representing one's school in the United States Academic Decathlon, working up a sophisticated project to enter in a science fair, competing for the privilege of playing as a guest soloist with a local symphony orchestra, or running for governor of Girls State, how does the church expect to appeal by plugging an aimless get-together as "a lot of fun," treating a roomful of passive youths to a popular speaker or one more film, or cultivating rote memory in games of Bible baseball or scriptural trivia? The plain fact is that many young people of intelligence, high idealism, and strong faith are bored to death by what the church serves up in its Sunday services and its youth programs. Young Steve Jobs, fabled genius in the development of personal computers, was "turned on" to their possibilities when as a freshman he began attending programs on electronics every Tuesday evening at Hewlett-Packard, along with about 20 other specially invited high school students.[70] Does any seminary similarly involve young people—or lay persons of any age—in regular, ongoing discussions of substance at the "cutting edge" of religion? Does any congregation challenge gifted adolescents to work on personal projects designed to call out their full potential intellectually, artistically, socially, and thus enlarge their spiritual vision?

As for college students, many congregations even in university towns rarely see them. They do not disbelieve; they too are bored, and church is so painfully predictable. Meanwhile the denominations, which have never adequately funded the programs of campus ministries have been cutting back on these efforts. Departments of religion in colleges and universities continue to increase in number; but in secular institutions these are academic operations, pluralistic, not missionary. Informed intelligence about religion is highly to be desired, and the church needs to take into increasing account the new minority of informed laity. But for the sake of the future, ministers, congregations, and denominations also need to strategize about their approach to students on the secular campuses. The church colleges were once major feeders for the seminaries and for lay leadership in the congregations, but that is no longer the case.

People contemplating midlife career changes also offer a pool of potential candidates for ministry. Mothers whose children have started to school or have left home are now undertaking further education and work outside the home. And many others, women and men alike, after spending ten years or more at a particular profession and finding it less and less satisfying, are seriously considering a change of vocation, with all that it may entail in further education and beginning over again.[71] A number of these are attracted to ministry. So also an occasional retiree decides to go to seminary and qualify for ordination.

All these adults deserve honest counsel about demands and difficulties as well as satisfactions, and should be helped to discover that any personal deficiencies which have made problems for them in their previous careers are likely to do so also in ministry. But many of these have already gained invaluable experience of congregational life through leadership in various lay offices and have developed a mature Christian faith; such "late bloomers" have much to bring to ministry, not least because they know how things are in the pew. They should find direction from reading the lives of two or three ministers such as Rosa Page Welch, Mae Yoho Ward, Margaret K. Henrichsen, Martin Luther King, Jr., Howard Thurman, Harry Emerson Fosdick, Ernest Fremont Tittle, F. E. Davison, Gilbert Courtney, and others.[72] Some will have the determination and resources to earn a seminary degree and still have a useful ministry of some years. Others may be well advised to continue earning their income in a job they know and to fulfill requirements for serving as a licensed minister. Yet others may need to discover the fullness of their Christian vocation as lay persons with special insight into and concern for the ministry.

As ethnic minorities take an increasing role in the common life, the church dare not overlook its responsibilities to raise up ministers out of these groups. Whereas ministry once offered almost the only opportunity for leadership among blacks and consequently attracted persons of outstanding ability, bright young blacks are now entering business and various professions, with few recruits for the service of the church. Hispanics have become a significant force among Disciples, and they need ministers familiar with their language and culture. Yet the number of black and Hispanic high school graduates going on to college has declined in the past decade. A few Americans of Japanese descent now serve Disciples churches, but the number from other Asian and from Indian American communities is negligible. Nevertheless 10 percent of Disciples seminarians now come from ethnic minorities.[74] Some scholarship programs to seminary have been set up explicitly for seminarians from the various ethnic minorities. Since 1970 Disciples also conducted a "Short Term Employment Experience in Ministry Program" (STEEM) designed to recruit ethnic minority youth into ministry. Of the 99 students who have served as interns, one-third have chosen to pursue a professional ministry. Numerous other STEEM participants have provided significant lay leadership to the church as a result of these summer experiences.

Persons with disabilities make up a forgotten minority, some of whom have significant gifts and insights to bring to ministry. For many such it has been difficult to find an opening in parish ministry because of popular concern about "image," but there have been notable exceptions. As "mainstreaming" continues in the schools and more persons with physical limitations take their places in the various professions, churches too will likely prove more accepting. Such specialized ministries as institutional chaplaincy, editorial work, and freelance writing offer additional opportunities for ministry.

Responsibility for Enlistment

In any initiative, "the pastor is the key." With dynamic ministerial leadership and a growing concern among the people, a few congregations have sent a continuing stream of young people to prepare for ministry, and once such a tradition becomes established, the candidates become role models for their younger peers. Certainly a pastor and staff can discuss the matter on occasion with the elders, with parents' groups, and with youth groups, avoiding undue pressure; can use The Week of the Ministry and other occasions to make this emphasis; can include the concern from time to time in the public intercessions. Of the 55 persons responding to questions at the 1984 Seminarians Conference, eleven indicated that a minister had approached them about considering the ministry; in six instances it was their pastor or youth minister. Three reported that a parent or grandparent had suggested the possibility, and six mentioned various other persons. But 33 said that no one had raised the possibility with them.

Elders, church school teachers, workers with youth, along with pastors and members of regional staffs, all need to be sensitive to the possibilities of persons in their community for ministerial work. Congregations can demonstrate regard for the profession in the way they deal with their own minister and minister's family.

Regions can take care to include in their continuing program for youth and young adults a concern for interpreting ministry and for counseling interested persons. Regional commissions on the ministry already carry heavy responsibility for candidates under care, applicants for ordination, and applicants for transfer of "standing," along with the requirement for periodic review of "standing" already granted; they may lack time or resources to conduct an ongoing program of enlistment. At least they can keep the urgency of the matter before the regional board and insist that any program be consistent with the stated policies of the commission.

Departments of religion in church colleges have worked at ministerial enlistment through the years, though the emphasis has diminished as the proportion of Disciples students has dwindled, new professors in the department lack ministerial experience or Disciples connections, and professional academic concerns claim priority on their agenda. Colleges which have entered into covenant with the Christian Church (Disciples of Christ) can make a much needed contribution to church and society by continuing to encourage programs which will attract superior young persons to consider ministry.

The responsibility of the seminaries is not generally understood to include enlistment for ministry as such, but rather the recruitment of students from among the already decided. Nevertheless in the visits of their representatives to college campuses and in conferences on the ministry which the seminaries sponsor, a considerable proportion of those who are reached have not yet declared a decision for ministry, and the interpretation given by the schools assumes considerable importance. Prospective students are now so dispersed and so hard to identify that, with a few exceptions, visits to college campuses are expensive and frustratingly unproductive. Yet seminaries need to develop opportunities to get faculty members together with college young people and with groups of high school youth. (More than once on being invited as a guest preacher, I have planned special words on ministry to the youth, only to discover that their leaders have scheduled an outing for them on that weekend, leaving me to talk to greyheads!)

Among the general units of the Christian Church (Disciples of Christ) the Division of Homeland Ministries should logically be involved because of its responsibility for Christian education, youth work, and ministry. In 1979, on the basis of data cited earlier in this chapter, the Department of Ministry concluded that a major program of enlistment was not called for. Until Disciples rid themselves of their "established church" mentality and develop a clear need for larger numbers of ministers, or until they determine to launch a program aimed at raising the quality of their ministry by deliberately going after persons of superior ability, or until demographic changes cut off the present steady stream of replacements, the Department does not appear likely to alter this conclusion. The Pension Fund, in addition to its contractual and voluntary responsibility toward retired and disabled ministers, sponsors The Week of the Ministry and develops materials for it, conducts research, and provides various services to ministers, not least of which is sustaining the morale of the corps. While it carries no responsibility for initial enlistment, the role of its officers as highly visible champions and interpreters of the ministry gives them significant influence. The Division of Higher Education, in representing the concerns of the church to the colleges, campus ministries, and seminaries, and in making known to the church the concerns of its educational institutions, has an obvious interest in a signficant program of enlistment, with emphasis on quality.

Screening the Aspirants

The concern for quality brings us to the responsibility of regional commissions on the ministry and of the seminaries to practice careful selectivity at every step among those encouraged to prepare for ministry. As representatives of the church, these bodies have a double-edged responsibility to the applicant: neither to turn aside one with latent gifts and requisite commitment nor to encourage any one unsuited for the ministry or for seminary work. Except in the case of an applicant wanting to do a year or two of theological study for personal enrichment, it is manifestly unfair to use up a student's time, money, and emotional involvement unless there is good reasons to believe that the student has the potentiality to become effective in some phase of ministry. The commissions and the seminaries have a like responsibility to the church, to donors, and to the general student body neither to shut the door on a person who can become a useful minister nor to prolong the academic retreat from reality for one who appears unlikely to do satisfactory work in school or in the parish. Academic records, charitably interpreted, give some indication of the capacity of an applicant to handle seminary courses, but equally important are personal integrity, religious development, ability to work with persons, motivation, and commitment to serve.

While it is notoriously difficult, in some cases, to predict usefulness in ministry on the basis of college transcripts or even participation in the seminary community, commission members and faculties are bound to follow their best judgment. If anything, the ministry will be harder and more demanding in years to come than it has been in the past, and selectivity becomes ever more important. Speaking impressionistically, for I know of no data to support the judgment, I believe that the schools in which I served would have been kinder to students and the churches had we taken a tougher line at this point. Careful annual review of the progress of each student, accompanied by appropriate counsel, is an obligation not to be shirked by seminary or commission,[75] though each may be inclined to defer to the other when it comes to "biting the bullet." In days of great pressure on institutional budgets the seminaries are under constraint to admit any warm body capable of paying tuition or boosting their income from the denomination. If in fact the church has too many ministers for available job openings, here is the place to begin rectifying the situation.[76]

Ministers of ability and commitment will attract young persons of ability and commitment into the service, and only such can deal with the needs of the coming age.

Chapter **7**

EDUCATION FOR TOMORROW'S MINISTERS

If seminary faculties are to redirect theological education from its orientation to a world that was and point it toward ministry to the coming age, they cannot avoid intensive dialog and difficult decisions. A young professor commented on the administrator of his school: "He is a good dean and a fine scholar, but he deliberately contrives to avoid dialog within the faculty. And the senior professors go along." These educators are not unique. Conditioned by the theological education that was, with its assumptions and system of rewards, overloaded with predetermined institutional and scholarly agenda, discreetly exercising their power to prevent interference with those agenda, they hold to commitments already fixed.

This book contends for a fresh look at our commonly held assumptions in theological education, an effort to envision a church and ministry prepared to confront the emerging new world, and a determination to redesign our programs to that end. No one person or commission can achieve such a consummation. It will require the widest possible discussion throughout the church, within the ministry, among seminarians, trustees, and professors. But as corporate keeper of the educational keys, the faculty bears greater responsibility than any other group for opening the door to the future. Dialog within the faculties concerning the common task is therefore essential. The issues raised in this chapter can be resolved only as those who together shape the teaching programs of the schools deal with them courageously and creatively.

Three Strands in a Ministerial Curriculum

The education of ministers requires a balanced combination of three essential elements twined like the strands of an Alpine rope for unity and strength. These strands are three differing but inter-related concerns—the scientific, the professional, and the fiduciary (designed to enlarge, strengthen, and transmit a trust).[1] Viewed separately, they constitute the respective goals of graduate education in religion, education for the exercise of ministry, and nurture in the faith. Ideally, a seminary will fulfill all three intentions within a common program, but they are not the same. The indiscriminate use of the term *theological education* to refer sometimes to the scientific concern, sometimes to the professional, sometimes to all three, serves mainly to blur the distinction and so to confuse our thinking about what the schools should really be trying to do. Each mode serves a valid and essential emphasis in the education of ministers; none alone is sufficient.

The Scientific Strand

The assumptions of the scientific mode so thoroughly pervade the thinking ot the university that the very term *academic* has come to imply a scientific approach to a particular subject matter. These assumptions also dominate the seminary. Confident that every phenomenon can and should be explained in naturalistic terms and that all true and useful knowledge is quantifiable, this mode of thinking is marked by a militant secularism and relativism; it fears dogmatism or even commitment.

The scientific ideal has led to ever narrowing specialization, to a dehumanizing of the life of the mind, to loss of the capacity to interpret the larger scene, to an almost total preoccupation with technology in applying the fruits of research.[2] It emphasizes logical-mathematical intelligence at the expense of other kinds, especially interpersonal and intrapersonal intelligence;[3] in education it is a central element of the industrial paradigm which arose with the Industrial Revolution.[4] Education has therefore become overwhelmingly secular and irreligious,[5] even in the teaching of religion itself. Recently a well known university cut down the cross from the spire of the building which houses its chapel. This mood contrasts sharply with the Christian humanism which so long prevailed in the colleges and universities. Intense competitiveness pervades the academic marketplace, often manifesting symptoms of destructiveness. Intellectual arrogance is all too common, a mindset which virtually ignores human beings outside the academy or even outside a particular department.

The dominance of the scientific model has spread from the secular academy to theological education, for the university graduate schools have shaped the academic ideals of the seminaries. It has made it both possible and necessary for professors to have careers in religion as a field of scholarship, and the university presupposes scholarship to be a good in itself. (A strong case can be made for that assumption.) But an institution committed to scientific investigation comes to exist more and more for itself or for those special interests which fund research, less and less for the public, or in the case of the seminary, for the church. The problems in religious studies which intellectuals are moved to address are often of little concern to persons outside a particular academic subfield,[6] with the result that the dominant interests of many seminary professors have minimal relevance to the work of ministry.

> Theology is becoming more like philosophy of religion, with theological faculty members seemingly academically respectable in the eyes of the secular and humanistic intellectuals on the campus. The danger is omnipresent that these theologians will abandon the gospel and forsake the church.[7]

Yet when the scientific mode functions at its best, commitment to truth determines methodology for each academic discipline in the seminary, and scholarly rigor rises to heights of nobility in dispassionate investigation and impartial analysis. Thomas N. Trotter has described scientific method from a Christian perspective, not as objective disinterest but as disinterested love.[8] As this ideal has pervaded the theological schools in the past century, the intellectual tone and excitement of the seminaires have been immeasurably enhanced. The displacement of sectarian polemics by scholarly objectivity has resulted in great gains for Christian understanding and ecumenical advance. While the seminary should beware of the secular, irreligious, competitive ethos so prevalent in the graduate schools,[9] it has no choice but to honor the canons of sound scholarship. Yet concern to sustain the humane values, once so prominent in liberal education and now so commonly slighted in the secular university, is also part of its scientific obligation.[10] The seminary, it has been argued, is the last stronghold of the liberal arts, and the values espoused by Christian humanism should not lose their home in the theological schools.

Standing between the university and the church, the seminary belongs by its very essence to both communities.[11] It needs to heed the admonition, "Render therefore to Caesar the things that are Caesar's, and to God the things that are God's"(Matt. 22:21).

The divinity school operating as part of the graduate program of a great university will of necessity give clear allegiance to the scientific mode. Though to some ministerial students that approach can seem cold and forbidding, the impressive record of such schools in scientific commitment and in educating pastors of remarkable effectiveness cannot be lightly dismissed.[12] No theological institution can serve the divine purpose for the coming age without allegiance to the highest academic ideals of the scientific approach.

At that same time a way must be found to lay to rest the widespread assumption that no truly great seminary is possible except as part of a university graduate school. True, the most celebrated scientific scholars are found in a university. The prevailing system of rewards for faculty members and of ranking seminarians for prestige sees to that. But the free-standing seminary, with equal devotion to the scientific ideal, may enjoy somewhat greater freedom in giving attention to the professional and fiduciary strands in ministerial education. The American religious community needs to find a way of honoring schools for devotion to and effectiveness in total education for ministry, not scientific distinction alone.

The Professional Strand

In the 1960s American seminary faculties put much effort into reflecting on their task as one of professional education. In changing the course leading to ordination from bachelor of divinity to master of divinity they emphasized its function as the "first professional degree." The School of Theology at Claremont and the Divinity School of the University of Chicago sent shock waves through the community of theological educators by devising new doctoral programs for the first professional degree, and a special commission of ATS recommended the general adoption of this pattern as member schools found resources to upgrade their offerings. The proposal did not carry, and the Doctor of Ministry degree now functions primarily as a program of continuing education or advanced professional work. But issues raised then still demand attention by seminary faculties. To what extent is the term *professional* useful in thinking about ministry? And how can the theological schools improve their service by approaching their task as professional education?

The term *professional* designates an occupation with distinctive characteristics.[13] 1) It is practiced as "a vocation of community service. . . to individuals, organizations, governments." 2) "The task requires technical competence and specialized knowledge," both theoretical and practical; the professional, initiated after apprenticeship under masters of the profession, has something to "profess." 3) Since the service offered is not readily available elsewhere, nor readily understandable by the client/patient, the relationship calls for trust and responsibility. 4) The members of a profession subscribe to a code of ethics. 5) The esoteric knowledge possessed by the members of the profession endows them with authority, which does not come from the persons they serve. 6) A guild or association of professionals determines rules for the profession, standards for admission, and procedures for control and discipline. 7) "The professional serves people. . . on a personal basis." 8) "The function performed by the professional is highly valued in the culture." It meets important needs of the society or of some social group.

After professional schools in law, medicine, and theology superseded education by apprenticeship to a master, the scientific spirit of the academy increasingly dominated these schools. Even so, American and British theological faculties managed to maintain a healthy balance between scientific and professional concerns through the common practice of appointing outstanding parish ministers to professorships in the various disciplines. These teachers were "old pros," integrating pastoral wisdom with scholarship and never losing sight of the congregation. Some of the best known ministers before World War II (Fosdick, Buttrick, Bowie, Scherer, Sockman, Ames,) taught courses in the great seminaries while continuing to serve in the parish; others (Niebuhr, Stewart) were appointed to fulltime faculty positions; and some of the most influential heads of seminaries (Coffin, Charles Reynold Brown, Stone, Palmer) came from the pastorate. Then the postwar requirement of the academic doctorate for faculty members and the new supremacy of theology crowded practitioners off the faculties, replacing them with young theoreticians innocent of pastoral experience (or even of divinity degrees) and not greatly interested in the life of the parish.

As the gulf between pastors and laity widened, seminaries took notice, and in the 1960s the cry went up for "professional education." Yet the new emphasis too often proved self-conscious and sterile, as faculties themselves failed to reach consensus on the nature and methodology of professional studies. Lacking for the most part the perspective of working pastors, faculties commonly hold grudging or negative attitudes toward field education, even while shifting the burden of professional concern to the professors in the "practical" courses. Moreover the ATS study on Readiness for Ministry resulted in few specific recommendations that could be proposed to the member schools.[14]

In the 1980s some schools began to back off from the earlier fascination with professional education. Meanwhile students too often perceived professionalism as specialized "know-how" analagous to that of attorney or physician and entitling the minister to social status. One recent seminary graduate sees a consequent loss of concern for servanthood, a compromising of the character of ministry; another calls for a "service ministry and personal integrity, in contrast to a professionalism dealing only with skills and personal fulfillment."[15]

The key to the problem of professional education lies in the attitude of the seminaries: professing to take ministry seriously, they seem not to take ministers seriously. With rare exceptions, working pastors are involved only marginally, if at all, in the educational program. At some schools there is sporadic consultation with select groups of ministers, and here and there a continuing advisory council, but the dominant concern often appears to be interpretation or promotion rather than substantive consultation about curriculum. Commonly an outstanding local minister offers a course in the practical field, giving students direct contact with someone actually involved in the profession, but such courses frequently lean more to reminiscence and advice than to systematic analysis. Members of the regular faculty, however, rarely devote attention, much less research, to a disciplinary analysis of effectiveness in ministry, except for an occasional statistical study by a sociologist or psychologist. Attention to religious leaders centers on their theology or their prominence in movements or in building denominational and ecumenical institutions, not their work as ministers of congregations with the intent of deducing patterns and principles for critical analysis.

A slight but intentional shift of focus, with no diminution of scientific rigor, could greatly enhance the professional usefulness of seminary studies.

Readings for biblical courses could well include examples of responsible hermeneutics in preaching and materials for Christian education as well as guidance in leading lay persons on their own pilgrimage of biblical discovery; for theological courses, selections from sermons or biographies of pastors dealing with their theological reflections, experiences in dealing theologically with problems of their members, procedures for helping Christians in the congregations learn how to think seriously, i.e., theologically, about faith and life, and good examples of doctrinal preaching; for church history, some use of ministerial biographies or congregational histories in every course; for arts of ministry, analysis of actual cases in parish life or pastoral experience.

Commitment to professional education remains a necessary ideal, demanding the attention of seminal thinkers.[16] It is not enough to leave matters up to common sense after graduation. One's natural response, for example, of sympathizing with a person who has lost a job may only increase the sense of depression; what is needed is a positive feeling of self-esteem.[17]

The difficulty lies in trying to devise an educational approach not subservient to the scientific model. Even a course on death and dying or on evangelism too readily becomes merely academic, losing the focus on persons. Some months ago a few of us listened to Earl Gibbs read a painfully honest autobiographical paper entitled "Grief: A View from the Inside."[18] His account of the recent unexpected death of his daughter impelled each person present to speak about the personal loss of a loved one. The author reflected on his own harrowing experience and the degree to which it "fit the pattern" he himself had earlier described in an academically respectable book on ministering to the grieving.

Ministerial education finds it too easy to stay with the safety of the book. All too rarely does it directly engage the human and divine reality of raw experience. How can that be done, bringing students into living encounter with persons who have known intense sorrow, fear, suffering, joy, conversion, hope? Perhaps it can be done only rarely. Few have the gifts and the strength to understand their own story and tell it with candor—and it would lose the power of freshness if told too often. But the concern for professional education will be met, not by increasing the number of formal courses detailing "professional" approaches to particular problems, but by bringing students to confront a human reality with all of the resources of their biblical, historical, theological, and technical knowledge. Clinical pastoral education has managed to do just this in hospital settings, though faculties have found difficulty in transferring the clinical methodology to the larger concerns of the parish.[19]

A disturbing question has particular relevance to professional education for ministry: Do seminaries treat seminarians like adults? Considerable evidence suggest not: the heavy required curriculum (to be discussed shortly), a prevailing authority-to-neophyte didactic model, the routine and unimaginative chracter of most assignments (writing papers out of reference books and recognized authorities, still recapitulating a dull process begun in high school), a relatively low ("realistic") level of expectation for student performance in fulfilling most of the requirements.

It should be observed with some acerbity that as young adults and college graduates seminary students have capacity for impressive, original work. Yet while their peers in age and education are as seniors in law school editing the nation's distinguished law journals, I know of no comparable theological journal edited by seminarians. Students in homiletics courses frequently do impressive and stirring preaching. Well along in my teaching career, once I had moved from traditional term papers to assignments calling for original investigation, I found that students demonstrated a sound use of historical method, and a number of them did intensive work in gathering data from printed journals, unpublished materials, and tape-recorded interviews. When treated as historians rather than as juveniles grinding out term papers, they did responsible historical work, and I was put to shame for so long having treated their predecessors as "just students."[20] A seminar in Faith and Order came alive when, instead of merely reading and discussing recent ecumenical documents, the group was constituted as a drafting committee to develop its own document on a current problem.

One of the great advantages of concurrent field education or contextual education is the opportunity to assign authentic ministerial tasks to be worked through in relationship to a course in Bible or theology, with an eye to the development of both scientific and professional maturity. Of particular importance are projects designed to give students a clear understanding of the contemporary situation, the shape of the world to come, the impact of social change on relgous ideas and institutions, and creative responses to the new situation.[21]

Faculties then could well docket for discussion such questions as these: "Do we deal with our seminarians as graduate students on the way to becoming professionals? What changes might we institute to recognize their maturity and evoke a more challenging performance? Are we preparing them for ministry in the church that was in a world that was? Or are we readying them to serve the coming age?"

The Fiduciary Strand

Is it possible for faculties today to conceive and commit themselves to a mode of education designed to impart faith, a view of truth, a cluster of commitments? In a secularized world dominated by technological assumptions academia has almost lost the capacity for talking in such language. It makes scholars squirm.

Yet wherever academics have spoken of "the great cultural tradition" (*ad fontes*) or "the black heritage" or "the legacy of classicism" or "democratic principles" or "moral values" or "our obligation to truth," the fiduciary character of education has been invoked.[22] Just as society entrusts its financial treasure to fiduciary institutions like banks and insurance companies, or the most valued artifacts from the human past to museums, so it has uniquely entrusted to the academy the responsibility for guarding, testing, enhancing, and enlarging its cultural and spiritual heritage.

Under the current dominance of the scientific model, academicians are prone to forget or even deny such a fiduciary responsibility. Yet to be true to itself and its unique vocation the academy must risk commitment;[23] research may be done by industry (R&D). The critical examination of current assumptions remains an implicit duty, but that task is not essentially destructive.

Such language can make professors highly nervous when the discussion has to do with national tradition or religious faith. Yet, though the issue is rarely acknowledged in academic literature or in faculty meetings, "All scholarship serves some purpose,"[24] and all but the most craven professors honor controlling allegiances. Indeed, academia's clear commitment to its fiduciary responsibility marks the great ages of human spirit. It particularly characterizes the work of the great Christian intellectuals. Even so, affirmation is not a notable element of the current academic style, either in the university or in the theological school.

A seminary rightfully resists the role of indoctrinator or sectarian propagandist. Liberal professors therefore in requiring their students to face hard questions about traditional faith and practice have tended to leave them to find answers for themselves. The enemy has been fundamentalism or pietism or traditionalism, the task of theological education to deliver the next generation of ministers from their clutches. Only rarely has a faculty articulated its academic vocation as one of positive witness to Christian faith, as in the case of Dietrich Bonhoeffer's outlaw seminary at Finkenwald during the Nazi regime.[25]

Yet any other role for a seminary is partial and self-defeating. To see its task merely as the scientific study of religion, like that of the university graduate school, is to overlook major obligations. To define ministry as a profession comparable to law, medicine, engineering, or teaching, as though its practice consisted of a particular set of skills, overlooks its true essence: humble but authentic service as an exemplar of life in Christ, a witness to the work of God in Christ, a spiritual director, a teacher of Christian faith, a leader of the Christian community.

Given the state of the church and the contemporary world, it is clear that the seminary must find a way of bearing authentic Christian witness within the church and to the secular mind, and of doing it in a way consistent with its obligaton to scientific investigation and to professional preparation.[26] Recent actions by the Vatican to silence certain theologians reveal an understanding of the fiduciary responsibility abhorrent to Disciples and Protestants generally, to all defenders of academic freedom, and to large numbers of Roman Catholics. Faith can hardly be instilled by coercion or the repression of doubt. Yet a seminary will regard its freedom as freedom in Christ. If "the voice of theology must be theological,"[27] faculties must come to terms with tradition and their fiduciary obligation as "stewards of the mysteries of God" (1 Cor. 4:1).[28]

This responsibility will require new engagement with the questions, "Are faith and piety proper goals of theological education?" It could well bring a new encounter with the intellectual pilgrimage of the great fourth-century doctors of the church: theirs was a quest for a particular kind of "knowledge," a knowledge of God and the human spirit and the church and human destiny. The search was in no sense anti-intellectual; rather it made full, honest, and convincing use of the philosophical tradition, integrating the best in secular education with the Christian witness to formulate a new, invigorating, and honest system of thought.[29]

Professors who accept their fiduciary responsibility will bear in mind the necessity of appropriation in all study, especially the study of religion.[30] It is not enough for ministerial students to work through the theology of Paul, of Mark of the Fourth Gospel, and to distinguish the essential elements of each. The crucial concern of each of these theologies is the faith it elucidates. Does the seminarian assimilate that? Lactantius spoke an urgent truth: "Never can that be investigated which is sought not through its own way."[31] Without loss of scientific rigor, the study of scripture, theology, church history requires a reverent exploration into faith as a particular discipline interacts with the life and mission of the church.

While shunning an anti-intellectual stance, the seminary cannot settle for an intellectualism without faith. It will give heed to the insight of the unlettered black preacher of an earlier generation: "He go to school and get his diploma. . . ; degrees on mathematics, and theology and what not and—now we witness, never hear a man gwine to schools to git his diploma on God."[32] Faculties could well re-examine the mode of the early Christian schools at Alexandria and Caesarea, and ponder the model of rabbinic education.[33] They will need to face corporately such embarrasing questions (embarrasing to minds long inured to the scientific mode of education): "Are faith and piety to be taught directly? Are they rather caught incidentally within the context of seminary life? How can they be legitimately taught in an academic institution? How can it order its life in such a way that they are caught? How do professors most helpfully relate to the struggles of students as the contours of their faith change in response to new learning?" If the theological school does not address such questions, but continues to drift in the wake of "scientific" assumptions, then it must face another question: "Where and how will the ministers of tomorrow find faith?"

The effort to answer such questions will require corporate commitment by the seminaries, their faculties, staffs, and trustees. It is not enough for presidents and development officers to speak glowingly of preparing ministers for tomorrow. As institutions the seminaries must embrace that as their fundamental task and faculties must come to terms with all that it implies.

Ministry to the coming age will require all three strands in its rope.[34] Therefore the seminaries owe equal attention to scientific, professional, and fiduciary concerns, and to their integration, in the education they offer. While a particular course may occasionally be developed in primary relationship to one of the three strands, it would be unfortunate to think of a curriculum which would segregate courses according to these separate categories. Rather it is important that the three strands be twined together in every course.

Designing a Curriculum

The planning of curriculum remains the chief corporate reponsibility of faculty. The task carries scientific, professional, and fiduciary obligations in the development of an integrated program of education for ministry.

A Continuing Problem

Faculties expend incalculable quantities of time and energy in periodic spasms of curricular revision. Often an ambitious round of papers and consultations on general issues precedes the proposals for a new design and the almost interminable negotiations that ensue. It is not easy for a scholar deeply involved in a particular discipline and engaged in projects of specialized research to retain a balanced concern for the curriculum as a whole. Every professor is troubled that students get so little work in one's own discipline, and "the territorial imperative" rages no less in the halls of ivy than in the jungle. In building curriculum, consensus may be an ideal, but log-rolling remains a fact of life.[35] Is it only a pious hope that greater common reflection on the needs of the world, on a theology of ministry, and on the three essential strands in ministerial education may lead a faculty to greater clarity regarding curriculum?

Individual faculties and the community of seminaries taken as a whole tend to oscillate between two traditional curricular models. One is a tightly prescribed program with a large number of required courses and electives; it is designed to introduce the student to each area of expected competence, normally by requiring stated courses in each academic field. Pedagogically, its chief weakness is the pattern of large classes in the required courses, with heavy reliance on lectures and the consequent limitation of interaction between students and professors, or even among students, in most of their seminary work. Furthermore, it leaves few opportunities for elective courses dealing with advanced topics and the professors' particular expertise; for the most part, such classes remain small. The process tends to depress morale by imposing a lockstep mood on the entire program and instills in the student the expectation of having one's education served up by experts rather than of taking initiative in working out a program. Despite its well-intentioned effort to assure a common grounding in the fundamental knowledge required for ministry, the three-year program is necessarily limited in the number of courses it can include and inevitably involves crucial omissions. Without doubt, it is the easiest kind of curriculum to administer; its requirements are the simplest for the dependent student to fulfill.

At the far swing of the pendulum is an open curriculum, with few specifically required courses and with competence in the major academic areas or fields demonstrated by examination. The intention is to develop student initiative in planning a program of study and to encourage independent investigation. As advantages it offers a large number of vital elective courses or seminars, resulting in greater freedom of choice, better student morale in class, and greater satisfaction for faculty members. Students like the flexibility, but dread the field examinations required to assure minimal competence in each area. Periodically their resistance approaches rebellion; not remembering the burden of many required courses, they persuade the faculty that the situation is intolerable; and the pendulum swings back to the tightly prescribed curriculum until that scheme again provokes an outcry.

It might be suggested that the problem in both cases arises from beginning, not with a commitment to the preparation of ministers, but with the traditional axiom that students should achieve minimal expertise in a number of academic disciplines, the number usually being determined by the local pattern of faculty organization into fields. So the student writes examinations, whether connected with particular courses or not, to demonstrate minimal knowledge, and the faculty in each discipline concedes that the level of achievement is probably enough for a minister, though clearly insufficient for a Ph.D. candidate. Similar condescension obtains toward the thesis in schools which still require it for the Master of Divinity. The graduate receives a seminary degree and, with a smattering of knowledge in assorted fields, goes out to minister.

The Integration of Learning

In the case of any particular graduate, those scattered globs of learning may or may not have fused into an integrated education for ministry. Theological faculties repeatedly affirm the ideal of integration, but almost universally lay the burden on the student.

In addition to whatever correlation and appropriation the student may accomplish intellectually and spiritually on one's own, certain academic requirements are commonly built into curriculm as a formal means of encouraging the process. Most frequent are clinical pastoral education, a seminar on ministry for seniors, and a paper by the student on "My Theology of Ministry." In D.Min. programs, the project or dissertation is widely specified as an exercise in integration, addressing an operational problem in ministry from the perspective of both a classical discipline (Bible, church history, theology, ethics) and a discipline in the practical field (Christian education, homiletics, liturgics, pastoral care).

An occasional seminary may commit itself to a particular pattern with the intention of "getting it all together"—a dominantly theological approach to all subjects in the required curriculum[36] or the goal of enabling the church to recover a distinctive sense of Christian identity.[37]

Here and there a professor is bold enough to undertake the work of integration. For example, a professor of practical ministry annually offers for seniors a course which addresses biblically, historically, theologically, and operationally a selected practical theme or parish problem. The student does a set of papers on the topic, each of which comes at it from the standpoint of a different discipline. Instead of appearing as a "visiting fireman" to give one more lecture, a professor from the biblical field critiques the exegetical paper; the theological essay and historical research are similarly analyzed for sound methodology. Each student then draws on this foundational work as a basis for programmatic proposals.[38]

Less comprehensively, but with a clear concern for integration, a professor of homiletics and a professor of New Testament may team-teach a course in "Preaching from Romans," or a single teacher may offer a course in "Historical Models of Ministry" with attention to biblical and theological perspectives, the internalizing of a sense of ministerial identity, biographical studies, and historical insights into the present situation.[39]

As a church historian, I discovered that a major paper requiring original research on the history of a congregation or the biography of a minister not only involved the student in a valuable exercise in historiography, but also contributed significantly toward integration as the student discovered how topics studied as abstractions in classroom and library actually affect work in the church. The reading of such papers in seminars evoked group discussion and thus enhanced the process.

Some professors in all fields try to demonstrate the relevance of their material to the life of the church and the work of the minister; the material is normally organized, however, as a unit within a particular academic discipline.

A Radical New Approach

The question now arises: Is the conventional sequence of required courses and electives in the traditional disciplines of graduate study in religion the most appropriate means of educating ministers? Might it not be possible that at least some of the malaise within the contemporary church, at least some of the inability of today's seminary-educated ministry to cope with the unprecedented situations in our world, may be traced to the unexamined assumption that meeting a given list of academic requirements in the scientific study of certain disciplines properly prepares them for the task? May it not be that a radical new approach is called for?[40]

As one whose mindset was formed by the traditional assumptions, who reveled in work in certain of the fields, who earned an academic doctorate and taught in one of the academic disciplines throughout most of my ministry, I find it most natural to approach any discussion of curriculum with the queries "How much church history can we get into the program?" and "What history courses will be most useful?" Perhaps these are the wrong questions.

In a flight of fancy (literally while flying at 35,000 feet) a seminary dean began to outline an entirely new approach to education for ministry. He noted first certain areas which must be included in any adequate curriculum: a study of scripture and theology (might I also insert church history?), prayer and spirituality, the social and human realities of the contemporary world, the skills or arts of ministry—1) teaching, 2) worship and celebration, 3) mission, 4) pastoral care, 5) oversight (management). Assuming these essential areas of knowledge, he undertook to conceive a curriculum organized around three central and inclusive elements in the mission of the church: witness, nurture, and service.

The first year of seminary would be given over entirely to the *witness* of the church, with primary attention to modes of proclamation and to the content of the faith, the latter involving intensive study of scripture, the forms of communication (theology), and the experience of witness (church history). The second year would center on *nurture* with attention to teaching, worship (celebration) and the spiritual life, prayer and spiritual formation, and oversight of the community. The third year would concentrate on *service*, with attention to the caring community (pastoral care), the social and human realities of the contemporary world, and organization for mission, service, and ministry.[41]

One can quickly see that any such approach to curriculm presupposes commitments on the part of faculty radically different from those which now obtain. The primary concern is education for ministry, involving the integration of all the constituent elements as a continuing and essential part of the program. The catalogue would not carry the customary array of course offerings in various fields arranged after the pattern of graduate school. A professor's primary contribution would be made not as a research scholar but as a master of a given field of knowledge dedicated to relating that to the work of ministry.

Many questions quickly come to mind. Would any existing faculty ever adopt such a program? Could a theologian, historian, or biblical scholar retain sharpness and expertise in one's field if one's teaching was oriented entirely toward functions of ministry? Would the student who finished such a program, no matter how well equipped with an understanding of the ministerial task, have a sufficient overview of theory and content in the various disciplines of divinity? Et cetera, et cetera.

Whatever the answers to these questions, the proposal has one supreme advantage. It exemplifies the kind of radical rethinking of ministerial education which the situation of the church and ministry demands on the approach of the twenty-first century. Perhaps after examining a series of such brainstorms, a faculty may conclude, not out of weariness but as an exercise of mature judgment, that the wisdom of many generations is not to be discarded, and that the conventional organizaton of curriculum by disciplines is the way to go. But in the process such a faculty would have discharged its obligation to reflect boldly on the best modes of integrating the knowledge, insights, and methods of the various disciplines into a holistic understanding of ministry and to reconsider responsibility for making such integration a concern in every course.

How fully does a seminary believe in the education it offers for ministry? Some schools of education have initiated a "teacher warranty program." If in the first two years after graduation a graduate proves unable to function satisfactorily in the classroom, a team from the school comes to the field to assess the situation and make recommendations; remedial work is provided for the teacher.[42] Will any seminary be so bold as to stand behind its graduates in this way?

One way of achieving the necessary integration is to give greater attention to the three essential strands in a ministerial curriculum, already discussed, and to the means of assuring an adequate emphasis on each, as well as on the interrelationships among them. Some professors in university divinity schools may feel compelled to maintain their allegiance to "pure" scientific scholarship, unsullied by the professional concerns of ministry or the fiduciary concerns of the church, and they may be justified in their decision. Or a seminary faculty may conclude that the scientific integrity of its formal academic program must not be compromised by fiduciary concerns and that its fiduciary obligations are properly handled outside the curriculum. Such a conclusion may well be legitimate—if the faculty builds into the total seminary experience of all ministerial students a responsible means of discharging the fiduciary responsibility.

But the faculty as a whole is obligated to come to terms with the issue: How are students, having been trained in their responsibility as critical exegetes or theologians or historians, to be prepared to work with equal responsibility as pastors or preachers or teachers of lay persons? A faculty's fiduciary duty may be not so much a matter of scrapping present curriculum or adding new courses as of explicitly avowing commitments, of going beyond the objective exploration of facts and issues to the raising of questions concerning value and relevance and to affirming a Christian witness. The scientific, professional, and fiduciary strands do more than intertwine; the distinctive color of each "bleeds" into the other two. A unified relationship among three strands makes for fullness of ministry.

Some Particular Needs

The analysis in our first five chapters calls for a major new look at the programs of the seminaries. That could result in sweeping revision of curricular patterns. In any case, it should take into account certain particular needs which cannot be ignored. Faculties will have to decide the best ways fo dealing with these essential concerns. They may find themselves driven to more rigorous demands regarding preseminary education through insistence on specific course requriements for entrance. They may radically revamp some elements of the current curriculum. They may conclude that three years give insufficient time for the basic professional degree. In any event, the following considerations are essential needs in the education of ministers.

Cultivating the Imagination

While imagery and story constitute the native idiom of faith, many persons schooled in the mindset of a technological age enter the seminary largely ignorant of the cultural legacy of art, music, literature, and religion. Moreover the conventional academic approach of most college and seminary courses instills in students the habit of reasoning in abstract concepts, using a technical vocabulary that makes communication with the lay mind virtually impossible, and attempting to give "flat answers" rather than launching on an adventure of discovery.[43] Even so, the relative decline of the liberal arts in the universities seems to have been accompanied by a similar decline of seminary courses designed to kindle the imagination, familiarize the mind with the great archetypes, and cultivate the power of imagistic thinking. Curricular requirements in literature, the arts, music, and the history of religions are virtually nil,[44] and even biblical content is often minimal.

The coming age will require ministers not only with keen minds and strong faith but with the power to project the intentions of God in appealing imagery.[45] "A person who doesn't think is a slave; a person who won't imagine is a prisoner."[46]

Imparting Knowledge of Society

For at least a century, while forces, principalities, and powers only dimly understood have battered the church that was and the world that was, American ministers have been far more ready to offer their people psychological diversions than sociological understanding. In trying to help members and congregations cope with life in a mass society they have offered little aid in understanding or altering it. They have painfully endured the decline of congregations under the impact of forces beyond their control, while popular nostrums like the church growth movement have addressed symptoms rather than the epidemic of change which debilitates the church as a social institution.

If the church has been baffled and ministers unenlightening regarding the present situation, the seminaries must accept a large share of the blame. "Theological education has adopted the pastoral-care model—a model consistent with a privatized gospel."[47] While professors with psychological credentials fill the catalogs with course-offerings, scholars in sociology of religion, history of religion, urban and rural sociology, and other social studies offering some understanding of the dynamics of the larger scene have all but disappeared form many faculties. Each of the four Disciples seminaries lists a professor in the area of church and society, who in most cases divides time with another field, and only one has a professor in history of religions.

Seminarians hear much talk about social conditions, but it comes from ethicists and theologians of liberation, whose wont is to speak normatively about right and wrong; they receive little or no guidance from scholars speaking descriptively about the way social institutions operate and why, or analytically about how institutions adapt or are changed. As a result, young ministers filled with fine prophetic fervor may fail to comprehend their members' and their own involvement in the system, may have little sense of realism regarding possibilities or methods of social change, and little understanding of the institutional facts of congregational life or the dynamics of the communites they try to serve.[48] Occasionally a church historian plows these fields; otherwise seminary faculties tend to let them lie fallow.[49]

The seminaries cannot continue to ignore or minimize the essential contributions of studies in religion and society to the preparation of ministers for the coming age.

Preparing Ministers to Teach

No skill will be more crucial to ministry and to leading the church in a constructive response to conditions traced in our first four chapters than the skill of the teacher adept at getting persons in a non-academic setting to see new visions and entertain new ideas. Yet while many ministers seem totally at sea with regard to the educational program of the church school and equally confused as to how to do their pastoral work as effective teachers, seminarians tend to avoid courses in Christian education and to go to their first parishes imitating the lecture method of their professors. Clearly the style of leadership required for the coming years is that of the person who can interest people in new ideas, involve them in experiences that enlarge their vision, and enlist them in translating new insights into action.[50]

A truly educational approach to ministry centers on persons and groups[51] and what happens in their understanding of self and world and God, rather than on mere transmission of facts. It requires not only knowledge but wisdom.[52] It asks not only what but why and how.[53] It eventuates in a comprehensive mode of ministering which interprets significant ideas and symbols and seeks to motivate action through preaching, courses of study, special events, conversation, prayer, and the deliberate sparking of creative interpersonal dynamics.

Teaching the Use of Scripture

An indispensible key to all the concerns here listed and to the need for spiritual maturity (discussed next in a separate section) is familiarity with the Bible, along with the ability to lead lay persons in responsible biblical study for the strengthening of faith, the sharpening of theological understanding, and the discovery of guidance for living. Here is a matter of crucial importance for Disciples of Chirst.

The dark side of the great advances in ministerial education in the past half century is the relative decline in knowledge of scripture and in the influence of the Bible on the life of the church. Much of that loss must be attributed to other causes—the waning of pietism and its devotional disciplines, so that many students come to seminary with no regular habits of reading the scriptures and only the vaguest familiarity with their contents;[54] and the heavy impact of secularism on the churches (the other side of the coin), so that few elders or teachers in the church school now have the ability of their predecessors to quote a passage pertinent to the point under discussion. The seminaries have made impressive strides in the teaching of theology and pastoral care and perhaps some other disciplines and in the sophistication of their biblical scholarship. But in finding their place within the total academic scene and accepting their new identity as theological schools rather than colleges of the Bible, the seminaries of the Disciples have unwittingly weakened the ministry at one point of peculiar vulnerability.[55]

The traditional declaration of Disciples, "no creed but Christ" continues to be sounded, but in the present situation it often indicates a void, whereas in earlier generations it pointed toward simplicity, freedom, and devotion to the person of Jesus Christ, while a constant preaching of the scripture, especially the New Testament, gave shape and substance to the faith. Without a warm and intelligent appropriation of the biblical witness, this non-creedal tradition has no other common source of guidance—no doctrinal confession, no official liturgy or book of common prayer, no teaching office with recognized authority, no authentic witness to Christian faith such as was once provided by the common pledge of adherence to the New Testament.

With no effective common guide, Disciples find themselves increasingly at loose ends, their laity confused, their ministers troubled over loss of identity, their seminarians subject to faddism. Unquestionably, Disciples have gained in theological maturity in the present century, and their ministry in intellectual sophistication. Some members respond eagerly to elective courses in theology and ethics, though frequently not knowing what to make of the contemporary thinkers. But popular ignorance of the Bible, not to mention the rudiments of biblical scholarship, causes some to use it unreasonably and others to reject it as unreasonable. More and more it is quoted in prooftexts rather than read for illumination.[56] Yet the Book continues to speak with power to ordinary folk when it is studied with theological responsibility.

It is time for the seminaries educating ministers for Disciples of Christ to reconsider their approach to biblical studies as well as minimal requirements in them. In five of the schools a student can graduate with no more than two courses in Old Testament and two in New Testament. (In the other two schools the student must complete three courses each.) With one of the two courses commonly an "introduction" and the other quite possible a thematic or historical study of limited scope, it is quite possible for a student to finish without intensive work in interpreting any major book of the Bible. Even at best, a course in one Gospel and one Epistle would meet the New Testament requirement. Eager for "relevant" electives, students tend to ignore biblical languages. Whatever justification seminaries in other traditions may have for such minimal demands in the study of scripture, the situation threatens the integrity of Disciples as a Christian community. Persons being educated for ministry in this tradition need a comprehensive command of the biblical material and the ability to use it responsibily in teaching and fiduciary witness. "The word of God alone makes theological education theological."[57]

Spiritual Discipline and Christian Maturity

A seminary curriculum fails if it does not enable a student to come "to know who one is as a minister."[58] While the matter has significant "scientific" and professional dimensions, its essence is not the information one has acquired, the functions one has learned to perform, the skills one has developed, but rather one's identity as a Christian and one's readiness to serve as a channel for the holy.

Spiritual integrity lies at the heart of authentic ministry; the responsible seminary simply cannot ignore its achievement and cultivation.[59] This is a central element in the school's fiduciary obligation. A minister looking back on his years at College of the Bible early in the century gave thanks for the "larger vision and deeper passion for suffering humanity" which came to him there.[60] Douglas V. Steere used to say that the world needs saints rather than a new theology, brilliant ministers, the union of all sects, a renewed religious movement or a revised program of evangelism.[61]

The Evident Need

Yet the need to be "taught of God" is a realm of learning commonly overlooked in seminary requirements, especially in schools which emphasize the scientific strand, or even the scientific and the professional, without comparable attention to the fiduciary. Still the people in the churches repeatedly express their concern for personal maturity, integrity of character, and authentic spirituality in their ministers.[62] How can the seminary contribute to the development of these qualities?

"Spiritual formation," the term often used for this process, is a monastic ideal, springing from the intention of life under the Rule and made possible by the vow of obedience taken by every monk in voluntary surrender of personal freedom for the sake of perfection. Protestant devotion to Christian liberty rebels at the concept; so do the convictions of religious liberals, who shudder at the thought of domination by one human being over another. Yet the phrase designates an essential element in the preparation of persons for ministry, even though serious attention to it in the seminaries may be honored more in the breach than in the observance.

The Problem of Responsibility

The problem arises in part from a lack of clarity as to where responsibility lies for the cultivation of the life of the spirit in candidates for the ministry. With the church? With the seminary? Elsewhere? Nowhere? Even though the answer "nowhere" seems best to describe actual practice, it must come as a surprise to many lay persons who tend to imagine involvement in prayer and Bible-reading as the major activity of students in seminary. Yet if an entering seminarian does not arrive with an authentic spirituality already growing, it is not likely to develop as a phase of fulfilling the requirements for graduation; these are almost exclusively academic in character, following a scientific or professional approach.

The growth of the life of the spirit in depth and power was once a product of the time spent within the seminary community, with its intense, intimate, and continuous contacts among students and professors. As previously noted, contemporary urban life has shattered that kind of community. For various reasons, most seminaries now conduct chapel once a week rather than daily, as was the custom some decades ago. There are few occasions of public prayer other than special ceremonial events. Prayer at the opening of class is rare, having been abandoned as a formality belonging to an earlier pietism. In one or two Disciples schools the president or the dean or the professor of worship functions as *de facto* chaplain, thus giving some direction and uniformity to the public worship, but if this person or any other serves as "spiritual director" to students it is more a matter of personal charisma than of official assignment.[63] It is not that seminaries are unconcerned about this need, but rather that their responsibility has been defined by tradition as primarily academic.

If a faculty should become concerned for spirituality, the problem of method would arise.[64] How can matters so interior and existential be made into requirements, academic or otherwise? How can spirituality be cultivated when community is shattered? Does not "formation" or "direction" smack of an authoritarianism alien to the Protestant principle, to liberalism to the scientific approach in education? Such questions point to formidable difficulties. Nevertheless, significant steps can be taken, some within the structure of the curriculum, some within other parts of the common life.

Introduction to the Spiritual Heritage

The content of the curriculum, even of required courses, can be expanded to include knowledge concerning the life of the spirit, without which there would be no theology nor religious institutions to study. Even the scholar exclusively committed to the scientific approach and acknowledging no obligation to professional or fiduciary concerns can see a responsibility to consider the phenomenon of faith in its varied expressions. Thus the curriculum can be strengthened by courses in the history of religions,[65] classics of religious autobiography and biography, liturgy, hymnody, mysticism, prayer and devotional practice, spiritual classics, history of preaching, history of religious art, and literature which grapples with issues of faith. The praxis ever implcit in theory can be made explicit, as we attempted in our chapter on a theology of ministry.

A biting cartoon has its character musing on the martyrs and the saints, "Just imagine what they could have accomplished had they gone to seminary!"[66] The irony suggests that courses in the standard curriculum—Bible, theology, church history, preaching, for example—often show no awareness of or concern for their spiritual dimensions, though these would seem to be inescapable. Since it is a mistake to separate mind from spirit, the study of a passage in Jeremiah or Luke, or atonement or the kingdom of God, of Gregory or Nyssa or Teresa of Avila, and certainly the writing of a sermon, should be more than a merely intellectual exercise.

The spiritual retreat, a major instrument in certain traditions, has been welcomed by Disciples students. (Most seminary retreats among Disciples have been "community events" focused on intellectual and professional concerns, or on a much-needed diversion from the academic grind, not on a spiritual quest.) In connection with a course on prayer and spirituality at Brite Divinity School, two retreats were scheduled, one under the direction of a Catholic retreat master, the other involving silence for private reading and meditation on scripture, along with significant acts such as giving blood and planting trees.[67] For some years the Commission on the Ministry for the Ohio Region has required all students under care to attend an annual retreat; part of its purpose has been orientation to the life and work of the church and maintaining ties between the students and the Commission, but spiritual growth has been a major concern. It is the proper business of both the church and the school.

A Full-Orbed Spirituality

In all their work in the seminary, students need to discover the difference between knowledge and wisdom, to seek openness of mind, humility of spirit, and a love for persons which will turn the very act of learning into a ministry and bring insights into realities they will proclaim across a lifetime. They need to come to an understanding of the mind of the apostle in celebrating our life in Christ Jesus, "whom God made our wisdom" (1 Cor. 1:30); Paul rejects all secular learning, especially rhetoric and philosophy, not as of no account, but as not offering salvation. The spirituality of the seminary, frightening though it may be to the scientific mind of the academician, is an existential involvement with the divine dimension of the studies. Otherwise the seminary dispenses

> Knowledge of words, and ignorance of the Word,
> and it will be true even there that
> All our knowledge brings us nearer to our ignorance,
> All our ignorance brings us nearer to death,
> But nearness to death no nearer to God.[68]

Neither scientific knowledge, even of theology or biblical texts, nor professional know-how can take the place of a living faith in Christ and a loving dependence on God. "We cannot expect experience to do the work of wisdom."[69]

The spirituality or wisdom being advocated is no pose of withdrawal from the world or condescension toward other persons, but a genuine relationship with God which controls all one's intentions, a spirituality integrated with the life of the mind, the intent of the will, the affections of the heart, and the use of one's bodily energies. An authentic Christian spirituality will manifest itself in openness to and loving concern for the persons one encounters in one's own experience and a commitment to the well-being of all people everywhere in justice and peace. Global awareness is a mark of Christian spirituality, including alertness to worldwide conditions, receptivity to the witness of the great world religions, special sensitivity to persons and movements from other cultures. The importance of ecumenical exchange becomes increasingly evident, especially bringing professors from abroad and developing programs for American students to study overseas, particularly in the Third World, thus reversing the prevailing imperialist model.[70]

Always there is need for honesty and realism. Spirituality turns false the moment it becomes a pose. Students need forthright instruction about the times of emptiness which have come to the greatest saints and to ordinary Christians. The essential element is commitment, not personal satisfaction even with so great a good as the Christian faith.[71] The seminary never wants one of its graduates to be in the position of the Greek herald pictured in a cartoon who arrives at the town square, surrounded by an eager crowd, only to say "I forgot the message."[72] Rather it should hope for graduates with the faithfulness and grace of a Latin American minister: after Emilo Castro was elected general secretary of the World Council of Churches, an old woman in a crowded church in Montevideo sought out a delegate to a forthcoming meeting to ask, "Please greet him for me. You know, he was my pastor. He introduced me to Jesus."[73]

The Seminary as Educating Community

Such spirituality is properly a corporate concern of the seminary. Even when Christians pray alone in joyful communion with God and in faithfulness to personal patterns of spiritual discipline, still they pray with the whole church for the whole of humanity.

Everything which contributes to the growth of Christian community among those associated with the seminary also makes for their spiritual growth. Facilities such as dormitories, apartments, refectory, gymnasium, and common room provide opportunities for casual contact and the means for strengthening the bonds of fellowship. A calendar of regular events—chapel, forums, music, drama, lectures, intramural athletics, organizations concerned with particular interests and causes, community meals—serves to build up the spirit of the place and to contribute to the spirituality of its members. Particularly important are special events conducted with flair and excitement, occasions making use of student experience, talent, and cultural diversity, and opportunities for informal meetings of students and professors (e.g., over lunch). Commonly berated as nonexistent during a student's days in school, the seminary's community life is later recalled as one of the most important elements in the graduate's seminary education.

As a more specific focus for the life of the spirit, worship celebrated according to the liturgies of various traditions broadens understanding and enlarges spiritual vision. It may also be instructive to Disciples students as they reflect that Lutherans and Episcopalians have done better in urban America than most mainline churches, have sustained a high level of ministerial morale, and have cultivated ties with the arts and with artists on the contemporary scene. Also important is the exploration of various traditions of spiritual discipline.

Life in community is the most powerful integrating force available to a school in its educational task. The Disciples Divinity House at the University of Chicago, for example, has long been noted for the intensive academic program offered its students by scholars engaged in scientific research, with little curricular attention to operational phases of ministry. Yet the House has an impressive record of preparing notable pastoral leaders. How is this fact to be explained? In discussing the question, a group of Disciples settled on a multi-faceted answer. Some of the factors are primarily academic: selective admissions (providing a pool of superior persons) and a demanding academic program. Perhaps equally important is the challenging intellectual and cultural environment of a university with a clear sense of vocation, a city with touches of greatness, and a Divinity School with unquestioned academic commitments.

No less significant have been the *esprit de corps*, so long characteristic of the House, the assignment of students to work as volunteers or interns with alumni engaged in active ministry, and especially the involvement of alumni in the activities of the House; these have included a weekly luncheon and evening discussion group, various lectureships sponsored by the House, the Divinity School, and the University, and an annual award to a distinguished alumnus. Also to be mentioned is the substantive character of the Divinity School journal, *Criterion,* which regularly publishes lectures by faculty members and visitors, and the traditional involvement of the Dean of the House, since its founding, at the cutting edge of Disciples life and thought.[75]

The point in exploring this example is to make clear that the program of a seminary is its total life as a community, not just what goes on in the classroom. Even when the academic curriculum is intensely scientific, the complete program of a school may have an impressive professional and fiduciary emphasis. The trick then is to involve students in that total program, not just the courses for which they register.

Chapter **8**

SEMINARY, CHURCH, AND MINISTERS IN PARTNERSHIP

Mission to the twenty-first century will demand the full dedication and enlightened insight of the church and of its ministers. Toward the shaping and conduct of that mission the seminaries bear an awesome responsibility. This chapter explores some possibilities for a highly intentional partnership with the church in their common mission.[1]

Concerns of the Partnership

Commitment to the education of a ministry prepared to serve the coming age will require careful attention by faculty, administration, and trustees to the impact of their decisions on the life and work of the church.

Faculty and Administration

In the selection of faculty, seminary professors naturally tend toward the mentality of the graduate school, this inclination increases with almost every addition of a young scholar to a teaching post. Any significant determination to make their first priority the preparation of ministers who will give authentic and effective witness in a new world, and to build faculty with that goal in mind, will require intensive internal dialog concerning this responsibility and a readiness to accept its implications—for academic policy, for the kind of awards and recognitions given to faculty, and for each professor's personal program of involvement, research, and writing.

It may be easier for faculties not offering the Ph.D. to accept such a priority and give it effect than for those with doctoral programs, for in making each new appointment the latter feel compelled to seek a scholar, i.e., a researcher dealing with narrow concerns rather than a teacher committed to a ministry for the future. While no seminary dare slack into an anti-intellectual stance or betray its responsibility for the scientific strand in education, it is bound to show equal concern for the professional and fiduciary strands and for the integration of these three elements in all that it does.

That primary commitment to ministerial education necessarily affects the formulation of qualifications for faculty members. Notices placed by search committees for seminaries seldom read differently from those placed by graduate schools except for the occasional reference to compatibility with a particular denominational tradition. Yet a seminary which takes seriously its partnership with the church will make all its concerns quite clear.

To honor its scientific obligations a seminary will rightly insist, with only the rarest exceptions, on a Ph.D. or Th.D. degree in the discipline to be taught or in one closely related, with a dissertation demonstrating superior intellectual gifts. It will want assurance that the candidate is abreast of new work in the field and participating in its scholarly society.

Ideally, a seminary will look for a candidate who also has the M.Div. or D. Min. degree, as evidence of a concern for ministry and general familiarity with the academic range of the curriculum. It will look especially for breadth of intellectual interest and learning based on a strong foundation of the liberal arts, for a mind that is active beyond the narrow bounds of one's specialization. To prepare students for ministry to the coming age a teacher requires the capacity to interpret movements, to make correlations, to help students see the relationship of technical knowledge to the needs of the world, the life of the church, and the work of ministry.[2]

Obligation to professional concerns impels a search committee to look for a candidate who not only holds a seminary degree, but who also has experience in the practice of ministry. Until midcentury most teachers in British and American theological schools came from the pastorate; their work had a "feel" for ministry now largely lacking. Going from graduate school directly into teaching and scholarly production may be the best route for upwardly mobile scholars in the university, but leaves something to be desired in seminary teachers. How can academicians prepare students for a profession of which they have no firsthand knowledge?

Concern for the fiduciary obligation appears even less frequently in the published notices, perhaps because it is difficult to formulate in acceptable academic jargon or to rate by objective criteria, perhaps because religious commitment is taken for granted. But such an assumption is not always valid. What should faculties seek in the realm of faith and commitment? Integrity of character, surely, including intellectual honesty. A respect for persons. An avowed Christian commitment and active involvement in the church. A theology not inconsistent with the mission of the school. The faculty must ask how its obligation to impart and strengthen Christian faith is enhanced or diminished by a contemplated appointment and make its decision accordingly.

The plea here is for each faculty to seek consensus on the importance of these considerations, scientific, professional, and fiduciary, and to state them openly and precisely when advertising for applicants.

A faculty will be the poorer if composed entirely of members of one denomination, and Disciples seminaries have expressed their ecumenical intention by appointing professors from various Christian traditions, including the Roman Catholic and the Orthodox. Some have also included a Jewish rabbi, and university divinity schools are likely to include Buddhists, Hindus, and members of other living faiths.

Other concerns may also weigh heavily in a particular appointment—consideration of gender, ethnic or cultural background, age—as faculties strive for representation and balance too long lacking. Matters of style and interpersonal relations cannot be ignored, nor can skill in teaching. Personal stability is important, for the tendency of academicians to want to be always on the cutting edge sometimes leads to faddishness; a minister who was in seminary in the late 1960s now feels that the faculty "caved in" at certain places to the detriment of their witness and the students' education.[3]

Qualifications for administrators include additional gifts beyond those indicated for faculty. While not every seminary president need be a research scholar, it requires great ego-strength and skill as a leader to preside over a company of Ph.D.s, especially if one does not have the degree. Commitment of both president and dean to the scientific, professional, and fiduciary obligations of the seminary is essential. In addition they must have gifts for maintaining *esprit de corps* by openness, honesty, consistency, mastery of the art of listening, and respect for differences; by providing abundant occasions for dialog and association; by a style of leadership that includes a quest for consensus; and by establishing sound and clearly-understood processes for internal communication and decision-making.

Seminary administrators hold posts of crucial importance not only to their schools but also to the intellectual and ecclesiastical life of the Christian Church (Disciples of Christ). Without a constitutional "teaching authority," Disciples once looked for religious and doctrinal leadership to their editors, pastors in their "great" pulpits, and heads of their colleges and seminaries. Now economic pressures have reduced their journalism to one major national publication, *The Disciple*, and for a time virtually eliminated the publication of books dealing with their intellectual tradition. Forces in society have reduced the stature of "big city" ministers. The "new breed of president" in the colleges and universities has been chosen for "technical and professional administrative skills" such as "capital development, financial management, technical administration, and institutional promotion" rather than religious leadership or theological expertise.[4] In a church whose regional ministers do not carry the historic teaching role of bishops, the most prominent figures left to serve as its theological mentors are the General Minister and President, the presidents of some general administrative units, and the seminary presidents and deans.

Thus the presidency or deanship of a Disciples seminary currently provides one of the key platforms for leadership in this church. Of its eleven moderators since Restructure, four have been theological educators. If seminary boards should follow the colleges in selecting promoters without theological concern, or should name presidents and deans who are not Disciples, the church would forfeit its first line of leadership to the bureaucrats, and Disciples with intellectual concerns would have a harder time finding a platform.

Not to be minimized are the motivation and spirit of non-faculty employees in positions of administration and service. Almost every one in ministry can look back to a business manager, a secretary for the director of field education or dean or president, a custodian, a cook, whose faithfulness, unfailing friendliness, and genuine concern for students are cherished in grateful memory. Careful selection of such persons on the basis of commitment to the goals of the school and devotion to persons as well as essential technical skills is an important factor in the welfare of the school. They too serve the partnership with the church.

Seminarians

The future of the Christian Church (Disciples of Christ) rests largely with its students, about 750 of them, now enrolled in seminary. With their academic work completed and a decade of experience in ministry, they will be coming into posts of responsible leadership at the dawn of the twenty-first century. More than 400 of them are studying in the four Disciples seminaries, another 120 in the divinity houses and seminary foundation; together these constitute nearly 70 percent of the total. The remaining 225 or so are in seminaries unaffiliated with the Disciples.[5] Partnership between the church and its schools requires common concern for the current crop of students and those who will come after them.

Such concern includes an active policy of holding the ministry as a significant vocational option before capable teenagers and young adults. The average age of Disciples students in seminary is 32;[6] for many, decision for the ministry has come after some working experience. The enlistment of qualified persons for ministry is a task of the church, not primarily of the seminaries. Disciples need some intentional modes as a denomination for seeking and attracting capable persons for this work.[7]

Undergraduate studies have much to do with preparing students for seminary, but at this point theological schools have lost ground in the past twenty-five years. It was once standard practice for them to require a strong college program in the liberal arts with work in literature, foreign language, history, philosophy, psychology, sociology, and science in order to gain admission. But the trend toward technical and vocational education brings increasing numbers of applicants who lack courses in some, even most, of these fields; many of them are mature, with families to support, having made a late decision for ministry. Reluctant to add to their difficulties (or lose them to another school) by assessing entrance deficiencies, most seminaries have settled for a bachelor's degree, whatever the major, insisting on no more than one or two stated undergraduate courses, as sufficient for admission.

The effect has been to weaken the "graduate" character of seminary work, since it is no longer possible to assume familiarity with Plato or Goethe or even Thomas Jefferson. A few years ago a student with a brilliant undergraduate transcript in engineering confessed to me his difficulty in doing the kind of thinking and reading taken for granted in seminary. He knew how to deal with formulas, but had no college work in literature, philosophy, or social theory. It is possible that the church will again come to prize the tradition of Christian humanism to the point of encouraging its youth to that kind of education that deals with meaning and value, and that out of such an emphasis will come a larger contingent of seminarians with a strong foundation for theological studies? In such a development both the churches and the seminaries have an interest.[8]

More important than specific courses and majors is the cultivation of a humane mind, responsiveness to the cultural heritage, capacity for critical thinking, commitment to the intellectual love of God, and readiness for lifelong adventure in learning. Greatly to be desired also is extensive work with a great college teacher, whatever the field. Some of the most fortunately prepared students still come to the seminary from the church-related liberal arts colleges. Congregations and regional church have reason to encourage their youth to attend one of these historic institutions of the Disciples. Church and theological school also have compelling reasons for upholding high standards for admission to seminary, including superior work and the completion of some courses in the various disciplines of the liberal arts.

Personal considerations are equally important: character, temperament, style in interpersonal relations, evident gifts for ministry. Of even greater concern is the quality of the applicant's Christian life and commitment. Is it vital and genuine or conventional and superficial? Seminaries normally ask the applicant to submit a personal statement concerning one's religious situation and desire to study for the ministry and to secure a letter of endorsement from an appropriate denominational official.

In view of the need for greater selectivity (see Chapter 6), it is important to the partnership that both church and school share responsibility for admissions (and rejections), especially since in some regions ordination follows almost automatically on graduation from seminary. When an applicant has been under care of a regional commission on the ministry, its approval normally indicates that some careful screening and counseling has already occurred.

Many students enroll in seminary, not as candidates for ministry but as seekers on a journey of faith. They want a chance to study Bible and theology in order to work through questions important to them and perhaps to explore the possibility of service in the ministry. Some of these persons leave seminary after a year or two, considering the time well spent and having found what they came for. Others finish a degree and apply for ordination. Both church and seminary have an interest in seeing that these latter persons have made a genuine decision, not just followed the line of least resistance.

The admission of qualified laypersons to seminary classes taken for personal enrichment has normally proved beneficial to all concerned. Various seminaries have also sponsored lay schools of theology, normally with shorter terms and less technical content than in seminary courses, but still with substance and a critical approach. Such schools conducted under congregational, district, or regional auspices seem to be on the increase, and frequently involve seminary professors in their programs. They heavy demands on professors' time and energy limit the number of such ventures in which the personnel of a seminary can be involved.

Vital to the partnership is the maintenance of ties with seminarians on the part of the church. For home congregations and pastors, as well as for the churches attended by the students while in school, it is important to show continuing concern. Lay persons who have taken courses in the seminary have a basis for relating to seminarians. Regional contacts occur chiefly through the commission on the ministry, in most cases through its routine formal processes, but these are quite important to the seminarian. Students under care have consistently spoken with high esteem of the retreats long conducted by the Ohio Commission. Also much appreciated are visits from regional ministers to the seminaries, keeping in touch with their students and conferring with those approaching ordination about finding a ministerial position. The concern of the general manifestation of the church is expressed in the program of the Pension Fund to pay the membership dues of theological students, the Seminarians Conference conducted by the Division of Higher Education with the cooperation of the other general units, the use of seminarians as ushers at the General Assembly, and the increasing practice of naming seminarians to the boards of administrative units or divisions of the church.

Links with Ministerial Practice

Every seminary has some faculty members closely attuned to the outlook of ministers in the parish and to the life of the congregation; these their graduates recall with special gratitude. Still the prestige and rewards in theological schools go to the scholars, too often aloof from church.[9] A pattern of acclaiming professors who contribute to the professional and fiduciary commitments of the seminaries, as well as to the scientific task, has yet to be established. At the least, the schools should expect a significant involvement of faculty and staff members in congregational life, alongside other Christians in worship, witness, and service. Seminary teachers need such "hands on" experience week by week in the church for the cultivation of their own Christian lives as well as a means of counteracting academic abstractions and the Ivory Tower syndrome. Students also need it. Many come to seminary with irregular habits of church attendance during college years, for various reasons, bad and not so bad. But now for the sake of their own discipleship and of integrating academics with real life, they need a regular involvement in church.

Equally crucial is the significant involvement of pastors, and regional, general, and ecumenical ministers in the educational process. In the effort of professional schools to incorporate current practitioners into their teaching force, schools of law and medicine seem to have done better than those of business and ministry, which still seek to dazzle their students with visiting academic stars, whether econometrists or theologians.[10] The real need is "the immersion of education-wise, experienced businessmen [and practicing pastors] in the very organization and operation of these schools."[11] "We need well-seasoned pastors and missionaries with about twenty-five years experience who would join seminary faculties, not simply as adjunct resource people but as respected mentors and models."[12]

Whether full-time or part-time, whether as adjunct professors or consultants or ministers-in-residence, whether taking sole responsibility for courses or joining with faculty scholars in team-teaching, such persons are needed as regular, continued, and honored members of the seminary community. For briefer appearances, persons engaged in ministerial practice are needed as preachers in chapel, lecturers, resource persons for particular class sessions, members of panels along with the scholars, and recipients of honorary degrees, citations, and alumni awards. The failure to use pastors in such ways and to hold them before the students as role-models demonstrates a greater interest in technical scholarship than in professional relevance. Nothing betrays the true agenda of the seminaries more quickly than the choice of celebrities to be invited to campus—not pastors, but scholars, bishops, and occasional bureaucrats.

The partnership between church and school is quite evident in field education, which involves the seminary, the student, the congregation, the supervisor (normally a pastor), and the regional church. In a generation the schools of the Disciples have come a long way from a primary concern for placement in "preaching points," income to keep students in school, and opportunity for practical experience, to a concept of field *education* which takes seriously the responsibility for supervision and the integration of professional experience with academic learning.[13] In evaluating their seminary education for this study, ministers overwhelmingly affirmed the need for field education as an introduction to the real world of ministry; some reported great help received from this work in seminary, others expressed disappointment over the inadequacy of the program.

Some congregations within range of a seminary have depended on student pastors for years and have contributed largely to the support of seminarians and the education of the ministry. The Christian Church (Disciples of Christ) acknowledges the contribution by presenting a "Certificate of Partnership" to each congregation which calls a student to serve as a minister-in-training. Representatives of the seminaries, regional staff, and commissions on the ministry share the partnership with congregational leaders through frequent conferences, visits to the field, and appropriate supervision, frequently given by a senior pastor nearby. From a too great reliance by many schools on student preaching as a source of income for seminarians the pendulum in ATS swung for a time to a doctrinaire abhorrence of any such distraction from academic duties until after graduation; in Disciples seminaries a balance seems now to have been reached, wtih attention to educational responsibility in the venture, though some students still are involved every week in excessive travel and diversion from their studies.

Many seminaries now require an intership, involving a period of a semester or more of full-time service on the staff of a church or other religious organization under the supervision of a carefully selected senior minister. The schools might well consider taking an additional leaf from medical education: the requirement of a period of "residency" after the award of the professional degree.[14] This would involve a planned program of observation, counsel, and review during a graduate's first pastorate or other assignment for an agreed two or three years after leaving seminary. The panel of counselors would include one or two carefully chosen persons from the congregation being served, from the regional staff or commission on the ministry, and from the seminary faculty. Such a program should facilitate the transition from classroom to effective practice of ministry.

Facilities, Budgets, and Financial Resources

Partnership between the church and its seminaries is quite apparent in the financial history and current income of the schools. In their early days of sacrifice and sometimes heroic struggle, most of them survived on offerings from the congregations, and most of the large donors who have underwritten buildings and endowment were Disciples. Major support now comes from the central budget of the church (see the following section), and the schools have joined the regional and general church in the major capital campaigns of the past two decades. Some of the seminaries have received impressive gifts from charitable foundations not related to the Disciples, but the bulk of their contributions comes from the churches and their members.

The four seminaries, two divinity houses, and the seminary foundation are well situated in impressive and serviceable buildings, constructed for the most part since World War II. Total value of land, buildings, equipment, and books (not counting the property of Phillips University used by the Graduate

Seminary) comes to $14,372,001. The seven ministerial institutions hold endowments totalling $51,414,376, and most of them enjoy a minimal level of financial security.[15]

Greatly increased scholarship funds will be required to release seminarians from monetary pressures in order to reap maximum intellectual and spiritual benefits from their studies. A major problem for students now entering seminary is educational indebtedness, oppressively increased by the time of graduation and ordination.[16] Given the low level or starting salaries, such burdens are more than the church should ask its future ministers to bear.

Equally grave is the low level of faculty salaries, which for Disciples schools runs $4000 per person less per year than the average for the accredited institutions in the Association of Theological Schools. It would require an additional $212,000 annually to bring Disciples faculty salaries up the the ATS average,[17] calling for an increase of 16.8 percent in denominational funding for the seminaries if all the gain were to be assigned to this one item. The partnership must continue to struggle with this discrepancy.

Ordination and Licensing

Even though early Disciples of Christ regarded ordination as the action of a congregation acting through its elders, the schools frequently took part. Ordinations at Bethany, for example, came at commencement time, and the most prominent bishops or elders in the laying on of hands were professors in the college. Through the decades the various colleges of the Bible and then the seminaries took initiative in planning and arrangements, with elders from congregations related to the ordinands coming to the campus or to a nearby church for a common service in which faculty members and other ministers took the lead. When ordination occurred in the candidate's home church or congregation served as student minister, graduation from seminary tended to make the examination by the elders or the ordination council largely *pro forma*; even if no official from the seminary participated in the service, it was the school which, in effect, made the decision to proceed, simply by granting a diploma, even though the faculty might argue internally that the conferral of a degree was purely an academic matter and that determining fitness for ministry belonged elsewhere. Persons familiar with the actual dynamics of the situation expressed increasing uneasiness.

With Restructure Disciples clearly affirmed ordination as a concern of the church in all its manifestations, and the partnership between church and seminary has become ever clearer. General provisions for the Order of Ministry are set forth in The Design for the Christian Church (Disciples of Christ), and policies and procedures for the church are adopted by the General Assembly. Through its commission on the ministry, the regional church is involved in counsel and care during the applicant's time of deciding and studying for the ministry, the examination, and the authorization for ordination. The sponsoring congregation expresses its reponsibility by recommending the candidate to the commission and by hosting the ceremony; other congregations related to the ordinand commonly join in the sponsorship. The seminary nearly always participates through its examination and recommendation of the student to the commission, often through membership on the commission, and usually through the participation of one or more professors, officers, and students in the ceremony. The partnership is clearly visible.

Two comments need to be made. For the ordinand the ceremony is the culmination of a long process of preparation and struggle, an occasion of high joy. Nearly always the ordinand requests the participation of certain persons who have been most influential in the pilgrimage—a former pastor, a campus minister, a chaplain, a college teacher, a seminary professor or dean or president, a fellow student. The array of mentors and colleagues witnesses to the partnership between church and school and would do so even more impressively if a few moments were taken to explain to the people the reasons these participants have been chosen.

A word of caution. The service is an action of the church acting through the commission and ought to be clearly under its control or that of someone it designates, perhaps the host pastor. An unfortunate development is a tendency for the ordinand to take over the planning as impressario, latching on to the first big chance to put on a special ecclesiatical event, and the service often becomes unbearably long, while the printed program centers on the person rather than on the church. Clearly the ordinand should contribute to the planning, especially in suggesting participants, but just as clearly the ordinand is the recipient, not the producer of the occasion; it should proceed within guidelines established by the commission. Nor should it ever be forgotten that the intention is ecumenical, not denominational, to provide a minister for the whole church of God.[18]

In licensing, the partnership of the seminaries is not so clear. They have been wary of, even downright opposed to, offering courses to prepare candidates for license. The Department of Ministry also declined to develop a program, leaving the matter to the regions. While regional commissions on the ministry examine candidates and authorize the issuance of licenses, no person or group has worked out a standard program of study.

Questions abound. Should such programs be offered by the seminaries? By the colleges? By both? How can candidates, most of whom have full-time jobs, reasonably schedule such courses? In evening classes? On a concentrated weekend schedule? What about access to a library? Should the courses be at the same level as the standard seminary program? (After all, are not most candidates for licensing college graduates?) How much less work than that required for the Master of Divinity is sufficient for a licensed minister? Are courses in a lay school of theology adequate? (Surely some additions would be necessary, such as the various "arts of ministry.") Have the seminaries the resources and the proper location for such programs? Do they need to put more effort into extension programs for this purpose?[18] Is the demand sufficient to justify the use of heavily burdened personnel in the seminaries?

Some breakthrough is needed if a ministry is to be prepared for the smaller churches having insufficient resources to support a seminary graduate in full-time ministry. Reading programs offered in the past to help candidates qualify for licensing are dreary and inadequate. If the church is to continue to recognize the office of licensed minister, as evidently it must for the foreseeable future, the seminaries have an obligation at the very least to give counsel on the development of a workable program of preparation. That would seem to be a minimal obligation of the partnership.

Sustaining a Vital Ministry

After ordination comes a lifetime of ministry, and while the joys may be great, the burdens are often heavy and the problems overwhelming.[20] One of the most crucial problems before the church is that of sustaining its ministry in good health, high morale, and ability to serve creatively through the decades. The partnership of the seminaries is of crucial importance.

A review of the ecclesiastical dynamics of ministry is needed, as noted in Chapter 4, to assess the effect of the uncoordinated accumulations of pressures and program demands from congregation, district, region, and various general units, not forgetting ecumenical and community service organizations which, if not formally ecclesiastical, nevertheless rely on ministerial leadership. Factor in the denominational mode of awarding "Brownie points" or recognitions that play a part in advancing a minister's career, and you have a "system" guaranteed to produce frustration and tension. It would be a revealing project for some minister to keep tabs on denominational meetings, reports, correspondence, mailings, and special events for six months, recording the denomination's picture of its ministers in terms of the expectations it imposes.

Vocational frustration or fulfilment makes up a large component of ministerial morale. "Burnout" is a recent expression for ministerial fatigue[21]— or for the self-pity which, ironically, too often seems endemic in a profession noted at its best for high morale that glories in suffering for the cause. Doubtless we too easily fall victim to the success syndrome of our secular society, resenting the religious celebrities seen on television, whose glamour accentuates by contrast our own feeling of getting nowhere. Clearly the church needs to formulate criteria of success consonant with Christian faith and to give these force in its life by using them as the basis for commendation and recognition. If the essence of the ministerial task is preaching the Word, ministering the sacraments, and caring for the church (recall Chapter 4), and if one does that to the best of one's ability, is not one's ministry a success? The seminaries could lead the partnership in formulating and interpreting among Disciples authentic Christian criteria of significant ministry.

The deployment of ministers is a key problem in morale.[22] Probably most ministers feel themselves qualified for more rewarding posts than those they presently hold, and since most of them serve in small, even marginal, churches, they often feel forgotten by their leaders and ministers in the most desired positions. Particularly when one wants to leave one's present situation or perhaps is forced to resign does this issue assume overriding urgency. Yet with decision-making in such matters left to congregations, Disciples have no ministerial placement system, as has been said, but only a process. Problems of location or relocation are especially acute for women and minorities. The seminaries can help the church to a clearer understanding of its obligations to the ministry and can sustain ministers themselves with a sense of the dignity of their service.

The current popularity of terms like "support systems" and "networking" indicates awareness of personal vulnerability and the need for affirmation and help from one's peers.[23] While churches and the helping professions have responded by providing such services for ministers who need them, they have tended to deal more with the hurts than with their causes—the massive array of social and ecclesiastical trends discussed in our opening chapters. In partnership with the churches, it befits the seminaries to devise programs for relieving the pain but also for dealing constructively with the unprecedented problems of the emerging world and the archaic expectations so often imposed on ministers. Attention to a few basic matters will also help.

Finances constitute a continuing trouble spot. Even though average annual compensation for Disciples ministers in 1985 was $20,979 ($24,666 when students, part-time, and bivocational ministers are omitted), more than 600 ministers received less than $12,000 for their services while barely 400 received more than $30,000.[24] When compared with starting salaries for engineers just out of college, not to mention professional athletes unable to earn a degree, these figures could well dissuade all but the most dedicated from entering the ministry, and they do discourage some of the church's most faithful servants and their families. Basic income is an essential consideration regarding ministry, especially in new situations with inadequate institutional strength. Is the establishment of endowments for the support of ministers in creative missions, rather than of particular congregations, a possible answer to the problem?[25]

An important element in ministerial morale is personal support from the regional staff. Pastors commonly express a desire for a personal relationship with the regional minister, involving some attention to one's current problems. ("No business treats its retail outlets and managers like the Church.")[26] While the office of regional minister is still being defined in practice, it sometimes seems in the danger of corruption after the demonic models of denominations with a managerial episcopate. Yet the honored tradition of Disciples regional ministers and state secretaries who truly were pastors to their congregations and ministers is still remembered, and conscientious successors try to follow it insofar as their workloads permit. The seminaries can throw their considerable influence behind every effort to establish the truly pastoral nature of oversight (episcope) as Disciples develop the concept and exercise of regional ministry.

The most crucial single element in the ministerial support system is the minister's family. The loyalty of devoted spouse, children, and "in-laws" to one's ministry, even at considerable personal sacrifice, has kept many a minister on track. Yet important as such support is, it must not be forgotten that these people need encouragement and support themselves.[27]

We come then to the need for a ministering church. Congregation, region, and general units each carry responsibility in support of individual ministers and of the ministerial corps. The General Minister and President is pastor to the whole church and particularly to its ministers. The Pension Fund serves in large areas of need in addition to income for retirees. The Division of Homeland Ministries through its Department of Ministry operates the central clearing house for placement and deals with general concerns. The General Board's Task Force on the Ministry takes up issues both of theology and practice.

Regional commissions on the ministry establish personal ties with each minister as a basis for the granting of standing. Most regions also contract for professional counseling programs for ministers who request them. Seminary staff and faculty members render their primary service in the education of ministers, but continue to serve as role models, counselors, and friends through the years of service. The support of Christian colleagues, ministerial and lay, is often a source of strength and encouragement. Even so, there are critical gaps in the safety net, and church and seminary as partners in mission to the coming age must continue to give concerted attention to the needs and to ways of meeting them.

The discipline of the ministry is a concern also requiring attention. For this task the Christian Church (Disciples of Christ) relies on a periodic review of standing by the regional commissions. While most professions by definition attend to the discipline of their own members, Disciples treat this as an ecclesiastical concern. The seminaries might stimulate some further thought on the issue.

Continuing Education

For the sustaining of a vital ministry no element is more important than lifelong growth in mind and spirit as the minister gains new knowledge and understanding through continuing education—"the only kind of education there is."[28] In partnership with the church the seminaries have a major responsibility at this point.

An ongoing program of personal study is basic to a minister's staying alive intellectually, yet many seminary graduates seem to lack motivation or ability to develop programs of continued growth, especially to maintain patterns of systematic reading and self-generated inquiry without the crutch of courses and assignments. This weakness is evident with respect to regular programs of meditation and prayer, as of signficant study on a variety of topics.

Why should it be necessary to enroll in more courses in order to keep on learning? Ten years out of seminary, too many ministers seem no more in touch with new developments in Christian thought than are licensed ministers who have completed only a minimal course of readings. A casual glance about many a minister's office—it used to be called a study—discloses a meager personal library in a deplorable state of obsolescence. Money is not the key problem, but rather a lack of intellectual curiosity or personal discipline. The director of a public library once spoke to me of her readiness to order new books when requested (most titles not on the shelves are now available through interlibrary loan) and registered her disappointment that so few ministers ever used the library. Interest in further learning seems to center on operational skills, chiefly counseling or dealing with particular problems of church or community, but to show little concern for staying abreast of biblical studies or theology, even less for enlarging one's grasp of history, history of religions, and the place of religion in a changing society.

We may properly ask: Are the seminaries themselves at fault here? Have they nourished, or at least failed to uproot, the passivity syndrome in the educational process? Has their emphasis on meeting requirements failed to awaken intellectual curiousity and creativity? What changes are called for now?

All kinds of organized programs of continuing education are available: religious book clubs, cassette series, subscriptions to journals: (*The Christian Century*, a major news magazine, *Mid-Stream*, theological quarterlies), classes offered by seminaries and colleges, annual lectureships (the Lyman Beecher Lectures at Yale, the Earl Lectures at Pacific School of Religion, the Oreon E. Scott Lectures at various Disciples schools, other named lectureships throughout the country), special institutes and seminars sponsored by various schools and organizations,[29] local lectionary groups and other study groups, advanced degree programs and other opportunities offered by seminaries, universities, or local colleges, traveling seminars with academic credit, the Academy of Parish Clergy, particular projects calendared for personal study. With discipline any minister can take a concern, study it indepth, and bring the matter to clusure in a period of six months or so.[30]

The issue is not lack of opportunity, but expectation on the part of the church and motivation on the part of the minister. The seminaries can use their influence with congregations and church organizations to interpret the need for continued intellectual growth and to establish study leaves in every minister's contract. And if their graduates are truly to serve the coming age, the schools will renew their efforts to awaken in their students a lifelong hunger to learn.

Covenant and Conference

The structure of the Christian Church (Disciples of Christ) provides an essential instrument of partnership in its general Division of Higher Education and, more specifically, in that Division's Council on Theological Education.

The Mission of the Division of Higher Education

For the seminaries the Division serves as their link with the general structure of the church. It also brings them into continuing relationship with the colleges and the campus ministries, establishes a means for cooperation among the seminaries with regular consultation regarding their mission, and provides counsel to seminary heads, trustees, and faculties. It interprets developments in the field of higher education generally to the member institutions and to the church. With support from two foundations, the Division commissioned the sesquicentennial study of higher education among Disciples, in three volumes, of which this book is one.

As a general administrative unit of the church the Division has attained significant stature in its common life. Prior to 1978 the old Board of Higher Education was an assocation for voluntary cooperation, consultation, and interpretation established by the member institutions, each of which made its own appeal to the churches for funds. By contrast DHE is not a board of institutions set up by them as a lobbyist for their common interests, but a division of the church. Its status affirms the conviction of the church that higher education is integral and essential to its life and mission. The Division brings the church and the seminaries into a relationship of mutual responsibility. The church's contribution to the funding of the related institutions now comes from the general budget of the denomination and is administered according to a formula adopted by the Division of Higher Education. Each school governs its internal affairs through its board of trustees and faculty, in accordance with its charter. It maintains its relationship with the Christian Church (Disciples of Christ) through the Division of Higher Education.

The Division is governed by a board of 24 members, nominated by its nominating committee, and elected by the General Assembly for terms of three years. Fifteen of the directors are members-at-large, not employed by any related institution, and three are nominated from each of the three councils, composed respectively of representatives of the related seminaries, colleges, and campus ministries. The Council on Theological Education is made up of two representatives from each of the four related seminaries, one representative from each divinity house and seminary foundation, two regional ministers, two ministers serving congregations, two educators in pre-theological work, two lay persons, two seminarians, the executive of the Department of Ministry, the chairperson of the General Board's Task Force on Ministry, and the Deputy General Minister and President who carries responsibility for policy with respect to ministry.[31]

Each institution which wishes to affirm its affiliation with the church through the Division enters into a covenant by action of its governing board and of the region(s) to which it is related. Each such region agrees to promote the school, to cooperate where feasible in field education, to provide counsel through its regional minister, and to conduct the work of its commission on the ministry in close concert with the seminary. The school agrees to serve as a resource center to the region, especially in implementing the priorities of the church, to serve as a center of continuing education for the region, to make its personnel available for service on the regional board or in other capacities, and to operate in close concert with the commission on the ministry.[32]

The Council on Theological Education continually re-evaluates the mutual responsibility of church and seminary in the education of the ministry and provides regular opportunity for conference and planning. The responsibility of the seminaries to come to terms with current trends in society and to prepare ministers for the future, the theme of this book, is a crucial concern of the Division. The Division also performs certain specific functions for the schools which require mention.

Conducting Theological Dialog

The Division fulfills a unique role in the church by sponsoring, in addition to interest groups and workshops at General Assemblies, a number of signficant programs which provide opportunity for theological dialog and give attention to many of the concerns addressed in this book.

The Seminarians Conference. A high point in any Disciple's education for ministry is the conference for seminarians sponsored biennially by the Division. Sessions held in both St. Louis and Indianapolis include visits to the offices of major administrative units of the church, presentations from various representatives concerning the general work of the denomination and the way it functions, occasions for asking questions, and opportunity for personal interviews. A Disciples leader or scholar may present a lecture on a substantive topic of current importance, and some interpretation is given concerning various types of ministry today.

The conference provides an intense experience of fellowship among seminarians, personal engagement with church leaders, and reflection about church and ministry in a highly stimulating context. A large and enthusiastic group of seminarians, commonly numbering around one hundred, comes from the seven related institutions and the many other seminaries across the land where at least a few Disciples are enrolled. Begun in 1955 as the Middlers Conference, the event was proposed by the Board of Higher Education's Commission on Seminaries after hearing a report of a visit to Indianapolis and Lexington by students of the Disciples Divinity House in Chicago.[33] The Conference has proved helpful to each new contingent of seminarians, though experience suggested the wisdom of holding it for students early in their middler or senior year, when existential interests begin to focus sharply on the life of the church and the realities of ministry.

Association of Disciples for Theological Discussion (ADTD). Feeling the need for an annual gathering of Disciples scholars to engage in serious dialog, Walter W. Sikes of Christian Theological Seminary and Royal J. Humbert of Eureka College called together a group of persons in 1957, who formed ADTD. Limited to thirty members in order to allow all members to participate in the dialog, the association received a small annual subsidy which, along with the sizeable annual dues paid by the members, covered the expense of meetings and travel. The Division of Higher Education now underwrites this annual subvention.

ADTD presents an opportunity for continuing dialog among a number of the church's intellectual leaders, though as the number of doctorates held by faculty members has increased, membership has become almost exclusively professorial. Discussions deal both with general themes and with topics of particular relevance to Disciples. In the 1960s the association sponsored the development of a number of books for Bethany Press (now CBP Press). Since the Division of Higher Education became a partner in the enterprise, ADTD has given special attention in its programming to issues before the church. Most of the papers have been published in *Encounter*.

The Disciples Theological Digest. As a futher instrument of dialog the Division of Higher Education has launched the publication of an annual review of scholarship in religion on the part of Disciples. The format includes a major substantive article on this intellectual tradition, biographical sketches with bibliographies for selected scholars, and abstracts of recent books and articles written by Disciples.[34]

Thus the Division fulfills an important function in the church's life by promoting through conference and publication signficant theological discussion among seminarians and on the part of mature scholars.

Church Funding for Theological Education

The Christian Church (Disciples of Christ) operates with approved askings for general outreach, established each year by the Commision on Finance; the Church Finance Council distributes the funds on the basis of actual income from the churches. The general budget includes an item for each major administrative unit and related organization, including of course the

Division of Higher Education. In addition, the Commission establishes for each year two allocations for higher education, one for the fifteen colleges and universities, another for the seven seminaries. For 1987 the allocation for the seminaries totals $1,251,540, which is 9.46730 percent of the church's budget for general outreach; for all institutions of higher education, not including the Division itself, this comes to 18.67040 percent of the total and is a declining percentage.

In 1985 the Disciples allocation for theological education considered as a proportion of the denominational budget, looked puny when compared to that assigned to its six seminaries by the Southern Baptist Convention, namely 20.5 percent. On a percentage basis, however, Disciples surpassed other mainline denominations: Presbyterians (5.3 percent), and American Baptists (3.5 percent). United Methodists assign to their thirteen seminaries 2 percent of *congregational* budgets, and Episcopalians do likewise with 1 percent for their ten seminaries. As for dollars generated for their seminaries, Southern Baptist lead with $24,166,757 from the denominational budget, followed by Methodists with $13,552,500, Episcopalians with $2,404,256, Presbyterians with $2,119,840, and American Baptists with $1,219,342.[35]

From the funds allocated to seminaries the Church Finance Council makes distributions among the seven institutions on the basis of a formula developed by the Division of Higher Education in consultation with the seven seminary executives. Before Restructure each school presented its case to the old Commission on Brotherhood Finance, and the transition to the new procedure has involved the institutions in some uneasiness. The original formula for distribution among the schools, developed in 1978 by a task force of the General Board, first relied on their "historic base," i.e., their previous allocations, which varied widely among the seminaries, reflecting more intense cultivation of the churches in some areas than in others in the days before Unified Promotion. This imbalance was gradually redressed by factoring in as a larger consideration each year the number of Disciples students enrolled in each school. The forumla was altered again in 1985.

Forty percent of the total sum available from the Church Finance Council is now distributed among the theological schools, the four seminaries receiving equal shares while smaller set portions go to the divinity houses and seminary foundation. The remaining 60 percent is distributed on the basis of total instructional hours offered through each institution; instructional hours taken by Disciples and students from the United Church of Christ are fully counted, those taken by students from other denominations are factored in on a basis of two-thirds. In addition, an emergency fund is held in reserve.

The intentions in moving to the current forumula are commendable: providing for the size of the instructional burden and "market viability," for the preparation of many kinds of ministers, for the education of both laity and ministry, and for the ecumenical component of Disciples mission.[36]

Any tinkering with the forumla immediately raises issues which the tinkerer may not have forseen. Naturally any given institution will favor giving a larger weight to factors which would increase its income and will resist those considerations which might decrease it. The following questions, however, merit consideration.

Is the heavily quantitative emphasis, i.e., distribution on the basis of instructional hours, justified? We have earlier advanced the argument that in preparing a ministry for the future, quality is a much more crucial issue than quantity. How can schools be encouraged to upgrade their student bodies by greater selectivity in admissions if that decision will cost them money, at least in the short run, not only in loss of tuition but in decreased support from the church? Professors sometimes give voice to the suspicion that admissions policies have grown more lax as a result of denominational formulas which count raw numbers without discrimination as to capacity or promise for the future. How can schools which tighten standards be rewarded rather than penalized?

Is the offering of courses, whether for future ministers or for lay leaders, the only function by which the service of the various schools to the church may be measured? The answer may well be that few objective standards are as easy to reduce to statistics as total instructional hours, that other modes of assessing a school's value to the church are too largely subjective. But might it not be possible for the Division to devise ways of giving weight to some other pressing concerns, to which this book calls attention? Its program of grants to particular colleges to underwrite research pertaining to the work of the church or other special services deemed of particular importance might be extended to the seminaries; or awards might be made for such work already done. This book takes up nearly every chapter areas of need in which the church and ministry should be able to look to the seminaries for help. How can the Division encourage the schools to give it? Funding may not be the best way, but "money talks."

A Channel for the Church's Concern

As a major administrative unit of the church, the Division of Higher Education is responsible for holding before the related institutions the express concerns of the denomination. While all the schools are aware, for example, of the mission priorities adopted by the General Assembly, the Council on Theological Education regularly reviews these, discusses specific ways in which the schools may address them, and asks for reports of their efforts to deal with the priorities.

Persons outside the seminaries often express a sense of need or their frustrations over the failings of a particular minister by anguished cries for the seminaries to offer, even to require, a course in the area of the perceived deficiency—decorum in the chancel, handling personal finances, the mechanics of baptizing by immersion, managing conflict, conducting an every-member canvass, dealing with one or more of the church's mission priorities. In 1983 the General Assembly passed a resolution (8316) calling on every seminary to institute required instruction in evangelism. Since it is the prerogative of faculty to establish curriculum, it would constitute a series infringement on academic freedom for the General Assembly to make any serious attempt to dictate that responsibility. Yet Disciples need a channel, individually and collectively, for referring their concerns to the seminaries. Sometimes they can talk with a president, dean, professor, or trustee. But the Council on Theological Education is a proper and expeditious channel for such matters. Issues placed on its agenda are likely to receive systematic and responsible attention.

The Division has given careful attention to particular research and reflection needed by the church. When the question of ordination for homosexuals was causing great concern in the General Assembly, the Division asked the Association of Disciples for Theological Discussion to address the issue, and its 1978 meeting dealt entirely with it; ADTD also gave over its 1984 meeting to a consideration of Disciples theology, and both sets of papers were subsequently published.[37] The Division looks to ADTD for scholarly work on concerns of the church and has drawn on help from its members in the preparation of "The Disciples Theological Digest."

The Division serves both as a point of reference and as an initiator in expressing the church's concerns regarding theological education in general and, more particularly, regarding the education of its ministry. That responsibility looms large as the church gives increasing thought to the twenty-first century.

The Mission of the Division of Higher Education to the Coming Age

Nothing will be more crucial in the work of the Council on Theological Education than to follow through on the issues raised in this study. The task is so great as to demand common study and reflection on the part of seminaries and knowledgeable people in the church. How can this best be accomplished?

The Council itself may well be the appropriate instrument. With analytical papers as a basis for discussion, perhaps some of them written by persons co-opted from outside its regular membership, it could seek a common mind on the task of the seminaries and especially on any new directions they might be asked to take. Alternatively, it might recommend to the Division the establishment of a panel for the Review of Ministerial Education in the Christian Church (Disciples of Christ), on the model of the Panel of Scholars. Such a step might call for involving other units of the church especially concerned with the theme in the sponsorship of the panel, particularly the Department of Ministry, the Council of Regional Ministers and Moderators, perhaps the Pension Fund. It should presuppose the full cooperation of the seminaries in its investigations and their sincere response to the recommendations growing out of the study. Membership in the panel should include selected seminary professors and administrators, regional and general ministers, pastors, undergraduate professors, and lay persons.

In being asked to formulate recommendations the council or the panel would go beyond the function of the Panel of Scholars, which produced and published papers for study but issued no corporate proposals. This review, by contrast, would be expected to issue in recommendations to be acted on by the Division and the General Assembly, and then referred to the seminaries. Care would need to be taken not to overstep the prerogatives of the schools, their boards, and faculties in the formulation of curriculum, but the review would offer on behalf of the church a perception of the most pressing needs and would call on the seminaries for help.

A seemingly small matter which may have larger import is a reconsideration of the name of the Council. Throughout this study it has been shown that the term "theological education," by begging the question of proper preparation for ministry, may be part of the problem. It has come to designate the traditional program in the "theological schools," a pattern which Disciples seminaries intentionally adopted in giving up their former designation as colleges of the Bible; yet it seems weighted toward a scholastic approach to a body of knowledge rather than toward the mission of the church to the future. Would not a name such as Council on Education for Ministry demonstrate far more clearly the rightful purpose of the seminaries?

The Division might well consider taking initiative on a program of education for licensed ministers, although any such step should properly await the outcome of the proposed review. While neither the seminaries nor the Department of Ministry have been inclined to develop such a program, the needs of the small churches are quite real, and some responsible party needs to address them. What kind of curriculum is both needed and feasible? Where and by whom would the essential courses be taught? How would the venture be financed? How would it be related to existing institutions? Is a reading course still an appropriate instrument? How does such a program qualify as higher education?

Drawing on its considerable success with the Seminarians Conference, the Division might consider sponsoring on that model a gathering for licensed ministers and candidates, perhaps as a one-time event, perhaps as a quadrennial. It might also recommend to the Department of Ministry a joint workshop for licensed ministers and candidates at the General Assembly.

No task for the future can be more important for the Division than helping the seminaries to become in far greater actuality than heretofore intellectual and spiritual centers for the life of the Christian Church. That aspect of their destiny will be the theme of the closing section in this study. It should be a major concern of the Council.

In addressing its ongoing mission and special responsibilities toward the coming age, the Division must realistically consider its need for staff. If it may be assumed that present personnel is sufficient for tasks currently being carried, it is hardly realistic to ask them to add the administrative burden of the proposed review and its interpretation to the church and to the seminaries or of a possible program for the preparation of licensed ministers. For the period of review at least the Division would need the services of an additional vice president and appropriate support staff. Unlike the president, who has responsibility for the entire program of the Division and needs not be a theologian, this vice president would need to be a seminary graduate, preferably with experience on a seminary faculty or staff, well acquainted with the life of the church and the realities of ministry, and alert to developments in the contemporary world. Any such addition to staff would of course require additional or special funding.

At the Center of a Church for the Coming Age

In the "New World Acomin'" the church of the future will necessarily be engaged with a multitude of complex issues raised throughout the study. The world that was will not return, and the church that was will not be able to serve the world tomorrow. Old-timers in the West speak of the "buffalo syndrome," the fantasy said to have caused the Indians to wait idly for the return of the buffalo rather than address their hard new conditions without the source of their former prosperity.[39] In a church still nostalgic for the lost glory of Christendom, or at least of a "Christian America," an essential part of the seminary's task is to free the mind of the church from the buffalo syndrome and turn it toward God's new day.

If government and major corporations have need of "think tanks" to examine their course with hard criticism and to propose creative options, so has the church. Naturally it will look to its seminaries, which H. Richard Niebuhr called the "intellectual center of the Church's life."[39] It has every right to turn to them for gudiance as they discharge their scientific, professional, and fiduciary obligations toward ministry for the future.

The Theological Center

Serious reflection about God's coming age and the church's witness to divine intention for our present and our future belongs high on the agenda. In the generation since Niebuhr put forth his remarkably attractive ideal of the theological school as intellectual center the dynamic of scholarship in religion has profoundly changed. The phenomenal growth of departments of religion in American colleges and universities has arguably made them the center of research and interpretation in the field.[40] On the current academic scene the independent seminaries now function less prominently as major centers of religious thought and research.

But "intellectual center" was only part of Niebuhr's slogan: it was completed by the phrase, "of the Church's life," and when that qualifier is added the formula fittingly describes the vocation of the seminaries. For the scientific investigation of religion conducted in the universities is not intentionally related to the work of the church. But in the seminaries the scientific work of biblical, theological, and historical study is committed both to scholarship and to relevance. Their reflection on the Christian tradition and the church's engagement with the mind of the coming age has a more direct involvement with the mission than does that in the department of religion.

The central object of theological inquiry, God (especially God's intention for humankind), is in the university one of many ideas in the cultural heritage to be impartially investigated, but in the seminary it is the controlling commitment of the academic community and of the church which sustains it. The seminary can tolerate no less intellectual rigor than the university, nor can it duck any of the hard questions that the university raises, but it can never be satisfied with detached theorizing.

As the church approaches the twenty-first century it needs more than ever before centers of intellectual vitality addressing the questions which are central to its witness in that new age. In an earlier chapter we noted the aloofness of contemporary intellectuals and opinion-makers from vital Christian thought, indeed their ignorance of it and their genteel hostility toward religion, which they seem to know about only in bizarre and authoritarian expressions. By contrast with the nineteenth-century intellectuals whose inability to believe the ancestoral faith was accompanied by great saddness, today's unbelievers seem to feel little sense of loss. But neither then nor now have they received much help from the church and its theologians.[41] No greater challenge confronts the seminaries than enabling tomorrow's ministry to participate vigorously in the struggle for the mind of a new generation, an enterprise in which the schools themselves must lead.[42]

The Missional Center

A major distinction between the seminaries and the university departments of religion is the seminaries' commitment to professional education. Their task is the preparation of ministers. They carry the responsibility for addressing the hard questions of mission, for helping the churches understand the radically changed context in which God now calls them to witness, for devising and refining techniques and procedures both faithful to the gospel and effective in the new situation.

Increasingly ministers and churches have been turning to organizations and leaders that have carefully studied the current situation and offer workable modes for dealing with them. These include the Glenmary Research Center, the Alban Institute, the Institute for Church Growth, Yokefellow House, the

208   THE EDUCATION OF MINISTERS FOR THE COMING AGE

Institute for Biblical Literacy, and the National Evangelistic Association, as well as individual entrepreneurs. It may be asked why so much of this work, which is at the cutting edge of research into professional problems, has taken its rise outside the seminaries and, with one or two exceptions, has no institutional connection with them. It is eagerly sought by pastors and lay leaders in congregations, and some of it is of unimpeachable quality, but ministers have to stumble on to it after seminary or outside seminary. In the teaching of preaching and of pastoral counseling most of the seminaries perform their missional task at a high level, and here and there one does notable work in worship or Christian education or church administration. But the institutes mentioned and others like them have rushed into a void which the seminaries should never have permitted to exist.

An impressionistic judgment suggests that a number of these programs propose short-term solutions to keenly felt needs, without addressing those larger trends overwhelming the church which we described in our opening chapters, and that they give more attention to matters of immediate institutional survival than to those of long-term mission. Those judgments are offered, not to discount the importance of the service being rendered, but to suggest priorities for the attention of seminary faculties. Throughout this study we have repeatedly affirmed the obligation of the theological schools to give special attention to congregational needs and problems and to ways of working effectively with ordinary groups of ordinary persons. These are essential items for their agenda.[43]

The seminaries also bear responsibility toward the ecumenical church. They are called to keep faith with the vision of the total Christian community in its wholeness, with students of various denominations and with the churches from which they come, with the schools' constituency beyond the Disciples, with all victims of human alienation and religious discord.

Toward the life of their own denomination the seminaries now carry almost alone, except for the Disciples of Christ Historical Society, the responsibility of continuous critical examination of its tradition and the development of proposals for reform. The health of any denomination constantly requires this kind of serious intellectual engagement and critique; otherwise it deteriorates into a mere sociological entity, an engine of production. It dare not allow its tradition to degenerate into a collection of slogans or a mere bundle of liturgical habits.

Can the seminaries help the churches to recover a sense of the rightful intellectual dimensions of their ministers' work? We have noted the decline of ministerial leadership in the general world of thought and the activistic preoccupation with management which denominations and congregations instill. Can such expectations be modified? In programs for the D.Min. degree, men and women, released briefly from pastoral demands, have demonstrated a level of intellectual performance beyond anything they have previously done. Will they ever reach it again? The church can ill afford another half century of loading down its ministers with busy-work which prevents them from signficant participation in the struggle for the mind of a new generation. This is no plea for preaching abstractions and irrelevancies which are "over the heads" of the congregations, but rather for the kind of exciting leadership in church and community by which a coach sometimes inspires a team to play "over their heads." The seminaries will make a signficant contribution to mission in the twenty-first century if they can help the church reform its ministry in such a manner.

The Spiritual Center

The scientific and professional obligations of the seminaries make fairly obvious their rightful role as theological and missional centers for the church. But is the seminary a spiritual center? Is such a role demanded by its fiduciary responsibility? And if so, is it in keeping with its purpose as a school? If readers review the questions so frequently posed thoughout this study, they will note that many of them point to the responsibility of the schools in this very area.[44]

The spiritual emphasis being called for here is holistically and religiously understood, as distinguished from the merely intellectual (theological) or the merely psychological. This is no vacuous or sentimental privatism, no outward pose of traditional religiosity, but rather a vital, joyful, loving, responsible relationship of Christians with God and with every human being, indeed, with every creature that shares life on this earth. This is the spirituality of the Yahwist, who discerned the purpose of God in creation and world history; of the Psalmists, whose communion with God caught up into sublime poetry all the concerns of their personal lives and national crises; of the prophets, whose vision of God led them to cry for justice and to suffer in the failings of their people; of the priests, who transmuted the ideals of the prophets into operable principles of law and themes of liturgy; of the sages, whose reverence flowered into wisdom; of Jesus, for whom prayer was discerning the will of God and yielding fully to it. This is a spirituality which integrates mind and soul, hand and heart, in self-giving service, which knows no area of life not open to the intention of God.

Where is the spiritual center in the contemporary church? That question finds no obvious answer. In the ancient church it was clearly "the sacramental person," the bishop presiding as head of the family of faith gathered about the holy table. In the medieval church it was the monastery or the convent where seekers after perfection lived quietly under the Rule, keeping the hours of prayer each day and night and offering intercessions for the church and the world. In Puritan New England it was the minister's study, where the local divine gave himself over to prayer and the spirituality of vigorous thought on the issues of sin and salvation. (Alexander Campbell also spent long hours in his study.) In Pietism it was the University of Halle, where great teachers imbued their students with the ideal of a practical spirituality in place of a polemical dogmatics and with the passion that pioneered the Protestant missionary movement.

It should be clear that the church which is called to serve the coming age also has need for places of concentrated attention to the gospel in relation to the needs of the emerging world, to the reality of God and to communion with God, to divine judgment, the standard by which everything earthly is measured, to the power of God to transform persons and society, to the empowerment of the church, the revival of religious zeal, the renewal of culture in truth, beauty, and goodness, to the nature of God's Coming Age. Granted, every communion table in every congregation, every pulpit, every minister's study, should be such a place.

But where in the contemporary church does this spiritual concern, so central to its existence and calling, come to focus? Not in its regional or general structures; such a responsibility is not even envisioned in their self-definitions or charters, though hinted at in the old charters of The United Christian Missionary Society and the Council on Christian Unity. It surely is not now seen as the function of the church college, though it was actualized at one time in some of them, e.g., Hiram College in the days of E.V. Zollars or the School of the Evangelists in the time of Ashley S. Johnson. Half a century ago G. Edwin Osborn shared with his students his vision for Phillips University, especially its College of he Bible, as the center of a great spiritual revival. (Does any theological school of the Disciples today hold such a notion of its calling?)

Again the question must be asked: Is it appropriate to think of the seminaries as such places in the life of the Disciples? Is such a vision compatible with their educational mission and academic commitments? Do faculties, students, trustees, and constituencies see such a responsibility as pertaining to their mission? While many in the theological schools would have to confess considerable personal discomfort at such a line of questioning, the fact is that not a few alumni look back on their seminary days as a crucial time of spiritual development and on the faculty or at least one or two professors as their spiritual mentors. Yet such a function appears to be incidental, even accidental, in the seminary's self-understanding. Are we justified in letting it remain so?

The responsibility of serving as spiritual center is not likely to be assigned to the seminaries or any other agency by the General Assembly, and if the schools acting on their own should see and accept it as part of their task, they cannot delegate it or pass it off to a committee. Rather the community, and especially the faculty, must voluntarily assume it, in humility and without piosity, in faithfulness to the admonition, "Sound no trumpet before you." The purpose will then require implementation in the routine patterns of the

SEMINARY, CHURCH, AND MINISTRY IN PARTNERSHIP

common life, perhaps in daily intercessions, perhaps in projects of public service which move outside the cloister. Without a commitment to its vocation as a spiritual center of the church's life the work of any seminary is incomplete, no matter how brilliant its faculty, how dazzling its scholarship, how relevant its program.

The seminary's ultimate obligation is to all the people of the Coming Age as they are addressed by the One who spoke through the prophet: "Not by might, nor by power, but by my Spirit, says the Lord of hosts" (Zech. 4:6).

Notes

Foreword

1. Thomas J. Liggett, "The Return of the God-Fearers: The Real Challenge in Evangelism," *Impact: Disciples on the Pacific Slope*, 11 (1983), pp. 48, 50-52.

Chapter 1: The World Rushing Toward Us

1. On the advent of futurology, consult Herman Kahn and Anthony J. Wiener, *The Year 2000: A Framework for Speculation on the Next 33 Years*, Macmillian, 1967. On the new industry see Robert B. Tucker, "Trend-Watchers," *United*, 29, 10: pp. 35-39. 118-124.
2. Review of Marvin Cetron and Thomas O'Toole, *Encounters with the Future: A Forecast of Life in the 21st Century*, McGraw-Hill, 1984 in *The Christian Century*, Feb. 15, 1984, p. 180. On the limitations see Mary Douglas and Steven Tipton, eds., *Religion and America: Spiritual Life in a Secular Age*, introd. by Robert A. Bellah, Beacon Press, 1983, pp. 25, 150, 277. cf. Joseph J. Corn and Brian Horrigan, *Yesterday's Tomorrows: Past Visions of the American Future*, Summit Books, 1984.
3. The best know recent example of extrapolating from present developments is John Naisbitt, *Megatrends: Ten New Directions Transforming Our Lives*, Warner Books, 1982. More profound is Daniel Yankelovich, *New Rules: Searching for Self-fulfillment in a World Turned Upside Down*, Random House, 1981. The most celebrated work of imagination in this vein is George Orwell, *1984*, Harcourt, Brace, Javanovich, 1949, thoroughly analyzed in scores of popular and scholarly journals as its titular year rolled around. As an example of projecting greater significance for a current trend than actually proves out in the future, consider McLoughlin's reading of the counterculture in the 1960s and early 1970s as a new and different religious revival destined to effect a profound renewal of modern society in the manner of earlier religious revivals; William G. McLoughlin, "Revivals, Awakenings, and Reform: An Essay on Religion and Social Change in America," *Chicago History of American Religion*, ed. Martin E. Marty, University of Chicago Press, 1978.
4. Ann McFeatters, *Indianpolis Star*, "At halfway point, '80s look more like past than 'experts' predicted," Trends, January 6, 1986, pp. 1, 3.
5. John Greenwald, "The Forecasters Flunk," reported by Frederick Ungeheuer, *Time*, Aug. 27, 1984, pp. 42-44; Alfred Zanker, "When Economic Forecasters Miss the Target," *U.S. News & World Report*, Nov. 12, 1984.
6. e.g. Daniel Bell, *The Coming of Postindustrial Society*, Basic Books, 1973; Robert Jungk, *Tomorrow Is Already Here*, trans. by Marguerite Aldman, Simon and Schuster, 1954; Herman Kahn and Anthony J. Wiener, *The Year 2000: A Framework for Speculation on the Next 33 Years*, The Macmillan Company, 1967; Foreign Policy Association, *Toward the Year 2018*, Cowles Education Corporation, 1968; Christopher Lasch, *The Culture of Narcissim: American Life in an Age of Diminishing Expectations*, Warner Books, 1979; Alvin Toffler, *The Third Wave*, William Morrow and Company, Inc., 1980; Naisbitt, *Megatrends*, Lesslie Newbigin, *The Other Side of 1984: Questions for the Churches*, Geneva: World Council of Churches, 1984.
7. "The Next Step: 25 Discoveries That Could Change our Lives," *Science* November, 1985, pp. 6, 9, a special issue. Arthur C. Clarke, *Profiles of the Future: An Inquiry to the Limits of the Possible*, Holt, Rinehart and Winston, 1982.
8. "Sliding toward Oblivion," *Newsweek*, July 23, 1984; "Financial Facts at the Fingertips," *U.S. News & World Report*, Sept. 18, 1986, pp. 53-54.
9. Douglas and Tipton, *Religion and America*, p. 19; "Wizards of Marketing," *Newsweek*, July 22, 1985, pp. 42-44; "Computers Make the Sale," *Newsweek*, Sept. 23, 1985, p. 46.
10. "Computers' Next Frontiers," *U.S. News & World Report*, Aug. 26, 1985, pp. 38-41; "A Threat to the Darkroom," *Time*, June 30, 1986, p. 67; "Solving the Chinese Puzzle," *Newsweek*, Aug. 18, 1986, p. 43.

11. See Parker Rossman, *Computers: Bridges to the Future*, Judson, 1986; William R. Johnson, *The Pastor and the Personal Computer: Information Management for Ministers*, Abingdon Press, 1986; Russell H. Dilday, Jr., *Personal Computer: A New Tool for Ministers*, Broadman Press, 1986; Philip Siddons, "The Church in the Digital Age," *The Christian Century*, April 16, 1986, pp. 380-81; "Computers, ethnicity, issues in education," *The Disciple*, June, 1985, p. 31.
12. Bernard Quinn, Herman Anderson, Martin Bradley, Paul Goetting, and Peggy Shriver, *Major Denominational Families by Counties of the United States*, Glenmary Research Center, 1980. See also Peter Halvorson and William Newman, *Atlas of Religious Change in America, 1952-1971*, Glenmary Research Center, 1971; *Nelson's Complete Concordance of the Revised Standard Version of the Bible*, compiled under the supervision of John W. Ellison, Thomas Nelson & Sons, 1957.
13. Michael VerMeulen, "Urban Flight: How three professionals joined the movement back to rural America, but kept their big-city careers," *TWA Ambassador*, May 1984, pp. 45-54; Craig Calhoun, "Computer Technology, Large Scale Social Integration and the Local Community," *Urban Affairs Quarterly*, (forthcoming).
114. "An Electronic Assault on Privacy?" *Time*, May 19, 1986, p. 104.
15. See Sherry Turkle, *The Second Self: Computers and the Human Spirit*, Simon and Schuster, 1984; Craig Brod, *Technostress: The Human Cost of the Computer Revolution*, Addison-Wesley, 1984; Naisbitt, *Megatrends*, chp. 2, "Forced Technology—High Tech/High Touch," Craig Calhoun, "The Microcompter Revolution? Technical Possibilities and Social Choices," *Sociological Methods and Research*, 9, 4, 1981, pp. 397-437; Andrew Nagorski and Russell Watson, "Moscow Faces the New Age: A closed society meets the information revolution," *Newsweek*, Aug. 18, 1986, pp. 20-22.
16. "The Video Revolution," *Newsweek*, Aug. 6, 1984, pp. 50-57; Harry F. Waters, "The Age of Video," *Newsweek*, Dec. 30, 1985, pp. 44-53.
17. A similar dynamic operated both in Europe with its established churches and in the United States with its denominations (and civil religion). Parents belonging to the radical sects took pains to instill in the young a sense of distance from the dominant culture, but often, except for certain points of emphatic distinctiveness (e.g. pacifism), the strain was not severe.
18. Neil Postman, *The Disappearance of Childhood*, The Delacorte Press, 1982; cf. Postman, *Amusing Ourselves to Death: Public Discourse in the Age of Show Business*, Viking, 1986; cf. "A Conversation with Neil Postman: 'TV Has Culture by the Throat,'" *U.S. News & World Report*, Dec. 23, 1985, pp. 58-59.
19. "The Stars of the Bottom Line," *Newsweek*, Aug. 26, 1985, pp. 42-43; "Heroes Are Back," *U.S. News & World Report*, April 22, 1985, pp. 44ff; Ralph Schoenstein, "The Modern Mount Rushmore," *Newsweek*, Aug. 6, 1984, p. 9.
20. J. Irwin Miller, *More Than Words Alone: The Hugh Th. Miller Lectures*, Christian Theological Seminary, Indianapolis, Ind., 1983, p. 40; "Targeting the Tiny Tots," *Newsweek*, April 14, 1986, p. 45.
21. William F. Fore, "Media Violence: Hazardous to Our Health," *The Christian Century*, Sept. 25, 1985, pp. 834-836; James M. Wall, "Out-of-Control Media Hear Harsh Criticism, " *The Christian Century*, Oct. 9, 1985, pp. 883-883; "Machine Gun USA, " *Newsweek*, Oct. 14, 1985, pp. 46-51.
22. "Big Media, Big Money," *Newsweek*, April 1, 1985, pp. 52-54.
23. "The people involved... aren't concerned about the political or social connotations," Alvin P. Sanoff, "What is Hollywood Saying to Us?" *U.S. News & World Report*, June 30, 1986, pp. 54-55.
24. "Media Elites Studied," *The Christian Century*, March 17, 1982, p. 296; John Dart, "Poll Cites Secular Orientation of TV Elite," *Los Angeles Times*, Feb. 19, 1983; cf. Kenneth Slack, "An Edinburgh Diary," *The Christian Century*, July 3-10, 1985, p. 636.
25. "Atomic Power's New Woe: How to Bury Old Plants," *U.S. News & World Report*, Nov. 12, 1984, p. 81.
26. Peter S. Prescott, "What Did You Do in the War?" *Newsweek*, Oct. 15, 1984, p. 98.
27. *Seeking God's Peace in a Nuclear Age: A Call to Disciples of Christ*, CBP Press, 1985.
28. Joseph M. Horodyski, "Space Odysseys on Tight Budgets," *Newsweek*, Sept. 24, 1984, p. 14; Robert A. Thomas, "What About Sin?" Sermon for Aug. 4, 1968, University Christian

214 THE EDUCATION OF MINISTERS FOR THE COMING AGE

Church, Seattle, Wash., p. 3
29. "Executives Who Look Beyond the Bottom Line," *U.S. News & World Report*, Oct. 22, 1984, pp. 61-62.
30. Randolph E. Schmid, "U.S. population growth seen coming to halt," *The Oregonian*, Portland, June 21, 1984; Harry F. Rosenthal, "Little to cheer about found in world outlook," *The Oregonian*, Portland, Dec. 26, 1984; "World energy outlook: Chevron forecasts supply and demand to the year 2000," *Chevron World*, Summer 1985, pp. 6-8.
31. e.g., Business Item 8314, "Report and Recomendations of the Task Force on Christian Life Style and Ecology," and Business Item 8315, "Resolution Concerning an Ecologically Responsible Christian Life Style," San Antonio General Assembly, 1983; see *Yearbook and Directory*, 1984, of the Christian Church (Disciples of Christ), Indianapolis, General Office, pp. 224-228.
32. *U/S: A Statistical Portrait of the American People*, Andrew Hacker, ed., Penguin Books, 1983, pp. 29-33; "Snapshot of a Changing America," *Time*, Sept. 2, 1985, pp. 16-18; "10 Forces Reshaping America," *U.S. News & World Report*, March 19, 1984, pp. 40-52; "Next: Young vs. Old?" *U.S. News & World Report*, Nov. 5, 1984.
33. "10 Forces," p. 48; "Asians: To America with Skills," *Time*, Special Issue on Immigrants, July 8, 1985.
34. Hacker, *Statistical Portrait*, pp. 144-154.
35. *Ibid.*, pp. 123-125.
36. Reported by Wayne Bell at Council on Theological Education, October, 1984.
37. James Bryse, *The American Commonwealth*, 2nd rev. ed., Macmillan and Co., 1891, pp. II, 584.
38. See Report of the North American Consultation on the Future of Ministry: "Ministry in an Age of Ambiguity," Toronto, Canada, Oct. 7-10, 1980, New York, Professional Church Leadership, National Council of Churches of Christ in the U. S. A.; cf. Robert J. Samuelson, "Global Matchmaking," *Newsweek*, Jan. 14, 1985, p. 63; "10 Forces," p. 48.
39. Investment banker Felix Rohatyn, quoted in "A Business Boom Defies Its Doubters," *Newsweek*, April 30, 1984, p. 64; cf. "Honoring the Auto's Past," *Newsweek*, Sept. 3, 1984, p. 9; "The Blue-Collar Blues," *Newsweek*, June 4, 1984, pp. 52-55; "Detroit's Torn Lifeline," *Newsweek*, Sept. 3, 1984, pp. 59-60; "Low-tech: Where the jobs will be," UPI, *St. Louis Globe-Democrat*, May 23, 1984.
40. Robert J. Samuelson, "We're Not a National Laundermat," *Newsweek*, July 9, 1984, p. 61.
41. Hacker, *Statistical Portrait*, pp. 122, 137, 152-53; "10 Forces," p. 47.
42. E. W. Linder, "Child Carelessness: Sexual Abuse in Day Care," *The Christian Century*, March 13, 1985, pp. 270-272.
43. Hacker, *Statistical Portrait*, pp. 143-144; "The Rich Get Richer," *St. Louis Post-Dispatch*, Oct. 7, 1984, p. 2B; "Poverty: The War Isn't Over," *Newsweek*, Sept. 9, 1985, p. 24.
44. "Americans—$6 Trillion in Debt and Sinking Deeper," *U.S. News & World Report*, May 21, 1984, pp. 84-85; "The Year of the Yuppie," *Newsweek*, Dec. 31, 1984, pp. 4-31; "Here Come the Baby-Boomers," *U.S. News & World Report*, Nov. 5, 1984, pp. 68-73; "The New-Collar Class," *U.S. News & World Report*, Sept. 16, 1985, pp. 59-65; Robert J. Samuelson, "The Best and the Brightest," *Newsweek*, May 26, 1986, pp. 44-46; "Golden Paintbrushes: Artists are developing a fine eye for the bottom line," *Newsweek*, Oct. 16, 1984, pp. 82-83.
45. "Revolution on a desktop," *Time*, June 30, 1986, p. 63; Michael Rogers, "The PC Printing Press," *Newsweek*, July 14, 1986, pp. 50-51.
46. "10 Forces," force 8.
47. T.J. Peters and R. H. Waterman, Jr., *In Search of Excellence: Lessons from America's Best-Run Companies*, p. 49.
48. Senator J. W. Fulbright quoted by Robert A. Thomas, "What About Sin," Sermon for Aug. 4, 1968, University Christian Church, Seattle, Wash., p. 3.
49. "As Cluster Suicides' Take Toll of Teen-Agers," *U.S. News & World Report*, Nov. 12, 1984, pp. 49-50; Barbard Vobejda, "Study Shows Many Teens Alienated," *The Oregonian*, Portland, Nov. 2, 1985; David Gelman, /Treating Teens in Trouble," *Newsweek*, Jan. 28, 1986, pp. 52-54; Kathleen Housley, "Churches Respond to Teen Suicide," *The Christian Century*, April 30, 1986, pp. 438-439.
50. See, e.g., Colin Wilbur Williams, *Where in the World? Changing Forms of the Church's*

Witness, Distributed by National Council of the Churches of Christ in the U.S.A., 1963; Williams, *What in the World?*, Office of Publication and Distribution, National Council of Churches of Christ in the U.S.A., 1964; *The Congregation in Mission*, Abingdon, 1964; cf. Richard H. Drummond, "Prolegomena to a Theology of the Christian World Mission," *Encounter*, 28, 2, Spring, 1967, pp. 2, 99-129; A. M. Pennybacker, "Congregation and Mission," *Encounter*, 28, 2, Spring, 1967, pp. 130-150.
51. I am indebted to President Herman Blake of Tougaloo College for this thought.
52. For the necessary struggle of the church against its present acculturation see Jan G. Linn, *Christians Must Choose: The Lure of Culture and the Command of Christ*, CBP Press, 1985.
53. Douglas and Tipton, *Religion and America*, p. 9.
54. *Ibid.*, pp. 5, 11-13.
55. Kenneth Slack, a quote by David Smith, "An Edinburgh Diary," *The Christian Century*, July 3-10, 1985, p. 636.
56. Douglas and Tipton, *Religion and America*, pp. 4, 6.
57. *Ibid.*, p. 20.
58. Miller, *More Than Words Alone*, p. 45.
59. Clark Williamson, "The Death of God: A Survey," *Encounter*, 27, 4, Autumn, 1966, pp. 283-296.
60. Gabriel Vahanian popularized Nietzsche's phrase about the death of God in the early 1960s, not to advocate a naturalistic secularity as a "theological" position but to depict the emptiness of life without God as set forth in contemporary literature. See Vahanian, *The Death of God: The Culture of Our Post-Christian Era*, Braziller, 1961.
61. F. Thomas Trotter, "Imagination and History," *Impact*, 11, (1983), p. 15.
62. Ronald E. Osborn, "Divinity's Need of the Humanities," *Impact*, 14, (1985), pp. 24-36; D. Duane Cummins, Address to the Council of College and Universities, Aug. 2, 1985.
63. See Jaime M. O'Neill, "No Allusions in the Classroom," *Newsweek*, Sept. 23, 1985, p. 14.
64. Hacker, *Statistical Portrait*, pp. 251; cf. 242-243.
65. Andrew Hacker, "The Decline of Higher Learning," *New York Review of Books*, Feb. 13, 1986, pp. 35-42; cf. Robert J. Samuelson, "Back-to-School Economics," *Newsweek*, Sept. 23, 1985, p. 23.
66. Larry J. Crockett, "My Buttoned-Down Students," *Newsweek*, Oct. 22, 1984, pp. 20-21. For recommendations, see Howard R. Bowen, *The State of the Nation and the Agenda for Higher Education*, Jossey-Bass Publishers, 1982.
67. Douglas and Tipton, *Religion and America*, p. 17.
68. *Ibid.*, pp. 7, 209.
69. *Ibid.*, pp. 4, 6, 7.
70. cf. Robert N. Bellah, Richard Madsen, William M. Sullivan, Ann Swidler, Steven M. Tipton, *Habits of the Heart: Individualism and Commitment in American Life*, University of California Press, 1985, in passim; cf. Douglas and Tipton, *Religion and America*, pp. 120, 132, 142.
71. See especially Albert C. Outler, *Psychotherapy and the Christian Message*, Harper, 1954; Don S. Browning, *Atonement and Psychotherapy*, Westminister, 1966.
72. For an address to the issue by sociologists rather than theologians, see Bellah et. al, *Habits of the Heart*. cf. Philip Rieff, *The Triumph of the Therapeutic*, Harper and Row, 1966.
73. Douglas and Tipton, *Religion and America*, pp. 20-21.
74. Recall Jewish reflection on a "History too brutal to admit a caring divinity." Douglas and Tipton, *Religion and America*, pp. 271-272.
75. For "postcountercultural" values and confusion, see Douglas and Tipton, *Religion and America*, pp. xii, 246.
76. For disenchantment, *Ibid.*, pp. xii, 218.
77. Jay R. Calhoun, observation to the author, Aug. 1, 1985; cf. "The Talk of the Town," *The New Yorker*, Sept. 23, 1985, p. 27.
78. The term is Ernest Campbell's, quoted by Elias S. Hardy in Robert T. Newbold, Jr., *Black Preaching: Select Sermons in the Presbyterian Tradition*, The Geneva Press, 1977, p. 127.
79. 1 Cor. 2:6; Moffatt.
80. Douglas and Tipton, *Religion and America*, p. 193.

Chapter 2: The Church in the World That Was

1. For a crucial distinction ("Tradition is the living faith of the dead, traditionalism is the dead faith of the living") see Jaroslav Pelikan, *The Vindication of Tradition*, Yale University Press, 1984, p. 65; quoted in Bellah et. al., *Habits of the Heart*, p. 140. cf. Jay C. Rochelle, "Pentecost as Memory, Pentecost as Hope," *The Christian Century*, May 22, 1985, pp. 534-535; for heritage and identity, see Douglas and Tipton, *Religion and America*, p. 268; for Rabbi Abraham J. Heschel's reflections on memory and faith see Perry LeFevre, *Understandings of Prayer*, Westminister, 1981, pp. 174-176.
2. On Christian freedom from the past, see Lactantius, *The Divine Institutes*, II, 7 (Fathers of the Church 49, 121); on the danger of nostalgia as thinking of oneself in the past, not the present, see Douglas and Tipton, *Religion and America*, pp. 223-224.
3. The phrase comes from Suzanne Langer.
4. Christopher Dawson, *Religion and Culture*, London, Sheed and Ward, 1948, pp. 1, 81-84. For a vivid account of the visions of one such shaman, see John G. Neihardt (Flaming Rainbow), *Black Elk Speaks: Being the Life Story of a Holy Man of the Oglala Sioux*, University of Nebraska Press, 1961.
5. Will Durant, *The Story of Civilization, I. Our Oriental Heritage*, Simon and Schuster, 1942, chps. II-VI.
6. See Northrop Frye, *Anatomy of Criticism: Four Essays*, Princeton University Press, 1957; Mircea Eliade, *Shamanism: Archaic Techniques of Ecstasy*, trans. Willard R. Trask, rev. and enl. Bollingen Foundation; distributed by Pantheon Books, 1964; Eliade, *Patterns in Comparative Religion*, trans. Rosemary Sheed, World, 1958.
7. Douglas and Tipton, *Religion and America*, pp. 208-209, 268.
8. Levine, "William Shakespeare and the American People," *American Historical Review*, Vol. 89, p. 48.
9. Hacker, *Statistical Portrait*, pp. 1-32, 24.
10. *A History of the Ecumenical Movement, 1517-1948*, Ruth Rouse and Stephen C. Neill, Westminster Press, 1954, pp. 594-595.
11. Hacker, *Statistical Portrait*, p. 27.
12. For a careful and not unhopeful analysis of this trend, see William R. Hutchison, "Past Imperfect: History and Prospect for Liberalism," *The Christian Century*, Jan. 1-8, 1986, pp. 11-15 and Jan. 15, 1986, pp. 42-46.
13. For a systematic overview see Eric G. Jay, *The Church: Its Changing Image through Twenty Centuries*, John Knox Press, 1977; Jaroslav Pelikan, *Jesus through the Centuries*, Yale University Press, 1985. For the apostolic age see Paul S. Minear, *Images of the Church in the New Testament*, The Westminster Press, 1960.
14. Hans Kueng, "A Christian Scholar's Dialogue with Muslims," *The Christian Century*, Oct. 9, 1985, pp. 890-894.
15. For a discussion of important topics related to this issue, see Clark M. Williamson, *Has God Rejected His People? Anti-Judaism in the Christian Church*, Abingdon, 1982.
16. See Ray C. Petry, *Christian Eschatology and Social Thought: A Historical Essay on the Social Implications of Some Selected Aspects in Christian Eschatology to A.D. 1500*, Abingdon, 1956.
17. See Royal Humbert, ed., *A Compend of Alexander Campbell's Theology*, with commentary in the form of critical and historical footnotes, The Bethany Press, 1961, pp. 265-269; cf. Vachel Lindsay, *Collected Poems*, rev. ed., Macmillan, 1946, "Alexander Campbell," pp. 352-358.
18. Matt. 7:13-14; 11:16-19; 13:1-7.
19. Matt. 6:1-18; 23:1-39.
20. Luke 13:31-32; 22:25; John 19:10-11.
21. Luke 19:41-44; Mark 13:1-37.
22. John 4:19-24.
23. See H. Richard Niebuhr, *Christ and Culture*, Harper, 1951.
24. See "The Church as Mother of Learning," in Quirinus Breen, *Christianity and Humanism: Studies in the History of Ideas*, ed. Nelson Peter Ross, Eerdmans, 1968.
25. Douglas and Tipton, *Religion and America*, p. 113.
26. *Ibid.* p. 210.

27. For treatment of this development, see the following section, "The Churches in the USA."
28. Douglas and Tipton, *Religion and America*, pp. 112, 209, 277; cf. 221ff, 276ff.
29. Vahanian, *The Death of God*, pp. 1-60, in passim.
30. See T. S. Eliot, *Idea of a Christian Society*, London, Faber and Faber, 1939; Miller, *More Than Words Alone*, pp. 1-30; John B. Cobb, Jr., *Christ in a Pluralistic Age*, Westminster, 1975.
31. See Rosemary Radford Ruether, "Catholics and Abortion: Authority vs. Dissent," *The Christian Century*, Oct. 3, 1985, pp. 859-862.
32. See Ronald E. Osborn, *Experiment in Liberty: The Ideal of Freedom in the Experience of the Disciples of Christ*, The Forrest F. Reed Lectures for 1976, The Bethany Press, 1978, chp. 3.
33. See *Theological Education*, 19, 3 (Spring 1983) for a special issue devoted to the problem of authority. cf. William Baird, *What is our Authority? Study Series #2*, Council on Christian Unity, 1983.
34. In suggestive essays in *The Lively Experiment* and *The Nation with the Soul of a Church*, Mead argues that the denomination is essentially an instrument of mission.
35. Observation by Art Morgan, May 25, 1984.
36. The flurry of excitement which attended the discussion of this theme a decade ago has subsided, skeptics deeming the purported "religion" a figment of imagination since it has no fullblown ecclesiastical structure, and theologians dismissing it as a form of pious jingoism. cf. Robert N. Bellah, *The Broken Covenant: American Civil Religion in a Time of Trial*, Seabury Press, 1975; Ronald E. Osborn, "Perils for Christianity or Opportunity for Ecumenism? A Consideration of American Civil Religion," *Encounter*, 37, 3 (Summer, 1976), pp. 245-258.
37. Lawrence Kilman, "Poll finds many oppose church-state separation," *The Oregonian*, Portland, Oct. 14, 1985, p. A10.
38. George Lyman Locke, "For Our Country," *The Book of Common Prayer*, 1928, p. 36; cf. Massey Hamilton Shepherd, Jr., *The Oxford American Prayer Book Commentary*, Oxford University Press, 1950.
39. Ronald E. Osborn, "Religious Freedom and the Form of the Church: An Assessment of the Denomination in America," *Lexington Theological Quarterly*, 9:3 (1976), pp. 85-106; Douglas and Tipton, *Religion and America*, pp. xi, 211, 219-221.
40. Sidney Mead has also dealt with this alliance.
41. Recall chp. 1.
42. "Religion will become increasingly treated as a consumer item," Ted Peters, "The Future of Religion in a Post-Industrial Society," *The Cutting Edge*, 11, 2, (March-April, 1982), p. 2. "The church [has become] a supermarket dispensing spiritual junk food to passers-by," Jon Johnston, quoted by Bruce Buursma, "Scholars forecast difficult era for Christianity in America," *The Oregonian*, Portland, Feb. 15, 1986, p. D5.
43. Edwin Scott Gaustad, *Historical Atlas of Religion in America*, Harper & Row, 1962, p. 158.
44. *Religion in America 1984*, The Princeton Religion Research Center, Inc.; cf. *Religion in America, 1982*.
45. Douglas and Tipton, *Religion and America*, pp. 274-275; cf. H. Richard Niebuhr, *The Social Sources of Denominationalism*, Meridian Books, 1957.
46. Edwin Scott Gaustad, "Did the Fundamentalists Win?" in Douglas and Tipton, *Religion and America*, pp. 170-178, 233.
47. Douglas and Tipton, *Religion and America*, pp. 168, 244-246, 248(n. 47).
48. Rodney Stark and William Sims Bainbridge, *The Future of Religion: Secularization, Revival and Cult Formation*, University of California Press, 1985; Douglas and Tipton, *Religion and America*, pp. 229-234.
49. *Ibid.*, p. 133.
50. Harvey Seifert, *New Power for the Church*, Westminster, 1976.
51. "Bilateral Conversations between Catholics and Disciples," *Mid-Stream*, VII, 2, (Winter 1968).
52. Douglas and Tipton, *Religion and America*, pp. 179-180.
53. Peter Berger, "From the Crisis of Religion to the Crisis of Secularity," in *Ibid.*, p. 17.
54. *Ibid.*, pp. 126-127.

55. Thomas Campbell, "A Declaration and Address," Proposition 9, reprinted by Bethany Press, 1955.
56. Robert Richardson, *Memoirs of Alexander Campbell, Embracing a View of the Origin, Progress and Principles of the Religious Reformation Which He Advocated*, J.B. Lippincott & Co., 1871, pp. I, 236.
57. The slogan long carried on the masthead of the *Christian Standard*.
58. Rupertus Meldenius is credited with the origin of the slogan; Winfred Ernest Garrison and Alfred T. DeGroot, *The Disciples of Christ: A History*, Christian Board of Publication, 1948, pp. 40-41.
59. A Campbell, *The Christian System in Reference to the Union of Christians and Restoration of Primitive Christianity as Plead by the Current Reformation*, Bethany, Va., 1835, Christian Board of Publication, p. 10; for "exactly where the Apostles left them," see Thomas Campbell, "A Declaration and Address," paragraph preceding Proposition I.
60. A Campbell, *The Christian System*, chp. xxv, III, p. 83; cf. Ronald E. Osborn, "Eldership among Disciples of Christ: A Historical Case-Study in a 'Tent-making Ministry," *Mid-Stream*, VI, 2, (1967), pp. 74-112; cf. Newell Williams, "Ministry Among Disciples: Past, Present and Future," Study Series 3, Council on Christian Unity, 1985.
61. Samuel C. Pearson, Jr., "The Association of Disciples for Theological Discussion: A Brief Historical Appraisal," *Encounter*, 37, 3, (Summer 1976), pp. 259-283.
62. See Eva Jean Wrather, *Creative Freedom in Action: Alexander Campbell on the Structure of the Church*, Bethany Press, 1968; Ronald E. Osborn, "The Structure of Cooperation," *Mid-Stream*, 2, 3, (1962), pp. 28-49.
63. Chapter 3 will give more extensive treatment to this development.
64. Chapter 4 will give more extensive treatment to this development.
65. Early reformulations include James Harvey Garrison, *The Old Faith Restated*, being a restatement by representative men of the fundamental truths and essential doctrines of Christianity as held and advocated by the Disciples of Christ in the light of experience and of biblical research, Christian Publishing Co, 1891; William Thomas Moore, *The Plea of the Disciples of Christ or the principles and aims of a religious movement, newly stated and critically examined*, Christian Century Co, 1906; and Byrdine Akers Abbott, *The Disciples: An Interpretation*, The Bethany Press, 1924. Classical liberal interpretations were advanced by H.L. Willett, E.S. Ames, W.E. Garrison, A.W. Fortune, Frank N. Gardner, and others. See James O. Duke, "Scholarship in the Disciples Tradition," *The Disciples Theological Digest*, I (1986), pp. 5-40; cf. Ronald E. Osborn, "Theology Among the Disciples," chapter 2 in George G. Beazley Jr., *The Christian Church (Disciples of Christ): An Interpretative Examination in the Cultural Context*, The Bethany Press, 1973.
66. See Clark M. Williamson, "Disciples Baptismal Theology," *Mid-Stream*, 25, 2, (April 1986), pp. 218-220.
67. Harold E. Fey, *The Lord's Supper: Seven Meanings*, Harper, 1948; Stephen J. England, *The One Baptism: Baptism and Christian Unity with Special Reference to Disciples of Christ*, Bethany Press, 1960; Joseph Belcastro, *The Relationship of Baptism to Church Membership*, Bethany Press, 1963; J. Daniel Joyce, *The Place of the Sacraments in Worship*, Bethany Press, 1967; Keith Watkins, *The Feast of Joy: The Lord's Supper in Free Churches*, Bethany Press, 1977. See also the papers on baptism and the Lord's Supper prepared by members of the Commission on Theology and Christian Unity in response to a request from the International Convention of Christian Churches (Disciples of Christ), *Mid-Stream*, V. 2, (Winter 1966).
68. W.B. Blakemore, "Reasonable, Empirical, Pragmatic: The Mind of Disciples of Christ," *The Renewal of Church: The Panel Reports*, W. B. Blakemore, ed., The Bethany Press, 1963, pp. 161-183.
69. See Kenneth L. Teegarden, *We Call Ourselves Disciples*, The Bethany Press, 1975; Ronald E. Osborn, "Theological Issues in the Restructure of the Christian Church (Disciples of Christ): A Not Unbiased Memoir," *Mid-Stream*, 19, 3, (1980), pp. 272-308.
70. Casiano Floristan, *The Parish: Eucharistic Community*, trans. John F. Byrne, London, Sheed and Ward, 1965.
71. I am indebted to the late Douglas Horton for a persuasive development of this thought in his little book on Congregationalism, not now availble to me.

72. See Vance Packard, *The Pyramid Climbers* on the comparative status of denominations, McGraw-Hill, 1962.
73. Douglas and Tipton, *Religion and America*, pp. 113, 173; Gibson Winter, *The Suburban Captivity of the Churches: An Analysis of Protestant Responsibility in the Expanding Metropolis*, Doubleday, 1961.
74. W.B. Blakemore argued this point in an eloquent series in *The Christian-Evangelist*; see also Ronald E. Osborn, *The Faith We Affirm: Basic Beliefs of Disciples of Christ*, The Bethany Press, 1979, pp. 87-91.
75. Consider, for example, James F. Hopewell, "A Congregational Paradigm for Theological Education," *Theological Education*, 21, 1, (Autumn 1984), pp. 60-70. Note also the focus of Thomas C. Oden, *Pastoral Theology: Essentials of the Ministry*, Harper & Row, 1983; cf. David Heim and Eugene C. Roehlkepartain, "Urban Ministry: Strategy and Faith for the City," *The Christian Century*, May 14, 1986, pp. 491-495; David Kelsey, "A Theological Curriculum About and Against the Church," (unpublished paper).
76. James L. Merrell, "Viewpoint," *The Disciple*, October 1984, p. 5.
77. Douglas and Tipton, *Religion and America*, p. xiii.

Chapter 3: Ministry in the Church That Was

1. Ronald E. Osborn, *In Christ's Place: Christian Ministry in Today's World*, The Bethany Press, 1967, pp. 146-152.
2. *Ibid.*, pp. 261-262.
3. Ronald W. Graham, "Women in the Pauline Churches: A Review Article," *Lexington Theological Quarterly*, 11, 1 (January 1976), pp. 25-34.
4. Osborn, *In Christ's Place*, pp. 60-70.
5. For a magisterial study see Bernard Cooke, *Ministry to Word and Sacraments: History and Theology*, Fortress Press, 1976; cf. *The Ministry in Historical Perspectives*, eds. Richard Niebuhr and Daniel D. Williams, Harper & Brothers Publishers, 1956; John T. McNeill, *A History of the Cure of Souls*, Harper & Brothers, 1951.
6. Urban T. Holmes III, *The Future Shape of Ministry: A Theological Projection*, The Seabury Press, 1971, part I.
7. *Ibid.*, p. 27.
8. See St. Gregory Nazianzen, "On His Sister, St. Gorgonia," *Fathers of the Church* 22:101-118; St. Gregory of Nyssa, "The Life of Saint Macrina," *Fathers of the Church* 58:161-194; cf. Ronald E. Osborn, "I'm Looking over a Four-Leafed Clover That I Overlooked...," *Impact*, 8 (1982), pp. 15-30. With Gregory's spiritual and intellectual humility before the superior wisdom of his sister Macrina, which he freely acknowledged, compare the similar respect paid by Augustine and his companions in philosophy to his mother Monica at Cassiciacum. In the dialogs there, just after his conversion, they repeatedly deferred not only to her saintliness but to her insight into the most profound themes under discussion, even though she lacked the formal vocabulary of the schools. See *Fathers of the Church*, Vol. 1.
9. *Baptism, Eucharist and Ministry*, Faith and Order Paper, No. 111, Geneva, World Council of Churches, 1982.
10. Henry Sloane Coffin, *Communion Through Preaching: The Monstrance of the Gospel*, Charles Scribner's Sons, 1952.
11. Luther, "Concerning the Ministry," addressed to the Senate in Prague as representative of the Bohemian Christians, 1523, *Luther's Works*, vol. 40, *Church and Ministry, II*, ed. Conrad Bergendoff, Concordia Publishing House, 1955-1976, pp. 21-34. Calvin, *Institutes*, Book IV, (LCC, XXI). See also Charles Clayton Morrison, *The Unfinished Reformation*; Robert Clyde Johnson, *The Church and Its Changing Ministry*, Office of the General Assembly, The United Presbyterian Church in the United States of America, 1961, pp. 30, 53-63.
12. Jane Dempsey Douglass, "Christian Freedom: What Calvin Learned at the School of Women," *Church History*, 53 (June 1984), pp. 155-173. For the Pauline texts, Ronald W. Graham, loc. cit.
13. See Elwyn Allen Smith, *The Presbyterian Ministry in American Culture: A Study in Changing Concepts, 1700-1900*, The Westminster Press, 1962. For a schematic analysis see Ronald E. Osborn, *Freedom to Serve: Models of Ministry in America*, forthcoming.

14. Only a generation after the Great Migration, however, Samuel Danforth lamented the decline of godliness in the colony and the passing of the great group of godly ministers; see "Errand into the Wilderness," in A.W. Plumstead, *The Wall and the Garden: Selected Massachusetts Election Sermons, 1660-1775,*. University of Minnesota Press, 1968; cf. Sacvan Bercovitch, *The Puritan Jeremiad*, The University of Wisconsin Press, 1978.
15. James W. Jones, *The Shattered Synthesis: New England Puritanism before the Great Awakening*, Yale University Press, 1973.
16. *The Great Awakening: Documents Illustrating the Crisis and Its Consequences*, Alan Heimert and Perry Miller, eds., Bobbs-Merrill, 1967; for educated clergy as a seeming barrier to spirituality, see Douglas and Tipton, *Religion and America*, p. 162.
17. Timothy Smith, *Revivalism and Social Reform*, John Hopkins, 1980.
18. Roger W. Stump, "Women Clergy in the United States: A Geographical Analysis of Religious Change," *Social Science Quarterly*, 67, 2, (June 1986), pp. 339-352, esp. 341.
19. The large number of women, married and single, who went as foreign missionaries has long been well known. Their important influence in the nineteenth-century denominational colleges has not received adequate attention, so far as I know, though the histories of particular institutions often pay loving tribute to one or two women, like Amanda Booth at Hiram, who profoundly influenced their students. Randi Jones Walker has detailed the major contribution of women as home missionaries in one of the territories; see her "Protestantism in the Sangre de Cristos: Factors in the Growth and Decline of the Hispanic Protestant Churches in Northern New Mexico and Southern Colorado, 1850- 1920," Ph.D. dissertation. Claremont Graduate School, 1972. Since the consciousness-raising on this issue, I have noted the names of women pastors appearing regularly in the narratives of small congregations among the Disciples contained in various state histories, especially for the western states. Harold E. Fey, as a youth in Nebraska before World War I, was converted by a woman evangelist; see *How I Read the Riddle: An Autobiography*, printed for the Council on Christian Unity of the Christian Church (Disciples of Christ) by The Bethany Press, 1982, pp. 27-29; cf. Nancy A. Hardesty, *Women Called to Witness: Evangelical Feminism in the Nineteenth Century*, Abingdon Press, 1984; Mary Ellen LaRue, "Women Have not been Silent. . . : A study of women preachers among the Disciples," *Discipliana*, January, 1963, pp. 85-89.
20. Dwight L. Moody was a layman when he rose to prominence as an evangelist; so was John R. Mott, moving spirit in the YMCA, Student Volunteers, worldwide Student Christian Movement, national Christian councils, and various ecumenical conferences which led to the formation of the World Council of Churches.
21. J.A. Seaton, "What is Expected of a Preacher?" in *Doctrine and Life by Iowa Writers*, G.L. Brokaw, ed., Christian Index Publishing, Co. 1898, pp. 54-64.
22. Robert Clyde Johnson, *The Church and Its Changing Ministry: Study Material Prepared under the Direction of the General Assembly Special Committee on the Nature of the Ministry*, Office of the General Assembly, The United Presbyterian Church in the United States of America, 1961, pp. 30ff.
23. *Church Management* was long the title of a professional journal for ministers. For professionalization and career specialization as a trend in society, see Lasch, *The Culture of Narcissism*, Warner Books, 1979, pp. 386ff. For ministerial take-over of leadership from the laity, I am indebted to an address by Barbara Brown Zikmund; see her paper, "The Contribution of Women to North American Church Life," *Mid-Stream*, 22, 3 & 4 (July/Oct., 1983), pp. 363-377. In a letter to the author (March 19, 1984) Herbert L. Minard pointed out the need for "an analysis of the effect of 'corporation theory of management on the Disciples of Christ, with upgrading of clergy and downplaying of laity," adding that the national YMCA "has suffered greatly from this [process] and our world service has become miniscule."
24. H. Richard Niebuhr, in collaboration with Daniel Day Williams and James M. Gustafson, *The Purpose of the Church and Its Ministry: Reflections on the Aims of Theological Education*, Harper & Brothers, 1956, pp. 79ff.
25. Kenneth Henry, "Unknown Prophets: Black Disciple Ministry in Historical Perspective," *Discipliana*, 46, 1 (Spring 1986), pp. 3-9; I am also indebted to Lorenzo Evans for a presentation at Christian Theological Seminary, May 1, 1969; cf. Joseph A. Johnson, Jr., *The Soul of the Black Preacher*, privately published, 1970; Henry J. Young, *Major Black*

Religious Leaders, 1755-1940, Abingdon, 1977.
26. Alexander Campbell, *The Christian System*, p. 83. Thomas Munnell, *The Care of the Churches*, (1888), the most significant treatise on ministry written for Disciples in the nineteenth century, will be discussed later in this chapter in the section on "The Work of the Minister." See also William Martin Smith *For the Support of the Ministry: A History of Ministerial Support, Relief, and Pensions among Disciples of Christ*, Pension Fund of Disciples of Christ, 1956 and *Servants without Hire: Emerging Concepts of the Christian Ministry in the Campbell-Stone Movement*, The Disciples of Christ Historical Society, 1968; Kenneth L. Teegarden, *We Call Ourselves Disciples*, The Bethany Press, 1975, pp. 74-82; John M. Hardy, "Nurture, Ordination, Standing for the Order of Ministry, the Christian Church (Disciples of Christ)," unpublished paper, January, 1980.
27. Alexander Campbell, *The Christian System*, pp. 330-331.
28. Recall Chaps. 1 and 2. cf. Dale E. Soden, "The Church vs. the University: The Struggle for Community Control in Seattle, Washington." I am grateful to Professor Soden of Oklahoma Baptist University for a copy of this unpublished paper, read to the Pacific Coast Branch of the American Historical Association. For a discussion of the decline across an even longer trajectory see Dumas Malone, *Saints in Action*, The Abingdon Press, 1939, chps. 2, 3.
29. See Chp. 6 for more extended discussion of the number and quality of ministers needed.
30. In the 1960s the name of the basic professional degree was changed from Bachelor of Divinity to Master of Divinity and many seminaries introduced a new advanced degree, Doctor of Ministry (D.Min.).
31. Johnson, *The Church*, p. 30. Aside from Thomas Munnell (see the next sub-section) Disciples produced virtually no books of a doctrinal or theological character on ministry before mid-twentieth century.
32. D. Duane Cummins, president of the Division of Higher Education, posed this question in an extended conference going over the prospectus for this study, Jan. 9, 1984.
33. The author's study, *In Christ's Place: Christian Ministry in Today's World*, thoroughly examines ministry in the New Testament.
34. See the Apostolic Fathers.
35. See especially the letters of Cyprian and his lectures to the African bishops regarding the lapsed, *Fathers of the Church* 36, 51.
36. See the catechetical lectures of Cyril of Jerusalem, John Chrysostom, Ambrose of Milan; also Agustine's lecture *De catechizendis rudibus*, a course of instruction for catechists.
37. Bernard Cooke's five-part analysis of the work of ministry, which provides the framework for his magisterial *Ministry to Word and Sacraments*, overlaps or subdivides the three-part arrangement of Word, sacrament, care. Cooke's five functions are Ministry as Formation of Community, Ministry to God's Word, Service to the People of God, Ministering to God's Judgment, and Ministry to the Church's Sacramentality.
38. Gregory Nazianzen, *Oration II (In Defence of his Flight to Pontus, and his Return, after his Ordination to the Priesthood, with an Exposition of the Character of the Priestly Office*, Schaff and Wace, eds., *Nicene and Post Nicene Fathers, Second Series*, Vol. VII.
39. John Chrysostom, *Treatise On the Priesthood*, trans. W.R.W. Stephens, ed. Philip Schaff, *Nicene and Post Nicene Fathers, First Series*, Vol. IX.
40. Saint Ambrose (Bishop of Milan), *Three Books on the Duties of the Clergy (De officils ministerorum)*, eds. Schaff and Wace, *Nicene and Post-Nicene Fathers, Second Series*, Vol. X.
41. Saint Augustine, *Christian Instruction*, trans. John J. Gavigan, *Fathers of the Church*, 2.
42. Gregory I (Bishop of Rome), *The Book of Pastoral Rule*, trans. James Barmby, eds. Schaff and Wace, *Nicene and Post-Nicene Fathers, Second Series*, Vol. XII.
43. K.D. Mackenzie, "Sidelights from the Non-Episcopal Communions" in Kenneth E. Kirk, *The Apostolic Ministry: Essays on the History and the Doctrine of Episcopacy*, London, Hodder & Stoughton Limited, 1946, pp. 468-469.
44. Calvin, *Institutes of the Christian Religion*, ed. John T. McNeill, trans. Ford Lewis Battles, *Library of Christian Classics*, XX, Book IV, chp. 11, 6, p. 1059; cf. Book II, chp. XV.
45. Richard Baxter, *The Reformed Pastor*, ed. Hugh Martin, John Knox Press, 1956.
46. Thomas Munnell, *The Care of All the Churches. Being a Scriptural Statement of the Character, Qualifications, Ordination, and Relative Duties of the Christian Ministry,*

Evangelists, Bishops, and Deacons, with Special Directions as to the practical details of a successful ministerial life, both in the spiritual and business aspects of the work, Christian Publishing Co., 1888. cf. D. Newell Williams, "The Minister's Task: A Nineteenth-Century View with Relevance for Today," *Discipliana*, 43, 1 (Spring 1983), pp. 12-14.
47. See *Practical Theology*, Don S. Browning, ed., Harper & Row, 1983.
48. Niebuhr, *The Purpose of the Church and Its Ministry*, pp. 27ff.
49. Samuel W. Blizzard, "The Minister's Dilemma," *The Christian Century*, April 25, 1956, pp. 508-509; "The Parish Minister's Self-Image and Variability in Community Culture," *Pastoral Psychology*, October, 1959, pp. 27-36.
50. *Ministry in America: A Report and Analysis, Based on an In-Depth Survey of 47 Denominations in the United States and Canada, with Interpretation by 18 Experts*, eds. David S. Schuller, Merton P. Strommen, and Milo L. Brekke, Harper & Row, 1980, pp. 25-26.
51. Edwin L. Becker and David S. Schuller, "Christian Church (Disciples of Christ)," *Ministry in America*, pp. 307-331.
52. See Response of Commission on Theology and Unity to *Baptism, Eucharist, and Ministry* in Newell Williams, *Ministry among Disciples: Past, Present, and Future*, Council of Christian Unity Study Series.
53. See "The Ordained Ministry in Ecumenical Perspective," *Study Encounter*, VIII, 4, (1972).
54. See "The Ministry of the Church: A Lutheran Understanding," *Studies*, Division of Theological Studies, Lutheran Council in the USA, 1974. For individual works reflecting on this theme from the standpoint of the free churches see Robert S. Paul, *Ministry*, Eerdmans, 1965, and Ronald E. Osborn, *In Christ's Place: Christian Ministry in Today's World*.
55. *Baptism, Eucharist and Ministry*, "Ministry", para. 26; *The COCU Consensus: In Quest of a Church of Christ Uniting*, ed. Gerald F. Moede, Consultation on Church Union, 1985, chp. 7, paras. 26, 51, 54.
56. Moede, *The COCU Consensus*, chp. 7, para. 56. Compare with the functions listed for the ministry of lay persons, of bishops, and of deacons in the same chapter.
57. Alexander Ganoczy, *Becoming Christian: a theology of baptism as the sacrament of human history*, Paulist Press, 1976, pp. 108ff.
58. Donald W. Shriver, Jr., "'Honest Ministry' in the Nineteen Eighties," an address delivered in St. Louis, October, 1981, pp. 6-9.

Chapter 4: Education for Ministry That Was...

1. See Neihardt, *Black Elk Speaks*, pp. 163ff.
2. See Will Durant, *The Story of Civilization, I. Our Oriental Heritage*, Simon and Schuster, 1942, in passim.
3. *Interpreters Dictionary of the Bible*, "Education OT," ed. Keith Crim, Abingdon, 1976.
4. For background see Gerhard von Rad, *Wisdom in Israel*, Abingdon, 1972, chp. II.
5. The title of a popular work by Charles Reynolds Brown, c. 1930.
6. cf. Paul's three years in Arabia (Gal. 1:15-17), commonly interpreted as his term of study in Christian theology in preparation for his ministry.
7. 1 Cor. 12:28; Rom. 12:7; Eph. 4:11; James 3:1; Acts 13:1. cf. Lewis Joseph Sherrill, *The Rise of Christian Education*, The Macmillan Company, 1944.
8. William D. Davies, *Paul and Rabbinic Judaism*, London, SPCK, 1955. For rhetoric see Dieter Betz, *Hermeneia Commentary on Galatians*, Fortress, 1979.
9. The layman, Didymus the Blind, continuing the great school at Alexandria, exercised large influence in biblical exegesis. Macrina, sister of Gregory of Nyssa, though lacking in formal secular education, had profound theological insight, which enabled her to participate in dialogue with learned theologians and to instruct them; the same is true of Monica, mother of Augustine.
10. Gregory of Nazianzus, *The Theological Orations*, trans. Charles Gordon Browne and James Edward Swallow, I. 1. 3, *Library of Christian Classics*, III, p. 129. For similar sentiments developed at length by Augustine of Hippo, see his "Soliloquies," *Fathers of the Church*, 5.
11. See *The Love of Learning and Desire for God*.
12. Dargan, *The Art of Preaching*, pp. 70-73.

13. *The Ministry in Historical Perspective*, eds. H. Richard Niebuhr and Daniel D. Williams, Harper & Brothers, 1956, p. 167.
14. *Ibid.*, pp. 240-241.
15. For a careful and critical book-length analysis of the trend summarized in this paragraph see Edward Farley, *Theologia: The Fragmentation and Unity of Theological Education*, Fortress Press, 1983; cf. Farley, "The Reform of Theological Education as a Theological Task," *Theological Education* 17, 2 (Spring 1981), pp. 93-117.
16. I cannot recall reading a treatment of this theme, impressed on me by contact, indirect and direct, with such principals as Nathaniel Micklem, John Marsh, J.S. Whale, Newton Flew, and William Robinson, and such British scholars as James Moffatt and Robert S. Paul.
17. From *New England's First Fruits*, 1643, quoted by Sydney E. Ahlstrom, *A Religious History of the American People*, Yale University Press, 1972, p. 149.
18. George A. Kennedy, *Classical Rhetoric and Its Christian and Secular Tradition from Ancient to Modern Times*, The University of North Carolina Press, 1980, p. 228. cf. Mark A. Noll, review of Richard A. Harrison's *Princetonians, 1769-1775: A Biographical Dictionary*, Princeton University Press, 1980, *Church History*, 51, 4, (December 1982), pp. 465-466.
19. *American Historical Review*, 78, 4, (October 1973), p. 1122.
20. Richard Hofstadter and Walter P. Metzger, *The Development of Academic Freedom in the United States*, Columbia University Press, 1955, gives important data on the high proportion of students preparing for ministry; see pp. 115-116 nn 3-4, 174, 186, 192 n 98, 222 n 30. 295-296 n 64, 299-302, 315, 350 n 111, 352.
21. W. Clark Gilpin, "The Seminary Ideal in American Protestant Ministerial Education, 1700-1801," *Theological Education* (Spring 1984), pp. 85-106. cf. John M. Imbler, "Theological Education in the Thought of Alexander Campbell," Christian Theological Seminary, Indianapolis, 1980, p. 4.
22. Robert W. Lynn, *Why the Seminary? An Introduction to the Full Report of the Auburn History Project*, Lilly Endowment, Inc., 1980; John C. Fletcher, *The Futures of Protestant Seminaries*, The Alban Institute, 1983, p. 2; cf. Heather F. Day, *Protestant Theological Education in America: A Bibliography*, ATLA Bibliography Series, No. 15, The American Theological Library Association and The Scarecrow Press, Inc., 1985.
23. Robert Wood Lynn, "Notes Toward a History: Theological Encyclopedia and the Evolution of Protestant Seminary Curriculum, 1808, 1868, " *Theological Education*, 17, 2 (Spring 1981), pp. 118-144.
24. Lynn, *Why the Seminary?* pp. 18, 23, 25, 50.
25. *Ibid.*, p. 28; cf. Arthur Wentworth Hewitt, *The Old Brick Manse*, Harper & Row, 1966, pp. 5-6.
26. Lynn, *Why the Seminary?* pp. 13, 16, 25, 29, 33.
27. *Ibid.*, pp. 44-46, 82, 88.
28. *Ibid.*, pp. 5, 46, 56-58, 88. cf. Gilpin, "The Seminary Ideal"; Robert T. Handy, "Trends in Canadian and American Theological Education, 1880-1980: Some Comparisons," *Theological Education*, 18, 2, (Spring 1982), pp. 175-218.
29. Lynn, *Why the Seminary?* pp. 83-87, 89-92, 95-99.
30. *Ibid.*, p. 75. cf. Niebuhr and Williams, *The Ministry*, p. 274; William Adams Brown, *The Education of American Ministers*, Vol. I of *Ministerial Education in America*, Institute of Social and Religious Research, 1984, p. 82.
31. See Lynn, *Why the Seminary?*, p. 100.
32. *Ibid.*, p. 99.
33. *Fact Book of the Association of Theological Schools in the United States and Canada*, cited in "Christian Theological Seminary Looks to the Future," 1979, pp. 7-9. Part of the increase in these figures is due to a larger number of schools reporting in the later year, part to the fact that the D.Min. was a new program in 1968.
34. Lynn, *Why the Seminary?*, pp. 100-101.
35. *Ibid.*, p. 102. In the United Presbyterian Church, 90 percent of their candidates for ministry in 1960 had attended a school belonging to the Presbyterian Council on Theological Education; by 1975 this figure had dropped to 57 percent.
36. Albert C. Outler applies this term to John Wesley; it is equally applicable to Campbell.
37. Winfred Ernest Garrison and Alfred T. DeGroot, *The Disciples of Christ: A History*,

224   THE EDUCATION OF MINISTERS FOR THE COMING AGE

      Christian Board of Publication, 1948, p. 298. Henry K. Shaw, *Buckeye Disciples: A History of the Disciples of Christ in Ohio*, Christian Board of Publication, 1952; cf. John M. Imbler, "Theological Education in the Thought of Alexander Campbell," (Christian Theological Seminary, 1980) pp. 39-40.
38. For a brief account of Bethany and its influence, see D. Duane Cummins, "From Buffalo to Claremont," *Impact*, 11, (1983), pp. 5-13.
39. A. McLean, *History of the Foreign Christian Missionary Society*, Revell, 1919, p. 106.
40. John M. Imbler, "By Degrees: The Development of Theological Education within the Disciples of Christ," (Christian Theological Seminary, 1981), S.T.M. Thesis, pp. 12-14.
41. Dwight E. Stevenson, *Lexington Theological Seminary, 1865-1965: The College of the Bible Century*, The Bethany Press, 1964, pp. 29-36.
42. First among Disciples, Drake University awarded the B.D. degree in 1882, but the development did not evoke wide enthusiasm. See Imbler, "By Degrees," pp. 24-25.
43. C.F. Swander, "Making Disciples in Oregon," Oregon Christian Missionary Convention, 1928, p. 145.
44. Ronald E. Osborn, *Ely Vaughn Zollars*, The Bethany Press, 1947, pp. 169-172; cf. Frederick Augustus Henry, *Captain Henry of Geauga: A Family Chronicle*, Gates Press, 1942, in passim.
45. For the 1915 recommendation see "The Yearbook: Churches of Christ (Disciples)," 1915, p. 46; cited in Imbler, "By Degrees," p. 40. For the 1939 action see *Department of Church Development and Evangelism, License and Ordination of the Christian Ministry, A Report Prepared by the Committee on Effective Ministry of the Home and State Missions Planning Council (Disciples of Christ)*, The United Christian Missionary Society, 1948, p. 10; cited by Imbler, "By Degrees," p. 50.
46. Garrison and DeGroot, *The Disciples*, pp. 378-379.
47. William E. Tucker and Lester G. McAllister, *Journey in Faith: A History of the Christian Church (Disciples of Christ)*, The Bethany Press, 1975, pp. 309, 322.
48. Earl Irvin West, *The Search for the Ancient Order: A History of the Restoration Movement, 1849-1906*, Gospel Advocate Company, 1949-1950, pp. II, 376.
49. Laurence C. Keene, "Heirs of Stone and Campbell on the Pacific Slope: A Sociological Approach," *Impact*, 12 (1984), pp. 46-51.
50. Samuel C. Pearson, "The Campbell Institute: Herald of the Transformation of an American Religious Tradition," *The Scroll: Journal of the Campbell Institute*, 62, 2, (Spring 1978), p. 1-63.
51. Conference of Bible Teachers in Schools Composing the Membership of the Board of Education, Indianapolis, Ind., Feb. 13 and 14, 1928, cited in Imbler, "By Degrees," pp. 51-52. For extensive background on the Disciples ministry during this phase, see Riley Benjamin Montgomery, *The Education of Ministers of Disciples of Christ*, The Bethany Press, 1931.
52. See Samuel C. Pearson, Jr., "The Association of Disciples for Theological Discussion: A Brief Historical Appraisal," *Encounter* 37, 3, (Summer 1976), pp. 259-283.
53. Each institution has its own way of marking out "fields" or "areas" in the curric ulum, none identical with the categories on this chart. A careful reading of the catalogs, including descriptions for required courses, suggests the distribution indicated here.
54. See Appendix II. The questions for minsiters were deliberately written in such a way as to encourage a broad variety of responses, trying to elicit concerns rather than percentages among stated options.
55. For the assessment by regional ministers and by congregations, see p. 74; a letter from Charles Malotte, 85:10:18, amplifies the concerns. cf. "Perceived Strengths and Weaknesses of Recent Theological Education." CTS study, 12 (reproduced as table in Appendix III); James L. Merrell, "Ministry: Reflections of a Survivor," MS, June, 1985. The various studies of theological education conducted throughout this century by predecessors of ATS report a similar failure of the seminaries to prepare students for the practical demands of life in the parish; see Lynn, *Why the Seminary/*, pp. 83-84, 87, 90-92, 95-101.
56. For the observation that theology is the "late child of an age in which prophecy ceased," see Douglas and Tipton, *Religion and America*, p. 267.
57. Quoted by Granville T. Walker, *Preaching in the Thought of Alexander Campbell*,

Bethany Press, 1954, p. 239; cited in Imbler, "By Degrees," p. 43.
58. Farley, *Theologia*, in passim; cf. Joseph C. Hough, Jr., and John B. Cobb, Jr., *Christian Identity and Theological Education*, Scholars Press, 1985, chp. 1.
59. Douglas and Tipton, *Religion and America*, p. 249; recall Gaustad on liberal religion's loss of allies in the general culture, mentioned in chp. 2, c8, *Ibid.*, pp. 169ff.
60. *Ibid.*, pp. 257, 259-260; Farley, *Theologia*, in passim; W. Clark Gilpin, "Theological Education and Its Communities," *Criterion*, 24, 2, (Spring 1985), pp. 2-6.
61. William O. Paulsell, letter to the author, para. 8; cf. Ellis Cose, "Our Elitist Journalism," *Newsweek*, June 3, 1985; Raymond Gaylord, "What Are the Big Questions?," *The Disciple*, January 1986, pp. 11-13.
62. cf. "Why Teachers Fail," *Newsweek*, Sept. 24, 1984, pp. 64-70.
63. Paulsell, letter, paras. 7, 10.
64. Remark by T.J. Liggett. cf. Robert L. Wilson, "Electing Bishops: Politics or Call?," *The Christian Century*, Oct. 10, 1984, pp. 918-919.
65. Isa. 29:11-12 Moffatt; format revised for emphasis.
66. Luke 11:5-13; this format for emphasis.
67. Some of these studies on new structures for ministry were related to the studies of the missionary calling of the congregation then being sponsored by the World Council of Churches and other ecumenical bodies. The liberal religious press was filled with articles on the theme. A good example of the discussion is Ruediger Reitz, *The Church in Experiment: Studies in New Congregational Structures and Functional Mission*, Abingdon Press, 1969. For engagement with the issues then troubling seminarians, see Walter D. Wagoner, *Bachelor of Divinity: Uncertain Servants in Seminary and Ministry*, Association Press, 1963.
68. Among the more ambitious experiments in helping congregations to combat racism was Project Understanding, developed by the School of Theology at Claremont under a grant from the Irwin-Sweeny-Miller Foundation. It may be said to have achieved some modest success.
69. A proposal will be made in chp. 8 for a Panel for the Review of Ministerial Education and the initiation of recommendations to the General Assembly, requesting the seminaries to take appropriate action.
70. Paul R. Lawrence and David Dyer, *Renewing American Industry*, The Free Press, 1983, p. 267; italics theirs.
71. *Ibid.*, pp. 298-299.
72. Langdon Gilkey, quoted by Newbigin, *The Other Side of 1984*, Geneva World Council of Churches, 1983, pp. 3-4.
73. Bellah et. al., *Habits of the Heart*, in passim.
74. Newbigin, *The Other Side of 1984*, p. 21.
75. Douglas and Tipton, *Religion and America*, p. 113.
76. "Furniture Made Fun," *Newsweek*, Nov. 4, 1985, p. 82.
77. "We are... faced with a new task...: how to embody in the life and teaching of the Church the claim that Christ is Lord over all life, without falling into the Constantinian impasse? The answering of that question will require decades of costly search and experiment." Newbigin, *The Other Side of 1984*, p. 34.
78. Winthrop S. Hudson, *The Great Tradition of the American Churches*, Harper, 1953. cf. the observation of a distinguished sociologist: "Yinger goes on to suggest that the theoretical point of maximum effectiveness for religious organizations is reached when the organization has achieved enough in numbers and power to exercise a strong influence, while at the same time not having given up its essential ideals. Attempting to locate this point involves a genuine dilemma.... Powers outside the church cannot be either dismissed or conquered." from Oliver R. Whitley, *Religious Behavior: Where Sociology and Religion Meet*, Prentice-Hall, Inc., 1964, p. 56.
79. Lesslie Newbigin, *The Other Side of 1984: Questions for the Churches*, postsript by S. Wesley Ariarajah, Geneva, World Council of Churches, 1983, p. 23.
80. "Deaths," *The Christian Century*, Nov. 13, 1985, p. 1026.
81. Jan G. Linn, *Christians Must Choose: The Lure of Culture and the Command of Christ*, CBP Press, 1985.

Chapter 5: Toward a Theology of Ministry

1. "Baptism, Eucharist and Ministry, Faith and Order Paper No. 111," pp. 20-32, *The COCU Consensus: In Quest of a Church of Christ Uniting, Approved and Commended to the Churches by the Sixteenth Plenary of the Consultation on Church Union, Nov. 30, 1984, Baltimore, Maryland*, ed. Gerald F. Moede, Consultation on Church Union, 1985, chp. 7, "Ministry."
2. Along with Alexander Campbell's *Christian System*, the classic work among Disciples is Thomas Munnell, *The Care of all the Churches*. A twentieth-century formulation is my study, *In Christ's Place: Christian Ministry in Today's World*, Bethany Press, 1967. An important historical survey of Disciples practice is Newell Williams' paper on ministry in the Council for Christian Unity's study series.
3. Delegates from the free churches to ecumenical conferences struggle with ecclesiastical protocol which specifies that certain dignitaries be addressed by such titles as Your Eminence, Your All-Holiness, Your Grace.
4. For "parallelism between the person of Jesus Christ as the incarnate Word and the Christian community as the residence or the site of Jesus Christ," see T. J. Liggett, "Contextualization and Catholicity: Can the Tension Be Creative?," *Impact*, 11, (1983) p. 21.
5. On imitating the nature of God see St. Cyprian, *Letters*, 55 (19), trans. Sister Rose Bernard Donna, S.J., *Fathers of the Church*, 51:145; St. Ambrose, *Flight from the World*, (4.17) trans. Michael P. McHugh, *Fathers of the Church*, 65, p. 295.
6. For reflections of C. S. Lewis on God as creative Artist, not Manager, see LeFevre, *Understandings of Prayer*, p. 97; for the divine creativity see Henry Nelson Wieman, *The Source of Human Good*, The University of Chicago Press, 1946.
7. Trotter, "Imagination and History," *Impact*, 11, (1983), p. 15.
8. See "The Awakening of a Cathedral," *Newsweek*, June 16, 1986, pp. 59-60.
9. LeFevre, *Understandings*, p. 98.
10. For me the classic discussion of this theme is that by Rabbi Abraham Joshua Heschel, great scholar-saint of our time, in his study *The Prophets*, Harper & Row, 1969.
11. In all honesty it must be acknowledged that much process theology must also play hermeneutical games with scripture when it comes to passages affirming the divine omnipotence.
12. See Frederick Herzog, "A New Spirituality: Shaping Doctrine at the Grass Roots," *The Christian Century*, July 30-Aug. 6, 1986, pp. 680-81.
13. Lactantius, *The Wrath of God (De ira dei)*, chp. 12, *Fathers of the Church*, 54, p. 89; cf. 96, 105.
14. Archbishop Nathan Soderblom, quoted by T.J. Liggett, *Impact*, 11, p. 25. ("Person" has been substituted for "man" in the original passage.) For reflections organized with reference to the ministry of Jesus see *Theological Foundations for Ministry: Selected Readings for a Theology of the Church in Ministry*, ed. Ray S. Anderson, Eerdmans, 1979.
15. The thought is Pascal's, as interpreted by A. J. van der Bent, "Three Wise Men in Geneva," *The Christian Century*, Sept. 12-19, 1984, p. 821.
16. "Concerning the Ministry" [1523], *Luther's Works*, ed. and trans. Conrad Bergendoff, vol. 40, Church and Ministry II, Concordia Publishing House, 1958, p. 34.
17. Thomas J. Peters and Robert H. Waterman, *In Search of Excellence: Lessons from America's Best-run Companies*, Harper & Row, 1982, p. 29.
18. *Baptism, Eucharist and Ministry*, "Ministry," para. 15, p. 22.
19. Geoffrey Barraclough, *The Medieval Papacy*, Harcourt, Brace & World, 1968.
20. Petry, *Christian Eschatology and Social Thought*; cf. Ronald E. Osborn, "Hope Beyond History and Fulfillment in History: The Christian Faith and Eschatology," *Encounter*, 24, 1, (Winter 1963), pp. 41-60.
21. Dante Alighieri, *The Divine Comedy*, Paradiso, canto xxxiii, Carlyle-Wicksteed translation, pp. 143-145.
22. See Browne Barr, "The Ordination of Women and the Refreshment of the Sacraments," *The Christian Century*, Sept. 25, 1985, pp. 823-34. An alumnus of a Disciples seminary responded to the Questions for Ministers: "People expect leadership.... The development and communication of a vision need to be more emphasized." C73j.
23. Alfred North Whitehead, *Adventures of Ideas*, Macmillan, 1933.
24. Peters and Waterman, *In Search of Excellence*.

25. As an example see John Shelby Spong, "The Urban Church: Symbol and Reality," *The Christian Century*, Sept. 12-19, 1984, pp. 828-831.
26. Geoffrey Wainwright, *Doxology: The Praise of God in Worship, Doctrine, and Life*, Oxford University Press, 1980. cf. *Baptism, Eucharist and Ministry*, "Eucharist," paras. 19-20.
27. See Donald Shriver, "'Honest Ministry' in the Nineteen Eighties," Address to the Council on Theologial Education, Oct. 6, 1981, pp. 5-6.
28. See above, "A New Mandate: Readapatation," pp. 98ff.
29. Newbigin, *The Other Side of 1984*, p. 35.
30. Robert S. Paul, *The Church in Search of Itself*, William B. Eerdmans Publishing Company, 1972, p. 354.
31. Father Buti Tlhalgale, "Introduction," in Desmond Mpilo Tutu, *Hope and Suffering: Sermons and Speeches*, William B. Eerdmans Publishing Company, 1983, pp. 25-26.
32. Charles H. Bayer—att. In 1930 A. W. Fortune, long a member of the faculty at College of the Bible in Lexington, published a book entitled *The Church of the Future*, Bethany Press.
33. Samuel F. Blizzard found that "The social roles of Protestant parish ministers [are] defined by the requests of parishioners, the denominational program, and the culture of the community"; see "The Minister's Dilemma," *The Christian Century*, April 25, 1956, p. 510.
34. Among Disciples of Christ, the president of the old International Convention was most commonly a pastor, but since Restructure the ministers of congregations have been accorded far less prominence. Of the eleven moderators from 1968 to 1987, four were ordained ministers serving in higher education, three were lay persons, three were pastors of congregations, and one was a regional minister. In a comparable nineteen-year period (1948-67) the International Convention had 17 presidents; ten of these were pastors, four were ordained ministers serving as educators, two were state secretaries, and one was a lay person. No provision in the Design or no doctrine of the restructured church mandated the striking change. But in our society and perhaps our kind of church, which takes more seriously than before its common life, the base for leadership has evidently shifted; it is more difficult than before for the minister of a congregation to exert influence throughout the denomination or even to gain wide name-recognition.
35. For an explanation of the eminence of Congregationalist ministers in American life, see Dumas Malone, *Saints in Action*, The Abingdon Press, 1939, pp. 47-53.
36. Keith Watkins, "Five Acts of the Congregation," *Encounter*, 34, 3, (Autumn, 1973), pp. 322-334.
37. Toffler, *The Third Wave*, pp. 390-395.
38. See "Ministry as Formation of Community," Bernard Cooke, *Ministry to Word and Sacraments: History and Theology*, Fortress Press, 1976, pp. 33-215; Ronald E. Osborn, "The Building up of the Church: Reflections on a New Testament Image," *Impact*, 7 (1981), pp. 1-25.
39. On the need for adult education see Carey, *Carlyle Marney*, p. 115. For historical reflections on intellectual leadership from the pulpit, see Daniel Calhoun, *The Intelligence of a People*, Princeton University Press, 1973.
40. See Eric Dean, "St. Benedict's Way: A Protestant Appraisal of Monasticism," *Encounter*, 31, 1 (Winter 1970), pp. 333-334. cf. Perry LeFevre, *Understandings of Prayer*, an examination of the view of major contemporary theologians, which discloses important insights on bringing human will into harmony with the divine will, but offers little help regarding intercession. For a theologian's reflections addressed to a lay audience, see John B. Cobb, Jr., *Praying for Jennifer*, The Upper Room, 1985.
41. See Charles H. Bayer, "Do we care about theological issues?" *The Disciple*, June 1986, p. 54.
42. See Robert K. Greenleaf, *Servant Leadership: A Journey into the Nature of Legitimate Power and Greatness*, Paulist Press, 1977.
43. Jay R. Calhoun in discussion with the author.
44. Among the resources are Langdon Gilkey, *How the Church Can Minister to the World without Losing Itself*, Harper & Row, 1964 and Oden, *Pastoral Theology*. For a discussion of "models," see Hough and Cobb. See also my forthcoming study, *Freedom to Serve: Models of Ministry in the American Church*.
45. See Charles H. Bayer, "Disciples Need a Spiritual Leadership," *The Disciple*, August, 1984,

p. 43. There is matter for sober reflection in the historian's observation: "The founders of Methodism, who were independent of its ecclesiasticism or were the creators of it, were greater men than their successors in the formal episcopacy." Dumas Malone, *Saints in Action*, p. 48.
46. Carey, *Carlyle Marney*, p. 92.
47. "Marney was prophetic and critical when dealing with social structures and grace-oriented when dealing with people." Carey, *Carlyle Marney*, p. 89.
48. This term is suggested by Josh L. Wilson, Jr., in a provocative personal letter, August 23, 1985. [p. 3, #2]
49. Sidney E. Mead, *The Nation with the Soul of a Church*, Harper & Row, 1975, p. 123. cf. Calhoun, *The Intelligence of a People*.
50. "Information is educative. The Media has emerged as the information society's chief magister.... the Media is teaching us, explicating meaning and value, and implying power and priority through the processing of the rising flood of information." Josh L. WIlson, Jr., "Eaglecrest: A Networking and Communications Community," a paper presented at IEEE National Media Briefing, New York, May 1, 2, 1985, p. 3. On creative use of the media by the churches see Martin E. Marty, "Religious Television: A Challenge Unmet," *The Christian Century*, Sept. 12-12, 1984, pp. 839-842; for use of radio on a regular basis by pastors, see Herb Miller, "Notebook," *The Disciple*, October, 1985, p. 41.
51. Toffler, *The Third Wave*, pp. 279, 320; Shriver, "'Honest Ministry' in the Nineteen Eighties," o, 8.
52. See *Theological Education* (ATS) Spring, 1983 for a special issue devoted to this theme.
53. Leo J. O'Donovan, S.J., quoting John Courtney Murray, in a tribute entitled "Ahead of Us Still," *Criterion*, Spring, 1985, p. 9. [for bibliog, pp. 7-9]
54. See Theodore O. Wedel, *The Coming Great Church*, The Macmillan Company, 1945, pp. 147-151.
55. See "Reshaping the Pastoral Task," Carnegie Samuel Calian, *Today's Pastor in Tomorrow's World*, rev. ed., The Westminster Press, 1982, chp. 6; for examples, good and not so good, see "New Shepherds to Lead Nation's Religious Flocks," *U.S. News & World Report*, Dec. 31, 1984/Jan. 7, 1985, pp. 86-87.

Chapter 6: Addressing the Need for Ministers

1. This chapter and those which follow deal particularly with the situation and needs of the Christian Church (Disciples of Christ). The Grant Request for funds to produce this study called for "analysis of the denominational range of and demand for ministers (fulltime professional, bi-vocational, administrative leadership and specialized ministries)" among Disciples from 1990 to 2020, p. 2. # 1a. For a brief analysis of the situation among American Baptists, see Paul O. Madsen, *Tomorrow's Ministers*, Commission on the Ministry, American Baptist Churches, 1983.
2. The Design for the Christian Church (Disciples of Christ), Article VI. Ministry, paras. 89-93.
3. "Policies and Criteria for the Order of the Ministry in the Christian Church (Disciples of Christ)," adopted by the General Assembly, meeting in Louisville, Ky., 1971.
4. *Year Book and Directory - 1986 - of the Christian Church (Disciples of Christ)*, Office of the General Minister and President, m2.
5. Some of these ministries are discussed in Marvin T. Judy, with the cooperation of Murlene O. Judy, *The Multiple Staff Ministry*, Abingdon, 1969, and Richard G. Hutcheson, Jr., *The Churches and the Chaplaincy*, John Knox, 1976.
6. See Lawrence D. Maloney with Kathleen Phillips, "What's Behind a Growing Shortage of Priests?", *U.S. News & World Report*, June 18, 1984, pp. 43-44. cf. Charles E. Curran, *The Crisis in Priestly Ministry*; *Today's Vocation Crisis*, Godfrey Poage, C.P. and German Lievin, C.S.S.R., trans & eds., Newman Press, 1962.
7. "Clergywomen: 10,470 are now ordained," *Time*, April 3, 1978, p. 44.
8. Jackson W. Carroll and Robert L. Wilson, *Too Many Pastors? The Clergy Job Market*, The Pilgrim Press, 1980.
9. Department of Ministry, "The Ministry: Supply/Demand Issues for the Christian Church (Disciples of Christ) - 1979," Division of Homeland Ministries, a six-page report; Pension

Fund of the Christian Church (Disciples of Christ), Clergy Supply Study, June 1984 [a analysis based on actuarial data - 11 pages].
10. Pension Fund Study cited in 9, pp. 10-11.
11. Board of Church Extension of Disciples of Christ, Report of New Congregations Organized, Second Quarter, 1984, a quarterly memo to regional executives, area executives, selected national staff.
12. John R. Compton, "There is a crisis in black ministry," reported by Disciples News Service, 85b-63, March 12, 1985; for Hispanics, see Albert L. Garcia, "Enrollment Losses," *The Christian Century*, April 17, 1985, pp. 395-396.
13. UCC, 400; Disciples, 388 in 1978; "Clergywomen," *Time*, April 3, 1978, p. 44.
14. LaTaunya Bynum, Report to Seminarians Conference, Indianapolis, Indiana, October 4, 1984. cf. Anna R. Jarvis-Parker, "The Situation and Trends in the Ministry of Disciples Clergywomen in the Last Seven Years," *Discipliana*, 45, 1 (Spring 1985), pp. 7-10; Deborah Casey, "Heritage and History: Hand in Hand," *Ibid.*, 38, 2, (Summer 1978), pp. 19-21, 28; Mary Ellen laRue, "Women Have not Been Silent . . . : A study of women preachers among the Disciples," *Ibid.*, 2, 6 *(Jan., 1963), pp. 85-89; "Bibliographies: Disciple Women and the Church," Ibid*, pp. 91-95.
15. "With Justice for Some," *Newsweek*, June 4, 1984.
16. The sole exception since the adoption of The Design in 1968 was Jean Woolfolk, who retired as president of the Church Finance Council in 1982.
17. Jarvis-Parker, Anna, "Women as Parish Clergy," *The Christian Century*, Jan. 23, 1985, p. 72.
18. Ruth Brandon Minter, "Hidden Dynamics Block Women's Access to Pulpits," *The Christian Century*, Aug. 19-Sept. 5, 1984, pp. 805-806; Maxine Walaskay, "Gender and Preaching," *The Christian Ministry*, 13, 1 (January 1982), pp. 8-11. cf. "An Analysis of Department of Ministry Staff Visitation to Regional Commissions, etc., August 1979 - June 1981, pp. 3-4; "Women in Ministry Concerns," Division of Homeland Ministries, 1981.
19. Rebecca Chopp of the University of Chicago Divinity School, quoted by Joseph Carey, "Women of the Cloth: How They're Faring," *U.S. News & World Report*, Dec. 3, 1984, p. 77. See *Women as Pastors*, Creative Leadership Series, Lyle E. Schaller, ed., Abingdon Press, 1982.
20. Martin E. Marty, "Trends in Seminary Enrollments," *The Christian Century*, Feb. 6-13, 1985, pp. 116-117; cf. "Female Seminarians," *Ibid.*, Feb. 3-10, 1982, p. 111.
21. "Seminary Enrollment Down," *The Christian Century*, March 5, 1986, p. 233. cf. Clergy Supply Study, Pension Fund of the Christian Church, June 1986.
22. D. Duane Cummins, *Disciples Colleges: A History*, CBP Press, 1987, chp. 4. cf. "Teen jobs go begging this summer," *U.S. News & World Report*, July 7, 1986, p. 59.
23. Undated release for church newsletters, Office of Communication, May 5, 1985.
24. It should be remembered that ministers serving congregations and recognized institutions who had received ordination prior to the adoption of the "Policies and Criteria for the Order of the Ministry" in 1971 were granted standing as ordained ministers; virtually all of these had been ordained by local congregations, and many who were serving smaller churches lacked a seminary degree. For the 1979 study, refer to Department of Ministry, "The Ministry: Supply/Demand Issues, etc." appendix.
25. For many of the insights in this paragraph, I am indebted to D. Duane Cummins, in an extended conference on June 30, 1985. A letter from Charles Lamb, regional minister for the Northeastern Region, states: "The majority of our 60 congregations cannot call a full time, seminary trained minister. Most of our churches must turn to lay ministers, part time ministers, or become involved in yoked parishes." See also David R. Ray, *Small Churches Are the Right Size*, The Pilgrim Press, 1982; Lyle E. Schaller, *The Small Church Is Different*, Abingdon Press, 1982; *New Possibilities for Small Churches*, Douglas Alan Walrath, ed., The Pilgrim Press, 1983.
26. R. Denniston, ed., *Part Time Priests*, London, Skeffington, 1960; Kenneth L. Woodward et al., "Church in Crisis," *Newsweek*, Dec. 9, 1985, p. 70. Claire Cooke, an American Protestant minister in 1950s, held a factory job for same reason as the worker-priests and wrote frequently on religion and labor for *The Christian Century* and other publications. cf. William W. Durden, "A Study of the Bivocational Ministry of Southern Baptist Pastors

in the Middle Georgia Area for the Purpose of Developing a Workshop Manual for Southern Baptist Bivocational Ministers," San Francisco Theological Seminary, D.Min. project, 1984.
27. For a study of husbands and wives both employed as ministers see E. M. (Bud) Rawlings and David J. Pratto, *Two-Clergy Marriages: A Special Case of Dual Careers*, University Press of America, 1985.
28. For stirring accounts of such ministries a generation ago, see Margaret K. Henricksen, *Seven Steeples*, Harper & Row, Harper Chapel Book edition, 1967, and Arthur Wentworth Hewitt, *The Old Brick Manse*, pp. 4-25. Henricksen served Methodist churches, Hewitt Congregational; she earned a seminary degree after some years in the pastorate.
29. See Hunter Beckelhymer, *Hocking Valley Iron Man*, Bethany Press, 1962; cf. the account of a professor of economics who ably served as weekend pastor; in Carey, *Carlyle Marney*, p. 21. See also Maloney & Phillips, "What's Behind a Growing Shortage of Priests?", *U.S. News & World Report*, June 18, 1984, pp. 43-44; cf. Sara Rubenstein, "Catholic parishes share enthusiasm for lay pastors," *The Oregonian*, Portland, Aug. 25, 1985. Department of Ministry, "The Ministry: Supply/Demand Issues for the Christian Church," appendix.
30. Alan Carter, for the Carnegie Commission, address to California Association for Institutional Research, San Francisco, Feb. 28, 1973, from "Proposed Graduate School M.A. Program in Public Policy Studies," Claremont Graduate School, April 1974.
31. General Assembly Resolution 8319; cf. "An Analysis of Department of Ministry Staff Visitation to Regional Commissions on the Ministry during the Period Aug. 1979-June 1981," pp. 2-3, "Lay Ministry Program." cf. *Handbook of Educational Opportunities for Lay and Bi-vocational Ministers*, Department of Ministry, Division of Homeland Ministries, 1981. At least one of the regions, the Christian Church in Mid-America, has joined with the School of Theology, University of the South (Sewanee) to sponsor Theological Education by Extension as a means of assisting candidates for licensing in their preparation. For some observations in this paragraph I am indebted to D. Duane Cummins.
32. Wayne Bryant, personal observations to author; D. Duane Cummins, "Knob Knoster, Lone Jack and Sinner's Union" [a study of small congregations in Missouri], unpublished paper; Lyle Schaller, "What Does Your Pastor Do Best?," *The Christian Ministry*, 15:2, March 1984, pp. 2-14.
33. Henrichsen, *Seven Steeples*, p. 238.
34. Charles F. Kemp lists sincerity of character, ability, emotional maturity, a love of people, a love of the church, a growing Christian faith, a sense of commitment. See his *Preparing for the Ministry*, The Bethany Press, 1959, p. 40.
35. For recent reflection see Neil E. Lindley, *Dynamic Discipleship for a New Age: A Manual of Discipline and Strategy for Ministry and Service on the Way to Century 21*, Brentwood Christian Press, 1984.
36. St. Augustine, "Faith, Hope and Charity," (*Enchiridion de fide, spe et caritate*), *The Fathers of the Church*, Bernard M. Peebles, trans., The Catholic University of America Press, 1947, p. 2, 467.
37. See Nikos Kazantzakis, *The Saviors of God: Spiritual Exercises*, Kimon Friar, trans., Simon and Schuster, 1960, A Touchstone Book; cf. H. Richard Niebuhr, *The Meaning of Revelation*, Macmillan, 1941, pp. 117-118 (quoted by Hough and Cobb, *Christian Identity*, p. 30). See also *The World's Great Scriptures: An Anthology of the Sacred Books of the Ten Principal Religions*, Lewis Browne, comp., Macmillan, 1946; *The Bible of the World*, Robert O. Ballou, ed., Viking, 1939.
38. See the plea for pastoral understanding of the ethical complexity of decision-making in business in M. L. Brownsberger, "From The Other Side of the Pulpit," *The Christian Century*, Aug. 27-Sept. 3, 1986, pp. 746-748. For a glimpse of reality, see "Playing Office Politics," *Newsweek*, Sept. 16, 1985, pp. 54-59.
39. Bennett W. Gerardy, "A ministry neglected," *The Disciple*, October 1984, p. 4.
40. This point is persuasively presented by Daniel Jenkins in *Protestant Ministry*, London, Faber and Faber, 1958, pp. 17ff.
41. Robert A. Thomas, "Re-ordering Priorities," Sermon for Aug. 10, 1969, University Christian Church, Seattle, Wash.
42. For issues here raised, see *Encounter*, 23, 1, (Winter 1962), special issue on enlistment.
43. *Webster's Deluxe Unabridged Dictionary*, 2nd ed., Simon and Schuster, c. 1979.

44. See "Vocation," *The New Columbia Encyclopedia*, ed. by William H. Harris and Judith S. Levey, Columbia University Press, 1975.
45. Tari Lennen and Randi Walker, "A Theology of Call: A Clergywomen's Perspective," unpublished paper for the 1986 meeting of the Western Association for Theological Discussion.
46. But two generations ago black students in college and seminary tended to regarded belief in a miraculous "call" as an element in the faith of the ignorant, not in their own experience; see W. A. Daniel, *The Education of Negro Ministers: Based upon a Survey of Theological Schools for Negroes in the United States Made by Robert L. Kelley and W. A. Daniel*, George H. Doran Company, 1925, pp. 70-78.
47. Recall Gilbert Tennent's sermon on "The Danger of an Unconverted Ministry," chp. 3.
48. See A. Vermeersch, "Vocation, Ecclesiastical and Religious," *The Catholic Encyclopedia*, The Encyclopedia Press, c. 1912. cf. Luigi M. Rulla, S.J., Sr. Joyce Riddick, S.S.C., and Franco Imoda, S.J., *Entering and Leaving Vocation: Interpsychic Dynamics*, Loyola University Press, 1976.
49. See Ronald E. Osborn, *In Christ's Place*, pp. 67-68, 191-193, 215.
50. *Ibid.*, pp. 261-266.
51. *Ibid.*, pp. 266-272.
52. *Ibid.*, pp. 207-241.
53. St. Cyprian, "Letter 38," *Fathers of the Church*, 51, pp. 97-102.
54. Johnson, *The Church and Its Changing Ministry*, p. 152.
55. cf. Calvin, *Institutes of the Christian Religion*, IV. pp. 3, 10-16 (LCC, 21: 1062-1068). cf. "An Invitation to Action: A Study of Ministry, Sacraments, and Recognition," ed. by James E. Andres and Joseph A. Burgess, The Lutheran-Reformed Dialogue, Series III, 1981-1983, Final Report, Fortress Press, 1984, p. 98; Robert G. Cox, *Do You Mean Me, Lord? The Call to the Ordained Ministry*, The Westminster Press, 1985; cf. the classical Puritan formulation in William Ames, *The Marrow of Theology*, trans. from the third Latin edition, 1629, and edited by John D. Eusden, Pilgrim Press, c. 1968, Bk I. XXXV, pp. 1-9.
56. Granville T. Walker, *Preaching in the Thought of Alexander Campbell*, The Bethany Press, c. 1954, chp. 11, "The Call and Ordination of the Ministry of the Church." Neither Campbell's Christian System nor Royal Humbert's *A Compend of Alexander Campbell's Theology* has a section on "call" or "Vocation." Nor does the classic nineteenth-century Disciples treatise on ministry, Thomas Munnell's *The Care of All the Churches*. But Munnell's chapter on "the Preacher" in an illustration about George Whitefield seems to presuppose the normalcy and propriety of "recruiting" a promising youth for the ministry as it emphasizes the necessity of conversion to God and of the power of the Spirit, pp. 177-197.
57. Charles F. Kemp, *Preparing for the Ministry*, The Bethany Press, 1959, pp. 15; cf. pp. 18-20.
58. Barton Hunter, "Listen You, How Long Will You Wait?" *World Call*, May 1945, pp. 5-6; cf. "The Call to Preach" in John Bunyan Hunley, *A Spiritual Argosy: The Romance of Fifty-eight Years in the Christian Ministry*, The Christopher Publishing House, 1958, pp. 54-66.
59. William O. Paulsell and Ian McCrae, letters to author regarding this study.
60. Cynthia Pearl Maus, *Time to Remember: The Memoirs of*, Exposition Press, 1964.
61. Hunley, *A Spiritual Argosy*, pp. 69-80; F. E. Davison, *I Would Do It Again: Sharing Experiences in the Christian Ministry*, The Bethany Press, 1948, pp. 11-13.
62. Osborn, *Ely Vaughn Zollars*, pp. 139-140.
63. See Charles F. Kemp, *Guidance for Church Vocations*, Authorized by Committee on Effective Ministry, Home and State Missions Planning Council, Disciples of Christ, Department of Church Development and Evangelism, The United Christian Missionary Society, n.d.; Charles F. Kemp, *Preparing for the Ministry*, The Bethany Press, 1959; James H. Parrott, *Recruitment for the Christian Ministry*, Authorized by the Committee on Effective Ministry, Home and State Missions Planning Council, Disciples of Christ, Department of Church Development and Evangelism, The United Christian Missionary Society, n.d. As director of the Department of Ministry, Jay R. Calhoun gave leadership in the development of the Disciples Guidance and Recruitment Program. See also Dennis B.

Savage, *One Life to Spend: A Co-operative Text Published for The Co-operative Publication Association*, The Bethany Press, 1962.
64. See *Careers in the Christian Ministry: An Ecumenical Guidebook for Counselors, Pastors, and Youth*, Consortium Books, 1976.
65. For a positive example, see Veneta Whitmer, "Pastoral Ministry Provides Opportunity for Women to Reach People of All Ages," *The Christian*, Aug. 5, 1973, p. 24; cf. Zelma Mullins Pattillo, "You Know Women Can't Be Preachers!" *The Christian Century*, May 30, 1984, pp. 566-567.
66. See "Are you making what you're worth?" *U.S. News & World Report*, June 23, 1986, pp. 60-67; "Where the jobs are for 1986 graduates," *Ibid.*, June 16, 1986, pp. 48-49; "What People Earn," *Parade*, June 15, 1986, pp. 1, 4-5; "Salary Survey," *AHA Perspectives*, 22:5, May-June, 1984, pp. 4-6; Martin E. Marty, "The Reverend Numbers Game," *The Christian Century*, Oct. 2, 1985, p. 879. cf. William J. Goode, *The Celebration of Heroes: Prestige as a Social Control System*, University of California Press, 1978.
67. Massey Hamilton Shepherd, Jr., *The Oxford American Prayer Book Commentary*, Oxford University Press, 1950, pp. 260-261. The manual which G. Edwin Osborn edited for Disciples, *Christian Worship: A Service Book*, Christian Board of Publication, 1953, addresses this concern in prayers 365 and 566.
68. Ernst Robert Curtius, *European Literature in the Latin Middle Ages*, trans. by Trask, Pantheon Books, 1953, pp. 167ff; cf. Richard W. Coan, *Hero, Artist, Sage, Or Saint?*," Columbia University Press, 1977.
69. See "A Different Sort of Sport," *Newsweek*, July 2, 1984, pp. 72-74.
70. "Jobs Talks About His Rise and Fall," *Newsweek*, Sept. 30, 1985, pp. 51-57.
71. "The Switch Is On," *Newsweek*, May 28, 1984, pp. 93-95; Martin E. Marty, "Trends in Seminary Enrollments," *The Christian Century*, Feb. 6-13, 1985, pp. 116-7. See also an important article supporting the thesis that "most people aren't ready for a critical vocational decision until several years after college" and listing a great company of influential religious leaders who did not make that decision until after 30; David L. Holmes, "After 20 Years: How a Professor's Mind Has Changed Since College," *The Christian Century*, Oct. 18, 1978, pp. 978-983.
72. Useful twentieth-century autobiographies include Frederick Buechner, *The Sacred Journey*, Harper & Row, 1982; Harry Emerson Fosdick, *The Living of These Days: An Autobiography*, Harper & Brothers, 1956; Georgia Harkness, *Grace Abounding*, Abingdon, 1969; Margaret K. Henrichsen, *Seven Steeples*; Joseph Fort Newton, *River of Years: An Autobiography*, J.B. Lippincott Company, 1946; Howard Thurman, *With Head and Heart: The Autobiography of*, Harcourt Brace Jovanovich, 1979. Memoirs of Disciples include Peter Ainslie, *Working with God* or *The Story of a Twenty-five-Year Pastorate in Baltimore*, Christian Board of Publication, 1917; *Beyond Theology: The Autobiography of Edward Scribner Ames*, ed. by Van Meter Ames, University of Chicago Press, 1959; Myron C. Cole, *Myron Here*, Mills Publishing Co., 1982; Frank Elon Davison, *Thru the Rear-View Mirror*, The Bethany Press, 1955; Harold E. Fey, *How I Read the Riddle*; Kirby Page, *Social Evangelist: The Autobiography of a 20th Century Prophet for Peace*, ed. by Fey, Fellowship Press, 1975; Cynthia Pearl Maus, *Time to Remember*; Myers, Oma Lou, comp., *Rosa's Song: The Life and Ministry of Rosa Page Welch*, ed. by Guin Tuckett, CBP Press, 1984; *The Seeking Heart: The Prayer Journal of Mae Yoho Ward*, ed. by Don Ward, CBP Press, 1985. For brief biographical sketches of black leaders among the Disciples see Black Disciples Legacy Series, National Convocation of the Christian Church, 1976.
73. Charles Shelby Rooks, "Vision, Reality and Challenge: Black Americans and North American Theological Education, 1959-83," *Theological Education*, Autumn, 1983, pp. 37-52; Ruben P. Armendariz, "The Preparation of Hispanics for the Ministry of the Church," *Ibid.*, pp. 53-57; John M. Imbler, "Not What It Used to Be!" *The Disciple*, October 1984, pp. 8-10; "Affirmative Action in Action," editorial, *Los Angeles Time*, Dec. 19, 1983.
74. Data supplied by conversations with Lawrence S. Steinmetz and Patricia A. Burris, Division of Higher Education, Christian Church (Disciples of Christ). For an important analysis, see Irving H. Allen, Sr., *The Christian Church (Disciples of Christ) Profile of the Black Ministers, the Black Church Congregations and Facilities, A Minority Ministers*

Research Project, sponsored by the Division of Homeland Ministries and the Division of Higher Education of the Christian Church (Disciples of Christ) in cooperation with Jarvis Christian College, June-Oct., 1985. cf. *The Untold Story: A Short History of Black Disciples,* CMF/CWF Studies, Christian Board of Publication, 1976.
75. A father with one son in seminary and another in a service academy spoke with disappointment of the former, where no one seemed to realize that the young man had been missing classes for some weeks or was struggling with a personal problem. By contrast, the military knew where the other son was all the time. We may write off the difference as that between the freedom of graduate school and the regimentation of the armed forces. But that is not the total explanation. According to the father, the government knows it has an investment in each candidate and monitors individual progress. And what of the seminary?
76. Comment by Respondent G61a to "Questions for Ministers"; letters from Jane W. Hopkins, Ian McCrae, Art Morgan, and William O. Paulsell to the author regarding this study register similar impressions.

Chapter 7: Education for Tomorrow's Ministers

1. Schleiermacher's reflections on three elements within theologia—science, prudence, and wisdom—may cast some light on the question. cf. Farley, *Theologia,* 95 n 7. A more colloquial way of discriminating the three emphases in Margaret Henrichsen's discussion of "know how" [professional], "know why" [scientific], and "know who" [fiduciary]; see her *Seven Steeples,* pp. 138-139.
2. For analysis of the academic movement toward specialization and its dehumanizing trend since mid-nineteenth century, see "Curricular Reform in Historical Perspective," *Perspectives: AHA Newsletter,* Nov. 1985, pp. 21-23. For proposals requiring the scholar to become involved in the integrative task, see Philip D. Curtin, "World Historical Studies in a Crowded World," *Ibid.,* pp. 19-21.
3. "A Conversation with Howard Gardner: Human Intelligence Isn't What We Think It Is," *U.S. News & World Report,* March 19, 1984, pp. 75-78.
4. Observation by Josh Wilson following session on theological education at 1985 General Assembly, Des Moines.
5. Douglas and Tipton, *Religion and America,* p. ix.
6. Douglas and Tipton, *Religion and America,* pp. 26-27.
7. J. Deotis Roberts, "Liberating Theological Education: Can Our Seminaries Be Saved?" *The Christian Century,* Feb. 2-9, 1983, pp. 98, 113-116.
8. Observations at consultation on theological education, School of Theology at Claremont, May 7, 1986.
9. See Stanley Hauerwas and William H. Willimon, "Embarrassed by God's Presence," *The Christian Century,* Jan. 30, 1985, pp. 98-100.
10. Osborn, "Divinity's Need of the Humanities," *Impact,* 14, (1985), pp. 24-36.
11. W. Clark Gilpin, "The Seminary and Its Communities," *Criterion,* 24, 2 (Spring 1985), pp. 2-6.
12. "The core of appropriate ministerial education is scholarly inquiry into religious faith and ethical practice and ... this is not essentially distinct from the same penetrating, fundamental inquiry that occurs in appropriate Ph.D. education." W. Clark Gilpin, "A Divinity Education," The Disciples Divinity House of the University of Chicago-*DDH Bulletin,* 56, 3 (Spring 1986) p. 4. Note the observation below, cf: pp 183f.
13. A most useful assessment of the idea of the professional with respect to ministry is Paul M. Harrison, "Religious Leadership in America," in *The Religious Situation: 1969,* ed. by Donald R. Cutler, Beacon Press, 1969, pp. 957-979. See also, as sources for the discussion in this paragraph, Fichter, *Religion as an Occupation,* p. 164, citing Talcott Parsons and other social scientists; Everett C. Hungers, "Professions," *Daedalus,* 92 (1963), pp. 655-668; Alfred North Whitehead, *Adventures of Ideas,* pp. 58-62, 73-74; Jack R. Frymier, *The Nature of Education Method,* Charles E. Merrill Books, Inc., 1965. For reflections on the passage from Whitehead and for some other suggestions in this section I am indebted to Professor Calvin L. Porter for an unpublished paper, "Theological Education for a Professional Ministry," which he presented to the faculty of Christian Theological Seminary in the 1960s.

14. David S. Schuller, Milo L. Brekke, and Merton P. Strommen, *Readiness for Ministry: Vol 1 - Criteria; Vol. 2 - Assessment*, The Association of Theological Schools in the United States and Canada, 1976.
15. Questions for Ministers.
16. See the impressive achievement represented by Thomas C. Oden, *Pastoral Theology: Essentials of Ministry*, Harper & Row Publishers, 1983, especially chp. 1, "The Discovery of Pastoral Identity." While Farley in *Theologia* repeatedly rejects the "clerical paradigm" and seems to wish to replace attention to methods with theological reflection in courses on the pastoral task, his discussion makes a significant contribution to thinking about professional education for ministers. For further important reflections see John H. Westerhoff, "Practical Theology: What Will It Become?" *The Christian Century*, Feb. 1-8, 1984, pp. 116, 131-33.
17. Edward M. Berckman (quoting Michael Kenney and Manuel Tamayo), "Ministering to the 'New Poor'," *The Witness*, 62, 6 (June 1984), pp. 21-23.
18. C. Earl Gibbs, unpublished paper presented to the Western Association for Theological Discussion, May 1985. cf. the engagement with persons and personal concerns rather than the usual objective account of AIDS in Peter Goldman and Lucille Beachy, "One Against the Plague," *Newsweek*, July 21, 1986, pp. 38-50.
19. The argument of Joseph C. Hough, Jr., and John B. Cobb, Jr., for preparing the minister to be a practical theologian represents one effort to integrate scientific and professional concerns; see their *Christian Identity and Theological Education*, pp. 18, 95-103. My point is that the seminarian needs to theologize not just about death, but about a particular experience of death.
20. For an account of treating even younger students like real historians see Barbara Oberg, "Editing and the Teaching of History: Notes from the Gallatin Project," *Perspectives*, AHA Newsletter, 23, 8 (Nov. 1985), pp. 12-14.
21. Funded by grants from foundations, two ambitious projects in contextual education conducted by the School of Theology at Claremont put students to working with congregations on the issues of white racism (Project Understanding) and the integration of spirituality with concern for world hunger (Project Burning Bush).
22. See Wilmore, "Blackness as Sign" in Newbold, *Black Preaching*, pp. 165ff; cf. W. Clark Gilpin's summation after reflecting on the educational vision of George Burman Foster for the Divinity School at the University of Chicago: "The possibility of 'faith on earth,' the meaning of human sense for the worthfulness of life, the ways in which the good, the true and the beautiful find fragmentary expression in human religiousness, these are to my mind the enduring issues that sustain a divinity school's dialogue and engender its sense of common calling." "A Divinity Education," p. 5. For the larger context see Edward Shils, *Tradition*, The University of Chicago Press, 1981, and Craig Calhoun, "Education and the Problem of Continuity," in *The Anthropological Study of Education*, ed. by C. J. Calhoun and F.A. J. Ianni, Aldine, 1976, pp. 327-346.
23. Hough and Cobb, *Christian Identity*, pp. 95-97.
24. Newbigin, *The Other Side of 1984*, p. 45.
25. Dietrich Bonhoeffer, *Life Together*, Harper, 1954.
26. See, for example, "Stimulating Faith by Way of Contradiction," *The Christian Century*, Aug. 13-20, 1986, pp. 703-704; Calvin L. Mercer, "Norman Perrin's Pilgrimage: Releasing the Bible to the Public," *Ibid.*, May 14, 1986, pp. 483-86; Richard Lischer, "Theology for Ministry: A Conversation with Edward Farley's *Theologia*," *Encounter*, 46, 2 (Spring 1985), pp. 107-115; and especially Mary Elizabeth Moore, *Education for Continuity and Change: A New Model for Christian Religious Education*, Abingdon Press, 1983.
27. Douglas and Tipton, *Religion and America*, p. 260.
28. See Leander E. Keck, "Babel and Beyond," *Theological Education*, 21, 1 (Autumn 1984), pp. 34-47, exp. 42-47. For the fiduciary obligation of liberal education see Alexander Astin, *Four Critical Years: Achieving Academic Excellence*, Jossey-Bass Publishers, 1977.
29. See St. Augustine's dialogues written at Cassiciacum after his conversion (*Fathers of the Church*, 1) and his Confessions; also Gregory Nazianzen, "On the Trinity," (NPNF). cf. *The Life of Learning and the Love for God*; Newbigin, *The Other Side of 1984*, pp. 24-54, especially 33.
30. See George Erik Rupp, "Theological Education as the Historical-Critical Appropriation of

Traditions," *Theological Education*, 17, 2 (Spring 1981), pp. 145-151.
31. Lactantius, "The Divine Institutes," *Fathers of the Church*, trans. by Sister Mary Frances McDonald, O.P., The Catholic University of America Press, 1964, Bk III, chp. 28, Vol. 49, p. 239.
32. William H. Pipes, *Say Amen, Brother! Old-Time Negro Preaching: A Study in American Frustration*, The William-Frederick Press, 1951, p. 17.
33. George W. E. Nickelsberg and Michael E. Stone, *Faith and Piety in Early Judaism: Texts and Documents*, Fortress Press, 1983, p. 32.
34. For important proposals see Janet F. Fishburn and Neill Q. Hamilton, "Seminary Education Tested by Praxis," *The Christian Century*, Feb. 1-8, 1984, pp. 108-112.
35. Joseph C. Hough, Jr., "Reform in Theological Education as Political Task," *Theological Education*, 17, 2 (Spring 1981), pp. 152-166.
36. This is the thrust of Edward Farley's *Theologia*, which seems to have had its impact on the curriculum of Vanderbilt Divinity School where he teaches.
37. Hough and Cobb, *Christian Identity*.
38. The professor is David P. Polk, who holds the chair of practical ministry at Brite Divinity School. In 1985 the theme was shalom; in 1986, ministerial responsibility toward child abuse. Other professorial initiatives toward integration include theologian John Cobb's seminal paper, "Leadership by Proposal," as yet unpublished.
39. The author worked out this seminar while dean at Christian Theological Seminary and later offered it in the School of Theology at Claremont.
40. The need for radical revision of professional programs is also becoming evident in schools of law, education, business. See "A New Kind of Law School," *Newsweek*, Sept. 26, 1983, p. 91; "Why Teachers Fail," *Ibid.*, Sept. 24, 1984, pp. 64-70.
41. Donald D. Reisinger, informal notes, "Thoughts on a New Seminary Curriculum and Faculty for the Year 2000," May 21, 1984. These suggestions are still in a formative stage, and I am grateful to Dean Reisinger for allowing me to use them here as an example of radical new approach to curriculum design.
42. "OSU-WOSC proposes teacher 'warranty,'" *The Oregonian*, Portland, July 3, 1984, p. B1; "Teacher warranty bill received cooly," *The Daily Astorian*, Astoria, Oregon, Feb. 15, 1985, p. 12.
43. J. Irwin Miller, "Religion and the Arts," in his *More Than Words Alone*, pp. 1-20, 35-37.
44. Ronald Goetz, "Art in Seminary: Revolutionzing Theological Education," *The Christian Century*, March 19-26, 1986, pp. 299-303; cf. James M. Wall, "Art Speaks to Us of the Unity of Life," *Ibid.*, June 18-25, 1986, pp. 571-572. cf. James Carley, "What is Religious Art?" and J. Gerald Janzen, "Gravity and Art," in *The Mind of a Faculty: Essays Presented to Beauford A. Norris*, comp. and ed. by Clark M. Williamson, Ronald E. Osborn, and Leslie R. Galbraith, *Encounter*, 34, 4 (Autumn 1973). For statistics on "the generally miserable job American seminaries do with church music," see paper by Paul Wohlgemuth in *Duty and Delight: Routley Remembered*, ed. by Robin A. Leaver and James H. Litton, Hope, 1985.
45. See Bishop Spong's "The Urban Church: Symbol and Reality," *The Christian Century*, p. 830; cf. Charles E. Winquist, *Practical Hermeneutics: A Revised Agenda for the Ministry*, Scholars Press, 1980. Recall Chp. 5, section on vision.
46. Daniel Dyer, "Imagine the world without imagination," *Cleveland Plain Dealer*, Jan. 3, 1986.
47. J. Deotis Roberts, "Liberating Theological Education: Can Our Seminaries Be Saved?" *The Christian Century*, Oct. 5, 1983, p. 98, 113-116; cf. Toffler, *The Third Wave*, p. 393.
48. James M. Wall speaks to this situation in "Pastoral Imagination Links Love to Action," *The Christian Century*, Oct. 5, 1983, p. 867.
49. A notable exception is Pittsburgh Theological Seminary, which offers jointly with other professional schools degree programs leading to dual competency in ministry and social work, ministry and law, ministry and business administration. The existence of such programs and the presence of students involved in them should infuse a seminary campus with sociological awareness and realism regarding social structures. See Carnegie Samuel Calian, "The Challenge of John 3:16 for Theological Education," *The Christian Century*, Feb. 5-12, 1986, p. 146.
50. Toffler, *The Third Wave*, pp. 418-420.

51. Dr. Susan Carver of Harvard Medical School says, "We want our students to learn how to talk with their patients, how to deal with the total patient and not just their sore toes." See "Hospital Hospitality," *Newsweek*, Feb. 11, 1985, p. 79. In an important unpublished paper, "The Quality of Aloneness," Jay R. Calhoun observes that because the public view of the minister is so often that of a person operating alone (litugist, preacher, teacher, counselor, student) and because theological education tends to major on requirements which the seminarian performs alone, many young ministers are totally unprepared, either in expectation or in expertise, for the necessity of working with groups of people which is such a large part of ministerial leadership.
52. See Augustine, "Free Choice of Will," *Fathers of the Church*, 59, p. 140.
53. Philip D. Curtin, "Depth, Span, and Relevance," *American Historical Review*, 89, 1 (Feb. 1984), p. 4.
54. Andra Moran, eight-year-old daughter of recent seminary graduates, showed her knowledge of the theological scene when she observed, "Seminary is where you learn what you should have learned in Sunday school." Letter from Geoff and Ruth Ann Moran, Dec. 1, 1984. cf. Charles H. Bayer, "Biblical teaching still main task," *Disciple*, April, 1985, p. 43.
55. The overwhelming majority of respondents to Questions for Ministers, among those who had finished seminary after the 1950s listed something like "learning to think theologically" as the most valuable part of their education; those who finished earlier listed "biblical studies."
56. On biblical illiteracy, I am indebted to papers by Roger Carstensen. For a critique of common misuse of scripture in resolutions presented to the General Assembly, see Dale Patick, "We've 'swung too far' on Bible," *The Disciple*, January 1986, pp. 52-53. Issues of modern scholarship will be thrust into the open by publicity concerning the "Jesus Project." See John Dart, "Experts try to find 'real Jesus' in Gospels," *The Oregonian*, Portland, Nov. 21, 1985, A2.
57. Thorwald Lorenzen, "Theological Education between Church and World," *Ministerial Formation: Programme on Theological Education (World Council of Churches*, 32 (December 1985), p. 17.
58 Donald D. Reisinger, cf f.n. 41, chapter 7.
59. See Iris V. Cully, *Education for Spiritual Growth*, Harper & Row, 1984; Robert S. Bilheimer, *A Spirituality for the Long Haul: Biblical Risk and Moral Standard*, Fortress Press, 1984; Urban T. Holmes III, *Spirituality for Ministry*, Harper & Row, 1982; David Lowes Watson, "Spiritual Formation in Ministerial Training — The Wesleyan Paradigm: Mutual Accountability," *The Christian Century*, Feb. 6-13, 1985, pp. 122-125. For concern with character as integral to education generally, see Earl Eugene Eminhizer, "Alexander Campbell on Moral and Quality Education — Some New Light," *The Iliff Review*, Spring 1984, pp. 27-31.
60. Hunley, *A Spritual Argosy*, (6-57), p. 111.
61. E. Glenn Hinson, "Douglas V. Steere: Irradiator of the Beams of Love," *The Christian Century*, April 24, 1985, pp. 416-419.
62. *Ministry in America*, ed. by Schuller, Strommen, and Brekke, (3- 50), p. 19. Recall chp. 6, especially "Christian Discipleship," "Appropriation of Christian Tradition," "Concern for Persons," and "Commitment to the Church."
63. To the best of my knowledge no Disciples seminary has a formally designated campus chaplain or spiritual director. Some of the persons to whom students have turned for such a ministry on the basis of personal charisma have been E. E. Snoddy at the old College of the Bible in Lexington, Harry D. Smith and G. Edwin Osborn at Phillips, O. L. Shelton and Frank Albert at Christian Theological Seminary.
64. For important reflection see D. Newell Williams, "Disciples Piety: A Historical Review with Implications for Spiritual Formation," *Encounter*, 47, 1 (Winter 1986), p. 1-25. cf. Tilden H. Edwards, Jr., "Spiritual Formation in Theological Schools: Ferment and Challenge - A Report of the ATS-Shalem Institute on Spirituality," *Theological Education*, 17, 1 (Autumn, 1980), pp. 7-52. cf. Report of "Spiritual Development Network" within the United Church of Christ, with its call for a training center to help pastors meet parishoners' spiritual needs and for the church to examine the role of seminaries in providing spiritual direction in theological education, *The Disciple*, January 1986, p. 41.
65. See, e.g., Daisetz Teitaro Suzuki, *The Training of a Zen Buddhist Monk*, University Books, 1959; William Johnston, *Christian Zen*, Harper & Row, 1971; Robert L. Moore,

"Ministry, Sacred Space, and Theological Education: The Legacy of Victor Turner," *Theological Education*, 21, 1 (Autumn 1984), pp. 87-100. cf. Kenneth L. Woodward, "A Scholar's Sacred Quest," [obit. on Mircea Eliade], *Newsweek*, July 15, 1958, p. 63.
66. Marlette, *The Christian Century*, Feb. 5-12, 1986, p. 105.
67. The course was first developed by Alberta and Harold Lunger. After their retirement it was taken over by Joseph R. Jeter, Jr., who introduced the retreats.
68. T. S. Eliot, Choruses from "The Rock," *The Complete Poems and Plays*, Harcourt, Brace and Company, 1952, p. 96.
69. Naomi Bliven, "Philosophy the Guide of Life," *The New Yorker*, April 21, 1986, p. 124.
70. See "Global Solidarity in Theological Education: Report of the U.S./Canadian Consultation Held at Trinity College, University of Toronto," 12-15 July, 1981, Geneva, Programme on Theological Education, World Council of Churches.
71. A letter from Charles A. Malotte and a comment by Don A. Pittman at the DHE consultation in Des Moines, 1985, emphasize this point. For times of emptiness, see Leonard I. Sweet, "The Four Fundamentalisms of Oldline Protestants," *The Christian Century*, March 13, 1985, p. 266; cf. "The Fellowship of the Inadequate" in Perry Epler Gresham, *Disciplines of High Calling*, The Bethany Press, 1954.
72. cartoon: "I Forgot the Message," *Saturday Review*, undated clipping.
73. Betty Thompson, "A Profile of Emilio Castro," *The Christian Century*, Aug. 29-Sept. 5, 1984, p. 792.
74. Jay R. Calhoun, alumnus and former assistant dean of Disciples Divinity House, has helped me with this analysis. See Wm. Barnett Blakemore, *Quest for Intelligence in Ministry: The Story of the First Seventy Five Years of the Disciples Divinity House of the University of Chicago*, The Disciples Divinity House of the University of Chicago, 1970.

Chapter 8: Seminary, Church, and Ministers in Partnership

1. For significant reflections on this theme, see W. Clark Gilpin, "Theological Education and Its Communities," *Criterion*, 24, 2 (Spring 1985), pp. 2-6. For a report of an earlier study of theological education among Disciples, see Carroll C. Cotten, *The Imperative Is Leadership: A Report on Ministerial Development in the Christian Church (Disciples of Christ) With Recommendations by the Study Commission on Ministerial Education, Christian Church (Disciples of Christ)*, Frank G. Dickey, chairman, The Bethany Press, 1973.
2. See an eloquent plea to historians for such breadth, without which interpretation and relevance are lacking: "History has broadened, historians have not." Philip D. Curtin, "Depth, Span, and Relevance," *American Historical Review*, 89, 1 (February 1984), pp. 1-9.
3. "Questions for Ministers," YDS 70 k.
4. D. Duane Cummins, "The Preacher and the Promoter," *Discipliana* 44:1 (Spring, 1984), pp. 3-7, 14.
5. D. Duane Cummins, "From Buffalo to Claremont," *Impact*, 11 (1983), p. 12.
6. *Ibid.*
7. Observations by W. Clark Gilpin at DHE workshop on theological education, Des Moines, Aug. 5, 1985.
8. David S. Broder recently commended to aspiring young journalists at Reed College the essential importance of an undergraduate major in the liberal arts rather than in journalism. See Jonathan Nichols, "Soft-spoken superstar," *The Oregonian*, Portland, Feb. 21, 1985.
9. Douglas and Tipton, *Religion and America*, p. 174.
10. Albro Martin, review of Steven A. Sass, *The Pragmatic Imagination: A History of the Wharton School, 1881-1981*, University of Pennsylvania Press, 1982, *American Historical Review*, 89, 1, (February 1984), pp. 216-217.
11. *Ibid.*, p. 217.
12. Robert A. Edmunds, "Practical Training," *The Christian Century*, April 16, 1986, pp. 397-398.
13. For a classical statement of the need for supervision, not practice alone, see Cicero, "De oratore," I, xxxiii, 150, *Loeb Classical Library I*, p. 103.
14. This idea was proposed by Dean Barbara Brown Zikmund of Pacific School of Religion at the 150th Anniversary Forum sponsored by the Division of Higher Education in St. Louis,

Nov. 6, 1986.
15. Totals gathered from 1986 reports to Division of Higher Education. For a recent commentary on Disciples seminary endowments, see Cummins, "From Buffalo to Claremont," p. 11.
16. T. J. Liggett, "Concern for Excellence," *Minister's Bulletin (Church Finance Council)*, 35, 5, (Oct.-Nov., 1984).
17. *Ibid.*
18. The Commission in the Pacific Southwest Region has adopted a declaration which makes explicit the ecumenical intention of the act.
19. Henrichsen, *Seven Steeples*, pp. 136-139.
20. See, e. g., *Concerns among Disciples Ministers on the Pacific Slope: A Summary Report*, Oikodome Reports, 3, Disciples Seminary Foundation, September 1984.
21. John W. Smith, "Burnout: The Clergy's Self-Destruct System," a paper prepared for the Western Association for Theological Discussion, May 25-27, 1983.
22. See C. Roy Stauffer, "Since You Asked," *The Disciple*, February 1985, p. 58. cf. "Placement Problems," *The Christian Century*, Nov. 21, 1984, p. 1090. The Department of Ministry, Division of Homeland Ministries has issued a series of booklets dealing with the process: Thomas E. Woods, *The Church Seeks a Minister*; John C. Updegraff, *The Minister Seeks a Congregation*; and Sidney J. Spain, *How to Help the Process Along*.
23. See *Clergy Resource Network: A Summary Report*, Division of Homeland Ministries, Department of Ministry, 1978. cf. Kenneth W. Scovill, "Clergy Support Systems among Disciples of Christ," D.Min. San Francisco Theological Seminary project, 1983; Rodney L. Parrott, "On Collegiality," *Oikodome Newsletter*, Disciples Seminary Foundation, No. 7, (Fall 1984), pp. 2-3. Letters from Art Morgan (June 5, 1984) and Jane W. Hopkins (Aug. 27, 1984) commented discerningly on ministers' sense of need for support.
24. "Annual Compensation (1985) Christian Ministers," *Pension Fund Bulletin*, 53, 2 (March 1986), p. 3.
25. A suggestion offered by D. Duane Cummins, May 22, 1984.
26. Art Morgan, letter.
27. Sally Wright, "Parsonage Wives Want Pastors, Too," *The Disciple*, October 1984, pp. 22-23.
28. John Claypool in *Glad Reunion* quotes Carlyle Marney to this effect. I am indebted to Bobby W. Cook of Shreveport, La., for the quotation. For the general theme of this subsection see Perry H. Biddle, Jr., "Continuing Education for Effective Ministry," *The Christian Ministry*, March 1982, pp. 17-19.
29. See the annual listing of Opportunities for Continuing Education issued by the Department of Ministry, DHM. cf. Connolly Gamble, *The Continuing Education of Parish Clergy: Report of a Survey*, Society for the Advancement of Continuing Education for Ministry, 1984; Barbara G. Wheeler, *The Educational Preferences and Practices of Talented Ministers: Report on an Exploratory Study*, based on research conducted by Durstan McDonald, Cameron Murchison, and Barbara G. Wheeler, supported by a grant from the Lilly Endowment, Inc.
30. Observation by Professor Laurence C. Keene of Pepperdine University, May 25, 1984.
31. Articles of Incorporation and By-Laws, Division of Higher Education, Christian Church (Disciples of Christ), Inc.
32. *Church Campus: A Report from the Division of Higher Education*, 4, 1, p. 32.
33. Report of Commission on Seminaries to Directors, Board of Higher Education, March, 1954.
34. See *The Disciples Theological Digest*, I, 1 (1986), ed. by D. Duane Cummins, The Division of Higher Education.
35. "Theological Education Viewed as Education of All Christians in the Faith: As Contrasted with the View of Educating only Professional Disciples Church Leadership," a study document prepared for DHE, Oct. 16, 1985.
36. *Ibid.*
37. For the papers on homosexuality see *Encounter*, 40, 3 (1979); for those on Disciples thought, *Classic Themes of Disciples Theology: Rethinking the Traditional Affirmations of the Christian Church (Disciples of Christ)*, ed. by Kenneth Lawrence, Texas Christian University Press, 1986.
38. "Sunset of an Era in the Northwest," *U.S. News & World Report*, May 5, 1986, p. 23.

39. Niebuhr, *The Purpose of the Church and Its Ministry*, p. 107. But note: "In the Protestant tradition theological education at its best does not have its primary commitment to the church as such, but with the church to the word of God." Thorwald Lorenzen, "Theological Education between Church and World," *Ministerial Formation*, World Council of Churches, 32, p. 19.
40. In some of the great universities the divinity faculties are related to these departments.
41. For the nineteenth century see John Baillie, *The Sense of the Presence of God, Gifford Lectures, 1961-2*, Charles Scribner's Sons, 1962, pp. 154-157. For overtones of regret at the inability to sustain the intense convictions of his Disciples forebears, see William Maxwell, *Ancestors*, Knopf, 1971, in passim.
42. For a plea that scholars return to the public life and engage vigorously in the discussion of issues of general concern, see Stanley N. Katz, "The Scholar & the Public," *Perspective*, AHA Newsletter, 23, 7, (October 1985), pp. 13-14.
43. See an important proposal for replacing the clerical paradigm: James F. Hopewell, "A Congregational Paradigm for Theological Education," *Theological Education*, 21, 1 (Autumn 1984), pp. 60-70. *Resources for People who Care about Congregations: Publications and Education Catalogue*, Spring/Summer 1986, The Alban Institute. I note similar observations in an unpublished paper by David Kelsey, "A Theological Curriculum About and Against the Church."
44. See Appendix I.

Appendix I
A Guide for Curriculum Review, Readapatation
(Prepared by Prudence Dyer)

I. **Societal Needs, Forces Challenging the Seminaries and the Churches**
   A. Questions for Faculty Analysis, Discussion, Decisions
      1. What effect are the new social developments likely to have on the life of the spirit?
      2. What are some ways the church might respond effectively to the new situation?
      3. In what ways can authentic Christian ministry best serve the new age?
      4. What are the implications for theological education in fulfilling its mission to such a future?
      5. Is there evidence that increased working with data/computers intensifies the hunger for more than knowledge?
      6. How will the church prove sensitive to the spiritual longing of persons caught in a world of high technology?
      7. How may a new generation of ministers be prepared to engage them with a gospel that addresses depths beyond the facts?
      8. In what ways can the church ameliorate racial and ethnic tension?
      9. Can the church replace society's mindless preoccupation with self-indulgence with a sense of global responsibility?
         a. What steps would be necessary to enable a community of faith to launch movement for the deescalation of the arms race?
         b. Can the church reestablish its leadership in community service in fields such as child care, respite care?
         c. How can funds be raised to exert a positive influence upon the media?
      10. How can denominations and ecumeical bodies in their own organizational life free themselves from bureaucratic assumptions, . . . with a dedication to the people to be served?
      11. In what ways is it possible for a Christian, a congregation, a denomination, a council of churches, a seminary to discover methods to affect the decisions of . . . massive bureaucracies?
      12. Can an authentic Christian theology be articulated capable of delivering the church in our generation from the trap of subjectivism?
      13. Can the seminaries lead in providing the appropriate programs currently being filled by the Institutes and Associations?
      14. How can the seminaries continue their historic leadership in the ecumenical church?
      15. By what process can the seminaries and the churches fill the spiritual void in many youth lured by cults with appropriate Christianity?
   B. Proposed Actions, Priorities

II. **Philosophy & Objectives of the Seminary**
   A. Do the Philosophy and Objectives of the Seminary
      1. ecompass a search for solutions to the needs confronting the emerging world?

2. see the work of ministry as loyal service to the gospel in all its range and fullness?
3. address head-on the crises in culture, church, and ministry and the relevance of their program to these needs?
4. guide the way in which the faculty teaches that God works?
   —in creativity?
   —in pathos?
   —in forgiveness, renewal?
   —in self-giving?
   —in intention?
   —in transformation?
   —in servanthood?

B. Proposed Revisions.

III. Curriculum Design and Evaluation

A. Questions to Consider
   1. Is a radical new approach needed for the curriculum of the seminary?
   2. Does the Seminary have a process for evaluating the curriculum in line with the present challenges and for redesign and readaptation?
   3. Does the Seminary have a process for examining and reflecting on the needs of the world, the theology of ministry, and the three strands of ministerial education?

B. Recommendations, Priorities

IV. Curriculum Content — Seminary

A. Does the curriculum consider/give attention to
   1. Involving students in life-giving contact with the Christian tradition so that its insights and power may truly inform their work?
   2. Guiding students in working out a realistic understanding of authority in a Christian community, the demands of leadership, the powers of persuasion, the appropriate use of authority?
   3. Counseling students on ways they might become ministers able to lead an agenda facing the churches?
   4. Helping students understand the work of the ministry and the importance of that work (as basis for self-esteem)?
   5. Helping students acquire authentic spiritual and intellectual vitality?
   6. Designing an appropriate balance among strands of the biblical, historical, theological, and technical studies?
   7. Integrating the comprehensive range within the strands of scientfic, professional, and fiduciary concerns?
   8. Understanding the use of scriptures?
   9. Achieving balance in the dual roles of manager and spiritual leader?
   10. Considering a systematic theology for ministry?
   11. Involving students in the suffering of the world's forgotten people?

B. Recommendations, Priorities

V. Curriculum, The Seminary Community, Field Experiences, Internships

A. Criteria for
   1. The Seminary Community

            a. What provisions are made for shared life in the seminary community?
            b. How is spirituality nurtured?
            c. How does/might the community relate to the suffering of the world's forgotten people?
        2. The Field Experiences
            a. How are field experiences selected? supervised? evaluated?
            b. How are active ministers selected, utilized within the seminary (adjunct faculty? occasional lecturers? consultants? ministers in residence?)
            c. How is the use of the active ministers established? evaluated?

VI. **Seminary Professors and Administrators: Characteristics and Qualifications**
    A. Selection of Faculty
    What are the criteria for selecting, retaining faculty members?
    B. Self Evaluation
    Are We (Am I)...
        1. Aware of needs cited above and creative enough to readapt curriculum to meet needs?
        2. Committed to its program of education for the ministry?
    Do We (I)
        3. Exhibit concern for and commitment to the pastoral ministry?
        4. Strive to manifest God's nature and replicate or duplicate God's way of working?
        5. Work individually or with colleagues (and/or churches/regional boards) to help students integrate the strands within the curriculum?
        6. Create new ways of integrating the skills and arts of the ministry?
        7. Believe in and work to cultivate the imagination?
        8. Devise ways for students to acquire knowledge of society?
        9. Contribute to the intellectual and ecclesiastical life of the Christian Church (Disciples of Christ) and the ecumenical movement?
    C. Recommendations

VII. **Instructional Methods**
    A. Criteria for Seminary Professors: Do we (I)
        1. Deal with seminarians as graduate students on the way to becoming professionals? and for the coming age?
        2. Use the methods of professionals in encouraging intellectual growth, understanding?
        3. Consider and evaluate how faith and piety might best be taught?
        4. Examine how a conversion experience and/or other encounters with God are to be explained and interpreted?
        5. Cultivate the imagination of students?
        6. Devise ways for students to acquire knowledge of society?
        7. Structure opportunities for students to examine and evaluate various management models?
        8. Provide ways for preparing ministers to teach? to guide parishioners in matters of faith, Bible study?
        9. Examine and value the contribution to ministry of the black preachers?

VIII. Assessment and Evaluation

IX. Students: Recruitment, Needs, Learning Styles/Challenges
  A. Criteria for Admission
   1. What admissions requirements other than a bachelor's degree should be established?
   2. Is it realistic to require studies in the humanities and other liberal arts?
  B. Questions to Consider
   1. Does the seminary, in conjunction with the undergraduate schools and churches find effective ways to recruit candidates?
      a. with authentic spiritual and intellectual vitality?
      b. by frequent contact with seminary faculty?
      c. by interpreting ministry to college students?
      d. from a variety of sources for ministry for small churches?
      e. with personal integrity, motivation, and commitment to serve?
      f. with commitment to Christian life of service?
      g. by offering intellectually stimulating and spiritually enriching opportunities?
      h. by careful screening, selectivity, periodic review?
   2. Does the seminary faculty foster in each student the qualities of creativity, imagination as well as understanding of teaching, and use of the scriptures?
   3. Does the seminary faculty cultivate the understanding of "who one is as a minister"?
      a. with study of models of ministry?
      b. with evidences of esteem?
  B. Recommendations, Priorities

X. Churches/Congregations
  A. Does the Seminary help the students, active ministers, and congregations understand the need to . . .
   1. cultivate effective discipleship in the oncoming generation?
   2. look beyond their present constituency to reach people from outside?
   3. rally people/organizations from their communities to participate in the struggle for peace with justice?
  B. Is there a true partnership between the church and the seminary? Do the local pastors have status with the seminary?
  C. What are the partnership provisions for ordination, licensing?
  D. How does the seminary provide for sustaining a vital ministry?
   1. in helping develop more satisfactory processes for relocating?
   2. in counseling with or resolving financial concerns?
   3. in providing a "safety net"?
  E. How can the seminary help the churches to recover a sense of the rightful intellectual dimensions of their ministers' work? In providing for appropriate continuing education?
  F. Is it appropriate to think of the seminaries as centers of spiritual renewal?

G. Can the church with the seminary articulate and interpret the relevancy of Christianity within the community?

H. Recommendations, Priorities

XI. **Disciples: Regional/General Offices, Divisions, Boards**

A. Is there a need to consider/resolve/think through
1. A theologically responsible formulation of their "noncreedal" or "non-theological" stance?
2. A forthright theology of the sacraments?
3. A consistent doctrine of ministry?
4. Faithfulness to the vision of oneness and wholeness for the church?
5. New confidence and effectiveness in evangelism?
6. The vision of the church articulated in the Design?
7. God's particular intention for this age?
8. The use of the moral influence of Christians/Disciples as a minority group?
9. The Division of Higher Education and the Seminaries:
   a. Is the current distribution formula based on instructional hours one which should be rethought?
   b. What are the current concerns within the church which the seminaries might help address? (minister as servant; the servant community, denominationalism)
   c. Should the traditional program in "theological schools" be followed? readapted?
   d. Who will take the initiative on a program of education for licensed ministers? What might that program include?
   e. How can the DHE help the seminaries to become greater intellectual and spiritual centers for the life of the Christian Church?

B. Recommendations

Appendix II
Perceived Strengths and Weaknesses of Recent Theological Education*

One phase of the CTS study attempted to assess the strenghts and weaknesses of recent theological education as judged by the performance of graduates of seminaries in the past ten years. Respondents were asked to make these judgments without regard to denomination or the school where young ministers had studied. In separate columns, we indicate the judgments of separate groupings of persons consulted. The composite ranking indicates the strengths (at the top) and weaknesses (at the bottom).

Column 1 Alumni Board, Ministers' Advisory Board, Department of Ministry of the Christian Church and commissions on the ministry of Disciples' regions (from Iowa to New York, including Canada) (86)
Column 2 Indiana Disciples (32)
Column 3 Laity (23)
Column 4 Representatives of Other Judicatories (11)

	1	2	3	4	Composite
1. Insight/Social issues	316	128	83	41	568
2. Ecumenical commitment	322	118	85	39	564
3. Pastoral counseling	317	122	82	37	558
4. Motivation for professional growth	296	128	80	44	548
5. Theological perception	309	115	79	42	545
6. Biblical knowledge	304	112	86	37	539
7. Worship leader	295	100	83	32	510
8. International horizons	292	98	79	34	504
9. Community leadership	293	98	79	34	504
10. Understanding of Denominational program	252	105	84	35	476
11. Christian education	272	93	77	33	475
12. Able to work in a pluralistic society	264	95	73	35	467
13. Preaching	265	81	80	37	463
14. Spiritual formation	247	99	74	42	462
15. Church administration	216	79	63	31	389

*From a working document, "Christian Theological Seminary Looks to the Future," Indianapolis, 1979. Used by permission.

Bibliography

Statistical Surveys and Reports
Christian Church (Disciples of Christ)

Allen, Irving H., Sr. "The Christian Church (Disciples of Christ) Profile of the Black Ministers, the Black Church Congregations and Facilities, a Minority Ministers Research Project." Sponsored by the Division of Homeland Ministries and the Division of Higher Education in cooperation with Jarvis Christian College, June-October, 1985.

"An Analysis of Department of Ministry Staff Visitations to Regional Commissions on the Ministry - August 1979-June 1981." Division of Homeland Ministries, 1981.

"Clergy Resource Network: A Summary Report." Department of Ministry, Division of Homeland Ministries, 1978.

"Clergy Supply Study." Pension Fund of the Christian Church (Disciples of Christ), June 1984.

"Handbook of Educational Opportunities for Lay and Bi-vocational Ministers." Department of Ministry, Division of Homeland Ministries, 1981.

Hardy, John M. "Nurture, Ordination, Standing for the Order of Ministry, the Christian Church (Disciples of Christ)." Christian Church in the Upper Midwest, 1980.

"License and Ordination" of the Christian Ministry. A report prepared by the Committee on Effective Ministry of the Home and State Missions Planning Council (Disciples of Christ). The United Christian Missionary Society, 1948.

"The Ministry: Supply/Demand Issues for the Christian Church (Disciples of Christ) - 1979." Department of Ministry report. Division of Homeland Ministries, 1979.

Osborn, Ronald E. Survey of Selected Alumni/ae of Disciples-Related Seminaries and Foundation Houses. Fall, 1985.

_____ , Meeting with Executives of Disciples-Related Theological Education Institutions. Sept. 24-25, 1984.

Osborn, Cummins, "To Serve the Coming Age: The Mission of Theological Education." Interest Group at the General Assembly, Christian Church (Disciples of Christ), Aug. 5, 1985.

Osborn, Cummins, McCormick, Report to the Council of Colleges and Universities. Drake University, Aug. 2, 1985.

"Policies and Criteria for the Order of Ministry in the Christian Church (Disciples of Christ)." Adopted by the General Assembly meeting in 1971.

"Report of New Congregations Organized." Board of Church Extension, Christian Church (Disciples of Christ), Second Quarter, 1984.

Spain, Sidney J., *How to Help the Process Along*. Department of Ministry, Division of Homeland Ministry, 1984.

Updegraff, John C., *The Minister Seeks a Congregation*. Department of Ministry, Division of Homeland Ministries, 1978.

Wood, Thomas E., *The Church Seeks A Minister*. Department of Ministry and Worship, Division of Homeland Ministries, 1973.

Unpublished Dissertations and Theses

Durden, William W., "A Study of the Bivocational Ministry of Southern Baptist Pastors in the Middle Georgia Area for the Purpose of Developing a Workshop

Manual for Southern Baptist Bivocational Ministers," Unpublished D.Min. project, San Francisco Theological Seminary, 1984.
Imbler, John M, "By Degrees: The Development of Theological Education Within the Disciples of Christ," Unpublished S.T.M. thesis, Christian Theological Seminary, 1981.
_____ , "Theological Education in the Thought of Alexander Campbell," Unpublished paper, Christian Theological Seminary, 1980.
Johnson, Joseph A., Jr., *The Soul of the Black Preacher*, privately published, 1970.
Lynn, Robert W., *Why the Seminary? An Introduction to the Full Report of the Auburn History Project*, Lilly Endowment, Inc., 1980.
Scovill, Kenneth W., "Clergy Support Systems among Disciples of Christ," Unpublished D.Min. project, San Francisco Theological Seminary, 1983.
Walker, Randi Jones, "Protestantism in the Sangre de Cristos: Factors in the Growth and Decline of the Hispanic Protestant Churches in Northern New Mexico and Southern Colorado, 1850-1920," Unpublished Ph.D. dissertation, Claremont Graduate School, 1972.

General Sources
Christian Church (Disciples of Christ)

Abbott, B. A., *The Disciples: An Interpretation*. The Bethany Press, 1924.
Ainslie, Peter, *Working with God, or the Story of a Twenty-five-year Pastorate in Baltimore*. Christian Board of Publication, 1917.
Ames, Van Meter (ed.), *Beyond Theology: The Autobiography of Edward Scribner Ames*. University of Chicago Press, 1959.
Baird, William, *What is Our Authority?* Christian Board of Publication, for the Council on Christian Unity, 1983.
Beazley, George G., Jr., *The Christian Church (Disciples of Christ): An Interpretative Examination in the Cultural Context*. The Bethany Press, 1973.
Belcastro, Joseph, *The Relationship of Baptism to Church Membership*. The Bethany Press, 1963.
Black Disciples Legacy Series. National Convocation of the Christian Church, 1976.
Blakemore, Wm. Barnett, *Quest for Intelligence in Ministry: The Story of the First Seventy-Five Years of the Disciples Divinity House of the University of Chicago*. The Disciples Divinity House of the University of Chicago, 1970.
_____ , (ed.) *The Renewal of Church: The Panel of Scholars Reports*. The Bethany Press, 1963.
Brokaw, G. L. (ed.), *Doctrine and Life*. Christian Index Publishing Company, 1898.
Browning, Don S., *Atonement and Psychotherapy*. Westminster Press, 1966.
_____ , (ed.), *Practical Theology*. Harper & Row, 1983.
Campbell, Alexander, *The Christian System*. (Bethany, WV, 1835) Christian Board of Publication, n.d.
Campbell, Thomas, *A Declaration and Address*. International Convention of Disciples of Christ, 1949.
Cole, Myron C., *Myron Here*. Mills Publishing Co., 1982.
Cotten, Carroll C., *The Imperative Is Leadership*. The Bethany Press, 1973.
Davison, Frank Elson, *Thru the Rear-View Mirror*, The Bethany Press, 1955.
England, Stephan J., *The One Baptism: Baptism and Christian Unity, with Special Reference to Disciples of Christ*. The Bethany Press, 1960.
Fortune, A. W., *The Church of the Future*. The Bethany Press, 1930.
Fey, Harold E., *How I Read the Riddle: An Autobiography*. The Bethany Press, 1982.

———, (ed.) *Kirby Page, Social Evangelist: The Autobiography of a 20th Century Prophet for Peace*. Fellowship Press, 1975.
———, *The Lord's Supper: Seven Meanings*. Harper, 1948.
Garrison, James H., *The Old Faith Restated*. Christian Publishing Co, 1891.
Garrison, Winfred E., and DeGroot, Alfred T., *The Disciples of Christ: A History*. Christian Board of Publication, 1948.
Gresham, Perry E., *Disciplines of the High Calling*. The Bethany Press, 1954.
Humbert, Royal (ed.), *A Compend of Alexander Campbell's Theology*. Bethany Press, 1961.
Joyce, J. Daniel, *The Place of the Sacraments in Worship*. The Bethany Press, 1967.
Linn, Jan G., *Christians Must Choose: The Lure of Culture and the Command of Christ*. CBP Press, 1985.
Lawrence, Kenneth (ed.), *Classical Themes of Disciples Theology*. Texas Christian University Press, 1986.
Lindsay, Vachel, *Collected Poems*. Revised ed. Macmillan, 1946.
Maus, Cynthia Pearl, *Time to Remember*. Exposition Press, 1964.
Montgomery, Riley B., *The Education of Ministers of Disciples of Christ*. The Bethany Press, 1931.
Moore, William Thomas, *The Plea of the Disciples of Christ*. Christian Century Co., 1906.
Morrison, Charles Clayton, *The Unfinished Reformation*. Harper & Brothers, 1953.
Munnell, Thomas, *The Care of the Churches*. Christian Publishing Co, 1888.
Myers, Oma Loru (comp.), *Rosa's Song*, ed. by Guin Tuckett, CBP Press, 1984.
Osborn, G. Edwin (ed.), *Christian Worship: A Service Book*. Christian Board of Publication, 1953.
Osborn, Ronald E., *Ely Vaughn Zollars*. The Bethany Press, 1947.
———, *Experiment in Liberty: The Ideal of Freedom in the Experience of the Disciples of Christ*. The Bethany Press, 1978.
———, *The Faith We Affirm: Basic Beliefs of the Disciples of Christ*. The Bethany Press, 1979.
———, *In Christ's Place: Christian Ministry in Today's World*. The Bethany Press, 1967.
———, (ed.), *Seeking God's Peace in a Nuclear Age: A Call To Disciples of Christ*. CBP Press, 1985.
Rossman, Parker, *Computers: Bridges to the Future*. Judson Press, 1986.
Richardson, Robert, *Memoirs of Alexander Campbell, Embracing a View of the Origin, Progress and Principles of the Religious Reformation which He Advocated*. J. B. Lippincott and Co., 1871.
Shaw, Henry K., *Buckeye Disciples: A History of the Disciples of Christ in Ohio*. Christian Board of Publication, 1952.
Smith, William Martin, *Servants Without Hire*. The Disciples of Christ Historical Society, 1968.
———, *For the Support of the Ministry*. Pension Fund of Disciples of Christ, 1956.
Stevenson, Dwight E., *Lexington Theological Seminary, 1865-1965*. The Bethany Press, 1964.
Teegarden, Kenneth L., *We Call Ourselves Disciples*. The Bethany Press, 1975.
Tucker, William E., and McAllister, Lester G., *Journey in Faith: A History of the Christian Church (Disciples of Christ)*. The Bethany Press, 1975.
The Untold Story: A Short History of Black Disciples, CMF/CWF Studies. Christian Board of Publication, 1976.

Walker, Granville T., *Preaching in the Thought of Alexander Campbell.* Bethany Press, 1954.
Ward, Don (ed.), *The Seeking Heart: The Prayer Journal of Mae Yoho Ward.* CBP Press, 1985.
Watkins, Keith, *The Feast of Joy: The Lord's Supper in Free Churches.* Bethany Press, 1977.
West, Earl Irwin, *The Search for the Ancient Order: A History of the Restoration Movement, 1849-1906.* Gospel Advocate Co., 1949-50.
Whitley, Oliver R., *Religious Behavior: Where Sociology and Religion Meet.* Prentice-Hall, Inc., 1964.
Williams, D. Newell, *Ministry Among Disciples: Past, Present, and Future.* Christian Board of Pubilcation for the Council on Christian Unity, 1985.
Williamson, Clark M., *Has God Rejected His People?: Anti-Judaism in the Christian Church.* Abingdon Press, 1982.
Wrather, Eva Jean, *Creative Freedom in Action: Alexander Campbell on the Structure of the Church.* Bethany Press, 1968.

Periodical Literature
Christian Church (Disciples of Christ)

"Church-Campus: A Report from the Division of Higher Education." Christian Church (Disciples of Christ). 4:1, (1984).
The Disciple. selected editorials and articles. August 1984 - June 1986.
The Disciples Theological Digest. Division of Higher Education. 1:1 (1986).
Discipliana. selected articles. Disciples of Christ Historical Society. Summer 1978 - Spring 1986.
Eminihizer, Earl Eugene. "Alexander Campbell on Moral and Quality Education - Some New Light," *The Iliff Review,* Iliff School of Theology. Spring 1984.
Encounter. selected articles. Christian Theological Seminary, 1962 - 1986.
Gilpin, W. Clark, "A Divinity Education," *DDH Bulletin,* Disciples Divinity House, 56:3 (Spring 1986).
_____, "The Seminary and Its Communities," *Criterion,* 24:2, (Spring 1985).
Graham, Ronald W., "Women in the Pauline Churches: A Review Article," *Lexington Theological Quarterly,* 11:1 (January 1976).
Hunter, Barton, "Listen You, How Long Will You Wait?" *World Call,* May 1945.
Impact: Disciples of Christ on the Pacific Slope. selected articles. Disciples Seminary Foundation, School of Theology at Claremont. Claremont, CA, 1981-1985.
Mid-Stream: An Ecumenical Journal. selected articles. Council on Christian Unity, Christian Church (Disciples of Christ), 1966-1986.
Osborn, Ronald E., "Religious Freedom and the Form of the Church: An Assessment of the Denomination in America," *Lexington Theological Quarterly,* 11:3 (1976).
Pearson, Samuel C., "The Campbell Institute: Herald of the Transformation of an American Religious Tradition," *The Scroll: Journal of the Campbell Institute,* Disciples Divinity House, 62:2 (Spring 1968).

Contemporary Books on Theological Education and Ministry

Anderson, Ray S. (ed.), *Theological Foundations for Ministry.* Eerdmans, 1979.
Baptism, Eucharist and Ministry. Faith and Order Paper No. 111, Geneva, World Council of Churches, 1982.

250 THE EDUCATION OF MINISTERS FOR THE COMING AGE

Barraclough, Geoffrey, *The Medieval Papacy*. Harcourt, Brace and World, 1968.
Bergendoff, Conrad (ed.), *Luther's Works*. Vol. 40, *Church and Ministry*, Concordia Publishing House, 1955-76.
Bilheimer, Robert S., *A Spirituality for the Long Haul*. Fortress Press, 1984.
Buechner, Frederick, *The Sacred Journey*. Harper & Row, 1982.
Calian, Carnegie Samuel, *Today's Pastor in Tomorrow's World*. revised ed. The Westminister Press, 1982.
Carroll, Jackson W., and Wilson, Robert F., *Too Many Pastors? The Clergy Job Market*. The Pilgrim Press, 1980.
Coan, Richard W., *Hero, Artist, Sage, or Saint?* Columbia University Press, 1977.
Cooke, Bernard, *Ministry to Word and Sacraments*. Fortress Press, 1976.
Cox, Robert G., *Do You Mean Me, Lord? The Call to the Ordained Ministry*. The Westminister Press, 1985.
Cully, Iris V., *Education for Spiritual Growth*. Harper & Row, 1984.
Day, Heather F., *Protestant Theological Education in America: A Bibliography*. ATLA Bibliography Series, No. 15. The American Theological Library Association and The Scarecrow Press, Inc., 1985.
Dilday, Russell H., Jr, *Personal Computer: A New Tool for Ministers*. Broadman Press, 1986.
Farley, Edward, *Theologia: The Fragmentation and Unity of Theological Education*. Fortress Press, 1983.
Fletcher, John C., *The Futures of Protestant Seminaries*. The Alban Institute, 1983.
Greenleaf, Robert K., *Servant Leadership: A Journey into the Nature of Legitimate Power and Greatness*. Paulist Press, 1977.
Holmes, Urban T., III, *The Future Shape of Ministry: A Theological Projection*. The Seabury Press, 1971.
_____ , *Spirituality for Ministry*. Harper & Row, 1982.
Hough, Joseph C., Jr., and Cobb, John B., Jr., *Christian Identity and Theological Education*. Scholars Press, 1985.
Hutcheson, Richard G., Jr., *The Churches and the Chaplaincy*. John Knox, 1976.
Jenkins, Daniel, *Protestant Ministry*. London, Faber and Faber, 1958.
Johnson, William R., *The Pastor and the Personal Computer: Information Management for Ministers*. Abingdon Press, 1986.
Judy, Marvin T., *The Multiple Staff Ministry*. Abingdon, 1969.
Kelly, Robert L., and Daniel, W.A., *The Education of Negro Ministers*. George H. Doran Company, 1925.
Kemp, Charles F., *Preparing for the Ministry*. The Bethany Press, 1959.
Niebuhr, H. Richard, and Williams, Daniel Day (eds), *The Ministry in Historical Perspectives*. Harper & Brothers Publishers, 1956.
Niebuhr, H. Richard, et. al., *The Purpose of the Church and Its Ministry*. Harper & Brothers, 1956.
Oden, Thomas C., *Pastoral Theology: Essentials of the Ministry*. Harper & Row, 1983.
Paul, Robert S., *Ministry*. Eerdmans, 1965.
Rallings, E. M. (Bud), and Pratto, David J., *Two Clergy Marriages: A Special Case of Dual Careers*. University Press of America, 1985.
Rulla, Luigi, M., S.J., et.al., *Entering and Leaving Vocation: Inter-psychi Dynamics*. Loyola University Press, 1976.
Schaller, Lyle E. (ed.), *Women as Pastors*, Creative Leadership Series. Abingdon Press, 1982.
Schuller, David S., et. al, (eds), *Ministry in America*. Harper & Row, 1980.

Smith, Elwyn Allen, *The Presbyterian Ministry in American Culture: A Study in Changing Concepts, 1700-1900*. The Westminster Press, 1962.
Thurman, Howard, *With Head and Heart*, Harcourt, Brace, Jovanovich, 1979.
Wagoner, Walter D., *Bachelor of Divinity: Uncertain Servants in Seminary and Ministry*. Association Press, 1963.
Winquist, Charles E., *Practical Hermeneutics: A Revised Agenda for the Ministry*. Scholars Press, 1980.

Contemporary Periodical Literature
On Theological Education and Ministry

Berckman, Edward M., "Ministering to the 'New Poor,'" *The Witness*, 62:6 (January 1984).
The Christian Century. selected editorials and articles. April 24, 1956 - August 27/September 3, 1986.
The Christian Ministry. selected articles. January 1982 and March 1982.
"Clergywomen: 10,470 are now ordained," *Time*, April 3, 1978.
Douglass, Jane Dempsey, "Christian Freedom: What Calvin Learned at the School of Women," *Church History*, 53 (June 1984).
Maloney, Lawrence D. with Kathleen Phillips, "What's Behind a Growing Shortage of Priests," *U.S. News and World Report*, June 18, 1984.
"New Shepherds to Lead Nation's Religious Flock," *U.S. News and World Report*, December 31, 1984/January 7, 1985.
O'Donovan, Leo J., S.J., "Ahead of Us Still," *Criterion*, 24:2 (Spring 1985).
"The Parish Minister's Self-Image and Variability in Community Culture," *Pastoral Psychology*, October, 1959.
Stump, Roger W., "Women Clergy in the United States: A Geographical Analysis of Religious Change," *Social Science Quarterly*, 67:2 (July 1986).
Theological Education. selected articles. Association of Theological Schools, 1980-1984.
"Women of the Cloth: How They're Faring," *U.S. News and World Report*, December 3, 1984.
Woodard, Kenneth L., et. al., "Church in Crisis," *Newsweek*, December 9, 1985.

Contemporary Associational and Denominational Reports
On Theological Education and Ministry

"An Invitation to Action: A Study of Ministry, Sacraments, and Recognition," The Lutheran-Reformed Dialogue, Series III, 1981-1983. Fortress Press, 1984.
"Careers in Ministry: An Ecumenical Guidebook for Counselors, Pastors, and Youth." Consortium Books, 1976.
Gamble, Connolly, *The Continuing Education of Parish Clergy: Report of a Survey*, Society for the Advancement of Continuing Education for Ministry, 1984.
"Global Solidarity in Theological Education: Report of the U.S./Canadian Consultation." Geneva, World Council of Churches, 1981.
Johnson, Robert Clyde, *The Church and Its Changing Ministry*, Office of the General Assembly, The United Presbyterian Church in the United States of America, 1961.
Madsen, Paul O., *Tomorrow's Ministers*. Commission on the Ministry, American Baptist Churches, 1983.
"Ministerial Formation: Programme on Theological Education," Geneva, World Council of Churches, 32 (December 1985).

The Ministry of the Church: A Lutheran Understanding. Division of Theological Studies, Lutheran Council in the USA. 1974.
Ministry in an Age of Ambiguity. Report of the North American Consultation on the Future of Ministry, Toronto, Canada, October 7-10, 1980. Professional Church Leadership, National Council of Churches, 1980.
Toward the Year 2018. A report of the Foreign Policy Association. Cowles Education Corporation, 1968.
Williams, Colin Wilbur, *Where in the World? Changing Forms of the Church's Witness*, National Council of Churches of Christ in the U.S.A., 1963.

Social Interpretations of American History, Education, and Religion

Alhstrom, Sydney E., *A Religious History of the American People*. Yale University Press, 1972.
Astin, Alexander, *Four Critical Years*. Jossey-Bass Publishers, 1977.
Bell, Daniel, *The Coming of Post-industrial Society*. Basic Books, 1973.
Bellah, Robert N., *The Broken Covenant: American Civil Religion in a Time of Trial*. Seabury Press, 1975.
──────, et. al., *Habits of the Heart: Individualism and Commitment in American Life*, University of California Press, 1985.
Bercovitch, Sacvan, *The Puritan Jeremiad*. The University of Wisconsin Press, 1978.
Bowen, Howard R., *The State of the Nation and the Agenda for Higher Education*. Jossey-Bass Publishers, 1982.
Brod, Craig, *Technostress: The Human Cost of the Computer Revolution*. Addison-Wesley, 1984.
Bryce, James, *The American Commonwealth*, Macmillan and Co., 1891.
Calhoun, C. J., and Iomi, F.A.J. (eds.), *The Anthropological Study of Education*. Aldine, 1976.
Calhoun, Daniel, *The Intelligence of a People*. Princeton University Press, 1973.
Carey, John J., *Carlyle Marney: A Pilgrim's Progress*. Mercer University Press, 1980.
Clarke, Arthur C., *Profiles of the Future: An Inquiry to the Limits of the Possible*. Holt, Rinehart and Winston, 1982.
Cobb, John B., Jr., *Christ in a Pluralistic Age*. Westminster, 1975.
Corn, Joseph J., and Horrigan, Brian, *Yesterday's Tomorrows: Past Visions of the American Future*. Summit Books, 1984.
Cutler, Donald R. (ed.), *The Religious Situation: 1969*. Beacon Press, 1969.
Douglas, Mary and Tipton, Steven (eds.), *Religion and America: Spiritual Life in a Secular Age*. Beacon Press, 1983.
Frye, Northrop, *Anatomy of Criticism: Four Essays*. Princeton University Press, 1957.
Frymier, Jack R., *The Nature of Educational Method*. Charles E. Merrill Books, Inc., 1965.
Ganoczy, Alexander, *Becoming Christian*. Paulist Press, 1976.
Gilkey, Langdon, *How the Church Can Minister to the World without Losing Itself*. Harper & Row, 1964.
Goode, William J., *The Celebration of Heroes: Prestige as a Social Control System*. University of California Press, 1978.
Hacker, Andrew (ed.), *U/S: A Statistical Portrait of the American People*. Penguin Books, 1983.
Hardesty, Nancy A., *Women Called to Witness: Evangelical Feminism in the Nineteenth Century*. Abingdon Press, 1984.

BIBLIOGRAPHY 253

Heimert, Alan, and Miller, Perry (eds.), *The Great Awakening: Documents Illustrating the Crisis and Its Consequences.* Bobbs-Merrill, 1967.
Hofstadter, Richard, and Metzger, Walter P., *The Development of Academic Freedom in the United States.* Columbia University Press, 1955.
Hudson, Winthrop, S., *The Great Tradition of the American Churches.* Harper, 1953.
Jay, Eric G., *The Church: Its Changing Image through Twenty Centuries.* John Knox Press, 1977.
Jones, James W., *The Shattered Synthesis: New England Puritanism before the Great Awakening.* Yale University Press, 1973.
Kahn, Herman, and Wiener, Anthony J., *The Year 2000: A Framework for Speculation on the Next 33 Years.* Macmillan, 1967.
Kennedy, George A., *Classical Rhetoric and Its Christian and Secular Tradition from Ancient to Modern Times.* The University of North Carolina Press, 1980.
Lasch, Christopher, *The Culture of Narcissism: American Life in an Age of Diminishing Expectations.* Warner Books, 1979.
Lawrence, Paul R., and Dyer, Davis, *Renewing American Industry.* The Free Press, 1983.
Lindley, Neil E., *Dynamic Discipleship for a New Age.* Brentwood Christian Press, 1984.
McLaughlin, William G., "Revivals, Awakenings, and Reform: An Essay on Religion and Social Change in America" in *Chicago History of American Religion.* ed. by Martin E. Marty, University of Chicago Press, 1978.
McNeill, John T., *A History of the Cure of Souls.* Harper & Brothers, 1951.
Mead, Sidney, *The Nation with the Soul of a Church.* Harper & Row, 1975.
Naisbett, John, *Megatrends: Ten New Directions Transforming Our Lives.* Warner Brothers, 1982.
Niebuhr, H. Richard, *Christ and Culture.* Harper, 1951.
───────, *The Meaning of Revelation.* Macmillan, 1941.
───────, *The Social Sources of Denominationalism.* Meridan Books, 1957.
Orwell, George, *1984.* Harcourt, Brace, Jovanovich, (1949) 1984.
Paul, Robert, S., *The Church in Search of Itself.* Eerdmans Publishing Company, 1972.
Peters, T. J., and Waterman, R. H., Jr., *In Search of Excellence: Lessons from America's Best Run Companies.* Harper & Row, 1982.
Petry, C. Ray, *Christian Eschatology and Social Thought.* Abingdon, 1956.
Pipes, William H., *Say Amen, Brother! Old-Time Negro Preaching: A Study in American Frustration.* The William-Frederick Press, 1951.
Postman, Neil, *Amusing Ourselves to Death: Public Discourse in the Age of Show Business.* Viking, 1986.
───────, *The Disappearance of Childhood.* The Delacorte Press, 1982.
Rieff, Philip, *The Triumph of the Therapeutic.* Harper & Row, 1966.
Ross, Nelson Peter, *Christianity and Humanism: Studies in the History of Ideas.* Eerdmans, 1968.
Shils, Edward, *Tradition.* The University of Chicago Press, 1981.
Stark, Rodney, and Bainbridge, William Sims, *The Future of Religion: Secularization, Revival and Cult Formation.* University of California Press, 1985.
Toffler, Alvin, *The Third Wave.* William Morrow and Company, Inc., 1980.
Turkle, Sherry, *The Second Self: Computers and the Human Spirit.* Simon and Schuster, 1984.
Vahanian, Gabriel, *The Death of God: The Culture of Our Post-Christian Era.*

Braziller, 1961.
Wieman, Henry Nelson, *The Source of Human Good*. The University of Chicago Press, 1946.
Winter, Gibson, *The Suburban Captivity of the Churches*. Doubleday, 1961.
Yankelovich, Daniel, *New Rules: Searching for Self-fulfillment in a World Turned Upside Down*. Random House, 1981.
Young, Henry J., *Major Black Religious Leaders, 1755-1940*, Abingdon, 1977.

Miscellaneous

Baillie, John, *The Sense of the Presence of God*. Charles Scribner's Sons, 1962.
Bonhoeffer, Dietrich, *Life Together.*, Harper, 1954.
Dories, William D., *Paul and Rabbinic Judaism*. London, SPCK, 1955.
Dawson, Christopher, *Religion and Culture*. London, Sheed and Ward, 1948.
Eliade, Mircea, *Shamanism: Archaic Techniques of Ecstasy*. Trans. by Willard R. Trask. Bollingen Foundation, (distributed by Panatheon Books), 1964.
Eusden, John D. (ed.), *The Marrow of Theology*. Trans. from the third Latin edition. Pilgrim Press, 1968.
Horistan, Casiano, *The Parish: Eucharistic Community*, trans. by John F. Byrne. London, Sheed and Ward, 1965.
Heschel, Abraham Joshua, *The Prophets*. Harper & Row, 1969.
Johnston, William *Christian Zen*. Harper & Row, 1971.
Kazantzakais, Nikos, *The Saviors of God: Spiritual Exercises.* trans. by Kimon Frior. Simon and Schuster, 1960.
LeFevre, Perry, *Understandings of Prayer*. Westminster Press, 1981.
McNeill, John T. (ed.), *Calvin's Institutes of the Christian Religion*, trans. by Ford Lewis Battles. Library of Christian Classics, Westminster Press, 1960.
Minear, Paul S., *Images of the Church in the New Testament*. The Westminster Press, 1960.
Moede, Gerald F., *The COCU Consensus: In Quest of a Church of Christ Uniting*. Consultation on Church Union, 1983.
Moore, Mary Elizabeth, *Education for Continuity and Change: A New Model for Christian Religious Education*. Abingdon, 1983.
Niehardt, John G., (aka Flaming Rainbow), *Black Elk Speaks: Being the Life Story of a Holy Man of the Oglala Sioux*. University of Nebraska Press, 1961.
Newbigin, Lesslie, *The Other Side of 1984: Questions for the Churches*. Geneva, World Council of Churches, 1984.
Newbold, Robert T., Jr., *Black Preaching: Select Sermons in the Presbyterian Tradition*. The Geneva Press, 1977.
Nickelsberg, George W.E., and Stone, Michael E., *Faith and Piety in Early Judaism:- Texts and Documents*. Fortress Press, 1983.
Outler, Albert C., *Psychotherapy and the Christian Message*. Harper, 1954.
Pelikan, Jaroslav, *Jesus through the Centuries*. Yale University Pres, 1985.
_____ , *The Vindication of Tradition*. Yale University Press, 1984.
Ray, David R., *Small Churches Are the Right Size*. Pilgrim Press, 1982.
Reitz, Ruediger, *The Church in Experiment: Studies in New Congregational Structures and Functional Mission*. Abingdon, 1969.
Rouse, Ruth, and Neill, Stephen C. (eds.), *A History of the Ecumenical Movement, 1517-1948*. Westminster Press, 1954.
Sherrill, Lewis Joseph, *The Rise of Christian Education*. The Macmillan Company, 1944.
Schaller, Lyle E., *The Small Church is Different*. Abingdon Press, 1982.

Seifert, Harvey, *New Power for the Church*. Westminster, 1976.
Suzuki, Daisetz Teitaro, *The Training of a Zen Buddhist Monk*. University Books, 1959.
Tutu, Desmond Mpilo, *Hope and Suffering: Sermons and Speeches*. William B. Eerdmans Publishing Co., 1983.
von Rad, Gerhard, *Wisdom in Israel*. Abingdon, 1972.
Walrath, Douglas Alan (ed.), *New Possibilities for Small Churches*. The Pilgrim Press, 1983.
Wainwright, Goeffrey, *Doxology: The Praise of God in Worship, Doctrine, and Life*. Oxford University Press, 1980.
Webber, G. W., *The Congregation in Mission*. Abingdon Press, 1964.
Wedel, Theodore O., *The Coming Great Church*. The Macmillan Co., 1945.
Whitehead, Alfred North, *Adventures of Ideas*. Macmillan, 1933.

INDEX

Age of Reason, the, 36
American Indians, 42, 158
Asian Americans, 10, 11, 158
Association of Theological Schools, 74, 83, 84, 90, 99, 137, 193; ATS, 154, 165, 192

baptism, 49, 63, 67, 73, 80, 92, 105, 126, 148
Baptism, Eucharist and Ministry, 50, 60, 103, 117
Baptists, 43, 146, 147; American, 202; Southern Convention, 43, 84, 202
Blacks, 10, 42, 43, 65, 133, 158
bivocational ministry, 66, 137
Brite Divinity School, 90, 91, 181; Texas Christianity University Bible College, 86, 89

Campbell, Alexander, 29, 45, 47, 48, 50, 51, 65, 71, 77, 84, 85, 94, 117, 135, 151, 209
Campbell, Thomas, 45, 51, 65, 84, 117
Christian Endeavor, 30, 63, 153
Christian Churches (Independent), 48; Christians ("Independents"), 43, 46, 89
Christian Church (Disciples of Christ) [in the United States and Canada], xi, 7, 8, 10, 47 49, 84, 92, 114, 143, 159, 160, 187, 188, 192, 197, 201, 204; Disciples: general, 10, 42, 45, 53, 65, 93, 123, 136, 138, 146, 147, 151, 155, 158, 178, 179, 188, 193, 201, 204; education, 49, 78, 83, 86, 87, 88, 89, 90, 91, 94, 95, 99, 137, 181, 183, 189, 191, 192, 210; ecumenical, 43, 44, 48, 69, 170, 202; history and polity, 46, 47, 49, 50, 51, 66, 67, 72, 135; ministry, 74, 102, 117, 132, 133, 134, 152, 153, 154, 196, 197; Disciples of Christ: general, 56, 87, 90, 101, 193; education for ministry, 78, 84, 179; theology and practice, 38, 40, 41, 45, 65, 69, 147, 152, 178
Christian Theological Seminary, 88, 90, 91, 201; Butler School (College) of Religion, 88, 89
Church(es) of Christ, 46, 48, 88
Congregationlists, 43, 82; also see United Church of Christ
Council on Theological Education (Division of Higher Education), 199, 200, 203, 204

deacons, 50, 58, 65, 66, 67, 70, 71, 72, 75, 149
Department of Ministry, Division of Homeland Ministries, 138, 154, 160, 194, 197, 199, 200, 204, 205
Design, the, for the Christian Church (Disciples of Christ), 48, 51, 55, 66, 75, 131, 193
Disciples Divinity House, University of Chicago, 89, 90, 91, 183, 184, 201; University of Chicago Divinity School, 89, 99, 165, 184

Disciples Divinity House, Vanderbilt University, 90, 91
Disciples Seminary Foundation, 90, 91; School of Theology at Claremont, 99, 165
Drake Divinity School, 90; Drake Bible College, 86, 89
Division of Higher Education, 108, 160, 190, 199, 201, 202, 203, 204, 205, 206; Board of Education, 87, 89; Board of Higher Education, 199, 201

elders, 50, 66, 67, 71, 72, 75, 135, 149, 159, 193
Enlightenment, the, 34, 36, 41, 59, 60, 81
Episcopal Church, 132, 155; Anglicans, 82; Episcopalians, 43, 183, 202
eucharist, 60, 61, 70, 72, 73, 126; also see Lord's Supper
Eugene Divinity School, Eugene Bible University, 86
evangelists, 47, 58, 65, 66, 67, 70, 72, 75, 76, 77, 135

General Assembly [of the Christian Church (Disciples of Christ)], 8, 10, 66, 138, 143, 190, 193, 199, 203, 204, 205, 210
Great Awakening, the, 41, 62, 82, 147; Second Great Awakening, 62

Hispanics, 10, 42, 51, 158

Industrial Revolution, 17, 30, 35, 163

Jesus Christ, 25, 34, 45, 49, 51, 56, 58, 69, 71, 117, 126, 129, 138, 139, 178; Christ, 11, 33, 34, 45, 49, 53, 54, 56, 58, 69, 110, 114, 115, 116, 121, 124, 169, 182; Jesus, 29, 32, 33, 48, 58, 67, 70, 79, 105, 109, 112, 116, 117, 145, 148, 183, 209; ministry of, 31, 42, 58, 66, 69, 75, 104, 113, 118, 148

King, Martin Luther, Jr., 5, 109, 120, 122, 146, 157

Lexington Theological Seminary, 90, 91; The College of the Bible, 86, 88, 89, 90, 179
licensed ministers, 50, 66, 131, 135, 137, 138, 158, 194, 195; license, 138, 194; licensing, 194, 195
Lord's Supper, 50, 66; also see eucharist
Luther, Martin, 35, 60

Millennial Harbinger, the, xii, 33

National Council of Churches of Christ, 43
Niebuhr, H. Richard, 64, 73, 114, 206f

ordained ministers(ry), 59, 75, 117, 126, 130, 131, 132, 138, 140; ordinand, 194; ordination, 66, 67, 72, 73, 89, 129, 134, 137, 142, 149, 150, 151, 157, 159, 190, 193, 195, 204; ordained, 50, 65, 66, 116, 131, 133, 134, 135, 148, 150, 151

Paul (Apostle), 24, 29, 69, 79, 114, 117, 121, 148, 149, 170, 182
Pension Fund of the Christian Church, 160, 190, 197, 204
Phillips Graduate Seminary, 22, 90, 91, 192f; Bible college, 46, 88, 89, 210
Presbyterians, 43, 82, 202

Reformation, the (Protestant), 21, 35, 60, 69, 80, 145, 151
Renaissance, the, 21, 81
Restructure [Christian Church (Disciples of Christ)], 50, 66, 133, 187, 193, 202
Roman Catholic Church, 9, 38, 44, 99, 132, 137, 181, 187; Roman Catholics, 10, 100, 144, 150, 170; Catholicism, 60, 147

Scott, Walter, 45, 65, 84, 85
Stone, Barton W., 45, 51, 65, 84
Sunday school, 30, 63, 64, 154

theology of ministry, 66, 72, 73, 103, 105, 106, 119, 126, 129, 172
Third World, 12, 14, 99, 182

United Church of Christ, 132, 202; also see Congregationalists
United Methodist Church, 136, 202; Methodists, 43, 63, 83, 146, 147

Vatican II, 1, 75

World Council of Churches, 7, 18, 140, 155, 183

Yale Divinity School, 89, 90, 198

Scriptural References
Gen 1; 107
Job 38; 107
Ps 49:7-9(NEB); 115
Ps 104; 107
Isa 53:4; 108
Isa 63:9; 108
Lam 1:12; 120
Jonah 4:10; 109
Zech 4:6; 211
Matt 9:15-16, 22:15; 155
Matt 10:7; 33
Matt 20:28; 118
Matt 22:21; 164
Matt 22:42; 116
Matt 25:40; 109
Matt 26:53-54; 109
Mark 1:15; 32f
Mark 4:30(NEB); 121
Mark 10:42-43(JB); 117
Luke 16:8; 98
Luke 16:8(Moffatt); 129
Luke 18:11; 113
Luke 19:10; 118
Luke 23:34; 110
John 5:17; 104
John 5:30; 118
John 10:10; 118
John 14:12; 104
John 18:37; 118
Acts 5:29; 33
Acts 6:1-6; 149
Acts 7:22; 79
Acts 9:15-16, 22:15; 152
Acts 13:1-3; 149
Rom 1:25; 107
Rom 11:36(NEB); 106
I Cor 1:23-24; 110
I Cor 1:30; 182
Eph 3:12; 18
Col 1:29(Wey); 106
I Tim 4:14; 149
Heb 2:10, cf. vs. 14; 116
Heb 5:4; 148
I Pet 2:5; 116
Rev 21:5; 111